THE THEORY OF
PLAY AND
RECREATION

ALLEN V. SAPORA
Professor of Recreation
University of Illinois

ELMER D. MITCHELL
Professor Emeritus of Physical Education
University of Michigan

THIRD EDITION

THE RONALD PRESS COMPANY • NEW YORK

Preface

This is a basic textbook for the introductory course in recreation. It aims to give the student a background in the history and significance of the play and recreation movement and to guide him in planning and implementing a community program.

The book describes the role of the play element, defines the attitudes toward and utilization of play in different civilizations, and traces the developments in those countries which have contributed significantly to the modern world-wide movement. It reviews and interprets different play theories for a better understanding of why people like and seek certain forms of activity. This analytical explanation affords a practical basis for the classification of activities in setting up and conducting programs. The need for play today is thoroughly investigated, with emphasis upon its importance in physical growth and development, in matters pertaining to health, and in the choice of leisure-time interests and hobbies.

The organization, administration, and promotion of public recreation and of school and community sports, youth agency activities, and camping programs are carefully covered. The book describes the areas, facilities, and equipment essential for these programs and sets up representative yearly, seasonal, weekly, and daily plans of scheduling. It also presents the responsibilities and contributions of public and private agencies for diversified areas in the total program, and delineates leadership standards for the profession, with suggestions on how they may be reached and possibly improved.

The authors wish to thank the following graduate students for their assistance in this revision: Edmund M. Bernauer, Albert E. Myers, and Wilburn E. Norman, of the University of Illinois; and Robert Ian Story, of the University of Michigan. Grateful acknowledgment is also extended to the Boy Scouts of America, Girl Scouts of the USA, Camp Fire Girls, Boys' Clubs of America, and Young Men's Christian Association for valuable help in the preparation of respective sections in the chapter on public and private agencies; and to the National Recreation Association for the use of their materials in this and earlier editions of the book.

ALLEN V. SAPORA
ELMER D. MITCHELL

January, 1961

Contents

Part IV

ORGANIZATION AND ADMINISTRATION OF PLAY
AND RECREATION

Part I

HISTORICAL BACKGROUND OF PLAY

1

Play Through the Ages

Play is both universal and old. Wherever life is found, there is play in some form or other. Birds sing, kittens chase each other, young foxes wrestle and pounce on each other; and so they must have done even before recorded time. Throughout the world girls play with dolls, boys wrestle, adults engage in crafts and all pursue a host of play forms. The excavations in the ruins of ancient Egypt and Babylon show us that these are not new. Dolls, tops, rattles, and various other trinkets of pottery and metal reveal that even in these remote times boys and girls were accustomed to play and adults to engage in artistic effort.

In other civilizations, the Spartan and Roman governments supported warlike play. The Athenians in the period of their ascendency trained through play in order to cultivate physical beauty as well to inculcate the Athenian moral code of citizenship. Throughout most civilizations, however, play has been unorganized, that is, unsponsored and not promoted as a function of society. It has been an activity in which children and adults have engaged in on impulse or, perhaps, because of a holiday occasion associated with merriment. Even as late as the beginning of the twentieth century this prevailed.

Today, however, play exists as a highly organized institution. The implications of play in contemporary society are, to a great extent, the result of the *play movement*, which is discussed at length in the following two chapters. Actually, the play movement, like other social movements about the

3

end of the nineteenth century, includes not only the growth of public provision for play but a general program of education and broadening participation in a wide variety of leisure-time activities. The type and extent of these activities are a direct reflection of the changing social, economic, and cultural conditions in our society. Like the free school movement, the health movement, the labor movement, and other social movements, the play movement, a part of the general humanitarian reform movement which began about 1880, was directed toward extending the general educational and cultural development of all in our society. Although the play forms and concepts are somewhat changed, play remains as an integral part of the social behavior and expression of people in the world today.

PLAY AMONG PRELITERATE PEOPLES

Human life and human institutions can be better understood by—and indeed cannot be thoroughly understood without—a study of the life of primitive peoples. Play patterns are an integral part of all human cultures wherever man is found and in whatever state of culture. A study of the play of preliterate peoples will throw needed light on the nature of the play tendencies of mankind as a whole. Books on anthropology contain full descriptions of primitive play; no more than a brief sketch can be given here.

In studying the field of preliterate play, one is immediately impressed with the fact that, while the modes of expression may differ, the same general types of play exist as in civilized cultures. Conspicuous among these are: (1) dancing and rhythmic movement, (2) mimicking and acting, (3) singing, (4) conversing and storytelling, (5) arts and crafts, (6) games and contests.

It is not surprising to find response to rhythm, and particularly through *dancing,* a salient characteristic of the play of preliterate man. For man the world around, and in every period of recorded time, has found rhythm contagious and a stimulus to participation. So, too, there is no contemporary culture, primitive or otherwise, that does not engage in dancing.

People joining in the rhythmic movement of the dance not only experience an intensification of emotion, a feeling of increased power, and an ecstasy that otherwise would not be possible, but they are welded together by a feeling of unity and harmony. Thus, the dance had a very important social as well as recreational function. It is for this reason that the primitive people dance before going to war, for example, and in association with all important social functions.

Many of the more advanced preliterate peoples developed dancing to a high degree of perfection and beauty, as witnessed, for example, in the culture of the Southwest Indians, and to a slightly lesser extent, in the cultures of the Plains and Woodland Indians. In the ceremonials of these peoples, so many elements are combined that the term dance seems scarcely adequate. Rhythmic motion, however, is the dominant feature; the drum beat is the controlling factor and brings order to the ritual. It is the song portion that expresses audibly human hopes and aspirations and addresses them to the All-One.

In many tribes these various elements are combined in a dance ritual that is not without purpose but is specifically an act of worship of divine beings. It may be a ritual of praise and thanksgiving, a supplication for life's needs and for success in human ventures, but, almost invariably, the element of pleasure seems to be present as an objective. Again, it may be secular, even for sheer fun and to satisfy certain appetites, but usually the relation to the spiritual seems to be present. In such cases the distinction between religion and play seems difficult. The dances become more than a dramatic representation of life activities. They become an effort to reflect and symbolize the group's life philosophy. To illustrate, the Bantus of Africa asked, upon meeting a member of another tribe, "What do you dance?" and thereby learned what was essential about the visitor's people, so fully is the dance a reflection of their whole life.

Mimicry and *imitation* as a means of preliterate expression

are illustrated also by reference to the Indian's dances.
These are the type of dance in which events or personal experiences are re-enacted and stories are told by rhythmic
pantomime. The hunting and fighting motion-language of
these dances is often vivid and dramatic. There are other
types of dances in which the chief expression is through
mimicry, some in representation of spirit bodies and others
in imitation of earthly phenomena. There are dances in
which masks and other disguising costumes are worn as an
aid to mimicry and others that rely on pantomime only, without special costumes. It is not surprising that many of the
Indian's dance themes should be taken from the natural
world around him, imitating animals and birds, for example.
Many of these portray the creatures' characteristics with surprising fidelity. Ernest Thompson Seton, whose long life
was devoted to the study of animals and birds, once witnessed a Pueblo Indian in an unannounced dance: no sooner
had it started than he exclaimed, "Why, it's the prairie
chicken," and upon inquiry found that it was, so accurately
had the dance reflected the bird's nature.

In pointing out the importance of dancing in the cultures
mentioned above, one is, in fact, also indicating the significance of *singing,* for in the phenomenon called dance, movement and song are merely different phases of the same thing.
Indeed, the terms were often used interchangeably, and it
was not uncommon for a Plains or a Woodland Indian to say
of the *dances* of a neighboring people, that he did not know
those *songs.* While dancing without song accompaniment
was rare indeed, singing was not restricted to dancing alone
but was an integral part of other types of play activities.
And among these preliterates, as among people everywhere,
singing was also indulged informally by individuals, at work
and at play, purely for the joy of it.

An indication of the important place *storytelling* holds in
the Indian's pattern of life are the volumes of recorded
legends and stories of Indian origin—legends and stories
which taken together constitute a mass legendary lore which,
in the opinion of some, approaches that of the Greeks both

in quantity and quality. While these legends may have served as a means of education, of religious training, and of transmitting social lore, no one would question their primary function as entertainment. In a preliterate culture the spoken word is the only adequate means of expressing and of perpetuating myth and history, and therefore the eminence of the storyteller is understandable.

Peoples of the less sophisticated cultures quite universally developed the *arts and crafts*, pleasing to the eye as well as the ear. Line and color were much played with. The craft art of the Indian was as accomplished as his dancing and indicated again the development in his culture of the higher play forms. He was, and still is, the weaver of the world's finest baskets, and his hand-woven rugs and handmade pottery are among the finest that have ever been produced. For example, Mexican art is very largely Indian, although affected in design and skills by Spanish influence. Through the symbolic meanings of their designs, the art of the Indian is related to all the rest of his life.

The play life of preliterate children was more or less directly related to many of the pursuits of adult life and was employed as a preparation for them. The utilization of play as a means of education, so much emphasized in recent years, is thus not new in history. The Plains Indian youth was confronted with the necessity of developing himself into a hardened, toughened warrior, a rider of the plains and a rover of the woods, and the adults saw to it that his play contributed to this end. Moreover, the duty of the old men of the tribe was to train and educate the children in the ways of life. Much attention was of necessity given to practice with the bow and arrow as soon as the boy was old enough to handle a small-scale weapon. The Iroquois, for instance, are said to have had five grades of shooting through which all boys progressed before being considered a full-fledged hunter and warrior.

Problems comprised much of the play education of many Indian tribes. The Iroquois boys, for instance, were told to go to a certain spot, set up camp, secure food, kill and strip animals and fashion clothing and moccasins for themselves, kill a deer and return with it to camp. If it took them longer than prescribed they were sent again. In a wide range of the serious pursuits of life, training through play was devised for them.

Girls were likewise educated by the older folk so that they could do all things skillfully which adulthood would demand of them; the girl learned the meaning of symbolism, the art of her tribe, the crafts which the women practiced, the songs and legends of her people, as well as the household arts.

Games and contests very similar to those found today in civilized countries occurred frequently in the life of preliterate people. Wrestling, running and throwing contests, riding races, and games using balls were played by the Indians. Much emphasis was placed on long-distance running, and outstanding feats of distance running by adult Indians are on record. Gambling was very common not only among the Indians but all preliterate peoples. There seems to be a quite universal fascination for man to play with chance. Tops, stilts, pop-guns and wad-shooters, quoits, and coasting amused Indian children. Snow-snakes or ten-foot staves were hurled for distance competition across the snow. Contrary to general opinion, team games requiring some little organization were common; our games of lacrosse and shinny originated as Indian games. Practically all of these games developed a religious as well as a recreational significance.

EVOLUTION OF PLAY

The play customs of people form part of their folkways. Their origin and transmission from generation to generation are much like other folkways.

FACTORS CONTRIBUTING TO EVOLUTION. Man is naturally active, both physically and mentally. When primitive man had met the needs of self-preservation, he enjoyed some leisure-time for self-expression. Because he was alive and possessed of the physiological need for activity, gratification could not be obtained by rest and sleep alone and consequently he played. As has been said, his play consisted largely of play-fighting and play-hunting, dancing and pantomime, singing and storytelling, artistic and constructive crafts, games and contests. A major part of his play was either competitive or a rhythmic and pantomimic representation of hunting and fighting and served the purpose of training future hunters and warriors for their serious pursuits.

Children, always forward looking and onward reaching, imitated these adult activities, both serious and play. Mankind in general is imitative, and the play customs of a few of the group tend very rapidly to become the play forms of many. Each new generation of children took on through imitation the accepted play patterns. In this way a background of play traditions developed which was passed on from generation to generation and spread out in ever widening circles. Society is organized and devoted to the end of implanting in children its folkways and mores. Thus through imitation and inculcation, games and play patterns persist over long periods of time. Most games can be traced back to the early history of the folk who play them; in fact, their origin can seldom be located. However outmoded the traditional forms possess great value to the group.

Through the process of social evolution which is going on everywhere and unceasingly, however, games and play activities are constantly *changing*. No succeeding generation can imitate exactly the customs of the past generation, and minor changes gradually creep in. Furthermore, as a game spreads out over larger and larger areas, people in different localities add variations of their own until the game is played in widely different ways and is known by different names. An American square dance, for instance, while recognizably the same, varies as one travels from one locality to another: we speak of the Vermont way of dancing a certain routine, the Kentucky way, the Indiana way, or the California way.

In addition to the fact that no generation can imitate exactly the play of preceding generations, there are other factors leading to the evolution of the forms of play. There is accidental variation: through accident or chance, a new way of playing a game is stumbled upon and, proving more satisfying and appealing than the old way, it is accepted, imitated, taught to children and thus passed on as a folkway.

With the occasional appearance of creative minds, new play methods are invented or improvements made in the old. In the history of the present-day play movement, creative minds have altered old games decidedly, such as football, and have produced seemingly new ones, such as volleyball and basketball. These, though apparently new, are combinations of, or are based upon, older ones. Creative minds may hasten the development of the new, may alter and combine old games in a new form, but they seldom, if ever, create a new game outright.

The cross-fertilization of cultures through war, travel, and ease of communication also leads to the appearance of new play customs in a society. A warring tribe, conquering or being conquered by its enemies, takes on from these strangers play and art customs which are adopted as the tribe's own. One of the popular dances of the Jemez Pueblo Indians, for instance, is the Comanche, a dance learned by them while held captive by their traditional enemies, the Comanches. Today, with much travel in foreign countries, ideas for recreational changes are disseminated quickly.

Old cultures, highly crystallized and stagnant with tradition, change very slowly, while new cultures and countries, relatively free from reactionary elements, possess an exuberance and accelerated tempo which leads to the rapid appearance of the new. Freedom from deeply entrenched traditions is therefore conducive to rapid change in forms of play; and play forms, which vary enough from the old to be apparent as new, emerge in these younger cultures and countries.

Another important factor in the evolution of play in any society is a large amount of leisure time. Leisure always gives an added importance to play and festivity. So it was in lands of plenty like Egypt, where the Nile overflowed and left a fertile valley, and in Babylonia, where the Euphrates, too, formed a fertile valley. Fertile land supported a heavy population and, in turn, certain tribes grew stronger and better organized, conquered others, and set themselves up as a ruling class. This increased still further the time for leisurely pursuits for play. With material wants satisfied, there was time for art, literature, philosophy, and other intellectual achievements that could be preserved for the benefit of future generations.

CHANGE IN SIGNIFICANCE OF GAMES. With the passage of the centuries and the inevitable change that occurred, ceremonies and rituals once affiliated with the supernatural and possessing sacred meaning lost their religious significance and, though continuing, were viewed in a secular light. Sacred customs easily degenerated into mock ceremonies as time went on. Thus, for instance, it is claimed that such customs as the bridal veil, throwing rice at wedding ceremonies, and the toast, are all survivals of once serious rites and profoundly solemn covenants. Many of our gambling games are remnants of old practices concerned with omens, superstitions, and magic. Our well-known children's singing plays are traced back to the old customs of dancing, the once serious ceremonial now garbed as play. Children's counting-out rhymes like "Eeny, Meeny, Miny, Mo" are said to have originated in primitive methods of selecting by lot a person to be a hostage or a victim. In the same way, the line games of today are compared to meetings between hostile groups of old; the circle games, to old customs performed by a group joined in friendship; the games like "Blindman's Buff," to old ceremonies of sacrifice; the serpentine games, to acts of worship in which a sacred tree was encircled.

Tag and goal games in general are likened to old tribal activities, such as flight, pursuit, capture, and escape, the last possibly depending upon reaching a place of refuge in time. In addition, games like "Fox and Geese" are supposed to be symbolical of a domestic animal striving to protect itself and young against a beast of prey; whereas, games like "The Bear" and "Hare and Hounds" represent the chase. Our children's marriage games in line form indicate primitive customs of marriage by capture or purchase; while the marriage games in circle form, on the other hand, mean an advance to the point where courtship and love were necessary preliminaries. The well-known dance "Round and Round the Village" is pictured as a survival of a periodical village festival, on which occasion marriages were celebrated.

Most of our modern contests of strength and skill, such as running, jumping, throwing, and wrestling, date back in recorded history to ancient Greece, but probably have a history of many centuries of evolution before the rise of Greek culture. Our first record of athletic contests is that given by Homer in his description of the funeral ceremonies that Achilles instituted in honor of his friend Patroclus. The origin of the great Olympic festivals is wrapped up in myths and legends, and it is not until the year 776 B.C. that the names of the Olympic victors were publicly recorded. These occasions maintained a religious significance throughout their existence.

The love for strenuous athletic sports and competition is inherent among peoples who possess a strong loyalty to their tribe or state and who have not as yet lost their primitive hardihood. Thus, in the republics of early Greece and Rome, where the citizens, though belonging to a superior class, were still ready themselves to take the field, there was a common willingness to engage in virile exercises which keep the body hardened and the spirit courageous and resourceful. Yet, while the Greeks and Romans must be credited with the origin of many of our popular athletic contests, their later history reveals a citizenship indulging in luxury, entirely content to watch hired performers play at active sports. In the period of chivalry, when knights fought for land, title, and love, new types of contests arose. Fencing, tilting, archery, and genteel horsemanship were popular; and along with skill in the new accomplishments, there came into existence a spirit of courtesy and respect for opponents.

All this is indicative of the fact that play in its various forms is representative of the customs and traditions of a people. It is a means of ascertaining the trend of national life. A mirror of national character can be found, for example, in the easy-going, long-drawn-out, conservative, and individualistic English game on the one hand, and the high-strung, tense, changing, and success-seeking American game on the other. Primitive peoples are attracted to elementary games which are imitative of the life around them. Autocratic nations specialize in the disciplined, machine-like, and systematic gymnastics, whereas, all through history, democracy has been accompanied by an interest in amateur sports. This is true of Greece in its Golden Age, and of Rome in its Republic. Their sports compared to those of today, however, were far lacking in the element of team play even as their governments were limited in democratic scope when compared with today's democracies. Democracy desires to develop leadership in its masses and therefore is willing to foster the athletic sports which call for initiative and a keen exercise of the reasoning powers. The social environment becomes thus a criterion for the type of play indulged in by any people, and the nature of the government, most especially, affects and determines the play forms.

ATTITUDES TOWARD PLAY

Play, it is true, has always been an activity of man, yet one thing should be kept clearly in mind: play as a function is not identical with play as a movement and as an institution. The uninformed regard play as a frivolous, aimless, and childish activity. Yet it can easily be seen how this attitude should exist. The material and content of play is largely: a make-believe of occupations and customs that were once serious and all important; an imitation, especially by children, of the present-day serious occupations of men and women; and lastly, a play gratification in creative accomplishment or achievement. The latter presents play and art as synonymous and has always been considered by adults seriously.

It is from the first two phases, however, that the attitude of the ordinary adult is often formed. People connect their play experience with their childhood; these activities reflect, on the one hand, childishness and immaturity, yet, on the other hand, they also reflect a spirit of youth and inventiveness which most adults do not wish to lose entirely. However, at the same time they feel that this exuberant spirit must be curbed and subordinated to the more serious responsibilities of life and should break forth only on appropriate occasions.

The study of the treatment of play in the philosophies and educational systems of various countries throughout civilized history discloses that five distinct attitudes have prevailed at different times and places: (1) the *military* attitude, (2) the *art* attitude, (3) the *religious* attitude, (4) the *scientific* attitude, and (5) the *social* attitude.

MILITARY ATTITUDE. In the earliest stages of the development of the human race men seem to have discovered that play could be directed toward a certain desired end. Play was used in primitive cultures as a means of training to accomplish desired objectives. In the history of recorded civilizations this goal has most often been military, as evidenced in the ancient Persian, the Spartan, and Roman cultures. The Persians made the training of the boy a matter of public concern. At the age of seven he was taken in charge by the state and taught to hunt and ride, to shoot with the sling and with the bow, and to throw the spear. Practically all his education was of the physical type. Certain moral virtues, particularly truthfulness and reverence, were emphasized. The girl's education was of the domestic type, but did include singing and legends.

Warlike Sparta went so far as to give its boys a scouting education that is somewhat similar to the outdoor life of the Boy Scouts of today, but the courageous, self-reliant, uncompromising, and hardened warrior was always the goal in sight; similarly, a health training for the girls was to produce strong mothers for the state. The whole of Spartan life, including play, was directed by the military attitude. Part of the boy's education was to bear all sorts of physical hardships and to bear pain unflinchingly in public. Obedience and reverence for parents were prized moral traits. All music was of the martial type. This was a country which, under the rule of Lycurgus, was so severely disciplined that the freemen lived in barracks, and iron money was used in order that the citizens could not carry enough to buy luxuries. No wonder the God-speed of the Spartan mother to her son: "Come home with your shield or dead upon it"—no wonder the taunt of the Athenians, their rivals: "The Spartan's life is so unendurable that it is not surprising he gives it willingly in battle."

This attitude of parent and state focusing on children's play from the standpoint of its military usefulness was taken up by the Romans, a stern and practical people. Their play training allowed the younger tots to go their way largely unhampered; and as children will do, they played with toy carts and houses, dolls, hobby horses, stilts, tops, hoops, and at catching a ball. However, when the state felt that the children were old enough to be given serious attention, a different kind of exercise was in store for them, especially the boys. Running and jumping, both armed and unarmed, wrestling, sword and spear play, swimming, and horse riding then comprised the play—if it can be truly called play under the rigid spirit in which it was carried out. So possessed were the Roman people with this one ambition of preparing mind as well as body to meet the conditions of warfare that their public games, the notorious gladiatorial shows, would not satisfy unless much blood was shed. This cruelty was considered of practical importance in keeping the people, even in time of peace, hardened to the sight of death and suffering.

None of these attitudes in respect to play can scarcely be dignified by the name of a *play movement*. Play was considered as an educational factor, to be sure, but only from the one standpoint—the making of a warrior. This same viewpoint was held later, in the period of chivalry during the Middle Ages, when knights held that their sons should learn to throw the spear, fence, swim, use the battle-ax, ride in armor, and otherwise play at war. It is a pleasure to note, however, that a gentler spirit was creeping in, and that the youth was brought up to be more generous toward his opponents and toward women.

The boy in the period of chivalry was trained from childhood with this attitude in mind. At the age of seven he became a page. For the next seven years he was trained in domestic duties and in the deportment of polite society, the latter including reading, writing, singing, dancing, chess and backgammon, gallantry, and listening to tales of brave deeds as sung by the troubadours. At fourteen he became a squire. He now waited in attendance upon a knight, and his duties were vigorous ones. He learned to hunt and to hawk, to vault and climb in armor, to ride, and to become proficient in the weapons of war, such as the lance and battle-ax. Running, jumping, wrestling, and swimming helped to harden the body for these feats. At twenty-one, when he was dubbed a knight, he had learned the art of war in company with his chosen knight, was ready to tilt in the tournaments, and was thoroughly imbued with a spirit of loyalty and gallantry and the desire to champion the cause of the weak and oppressed.

ART ATTITUDE. By far the brightest page in the history of play in civilized nations down to the present day is that which tells the story of the small republic of Athens, during the Golden Age of Pericles in the fifth century before Christ. The concept of the art attitude is encompassed in the Athenian objective of developing the ideal, balanced citizen who was soldier, athlete, artist, statesman, and philosopher all in one. Play as an art form was exalted to the level of being an integral part of education and daily living, hence it can be called a play movement, the only true play movement outside of our own today.

An examination of the curriculum of studies shows the importance attributed to play in the making of this all-round citizen who could so enjoy the higher things of life. At an early age the boy and girl were given a nursery training similar to our modern kindergarten. There were infant chairs similar to our baby swings, colored rattles, many types of dolls, and toy boats, carts, and houses. The familiar toys —marbles, jackstones, hoops, hobby horses, stilts, skipping ropes, kites, swings, and see-saws—were in evidence, though often in a form that appears to us crude and amusing. Then there were also childish games that resemble our tag and our hide-and-seek, guessing games like "Odd or Even," prisoners' games, simple ball games, and so on. After this stage girls received little attention, women having but little part in public life.

At the age of seven, however, the boy enrolled in a school conducted by a private tutor. Two subjects mainly were followed: gymnastics (for the body) and music (for the soul). At that time, the latter included instruction in reading, particularly of Homer, also in writing, arithmetic, singing, rhythm, and in the use of the lyre and flute. But it is in the palaestra, the school of gymnastics, that we see our modern conception of play carried out. Here, the boys continued their free play, and were given instructions in running and leaping (for the lower limbs), discus and javelin throwing (for the arms and eye-hand coordination), and wrestling (for the whole body as well as the control of temper). Dancing was also fostered as an art that would add grace to the movements of the body. Other activities were swimming, games with balls, and simple boxing.

At the age of eighteen the youth was initiated into the company of the grown men and went through an apprenticeship of two years before being received into full citizenship. He continued his bodily exercises but left the palaestra and associated with the elders in the gymnasium. In addition to the sports he had known he was now introduced to a fivefold exercise called the pentathlon, and to a combination of boxing and wrestling, the pancratium. The gymnasium also possessed a great influence as a social and intellectual center, and the youth was brought into contact with great philosophers and statesmen.

The athletic skill which the Athenian training developed was tested out and exhibited in the wonderful spectacle of the Olympic games. So important were these games to Greece as a whole that the reckoning of time was dated by the Olympiads, the four-year intervals between the festivals. All hostility ceased between warring states and the occasion was one of general rejoicing and celebration. The athletes contended for the championship in all the popular athletic events as well as horseback races and chariot races. Not only did athletes vie for superiority, but the great poets and sculptors contested as spiritedly in their fields of endeavor. To attain the prize, the simple wreath of olive, was considered the peak of Greek ambition. But there was further honor forthcoming to the Olympic victor. His home city heaped honors upon him. Poets like Pindar celebrated his name in odes, and sculptors like Myron made him immortal in marble. Thus we can see why the great Olympic games could not remain unstained. The temptations to attain these honors were so great that athletes of the professional type did nothing but prepare for the games, and disreputable practices which often accompany uncontrolled professionalism crept in until, by the time the Romans had conquered Greece, all the wonderful spirit that had once accompanied the games had been entirely lost.

The words of the Athenian men of wisdom still preach that the play of the children is important and must be directed. To quote Plato: "Education should begin with the right direction of children's sports. The plays of childhood have a great deal to do with the maintenance or non-maintenance of laws." Aristotle states: "It is also very necessary that children should have some amusing employment." Pericles, the statesman, in his great funeral oration implies what the broad aim of Athenian education should be: "We cultivate the mind without loss of manliness . . . whereas our adversaries from early youth are always undergoing laborious exercises which are to make them brave, we live at ease and yet are equally willing to face the perils which they face. . . . We have our regular games to provide our weary spirits many relaxations from toil."

The art attitude of the Golden Age is summed up in the words of Plato when he says: "The mere athlete becomes too much of a savage, and the mere musician is melted and softened beyond what is good for him . . . the two should therefore be blended in right proportions."

RELIGIOUS ATTITUDE. Following the break-up of the Roman Empire, A.D. 486, there ensued a period of such great chaos that it is known as the "Dark Ages." Barbarian tribes overran all civilized Europe. People turned for solace to a spiritual conception of life. Everything was sacrificed to preparation for the hereafter. Inasmuch as the body was looked upon as an impediment to the higher yearnings of the soul, every means possible was taken to deny the body its natural comforts, and self-torture was even practiced. It is quite natural that play should not only be ignored but vigorously combated in such an age. The religious considered it derived from heathenish practices and an instrument of Satan leading one through the physical self into pleasure and temptation. The following expresses a saintly warning against allowing children to play: "Play of whatever sort should be forbidden in all church schools, and its vanity and folly should be explained to the children with warnings of how it turns the mind from God and eternal life."

During the Medieval and Renaissance periods aesthetic play was not only sanctioned but encouraged, so long as it had a distinct religious flavor. Beautiful cathedrals were constructed, masterpieces of painting produced, and enduring music created. It was in the spirit of creative play that these things came into being. Sanction was given these creative achievements, however, only when they were of a religious or semi-religious character.

The strict viewing of all amusements as sinful is found recurring later in the Puritan era. Even today people have not entirely outlived the religious fanaticism of the days of Cromwell, and much of the opposition to the play movement has come from people who feel that the only way to salvation is to practice rigid self-denial even as regards the most harmless type of pastimes. On the whole, however, the church today has swung over to a liberal attitude which even makes it an active promoter of the play program.

SCIENTIFIC ATTITUDES.   Man by nature could not long remain in such an unworldly atmosphere as the monastic and the chivalric. Toward the end of the Middle Ages a large number of influences brought about a change in attitude. The invention of gun powder meant an end to the ascendancy of the knightly class; and that of the printing press to the clergy's monopoly on learning. The common people began to assert an independence they had never manifested before. The spirit of the age was one of questioning and of critical research: men no longer were satisfied with superstitious beliefs and theoretical speculations. They wanted to measure life for themselves; to understand themselves and the actuality of the world about them. Contact with the Saracens, a scientific people, and the rediscovery of the long lost knowledge of the ancients, especially of Aristotle, satisfied for only a shore time. Then there ensued discovery after discovery in the field of science.

The great progress in the field of physical, biological, social, and medical sciences revolutionized the place of physical exercise in education. The unity of mind and body was made evident. In the Renaissance writers like Rabelais and Montaigne in France, Mulcaster and Ascham in England, and Comenius in Germany pleaded the necessity of play in the life of children. Rousseau and Froebel followed later; soon after 1800, experiments were commenced in the practical application of play in the school curriculum.

The scientific attitude not only evolved the idea of play having educational value to the young child, but it attempted to place physical exercise on a scientific basis from the health standpoint. Patriotic motives were largely responsible for this latter experiment, which resulted in the great national systems of gymnastics in Germany and Sweden. These in turn have affected all of Europe and even the United States. To reduce the body to a machine-like basis is faulty because of the repression of natural interests and of individuality. Such training provides easy exploitation should a militaristic class or ambitious dictatorship gain control. Today's attitude goes further and considers interest a factor. The newer studies in psychology have shown that the value of any pursuit is largely dependent upon the liking shown for it, and therefore individual tastes and preferences must be taken into account. Play has thus superseded the formal gymnastics of the past.

SOCIAL ATTITUDE. The present play movement surpasses previous play attitudes in magnitude and in breadth of aims. While to date it has placed less emphasis on the aesthetic side than that of the Athenians, in other ways it has broadened in a manner unknown to the ancients. Above all it is democratic. In the past the leaders alone were allowed free scope for their impulses. There were slaves or a downtrodden peasantry to do the work. Then, too, the modern freedom of women was unknown. The play movement of America fosters no class. In fact, through the opportunities offered, the tenement child may become better fitted for life than the pampered, secluded child of the rich home.

The democratic tendencies of the twentieth century have changed social understanding. Our whole structure of society is built upon team play. Life is now looked upon as a great game. The rules allow complete freedom to the individual just as long as he acts in accordance with the ideals held by the people as a whole. Therefore, he must be trained as a social agent, to act of his own accord for the common good. Each individual must do his part or the co-operative whole suffers. The state is for the people, not the people for the state. As a consequence, the scientific attitude, so long focused on natural phenomena alone, has now been turned toward man himself. The social sciences are slowly being brought to the advanced level of the natural sciences.

Play, then, is a medium through which social intercourse may be promoted in our contemporary society. In many instances intolerance, prejudice, and misunderstanding can be substantially reduced or resolved only by close personal association in activities having an impelling appeal which of themselves show unmistakably the value and wisdom of the democratic way of life. Play and recreational activities provide such a medium. Sports, dramatics, music, and other recreational activities provide a desirable means of expression in which people may gain acceptance for their achievements regardless of their race, creed, or position in society. In this sense, play and recreation activities serve as a catalytic agent in that they accelerate positive, desirable social relations that might not take place in the absence of such stimulation. The end result is the possibility of a better understanding of each individual's position in a democratic society.

As never before in history, schools are attempting to turn out an individual well trained in social relationships. The school has linked itself with the community and has taken on the aspect of a social center. Here, young and old alike are taught the fundamentals of citizenship through history, economics, geography, and other social studies; in languages, guidance-type courses, and vocational arts, as well as on the higher educational levels in social psychology, sociology, and group dynamics. There is a growing realization that the hallways and play areas of the school are as important as the classrooms. Possibly, in respect to the formation of character habits and attitudes and the socialization of the individual they are more important, for it is in these close, intimate, informal relationships in real-life situations that human nature is affected most profoundly.

This new attitude makes the school today a promoter of the playground and the gymnasium, as well as of extra-school activities such as athletics, dramatics, music, debating, and boys' and girls' clubs. Moreover, adults' leisure time is also provided with recreation and opportunities for personal growth through adult recreation clubs and interest groups, including clubs for adults over sixty-five years of age.

This social attitude of the school is reflected now in other community institutions, and the combined efforts of all are creating a high play level for the life of the people of our nation.

LEISURE AND CULTURE

Much has been said of the new leisure and how it has come about, yet one thing stands out: in America today there is more leisure than there has ever been in any other era of society. Further, this new leisure is a pressing social problem. Previously, leisure was the possession of a privileged class, produced by the labor of slaves, serfs, peasants, or lower classes, but today every man has mechanical slaves working for him so that free time is placed at the disposal of *all* men instead of only a fortunate few. While this situation is a happy, democratic one, it also presents a stupendous problem: the leisure time of an entire society—all ages, all kinds, male and female—must be accommodated in some way. In other words, there is a need for mass utilization of leisure at the same time there is mass production in industry.

Even so, the size of the leisure-time problem would not be so formidable if men could simply develop the old ways of using leisure more intensively and extensively. However, as the American people have been acquiring their newly found leisure, they have also been changing their attitude toward the whole question of leisure and the acceptable ways of using it. This is not unusual because throughout history the term "leisure" has been constantly changing in meaning.

EARLY CONCEPTS. The American pioneers frowned upon leisure. There was so much for them to do—forests to clear, swamps to reclaim, roads to build, large families to feed and to protect—that the person who took time for relaxation seemed an idler and a shirker. Our forefathers were building a continent and, naturally, they hated to see energy wasted. Leisure was not a problem with them.

When organized industry first came into being, the twelve-

hour day seemed the natural and obvious period of toil.
Then followed the ten-hour day and the six-day week for
manual labor. Sunday was the only day of leisure, and this
leisure was utilized to rest the tired body and the weary
spirit.

Then came the years of plenty following World War I—
work for everyone and wages incredible. The day of eight
hours and the week of five and one-half days came hand in
hand. Saturday afternoon had become a holiday. There
was a surplus of energy over and above the demands of the
work. How to use this extra time presented no problem,
for many new devices had grown up with prosperous times
—movies, automobiles, radios, professional sports, golf clubs,
bathing beaches, Coney Islands, and many other ways and
places to find amusement. Leisure was no longer frowned
upon as idleness; no longer merely rest time to recuperate
for more work. Instead, it became free time for a good time.
A solution to the leisure problem seemed simple so long as
prosperity continued, and workmen had both energy and
money to spare.

Then, in the 1930's, came the depression and the despair
of disillusionment. Once more, leisure was viewed in a new
light. For a time the word was not popular. It became con-
founded with unemployment and leisure time to the unemployed was nothing more than the specter of hours seeking
work, of time to brood on the loss of savings or the collapse
of life's cherished plans, of time spent in worries over the
future welfare of self and family. True leisure, however,
could come only when material wants were again satisfied
and when there were means of fulfilling spiritual wants of
men. True leisure was freedom from compulsion, time to
do what one wanted to do apart from earning a livelihood.

THE NEW LEISURE. Out of the darkness of the depression, there arose a new and nobler conception of leisure than
America or any other nation has ever known. People became leisure-conscious, leisure-minded. They came to realize that leisure is an inevitable part of the new social and

economic order, a permanent part of their lives, and so took a challenging attitude toward it. They no longer conceived of it as merely time for rest and entertainment. They infused leisure with something of its original Greek meaning, namely, devoting this time to schooling and education. And even though, as yet, no one has surpassed the ancient Greeks in the use of leisure for the cultivation of the possibilities of human genius in the way of art, literature, philosophy, and athletics, it is entirely conceivable that the future will grant that during the late 1930's America went beyond them in using leisure for social improvement and for bestowing happiness upon the masses of its people.

Such a situation was developing before the outbreak of World War II. Under the impact of this crisis came another, even if temporary, attitude toward leisure. Implicit was a sense of obligation; it connoted time for service, for the fulfillment of duty, for personal preparedness. The duty of being physically fit was imbued in the loyal citizen's consciousness. This was a part of the over-all patriotic duty of rendering service to a greater degree than one's output under ordinary peace-time circumstances. For those individuals who were not inducted into the armed services there were other emergency obligations. Theirs were the civilian, but none the less important, services of engaging in wartime industry with its twenty-four hour shifts, of acting as air-raid wardens, of volunteering as Red Cross or USO helpers, for assisting in Victory Loan and other government fund-raising drives, of reading to disabled veterans in the hospitals, of directing Boy Scout drives for needed scrap materials, and of volunteering for many other needed patriotic services. Such is the attitude toward leisure that crises always bring.

The postwar period, with its fuller recognition of automation, has increased hope of greater prosperity for all and, hence, even more leisure time. Although some of the frivolities that characterized the 1920's again made their appearance, the real social gains fostered in the 1930's should nevertheless be secure. These gains have been extended by expanding the programs of recreation departments; through opportune and attractive vacation offerings; through the integration of adult education and adult recreation programs; through the extension courses of colleges and universities; and through the rapid growth of the community college movement, bringing educational and cultural opportunities nearer to the home on a local basis. It would seem that the values crystallizing in the 1930's, namely, those of creative endeavor and of enriched personality, will be retained and advanced—they have come to be regarded as so important in the pattern of human life.

CONCEPT OF LEISURE IN MODERN SOCIETY. In the current use of leisure there is the entertainment-seeking that characterizes good times and prosperity along with shorter work days. But, possibly, underneath is another attitude toward the use of leisure—one harder to recognize because it is so close at hand and one that will be attributed to this era in future years when a look backward will offer perspective.

It seems that a new attitude toward leisure not hitherto prominent in our American society is shaping. This is the use of leisure as a time for escape. The troubled times that have come as the aftermath of World War II have been filled with apprehensions, fears, worries, uncertainties, and insecurities. There has been the cold war with its threat of another World War and the catastrophic possibility of atomic, H bomb, and nuclear warfare; there have been racial and nationalistic upheavals as well as political ones; there has been class consciousness as never before between labor and management in industry; there has been the feeling that the all-time prosperity of today may result in another financial crash reminiscent of the late 1920's and the depression that followed; there has been a mistrust of financial security by those elderly people whose retirement earnings have been devalued by inflation. In the midst of this confused, distraught, embroiled postwar world, leisure has emerged as time when people act to escape from the harsh realities of life. In it, people can temporarily forget the turmoil about them. The leisure of today has such a saving grace. The intellect is occupied in varying degrees of intensity with the absorbing pursuits at hand and, at the same time, concern for those problems, which momentarily had best be forgotten, is excluded. In such forgetfulness come recreation and recuperation for tasks ahead.

It has been seen that the type of society determines the ways in which leisure will be utilized. In other words, the attitude of any given society toward life will direct the uses of leisure time to specific ends. And, conversely, the uses of leisure can be seen to reflect the society itself—its elations, its depressions, its drives, its creative aspirations.

SUMMARY

The play life of preliterate peoples was an integral part of the full scope of life activities, inseparably related to all of them and a preparation for them. When life is so integrated, a play movement is not needed. Play movements become necessary only when life and education become fragmentized, divided and subdivided, specialized and ultra-specialized. As modern civilization developed, each culture developed its own play patterns. Some play habits of earlier civilizations were retained, but as the physical and social environment changed, new play habits were formed through accidental variation, by creative minds, or through lack of deeply entrenched traditions. The rapid improvement of methods of travel and communication also brought a cross-fertilization of cultures, producing changes and mutations of various play habits throughout the world. Men have also attempted to direct play toward certain desired ends; consequently the attitudes—(1) the military, (2) the art, (3) the religious, (4) the scientific, and (5) the social—toward play reflect this direction. The development of play throughout the world since the beginning to the twentieth century will be treated in more detail in the following discussion of the modern play movement.

SELECTED REFERENCES

The Annals of the American Academy of Political and Social Science,
CCCXIII (September, 1957). The entire volume is devoted to a
series of articles centered around "Recreation in the Age of Automation." Of particular importance to the material in this chapter is the
discussion of the philosophy and the economics of leisure and the pattern of leisure in our contemporary culture.

Duquesne University. *Leisure Living: A Series of Lectures Given at the
Community College.* Pittsburgh: Duquesne University, 1959. This
series of lectures indicates clearly the impact and importance of increased leisure in modern society. Specific emphasis is given to the
economic, social, psychological, and educational implications of more
leisure in a capitalistic economy.

LARABEE, ERIC, and MEYERSOHN, ROLF (eds.) *Mass Leisure.* Glencoe,
Ill.: The Free Press, 1958. This is a series of articles by writers expressing various disciplines regarding the ramifications and the effect
of leisure in our society. A comprehensive bibliography on leisure,
listing important publications about leisure from 1900 to 1958, is also
included.

The following three books contain basic material relating to the development of the concepts of play and recreation and the effect and growing
importance of leisure in modern society.

BRIGHTBILL, CHARLES K., and MEYER, HAROLD D. *Recreation: Text and
Readings.* Englewood Cliffs, N. J.: Prentice-Hall, Inc., 1953, Chaps.
1 and 2.

BUTLER, GEORGE D. *Introduction to Community Recreation.* 3d ed. New
York: McGraw-Hill Book Co., Inc., 1959, Chaps. 1 and 2.

NEUMEYER, MARTIN H., and NEUMEYER, ESTHER S. *Leisure and Recreation.* 3d ed. New York: The Ronald Press Co., 1958, Chaps. 1 and 2.

DEWHURST, J. FREDERIC, and others. *America's Needs and Resources: A
New Survey.* New York: Twentieth Century Fund, Inc., 1955. Chap.
11.

GARDINER, EDWARD N. *Athletics of the Ancient World.* New York: Ox-
ford University Press, 1930.

PIEPER, JOSEF. *Leisure, the Basis of Culture.* New York: Pantheon Books,
Inc., 1952.

ROSENBERG, BERNARD, and MANNING, DAVID (eds.). *Mass Media.* Glencoe, Ill.: The Free Press and Falcon's Wing Press, 1957.

STUMPF, FLORENCE, and COZENS, FREDERICK W. "Some Aspects of the
Role of Games, Sports, and Recreational Activities in the Culture of
Modern Primitive Peoples," *Research Quarterly,* XVIII (October,
1947), 198–218.

SUMNER, WILLIAM G. *Folkways: A Study of the Sociological Importance
of Usages, Manners, Customs, Mores, and Morals.* New York: Dover
Publications, Inc., 1959, Chap. 17.

WOODY, THOMAS. *Life and Education in Early Societies.* New York: The
Macmillan Co., 1949.

2

Modern World
Play Movement

The modern play movement is not the characteristic of a single country. It had its peculiar beginnings in practically every country and has shaped itself according to the special social and physical environments of each nation. The countries of Europe and the United States have been most prominent in the rise of the play movement and a general survey of their respective backgrounds, developments, and influences is needed for an adequate understanding of the significance and trends of the present-day world movement.

Before discussing further the implications of the play movement, it is necessary to define what the movement is, how it began, and why it has been such a significant social force in various countries throughout the world. Actually, the play movement is a typical example of a social movement, which in turn is the result of many complex social forces and conditions. What, then, is a social movement? Clarence E. Rainwater, sociologist, describes a social movement as "a mode of collective behavior occasioned by social disorganization or contacts, involving intercommunication of desires, and manifested by an organization of social activities intended to accomplish a common object. These activities consist of adjustments to the given social situation." [1]

A social movement is further explained by Neumeyer and Neumeyer in the following paragraph.

[1] C. E. Rainwater, *The Play Movement in the United States* (Chicago: University of Chicago Press, 1922), p. 1.

(1) Movements grow out of unsatisfactory and disorganized social situations causing social unrest and concern . . . (2) the situation must be defined by competent observers as constituting a social problem . . . (3) there must be a conscious effort to meet the situation . . . (4) to become a movement the reaction to the social need must be connected by cause and effect relations and extended in time and space . . . (5) the setting up of objectives and standards and the organization of social activities intended to accomplish them are evidences of maturation of a movement . . . (6) the final phase is the gradual realization of the objectives as disclosed through the stages in its development, transitions in its policies and activities, and trends in its organization.[2]

In some instances, as in the prohibition movement, the social movement is unsuccessful and is temporarily or sometimes completely abandoned.

Perhaps the first of these social movements was the sanitary or public health movement in various industrial areas of Europe during the late 1800's and in the United States immediately following the Civil War. The health movement picked up momentum and by the turn of the century became a drive to improve personal health as well as to obtain sanitary living conditions in congested urban areas.

The modern play movement, then, like other social movements, includes not only a rapid expansion of recreation facilities but a general program of education and increased participation by people in a wide variety of leisure-time activities characteristic of the changing social and economic conditions in Europe and America. The play movement has been a part of the general humanitarian reform movement which began in the latter half of the nineteenth century and was directed toward broadening the general educational and cultural development of all people.

Rainwater, who first analyzed the play movement in the United States, defined the movement as an attempt to bring about an adjustment of both the play life of children and the recreation activities of youth and adults to the changing social situation in urban as well as rural areas. He described

[2] M. H. and E. S. Neumeyer, *Leisure and Recreation* (New York: The Ronald Press Co., 1958), pp. 62-3.

the early play movement as the playground movement, relating the initiation of playgrounds in industrialized Germany to the initiation of playgrounds in the United States in the early 1880's. Neumeyer and Neumeyer broaden the scope of the movement and call it the recreation movement. The use of the term play movement in this work implies not only the scope of Rainwater's definition, but also what the Neumeyers call the recreation movement, as well as what has been termed more recently community recreation. The modern play movement, as it is understood in its entirety today, has grown to encompass all recreation opportunities existing in the urban and rural community of a private, voluntary, commercial, or public character.

The specific formal concept of organized public recreation and play had, to a great extent, its origin in nineteenth century German society. The play movement in Germany grew out of the activities of Guts Muths and Jahn, the growth of school physical education and play activities, the Turnverein, the sandgarden playgrounds in Berlin, and the practice of a wide variety of informal, outdoor recreation activities by all classes of the population. On the other hand, consideration must be given to the informal concepts contributed to the movement through games, sports, and social activities as practiced in England and several other countries throughout the world. These early developments in England and Germany actually brought together various interest groups which finally became the forces behind the growth of the play movement in America and elsewhere. These forces united the efforts of many people to stimulate participation in all types of traditional recreation activities, to train leaders to conduct these activities, and to provide playgrounds and other public and private facilities for the operation of recreation programs and services.

PLAY MOVEMENT IN EUROPEAN COUNTRIES

Although each country has developed its play system along more or less different lines from its neighbors, depending on the degree to which the cultural backgrounds vary, there are nevertheless certain similarities among the European systems which characterize them as a whole and set them off from the American movement. Both in the way they were conceived and in the way they are carried out, they differ in rather marked fashion from that found in this country. In his study of European play, L. H. Weir of the National Recreation Association, after an extensive study abroad, pointed out the following reasons for the differences between the situation in Europe and America:

1. The recreation movement in Europe began chiefly with the adults whereas in America it began with the children.

2. The highly specialized, formalized systems of gymnastics long established in many of the countries did not look with special favor upon mere play.

3. The rapid development of sports among the young people and adults tended to place the chief emphasis upon the activities of these groups rather than upon the needs of children, hence the great numbers of sports fields, stadiums, swimming centers, etc., chiefly for adults.

4. The public care of the children was chiefly in the hands of the educational authorities who, in spite of the great examples of Plato, Froebel, Pestalozzi and others, were backward (as in America in many instances) in recognizing the great social and educational values in the play of children. Moreover, the educational authorities had chiefly adopted the gymnastic systems of physical activities as more in conformity with the practices of highly organized, formalized educational methods and processes.

5. The close knit family life, as in most of the Latin countries and in Europe in general, was a factor in the lack of attention to children's play and public provisions for it. It was believed that the place for the children, outside of school, was the home. There was, therefore, no definite realization by municipal authorities of responsibility for children's play, a situation that is widely prevalent in many countries today.

6. In many of the countries a very large per cent of the

population is rural. There are many natural advantages for the play of children under such conditions and it was not deemed so necessary to make special provision for it.[3]

These conditions described by Weir were altered considerably by the events of World War II. The effects of destructive aerial bombing and land warfare was especially evident in postwar Europe. The refugee problem, along with significant political changes in many areas on the Continent, left many people with a feeling of insecurity; people in Europe as well as the Near and Far East faced serious social and economic problems in planning for the future.

Recovery in Europe, however, especially on the continent, has been surprisingly rapid. Everywhere people are impressed with the excellent condition and permanence of new public facilities such as streets, public buildings, and park facilities. The new emphasis is upon providing services of benefit to all people, stimulating civic spirit, and encouraging more citizen participation in municipal affairs.

Specifically, in sports and recreation, this new outlook is immediately noticeable. Sports facilities of private clubs have increased considerably; many new ultramodern sports stadiums, arenas, sports centers, and playing fields have been constructed throughout Europe. Public control of land on the fringe of towns has improved the appearance of urban areas, and many municipally owned, fringe area lands are being used for playfields and various other types of public recreation facilities. In addition, many cities promote cultural activities through a city department of culture, and municipalities bear the cost of promoting orchestras, operas, theatre programs, and similar local activities. Then, too, the authorities of the Swiss city of Geneva support private organizations devoted to art, welfare, sports, drama, vocational schools, and other specific cultural activities.

GERMANY. Probably Germany has had the most extended modern background in the development of physical education. Physical exercise first found a place in a modern

[3] L. H. Weir, *Europe at Play* (New York: A. S. Barnes & Co., 1937), pp. 83-4.

school when Basedow, in 1774, founded the Philanthropinum at Dessau. Some of the exercises were dancing, riding, fencing, vaulting, planing, carpentry, running, and wrestling. The emphasis was on the first four, the "knightly exercises" of chivalric times. The Philanthropinum attracted wide attention and many institutions were founded as offshoots. A famous schoolmaster, Guts Muths, elaborated on Basedow's scheme, giving great emphasis to the recreational phases of physical education. His work, in particular, influenced continental Europe to a great extent: through Pestalozzi and Fellenberg in Switzerland, Nachtegall in Denmark, Ling in Sweden, and Father Jahn and Adolf Spiess in Germany. It is noteworthy that the first one to stress strongly the educational side of play was Froebel in 1826 and that his studies and experiments resulted in the present-day kindergarten.

These early beginnings in Germany partook more of the nature of physical education than of informal or voluntary play. It was during the initial influence of a political leader, von Schenckendorff, in the 1880's, however, that the play movement actually began and the first play areas were established in Berlin. These were simply open play areas completely covered with sand, resembling a huge sandbox, and contained special play apparatus and materials for children from two to eight years of age. It was under the leadership of von Schenckendorff also, in 1891, that the Central Committee for the Promotion of Games in Germany was launched, an organization which included prominent play leaders representing the sports and play interests of various groups from all sections of the land. This organization helped to secure facilities, arrange teacher-training courses, publish rules of games, promote national conventions, and provide promotional leadership through the press.

While the formalism for which Germany is famed still receives a major emphasis, games and sports have played an ever increasing part in recent years. Popular among these are German handball, tennis, swimming, skiing, soccer, track and field, rowing, canoeing, bicycling, and fencing.

It was not until after World War I that widespread attention was given to city planning for recreation activities. Between 1918 and 1933, during the Weimar Republic, no country surpassed Germany in the realization of the importance of space for both indoor and outdoor play facilities. During the same period, significant advances were made in physical education through official government support which culminated in the acceptance of physical education in the school curriculum on the same basis as other subjects.

But even greater than the expansion of physical education during this era was the tremendous growth of private sports clubs, voluntary sports associations, and a myriad of organizations promoting informal physical and social recreation activities. Exemplifying this was the Youth Hostel movement, which spread rapidly throughout the nation. Founded by Richard Schirrman, a leader in the earlier German youth movement, the Youth Hostel activities became a wandering school of self-discipline and independence, comradeship, and outdoor living. Hostels were provided throughout the land at which overnight lodging was available for a few cents. Started in 1910, it grew to great popularity after World War I and by 1935 had about seven million participants. Hiking and bicycling across the land, singing folk songs, and engaging in serious discussions of political and social matters, youth found in this movement both a recreational outlet and an educational opportunity of great importance.

Although the German people had many political difficulties under the Weimar Republic, the period marked the culmination of a general pattern of informal sports and recreation participation that has become characteristic of Germany. The Germans learned to make great use of their rivers and mountains for boating, hiking, and camping. Canoeing and kayaking were popular. Hiking was a sport of major enjoyment. Once a month school children and teachers went on a required day-long hike. Bicycling was enjoyed informally and in organized groups. Whole families would often go on a cycling trip, the mother leading, the father bringing up the rear with the baby in a basket over the front wheel. Train and boat excursion travel was available at exceptionally low rates. The Germans also delighted in spending hours talking with one another. They sat for long periods over their beer steins, wine glasses, and coffee cups, just talking and seeking the enjoyment of one another's company.

After the Nazis came into power, the Government in 1933 seized direct control of all physical education, organized sports, and recreation activities of the German people. Physical education in schools was rigidly controlled through a special curriculum; out-of-school youth activities were systematically organized through the prominent Hitler Youth organization. This program provided activities for both boys and girls from six to eighteen years of age, including sports and games, hiking, camping, first aid, hygiene, reading, and general cultural activities under leaders carefully selected and indoctrinated in the Nazi political, social, and economic philosophies. Similarly, sports and recreation activities for adults, formerly under a number of independent private and public club organizations, were consolidated and controlled under sixteen unions directly under the supervision of a Nazi national sports commissioner. In addition, the vast informal sports and recreation programs of German labor groups were brought under control through the Nazi-directed Kraft durch Freude (Strength through Joy) organization, which effectively brought recreational, cultural, and travel opportunities to the German people at relatively little expense.

Since World War II, in East Germany the Communist government has rigidly controlled all sports and leisure-time activities. In West Germany, under the Allied Occupation, special funds have been allocated for the operation of youth centers under trained leaders, recreation facilities are being rebuilt, and the national character of German sports and leisure-time activities of the 1920's is rapidly being restored. In the bombed-out city of Cologne, for example, the new city plan has made possible a green belt, a little over a half mile wide and approximately three miles long extending along three sides of the city, devoted exclusively to sport and outdoor activity. Sports centers in Berlin, Garmish-Partenkirchen, and Frankfurt have been restored, and municipal stadiums and recreation centers similar to those enjoyed before are being built rapidly.

ENGLAND. The English play system has developed as an integral part of the cultural history of the people, rather than as a result of ideas innovated or promulgated by educators. Although trustworthy accounts of this growth are not too plentiful, there is no question that the liberty-loving Anglo-Saxons enjoyed sports, games, and amusements since the earliest times.

During the age of chivalry recreations involved archery, dancing, leaping, vaulting, wrestling, weight throwing, and ball games; but with the ascendancy of the Puritans all these were rigidly suppressed. It was not until the eighteenth century that games came back into universal favor again. This was due to the rise of the boarding schools for boys of the upper classes. These served as the nurseries of the national pastimes. At first the teachers merely tolerated the sports but with a new generation of teachers, who themselves had played, a new interest was added. Arnold, as headmaster of Rugby about 1840, recognized the character value of athletics and made them a necessary part of the curriculum. Since then, headmasters of all schools through the force of their opinions have made participation obligatory.

The English public schools of this type, which correspond to private secondary schools in our country, demonstrate the spirit of athletic play at its best. There are large and wonderfully kept fields to provide facilities for everyone. As a result of long vacations, frequent holidays, and considerable freedom in the afternoon there is much time available for play. Practically every season has its round of sports. A very commendable feature of the English schools is the close mingling of masters and pupils on the playing field. The result is a clean type of athletics and an amateurism that is of the highest grade. The higher schools for girls give the same emphasis to outdoor sports.

In the educational process as it operates in the British schools, games and sports are valued as much for the social training they afford as for the physical. The emphasis is the result of tradition and practice, however, and not of educational theory. The universities do not make play compulsory; yet, the habit persists and many athletic clubs are organized. Sport in the universities is casual and entirely up to the choice of the individual.

Professional athletic leagues flourish but to a lesser extent than in America, and since games are regarded essentially as play rather than work, the line between the professional and the amateur is very strictly drawn. It can be seen that the English system gives its primary emphasis to sports and competitive play. Even in the elementary schools, this type of play is introduced at an early age. These Council schools, as they are called, have gymnasiums, and a certain amount of gymnastics of the Swedish type is required. In the crowded districts some of these schools have roof gardens for the purpose of organized play.

Since World War II the greatest progress in general sports and recreation participation in England has been brought about by a major sports group, the Central Council of Physical Recreation (CCPR). The Council was formed in 1935 as a practical step toward bringing together all national organizations interested in the promotion and development of various types of sports participation. By 1956 the Council consisted of a federation of over two hundred major amateur athletic bodies governing practically all sports activities throughout England, Wales, and Northern Ireland. The Council is not a controlling body but rather a coordinating agency having an executive council employing more than fifty sports and recreation specialists who are available to help local sports clubs and groups. Although it is not a government body, the Council is subsidized to a large extent by the Ministry of Education. Among other things, the activities of the Council include the training of leaders, consultant services, promotion of special sports events, making films and visual aids materials, and the operation of National Recreation Centers. Sports enthusiasts of varying skill visit these centers for one- or two-week courses called Sports Holidays. The CCPR also sponsors many sports activities for women. It also cooperates with groups such as the English Folk Dancing Society in sponsoring folk dance festivals.

The Youth Hostel and camping movement, borrowed from Germany, has also been popular in England. In 1955 over three hundred low-cost hostels were in operation throughout England and Wales. The Camping Club of Great Britain and Ireland, with over 13,000 members, and the Youth Camping Association, the Canoeing Union, and the Rambler's Association affirm the broad interest of all age groups in camping and outdoor activities. The Boy Scouts of America and the Girl Scouts of the USA are offsprings of the English Boy Scouts and Girl Guides.

England's play system, so largely spontaneous, has had world-wide influence. European countries have taken to English recreative sports, such as golf, tennis, badminton, swimming, rowing, and soccer. The early colonists introduced outdoor sports into America with the result that athletic games furnish the major part of the physical education program in this country. In certain aspects, the English system is most commendable: the love of sport for sport's sake (less emphasis on winning), and the practice of maintaining participation in sport throughout life instead of its ceasing abruptly after leaving school.

SWEDEN. In Sweden the impulse towards gymnastics was generated by Peter Ling, who was, in turn, influenced by the writings of Guts Muths in Germany. Ling's motives were primarily patriotic so that his methods were at first almost entirely of a military nature. He urged his views so strongly and continually that in 1814 the Royal authorities established a Royal Central Institute of Gymnastics and appointed Ling as the director. This institution trained teachers of gymnastics first for the army and then for the schools. Peter Ling's son, Hjälmar, systematized the exercises for use in the schools and added new ones.

The Swedish system has influenced other countries to a great extent, especially France, Belgium, Norway, Denmark, and Greece. England employs the Swedish exercises in its public schools to supplement the effects of games; and for many years they were also used in the British navy. The United States owes much of its early progress in physical education to the exercises imported from this same source. The Swedish system of exercises is unexcelled for its developmental and therapeutic effects.

The emphasis in the Swedish recreation movement is definitely swinging toward games to supplement the formal gymnastics. Soccer is now the most popular sport. Skiing is second, followed by track and field athletics. Tennis, skating, golf, outdoor handball, and swimming also find broad participation. Play activities in Sweden are not confined merely to various forms of outdoor life. Folk dancing is enjoyed by large elements of the population and there is a widespread interest in the theatre and music.

The average individual takes part in mass competition and develops sufficient skill to pass tests to obtain sports badges. Busses at public expense transport children from Stockholm to nearby lakes for swimming. Bicycling has long been their mode of traveling. The Swedish athletes have always ranked high in the Olympic Games, excelling in the all-round track events such as the decathlon and pentathlon, in distance running, and in winter sports.

Sweden, with its seven million population, is well provided per capita with sports facilities. Also, sports centers such as Boson, located near Stockholm, provide special instructors and coaches who specialize in all kinds of sports programs operated by the National Sports Federation of Sweden. Local groups give some financial support to sports operations, but the majority of the funds for the sports movement have long been derived from national lotteries and more recently from the proceeds of government-supervised soccer and football pools.

DENMARK. Denmark has the oldest school of physical education in the world. In 1804 the Gymnastic Institute was founded for the training of army officers in physical education and Franz Nachtegall, the founder of the Danish system of gymnastics, appointed director. This school still flourishes and has had a far-reaching effect in the promotion of physical education. Games and track and field events came into popularity during the last quarter of the last century. Soccer, tennis, boxing, and fencing have become particularly popular. The Copenhagen Playground Association was organized during the 1890's and was instrumental in persuading the national government to appropriate funds for the promotion of group games in the schools. Niels Bukh, another great leader of Danish physical education, developed a new interpretation of the traditional Danish system of gymnastics and of the Ling system of Sweden in 1921. This interpretation, known as "primitive gymnastics," has had a great influence throughout Europe and America. In general the Danish people have always been most enthusiastic in respect to recreation and there has been an almost universal participation. Travelers in Denmark are immediately impressed by the number of bicyclists traversing the main thoroughfares—it is said there is one bicycle for every two inhabitants of the city. Boating and swimming are widely popular, and skating on old castle moats is a winter favorite. Folk dances are common at social gatherings.

FRANCE. The first attempt to introduce gymnastics into France was in 1817 following close on the Napoleonic Wars, but gymnastics soon centered almost entirely on the training of teachers for the army. The first concerted effort to introduce physical education in the schools came in 1890 through the adoption of the Swedish system of gymnastics and the issuance of a manual on physical training.

It was not until after World War I that physical education was made compulsory in the schools. In 1934 the Supreme Council for Physical Education was formed as a government agency to promote: (1) physical education in schools, (2) camps and Boy Scouts, (3) sports and contests, and (4) preparation for military service. A daily period in gymnastics was then required for all from six years of age on until military conscription. All teachers are obligated to teach these classes.

Since World War II, the French people have been revising their school study programs. It is clearly recognized that one great weakness is the limited attention given physical exercises and outdoor pursuits. Recent experimental work in French schools has indicated that regular school periods devoted to physical education and games have not endangered the traditional French curriculum but rather have been of benefit to the children's studies.

The playgrounds of the larger cities are for the most part small and cater mostly to young children. There are sports stadiums built for track and field and dog racing, for example, but these are maintained largely by gate receipts. The French government has not permitted the use of funds from soccer pools and similar sources to construct sports facilities or to provide sports and recreation leadership. On the other hand, since World War II, the Director General of Youth and Sports, a Minister of Cabinet rank, has been given the responsibility of promoting physical activities, sport, and recreation.

In the way of sports, the French people traditionally have inclined toward recreation of a milder type in which the element of team play is minor—handball, tennis, walking, cycling, croquet, fencing, and shooting. In recent years, however, participation in soccer has grown in numbers considerably; basketball also has become well liked as a team sport and there is significant progress in initiating it in larger urban centers. Bicycling, hiking, and hosteling are popular as always.

Traditionally there has been a relative indifference in France to recreation as a problem and a conspicuous lack of widespread provision for recreational leisure needs. Individualism is a marked characteristic of the French, and the Frenchman's feeling of social responsibility aside from his patriotism does not in general extend beyond his immediate family.

SWITZERLAND. Few countries of continental Europe, if any, have a longer or more brilliant history of physical activities, or a more efficient present day state of development than little Switzerland. This country proudly reports that it has as members of sport and gymnastic associations a greater percentage of its population than any European country. A century of gymnastics on the Turnverein or Turnen pattern was celebrated in 1932 when the Swiss Gymnastic Confederacy reached the hundredth anniversary of its aggressive history, with an active membership numbering upwards of 150,000. Following the trend of the present century, athletic sports and recreational games have entered, supplementing the gymnastics. The Swiss Football and Light Athletic Association has been active since 1895. Every four years the various athletic and gymnastic clubs and associations unite in a large and spectacular national festival.

There are many independent local sports clubs, particularly of wrestling, basketball, soccer, rugby, and mountain climbing. The marked increase in emphasis on sports and games rather than the traditional body training is marked further by the program offered at the famous national Swiss sports center, Eidgenossische Turn- und Sportschule, at Magglingen. This center reached its full operation in 1956, offering the most modern facilities for sports participation, maintaining training institutes in a variety of activities for special instructors, and conducting advanced research in sports and physical education activities. Schools have, especially since World War II, developed an excellent system of physical education.

Municipal play areas have been developed in urban areas, particularly public beaches and boating facilities, skiing centers, and public camping grounds in municipally owned forests. The Youth Hostels are prominent, and hiking, mountain climbing, skiing, and cycling are very popular in this country of unsurpassed variety of scenic appeal.

RUSSIA. As late as 1922 in Russia there were only hints
of physical education or of sponsored play. But in the years
since, and particularly following World War II, the movement has spread like a huge tidal wave. Backed by a distinct realization that the strength of a nation depends upon
the strength of individuals and that health is essential to
happiness, interest in sports has increased as in no other
country in a similar period of time.

The measures taken during this period to provide athletics
and physical education in the schools are truly remarkable.
By 1937 there were six graduate schools for physical education to train the necessary instructors. In 1953 the Soviet
Union had eleven institutes of physical culture, thirty-nine
physical culture high schools, and three special institutes
engaged in physical culture research. Institute students
participate in a broad, university-type training in all phases
of physical culture and recreation. Basically the Soviet
school physical education program is designed to develop
all-round fitness as well as interest and skill in sports. The
system of training begins in the nursery school and continues
long after school years into old age. The All-Union Committee of Physical Culture coordinates the work in the
schools of each district, county, and local soviet. The curriculum in physical education in the early grades includes
games, rhythmic activities, and calisthenics; in the fifth
grade sports are introduced and special attention is given to
gymnastics. Finally, a broad program of sport and leisure-
time activities is carried on in the vast network of Soviet
technical, trade, and secondary schools and at the university
level. Mass gymnastic demonstrations are common, with
boys and girls performing a wide variety of traditional exercises in colorful settings.

In Russia, however, training in physical culture, health,
and activities for leisure goes far beyond the limits of state
schools. It is the objective of the Russian government to
maintain the skills developed in the schools—to achieve mass
fitness of the entire population in conjunction with the development of a common culture based heavily upon tradi-

tional games, sports, music, drama, art, and other recreation activities. Sports clubs are directly supported by the government. Although these collective organizations are sponsored mainly by labor unions, many of them are organized and promoted by youth groups and voluntary sports societies. One of the thirty odd labor union groups, Shakhytor, owns and operates over 76 stadiums, 83 gymnasiums, and 3,800 sports fields throughout Russia.[4] Athletic and sports competitions are conducted throughout the country, even in the rural areas. Soccer is the favorite team sport. Basketball and volleyball are also gaining in popularity, as are gymnastics, wrestling, tennis, and Russian handball.

The government has built a series of public camps, hostels, parks of culture and rest, workers' rest homes, sanitariums, swimming pools, and recreation facilities of various types, all either free or at low cost to the masses. In 1954, the government appropriated for health and recreation an amount representing nearly half the entire budget for general education. In addition, approximately 20 per cent of the profits of all trade unions is channeled into sport and related activities.

Gifted athletes are trained in special schools. Thousands of boys and girls are given this special instruction at public expense to train for local, national, and international competitions. The success of Russian athletes, both men and women, in recent Olympic Games shows the phenomenal strides the country has made in a short space of time.

Russia, a communist state, has woven its entire social, economic, and cultural life about the specific political doctrines of Marxism. Not only is all sport and recreation participation by the people directed along these lines, but the physical structure of cities and villages represents a precisely executed master plan for all phases of life. As early as 1937 a very carefully planned pattern which provided playgrounds, playfields, community centers, and other basic leisure-time facilities was approved by the Russian State In-

---

[4] W. L. Steel, "Soviet Sport," *Physical Recreation*, VIII (April, 1956), 20.

stitute for City Planning. Since World War II, city planning
standards governing recreation and leisure-time facilities
have been altered to meet new needs created by the rapid
development of large urban Russian industrial areas.

The Russians are also justly noted for their cultural forms
of recreation including folk dancing and folk music, ballet,
concert and symphony music, and art.

PLAY MOVEMENT IN THE NEAR AND FAR EAST

In 1922 a model playground complete with equipment
for all sports was established in Ankara, Turkey, by the
American Friends of Turkey, and in 1927 they established
a second model playground at Smyrna which the city government took over two years later. Such important demonstrations were needed to implement the movement and supply patterns for other cities to copy. Turkey, like most of
the countries of the Near East, including Israel, Iran, Iraq,
Egypt, Jordan, and Syria, has taken radical steps to improve
physical education and to develop sports and recreation activities according to its social, cultural, and nationalistic
interests and needs. Physical education, based on Swedish
gymnastics, is required in schools. Sports clubs for both
youth and adults, indicating the growth of European-type
sports organization at the local level, are becoming more
prevalent throughout the Near East. Turkish sports include
soccer football, track, volleyball, basketball, skiing, and
swimming. Wrestling has long been practiced in Turkey,
and many Olympic gold medals have been won by Turkish
wrestlers. The country-wide interest in sports in Turkey,
as well as other countries in the Near East, is reflected in the
initiation of the Olympic-type Mediterranean Games in
October, 1951, and the Pan-Arab Games in 1953.

China has bestowed her art, literature, philosophy, and
culture on the world, but her traditional point of view regarding physical activity has been that no gentleman would
engage in play. Physical education was neglected for 4000
years, and consequently no system of physical training de-

veloped. As a result of recent European and American influence, however, a strong interest in physical education and public recreation has developed. By 1920 there were playgrounds and play teachers connected with practically all schools, and public playgrounds have been established in many of the larger cities. By 1940, the national government had built stadiums in a number of cities; and teacher-training schools were graduating instructors of physical education and recreation. Also, the National Physical Education Committee, organized in 1941, inaugurated a standardized curriculum in physical education. The new movement also included a broad program of sports and recreation activities for women. Since the Nationalist Government lost control to the Chinese Communists, the typical pattern of Soviet Russian sports and leisure-time activities has prevailed.

Japan until 1925 had an occasional baseball and football team, but there was very little interest in the sports. Then two huge stadiums, one seating 65,000 and the other 30,000, were built in Tokyo, and another accommodating 80,000 in Narmo; and upwards of a dozen universities built accommodations for 10,000 or more spectators. First class baseball is being played and the game is now as popular and universal throughout even the rural districts of Japan as it is in America—it is at the present time the most popular national sport. Cricket has never been taken up extensively in Japan, but hockey, association football, basketball, boxing, track and field events, and tennis are extremely popular and widespread. Golf has been taken up enthusiastically by business men and officials, and excellent courses are to be found. In the last quarter century the Japanese swimmers have met with outstanding success in competition. Wrestling has long been popular in Japan and boxing now has an ever increasing number of followers. With the advent of cafés, dancing of the western type has sprung into popularity, and a craze for it has swept the country. Much of the credit for the introduction of sport into Japan and China belongs to the YMCA.

The people of the Indian Union (India) and Pakistan, becoming independent nations in 1947, have taken definite
steps toward establishing physical education and leisure-
time facilities and programs. Reforms, only a part of the
tremendous social, economic, political, and cultural changes
that have swept over India, are quite evident. Physical education and recreation, like other new programs, are being
carefully integrated with the needs and interests of the vast
throngs of the population consisting of a variety of religious,
social, and cultural groups.

Provincial governments and local councils are developing
universal, free public education as rapidly as possible.
Physical education is required in the schools, but as yet
teacher training in this area is relatively undeveloped. Private, voluntary, and organized public groups are, at present,
carrying the burden of providing sports and recreation facilities and services. The YMCA, the Scouts, and similar
groups have a wide influence; private sports clubs are popular. In 1950, sixteen recreation centers for teachers, leaders,
and participants, partly supported by the government, were
opened in India. Physical education camps have become
popular, and it is the plan of the Indian government to
provide informal sports and recreation services for every
village. Included in these local services will be facilities
for libraries, art, music, and similar activities to foster national Indian customs and traditional cultural mores and
folkways.

Sports competitions are general throughout India and
Pakistan. In India particularly, field hockey is played.
India has won the Olympic field hockey championship each
Olympiad since the 1928 games at Amsterdam. Gymnastics,
basketball, volleyball, tennis, wrestling, track and field, and
other games are common. Traditional activities such as
yoga and a number of tag games are popular throughout
India. Bombay, Calcutta, and other large cities are developing Olympic-type stadiums and facilities for mass
sports and cultural activities for all the people.

Australia and New Zealand have felt the effects of the

world-wide play and recreation movement. Physical education is coordinated through the National Director of Training in a highly centralized, federal school system. School programs include both gymnastics and games and sports. Professional training in physical education, though recent in origin, is developing rapidly. Independent sports clubs are the centers of sports activities. Cricket, soccer, tennis, and swimming are the most popular sports but wrestling, track and field, and sailing are also widely pursued. The interest and enthusiasm in Australia for indoor as well as outdoor sports was demonstrated by the success of the Olympic Games held in Melbourne in 1956.

PLAY MOVEMENT IN MEXICO AND CANADA

The educational system in Mexico has, in recent years, been marked by rapid progress. Physical and health education have been recognized as regular school subjects in the revised public education program of the Ministry of Education. Cultural missions have been instituted to meet the social, educational, and recreational needs of the predominantly rural population. Sports and recreation activities are now commencing on an inter-school basis, and some intercollegiate competitions are taking place. Sports outside schools are promoted by local clubs and by industries which conduct outstanding sports and recreation programs for industrial workers and their families in the larger urban areas. The Mexican Sports Federation and its affiliated groups promote organized sports competitions throughout the country. Most popular sports are jai alai, gymnastics, track and field, boxing, and wrestling. American basketball and baseball have "caught on" in Mexico and are being played widely. In addition, traditional games and sports, characteristic of Indian life in Mexico, are being studied and recreation leaders are promoting them to preserve them as a part of Mexican cultural life. The people of Mexico enjoy dancing, folk music, and fiestas, in which all ages of the population participate according to age-old local customs and folkways.

A keen awareness of the importance of physical education, health education, and recreation is evident in Canada. Although still many areas of the country remain undeveloped, Canada harbors tremendous potential for future development. Despite a dual public and private school system operated in many parts of the country, there has been rapid progress in the development of leisure-time and physical education programs and services in all of Canada's Provinces.

Before World War II, physical education programs were carried on mainly in the larger urban centers. During the war, however, the number of draft rejections and other research data prompted the enactment of the National Physical Fitness Act in 1943. The Physical Fitness Division, under the Department of National Health and Welfare, acting primarily as a coordinating and advisory body, served as a clearing house for information and education concerning sports, athletics, recreation, community centers, physical education, and research. It conducted surveys, trained personnel, and created visual aids and other public relations material that stimulated provincial governments in developing local health, physical education, and recreation programs. Although repealed in 1954, the National Physical Fitness Act, to a great extent, developed the pattern upon which future development in health, physical education, and recreation in Canada can be based.

Public park, playground, and community recreation programs are providing excellent facilities and leadership for well-balanced, year-round recreation programs at the community and neighborhood levels. Many Canadian communities have laws permitting them to use tax funds for the provision of public recreation programs and resources. Sports participation between schools, colleges, and local independent clubs is widespread. Winter sports, particularly hockey and curling, are most popular. Facilities and leadership are provided in local areas. Basketball, baseball, soccer, and Canadian football are played extensively. Lacrosse is considered one of the national pastimes. Tennis and cricket competitions are carried on between local sports clubs. The great Canadian outdoors, containing some of the most fascinating natural areas on the North American continent, make Canada a mecca for hunting, fishing, boating, camping, and other outdoor sports and recreation activities.

PLAY MOVEMENT IN LATIN AMERICA

The nations of Central and South America, too, have felt the impetus of the modern play movement. The first interest came as a matter of chance, with many foreign inhabitants bringing their games with them. In this way soccer, pelota, tennis, cricket, golf, track, and baseball became known. The first efforts at actually promoting play were made by the YMCA. Then basketball and volleyball were added to the list of popular sports. Of late, many soccer associations have sprung up and compete in championships which finally lead to international competitions, with great throngs attending.

Since 1950, the development of modern sports and recreation programs in various Central and South American countries has developed very rapidly. Puerto Rico has established a modern school, playground, and recreation system closely resembling the most advanced systems in the United States. The population is very sports conscious, and baseball has grown to be the national sport. In Peru, a regular physical education program has been developed in both elementary and secondary schools, and sports are highly developed on a local club basis. The entire program is coordinated by the Department of Physical Education in the Ministry of Education. Playgrounds of the American type are found in Argentina, Brazil, and Uruguay. In Montevideo, a city of over 900,000 people, the latest planning principles are being applied to determine land use. Public recreation and other leisure-time facilities are being carefully designed and located. These developments are part of a vast master plan to provide the most modern parks, beaches, and general community recreation facilities and services for all the people. Significant progress has also been made in Venezuela, Bolivia, Colombia, and many other South American countries.

Indicative of the growth of sports in these countries and in Central America was the initiation in 1938 of the Bolivarian Games, which have been held at regular intervals since that time, and the Pan-American Games, another Olympic-type sports festival that has grown in popularity. More recently, basketball and baseball have become very popular in South America and have been added to soccer football, gymnastics, fencing, track and field, and swimming as the most popular of the imported sports.

AN INTERNATIONAL PLAY AND RECREATION MOVEMENT

As indicated, the impetus for the world play movement came from Europe, principally England and Germany, where social problems similar to those facing people in other parts of the world were handled with some success. Acute social problems caused by rapid industrialization, the concentration of population in urban areas, and the mass social disruption resulting from wars and changes in national boundaries caused people in Europe to formulate new social horizons. Thus, the play movement grew out of the social needs of people in the western world. More specifically, however, the movement was implemented in Europe by (1) the importance of physical fitness activities accentuated by the constant threat of aggression which hovered over Europe; (2) the growth of gymnastics on the Continent as a method of physical education together with the contrasting growth of games and sports in England in response not only to the need for fitness but as a means of expression through physical activities; (3) the national patriotic expression generated through sports and recreation activities, marked particularly by the revival of the Olympic Games and international competition, and finally (4) the realization of the value of individual expression and of national cultures and civilizations through all types of leisure-time activities such as games and sports, dance, music, art, drama, and hobbies of collecting and an experimental nature.

It is evident from these sketches of the growth of sports and recreation that there is a consciousness of the need for play, not only as a means to health, but as a means of social and moral education. There are several notable postwar changes in the character of sports and leisure-time participation which support the contention that there is literally a boom in the development of these activities throughout Europe, America, and the rest of the world as well.

First, there are more participants now in all sports and recreation activities than ever before, and all indications point to a further increase in participation in the future.

Second, there is a steady increase in interest as well as participation in sports and games in preference to the traditional European body-building and gymnastic activities.

Third, there is a marked increase in the number as well as the quality of both physical education teachers and sports coaches being trained. Teacher-training methods have improved considerably. A most notable advance has been made in the rapid growth of the Sports Medicine movement in Europe. This group of doctors and their associates, now organized into an International Sport Medicine Federation, provide research data to improve present sports practices and to guide their development in the future.

Fourth, there is evidence which clearly indicates that hiking, soccer, gymnastics, skiing, cycling, and swimming are the most popular sports for the participant in Europe. For the spectator, soccer, automobile and cycle endurance racing, horse racing, boxing, and track and field athletics are most enjoyed. Camping, practiced only in a limited way in 1940, is now very common. Basketball and volleyball are growing steadily; baseball and softball, despite American influences during World War II, have not been generally accepted in European countries but are played in several countries in Central and South America and in the Far East, particularly Japan.

Fifth, there is definite evidence to show that, on the whole, participation in sports, games, and recreational activities in Europe and most other areas of the world is still centered around private clubs and local sports associations. A new development, however, which strengthens this entire structure immeasurably, is the growth of national sports centers. Unlike any services existing in America, these centers, such as Lilleshall in England and the Swiss Sportschule at Magglingen, provide national sports and recreation leadership as well as accessible mass facilities for all types of sports participation which have been so vitally needed. The sports center idea has spread to South America, Australia, and other countries.

Sixth, there has been, since 1948, a great increase in the construction of sports, games, and recreation areas and facilities throughout the world. This has involved everything from providing more outdoor playing fields in land-poor England to the construction of massive indoor and outdoor facilities for participation in all types of sports, games, and leisure-time activities by the masses of the people in all walks of life.

Seventh, there has been, in most countries, a considerable increase in the financial support given to private as well as public agencies and groups promoting sports and recreation activities. These funds have been mostly taxes collected and distributed by the various federal governments. In Europe, these funds have been derived mainly from legalized betting on football, horse racing, and dog racing. Much of the post-World War II expansion of sports and recreation in Europe can be attributed to this great increase in funds.

People all over the world are conscious of the need for moving closer toward an understanding of common problems and interests in all phases of life. This is particularly evident in world activities in sports and recreation. In 1952, the National Recreation Association initiated an International Recreation Service which has made rapid strides in bringing together people from all parts of the world who are interested in or responsible for operating sports and recreation programs and services of all types. Also, the Preamble of the Charter of the United Nations states that the member nations are pledged to "promote social progress and better the standards of living in larger freedom . . . to employ international machinery for the promotion of economic and social advancement of all peoples." International progress is being made through the United Nations toward a greater understanding between all peoples of the world in the future. People in every country have something to contribute and something to learn. All people associated with the development of human understanding, and especially people closely involved in sports and recreation activities, have an obligation to promote the world-wide exchange of ideas and methods prevalent within each country.

SUMMARY

The play and recreation programs of countries discussed have greatly influenced the play movement throughout the rest of the world. However, in countries not mentioned, including the play movement in the United States which will be discussed in Chapter 3, rich contributions to the present world play movement have also been evident. Each country has its own unique pattern of recreation and has given some special meaning to the universal movement.

Even though other countries may have followed the patterns set by the European and American play movements as international exchanges took place, something characteristic was always added in the leavening process. These other countries still held to their indigenous and picturesque play customs, and at the same time wove them into a general pattern which embodied outside influence as well. The interchange of cultures took place in a noticeable way during the two World Wars when troops of various countries were stationed on foreign soils. To trace these developments in more detail is not possible within the space limitations of this book. Consequently, the reader with historical interest is referred to the reference list following. The primary emphasis of this chapter has, of necessity, been given to those countries in which the play movement, as such, originated.

SELECTED REFERENCES

KIERAN, JOHN, and DALEY, ARTHUR. *The Story of the Olympic Games.* Rev. ed. Philadelphia: J. B. Lippincott Co., 1957.

MENKE, FRANK G. *The Encyclopedia of Sports.* 2d ed. New York: A. S. Barnes & Co., Inc., 1960.

NEUMEYER, MARTIN H., and NEUMEYER, ESTHER S. *Leisure and Recreation.* New York: The Ronald Press Co., 1958, Chap. 4.

RAINWATER, CLARENCE E. *The Play Movement in the United States.* Chicago: University of Chicago Press, 1921, Chap. 1.

RICE, EMMETT A., HUTCHINSON, JOHN L., and LEE, MABEL. *A Brief History of Physical Education.* 4th ed. New York: The Ronald Press Co., 1958.

RIVERS, THOMAS E. "International Relationships," *The Annals of the American Academy of Political and Social Science,* CCCXIII (September, 1957), 105.

VAN DALEN, DEOBOLD B., MITCHELL, ELMER D., and BENNETT, BRUCE L. *A World History of Physical Education.* Englewood Cliffs, N. J.: Prentice-Hall, Inc., 1953.

For information about sports, including a wide variety of activities; such as sailing, racing, mountain climbing, camping, and dancing, see *Physical Recreation,* the quarterly journal of the Central Council of Physical Education, London, England. Included in each issue is a summary of current developments in sports throughout Europe and other parts of the world.

3

Play Movement
in the United States

The play movement in the United States is generally considered to have appeared in the late nineteenth century, but it is only too evident that this was a feeble start. According to records of the National Recreation Association there were only ten cities that had established playgrounds in charge of play leaders previous to the year 1900. These were: Boston in 1886; then from 1890 to 1900, Chicago, Philadelphia, Pittsburgh, Baltimore, Hartford, New Haven, New York City, San Francisco, and Albany. Moreover, Brooklyn, Providence, Milwaukee, Cleveland, Minneapolis, and Denver have legal documents showing that at that time the play movement was receiving consideration at the hands of the various city fathers. The interesting part of the origin of play in the United States is that practically all the early cities having playgrounds initiated play independently of one another.

EARLY INTEREST IN PLAY PROJECTS

To find the origin of public interest some would refer to the time when the old New England town commons were used by the boys in their games and by the forces training under arms. Others would select the year 1821 when efforts were made at out-of-doors physical education by the Latin School of Salem, Massachusetts; or 1825 when the Round Hill School of Northampton, Massachusetts, conducted an outdoor playground and gymnasium. These attempts, unfortunately, were of short duration. Similarly, from 1825 and 1830 outdoor gymnasiums were established at Harvard, Yale, Williams, Brown, and Amherst College, and at the New York High School, but held public interest for a short time only.

The incentive for these experiments was largely furnished by the efforts of German political refugees who strove to make their gymnastic system popular in this country. About 1850 the new German immigration to the United States led to the organization of gymnastic societies (*Turnvereins*) and ultimately to an endeavor to incorporate gymnastics in the public schools. Somewhat later there arose the rival movement to popularize the Swedish system of gymnastics. Both systems have influenced American trends in physical education.

It was in the 1860's that athletic clubs began to be found in colleges. Forerunners of municipal interest in recreative projects were the free public baths established by Boston in 1866 and the vacation school started by the old First Church of Boston in the same year. Private influence opened a vacation school in Providence in 1868. The vacation school introduced subjects like carpentry, singing, nature-study, and others different from the usual course of study in the regular schools. In 1872 Brookline, Massachusetts, became the first city to vote funds for land to be used for playground purposes, but no purchases were made at the time. Then in 1876 Washington Park in Chicago became the first known park to possess recreation facilities, but there was as yet no thought of supervision.

During this same period the beginnings of the group work movement were witnessed. The YMCA, which was started in London in 1844 and in Boston in 1851, organized its boys' department in 1860. The first gymnasiums in connection with YMCA buildings were installed in 1869. In the early years of the boys' department the emphasis was on religious and moral discussion, and it was not until much later that a significant trend in the direction of play was noticed. The YWCA was organized in London in 1861 and in Boston in 1866.

In 1880 the first organized camp for boys was established
by Ernest Balch at Chocorua Island, near Holderness, New
Hampshire.

SANDGARDEN STAGE. All these attempts were preliminary
to the experiment which took place in Boston in 1886 in the
form of sandgardens for little children. The idea was borrowed from Germany. A visitor to Berlin, Dr. Marie
Zakrzewska, was much impressed by seeing little children
playing at seashore games in sand heaps placed in public
parks. She wrote of this to the chairman of the committee
of Massachusetts Emergency and Hygiene Association. Interested women were responsible for the subsequent placing
of three piles of sand in the yards of the Children's Mission
on Parmenter Street. This was the beginning in Boston,
and it led to inquiries from other cities. Miss Ellen Tower,
Chairman of the Association, lectured in several cities regarding the success of the sandgardens. Other cities were
in a mood to follow Boston's lead. It was becoming only
too evident that there must be found some solution for the
many problems confronting child life—in fact adult life—in
the rapidly congesting cities. Foremost of all stood out the
need for removing the children from the danger of playing
in the streets and of offering them instead wholesome environment which would tend to cut down the amount of
juvenile crime and delinquency. These were phases of an
Anti-slums Campaign of which Jacob Riis of New York
City was one of the most active leaders. The danger of
play in the streets, prohibited by law, citizens' complaints of
children playing on their lawns, accidents and arrests from
play in the streets, loss of life from swimming in dangerous
waters—all these things showed how impossible it was for
the child to grow up normally in the cities. The passage of
the child labor laws, the inclusion of long summer vacations
from school, and the shortened working hours for the laboring man were other factors that quickened the agitation for
more municipal provision for play and recreation.

LOCAL DEVELOPMENTS IN THE MOVEMENT. Significant
developments began to follow on the sandgarden stage,

which meant supervised play for children of very tender years only. In 1888 the City of New York allowed use of its public school buildings for lectures in the evenings and later extended the privilege to other types of recreation.

In 1889 the Charlesbank Outdoor Gymnasium in Boston was opened, equipped with apparatus, running track, and space for games, and also provided with supervisors. This accommodated older boys and men, and two years later a section was added for women and girls. The Charlesbank Gymnasium was the forerunner of the movement for park playgrounds which followed reaching its climax in the South Park Playgrounds of Chicago. Another event which reflected the beginnings of the new social attitude toward play was the opening in 1894 of the Hull House Playground, which became famous under the leadership of Jane Addams. It was equipped with leaders and modern apparatus and it bestowed the name "model playground" on this type which became popular at this time and has since been the standard of most school playgrounds. The model grounds, inadequate in size for sports like baseball, contributed to the invention of space-economizing games like softball and to the adaptation of indoor games, like volleyball and basketball, to outdoor use.

In the year 1899 New York opened several schoolyard playgrounds, and the significant thing about this step is that it showed a growing tendency for public support to the new movement. Chicago assumed public responsibility when in 1903 it opened up the South Park Playgrounds. In the short time of two years Chicago taxed itself to the amount of $10,000,000 for park playgrounds—an amount that seemed enormous at that time. Theodore Roosevelt characterized this "the most notable civic achievement of any American city." A feature of the new parks was that they provided both outdoor and indoor recreational facilities, the latter being handled by buildings called "field houses." A typical field house contained gymnasiums, shower baths, an auditorium (for concerts, lectures, and dramatics), a dance floor, club rooms, and sometimes even a restaurant. The field house facilities have been provided elsewhere largely by the more economical use of school buildings for community recreation.

Los Angeles was the first city to appoint a separate recreation commission to avert the confusion in administration which usually results when different agencies like the park board, school board, and private interests work independently.

In 1903 Luther Gulick organized in New York City the first Public School Athletic League. This meant that an interest in promoting amateur athletics was in its beginning. In 1906 a great rural play festival and field day at New Paltz, New York, was interesting inasmuch as it expressed the need for play which was being felt in areas other than city districts. In the same year was organized the Playground and Recreation Association of America (now called the National Recreation Association), mainly for propaganda and consisting of leading men and women in the field of play and recreation, health, and social work. This organization helped unify the playground movement. In addition, its field workers went from city to city putting on campaigns of publicity, stirring up local interest, and giving practical aid to help each municipality launch its individual movement.

EXPANDING TRENDS. There were other events which helped to determine the course of the play movement. In 1902 Ernest Thompson Seton organized the Woodcraft Indians, a club movement for boys emphasizing a varied program of outdoor activities along physical, woodcraft, nature lore, and dramatic lines. The organization had a far reaching effect in influencing the nature of future group-work programs for children. As the program broadened, nature lore and campcraft found their way into the playground. A new appreciation of the use of music and singing as recreational mediums arose, and social dramatics in the form of playground and community center plays also entered the picture. Arts and crafts were inserted in the playground programs and an emphasis was placed upon a year-round program giving the social-recreational activities more of an opportunity.

The use of school buildings as social centers received its first practical demonstration in 1907 in Rochester, New York, where an appropriation was made by the city government and a director appointed. Gary, Indiana, in 1908 emphasized the wider use of the school plant by constructing buildings designed to serve admirably as social centers. In 1911 the National Education Association proposed a resolution approving the use of school buildings as social centers.

Among the leaders of the early play movement were Joseph E. Lee, George E. Johnson, Henry Curtis, Luther Gulick, and Clark Hetherington. Through their writings and personal influence they helped to keep the movement before the public and to shape its course.

The boys' and girls' club movement which had been gradually growing since 1902, received its greatest impetus about 1910 when the Boy Scouts of America were organized. In 1912 under the organizing leadership of Luther Gulick the Camp Fire Girls followed and the Girl Scouts were started.

The decade from 1910 to 1920 witnessed marked expansion in camping. Camps were organized in great numbers, under the leadership of both private concerns and organizations. The automobile had a significant effect upon the growth of the camping and outdoor movement during this period, by making the open country available to city-dwellers.

In this same period the athletic movement in high schools and colleges gained momentum and recognition. Athletics fell under faculty control, became better organized, and better facilities became available. Around 1915 the intramural movement, with its ideal of athletics for all, had its first trials in colleges and grew rapidly thereafter. It did not find its way into the high schools, however, until about 1925.

AFTER WORLD WAR I

Following World War I, with its revelation that one-third of the army recruits were unfit physically, many states passed physical education and recreation laws. James E. Rogers of the National Recreation Association was instrumental in achieving these results. The new importance given to physical education in the schools necessarily meant a temporary shortage of teachers, and teacher-training schools and universities rapidly instituted appropriate courses. By 1930, graduate training was offered in most large universities.

Evidence of increasing recognition and acceptance of play is seen in other events. In 1918 the National Education Association adopted its seven cardinal principles of education which showed a distinct appreciation of the contribution which recreation makes to child training. They are: (1) health, (2) command of the fundamental processes, (3) worthy home membership, (4) vocation, (5) citizenship, (6) worthy use of leisure, (7) ethical character.

In calling the National Conference of Outdoor Recreation in 1924, President Coolidge focused national attention on the leisure-time problem and the need for added facilities. The American Child Health Association was organized in 1923 and the National Amateur Athletic Federation in the same year. The President's Research Committee on Social Trends, appointed in 1929, gave particular attention to the recreation problem. The American Physical Education Association, always interested in the promotion of play, adopted its ten cardinal principles in 1931, one of which pledged the Association to the "promotion of the idea of play and recreation as aspects of the finest living." The American libraries in 1933 sponsored a three-point program of recreation, avocation, and occupation. The Parent-Teachers Associations have also been active in establishing, equipping, and supplying leadership for many playgrounds throughout the country.

The prosperous 1920's witnessed a great upsurge in recreation interest in the history of the movement. It was during this decade that recreation came of age, so to speak, and took its place full fledged and unassailed as a major and indispensable institution in American society.

In 1930 the White House Conference on Child Health and Protection was called by President Hoover and its many committees studied all phases of the recreational life and needs of childhood. It was one of the most significant gatherings in the history of child welfare, and its Children's Charter was one of the most impressive statements of the rights of childhood in all of history.

THE DEPRESSION YEARS. The depression of the 1930's at once increased the demand for, and reduced the supply of, recreation. Countless thousands of unemployed, with time on their hands and with spirits depressed, sought out the play centers. People once able to purchase the use of play facilities now were dependent on public facilities. At the same time, municipal recreation budgets were drastically reduced so that leadership staffs had to be cut to a minimum in many cities, and the operation of many play centers were jeopardized.

Into this emergency the federal government stepped with its Works Progress Administration (replacing the Civil Works Administration and the Federal Emergency Relief Administration), its National Youth Administration, and its Civilian Conservation Corps. The federal efforts fell into two categories, the developing of facilities and the providing of leadership.

It is estimated that as a result of federal relief funds, the recreation and park facilities of the country were, by and large, developed a full decade ahead of what otherwise would have been possible. It is unquestionably true that many communities now possess facilities that they would not otherwise have had within a quarter of a century. The national parks were likewise expanded and developed, and new wilderness "recreation demonstration areas" equipped as camps sprang up across the land. The Civilian Conservation Corps, itself a recreation institution of significance for its members, contributed outstandingly to the development of the marginal and outlying recreational facilities.

The second significant use of federal relief funds was the employing of relief workers to work under the supervision of the local recreation organizations. These workers, trained by local experts, permitted the carrying on of programs which otherwise would have been abandoned or drastically curtailed due to the fund shortage. These workers brought with them backgrounds of experience that provided varied leadership in crafts, dancing, music, drama, and similar areas, in addition to the areas of vigorous play. Other contributions of these workers were community surveys and researches which enabled the communities to have a better understanding of their resources and needs, of lasting value in planning for future expansion.

It is interesting to note that, as a result largely of these federal relief funds, local programs whose budgets had been deeply cut in the depression years were able not only to continue to operate but to *expand* their facilities and their programs ahead of the rate of normal years. As the economic crisis diminished and the federal funds were reduced, the local funds were gradually restored.

WORLD WAR II RECREATION PROGRAMS. During World War II the work of existing agencies was supplemented by programs especially devised for the needs of servicemen and industrial workers. These were headed up by the armed services themselves, and by the American Red Cross, the United Services Organization (USO), and the Federal Security Agency. The Red Cross supplied leadership and recreation materials at home and abroad for the use of servicemen. The USO furnished entertainment, hospitality, and information service to servicemen on leave. The Federal Security Agency provided recreational offerings for servicemen and civilian defense workers in wartime industrial centers.

SINCE WORLD WAR II

The growth of recreation through the 1920's and even during the economic depression that followed was rapid. But the developments in all phases of recreation programs, facilities, and services across the nation since the end of World War II have resulted in still another period of tremendous growth at all levels. Basically, the general underlying factors causing this latest expansion in recreation have been: (1) the economic prosperity during and following the war, (2) the unprecedented growth in population, (3) the physical growth of cities and the need for new schools and public facilities of all types, (4) the tremendous new interest in informal recreation and leisure-time activities through travel, television, and new areas of interest developed since the war, (5) the unparalleled development of organized labor, bringing more leisure and more money to millions of people, and (6) finally, and not the least important of these causes, a greater realization by government at all levels and by people in general that recreation programs, services, and facilities staffed by trained personnel are an essential part of the total community education and welfare services.

PUBLIC AGENCIES. Specifically, the statistics show clearly how significant the changes have been in the recreation movement during the past fifteen years. The National Recreation Association's *Recreation and Park Yearbook* shows the growth of the movement, particularly in the programs sponsored by public agencies. We quote only a few illustrations here.

For example, visitors at our National Parks in 1940 totalled almost 17 million persons; in 1948, over 25 million visited these parks, and in 1956 attendance had reached 50 million. A similar growth in need of, and services by, recreation programs of the Armed Forces, in Veterans Hospitals, and other federal agencies having responsibility to provide recreation facilities and services is noted.

Similarly, state recreation services have been expanded and many new services initiated at this level. State Recreation Commissions and their counterparts were created in New York and North Carolina in 1945, in California and Vermont in 1947. The Inter-Agency Council for Recreation, such as that found in Michigan and several other states, has been effective on a voluntary basis in coordinating recreation functions at the state level. Expenditures for state park services throughout the 50 states has increased from $33,000,000 in 1949 to $55,000,000 in 1955.

Local development, too, has been equally as marked in counties, cities, park districts, park-school operations, and similar subdivisions of local government providing recreation programs and services. Here, again, statistics relating to the recreation movement bear out the broad and extensive changes that are taking place. This is reflected also most accurately in the data compiled in the National Recreation Association Yearbook. In 1956, there were over 45,000 full-time, year-round paid workers doing some type of recreation work and 142,000 persons working part or full-time in all positions directly related to recreation.

VOLUNTARY AGENCIES. Although the increase in the scope of the recreation movement is quite evident in public agency operations, its growing stature in other settings also deserves mention. Recreation and leisure-time programs and services have multiplied in traditional agency operations. For example, public schools have more liberal curriculums and have gradually increased the amount of time devoted to education for leisure; voluntary agencies have provided new services to meet the needs of our growing population. Even the church has brought specific emphasis upon the leisure-time needs of people.

COMMERCIAL AND INFORMAL RECREATION. It has been reliably estimated that people in the United States spend over 30 billion dollars annually for various types of leisure-time activities. Upon close inspection it is found that expenditures for fishing and hunting are over 2 billion dollars annually. Money spent for boating totals nearly a billion, and expenditures for bowling are over the half-billion mark. The amount of money spent for travel and vacation trips is over 15 billion dollars. Home workshop and do-it-yourself expenditures have risen sharply, and money for television and for horse racing, baseball, football, and other professional sports offerings involve a staggering amount of the income of people throughout the nation.

PROFESSIONAL ORGANIZATIONS IN RECREATION

After 1930, as the need for trained leaders became more evident by increased participation in recreation, there was a trend toward establishing a formal professional recreation education program at the university level. (The rapid development of professional education for recreation since World War II is discussed in more detail in Chapter 21.)

Accompanying the expansion of park and recreation programs since 1946 was a realization of the plans and efforts of several professional park and recreation organizations which were established in the early years of the recreation movement. These organizations have grown independently, centering around various interest areas of the total recreation movement. In recent years efforts have been made to unify their work and bring more understanding of each other's contributions. Brief outlines of these professional organizations follow.

FEDERATION OF NATIONAL PROFESSIONAL ORGANIZATIONS FOR RECREATION. This organization represents park operators, public recreation administrators, college recreation educators, camp operators, physical education teachers, and other interested individuals, who in 1953 banded together to coordinate their efforts and strengthen the total recreation program. There is a growing interest in this type of organization by professional recreation workers because of the complications caused by the constant increase in the number of service and professional groups and by the overlapping functions of these various organizations.

THE AMERICAN INSTITUTE OF PARK EXECUTIVES. This organization, since its origin in 1898, has represented those particularly interested in parks. The purpose of the organization is the gathering and disseminating of facts and information regarding total park operations and cooperating with all other groups and agencies to promote park and recreation programs. Its members include park commissions, individual park board members, professionally trained park executives, and other professionals involved in park and recreation management throughout the United States and Canada. The Institute, with a membership of well over two thousand, holds annual conferences and publishes *Parks and Recreation*. The AIPE has given the widest application of the term recreation, by promoting the use of natural areas, zoological parks, outdoor recreation areas, games and sports facilities, and a wide variety of general park services basically educational and cultural. It has contributed greatly to the postwar park and recreation movement throughout the United States as well as Canada.

THE AMERICAN RECREATION SOCIETY. First organized in 1938 as the Society of Recreation Workers of America, changing its name in 1946, the Society has about thirty-five hundred members. It is a national, voluntary fellowship organization designed to improve the quality of professional leadership. Sections in the Society include the Armed Forces, Federal and State Services, Hospital, Industrial, Local Government, Rural, and recently a section designated as Professional Education for Recreation. The annual meeting of the Society is held during the National Recreation Congress and deals specifically with problems of the professional recreation worker in the field. The Society publishes a bulletin, the *American Recreation Annual* (1960). It promotes legislation for recreation and has published principles to guide the profession.

THE AMERICAN ASSOCIATION FOR HEALTH, PHYSICAL EDUCATION, AND RECREATION. This organization was founded in 1885 as the Association for the Advancement of Physical Education. In 1903, its title changed to the American Physical Education Association. In 1937, it became a Department of the National Education Association (NEA); and in 1938, adding a Recreation Division to its structure, it assumed its present title. Although the Association has over twenty thousand members, they are physical education teachers and health educators mainly, and the exact number of persons in the Association *primarily* concerned with recreation is difficult to estimate. In 1950, the Association adopted a Recreation Policy Statement which described its services and interests in recreation as centering around promoting: (1) recreation education programs in schools and colleges, (2) programs that will help the individual attain the aims and objectives of education, (3) utilization of existing facilities and construction of new facilities for the operation of recreation programs, (4) promoting research and evaluation in the field of recreation, and (5) the all-important factor of professional preparation of recreation personnel. The Association has annual national conferences which include special sessions in recreation. It also publishes a *Journal* and a *Research Quarterly*.

THE NATIONAL ASSOCIATION OF SOCIAL WORKERS. This organization was formed in 1955, combining the organizations formerly known as the American Association of Group Workers, American Association of Medical Social Workers, American Association of Psychiatric Social Workers, National Association of School Social Workers, Association for the Study of Community Organization, and the Social Work Research Group. The Group Work Section of the Association is particularly concerned with promoting cooperation among professional persons working in various private and voluntary leisure-time and informal education agencies and groups. It seeks to raise standards, improve professional competence, and encourage research.

OTHER AGENCIES. Since so many groups and organizations, in addition to those mentioned above, provide a variety of professional recreation services, it is possible to mention only a few more: The American Camping Association seeks to raise standards in camping and promote all phases of camping throughout the country; The College Recreation Association, founded in 1948, is an organization composed of college faculty members engaged in professional recreation education, and (now reorganized as the Recreation Education Section of the American Recreation Society); The National Association of College Unions, a group of persons that since 1914 has been promoting the development of professionally trained leaders in college union administration, which has developed very rapidly since 1946; the National Industrial Recreation Association, an organization of individuals engaged in personnel and recreation work in industries. There are, of course, numerous organizations such as state Recreation Societies, state Park Associations, and similar groups in Canada which are active in practically every province. These groups constantly work to improve standards through registration and certification, development of desirable ethical practices, dissemination of information, and the maintenance of training institutes.

PROFESSIONAL SERVICE ORGANIZATIONS

Several organizations provide professional services in the recreation field and have been particularly important in the growth of the recreation movement.

NATIONAL RECREATION ASSOCIATION. Formed as the Playground Association of America in 1906, this organization has undoubtedly been the major force in the growth of recreation in the United States. It is a national, nonprofit service agency providing general information about recreation. In 1957, the Association included almost 19,000 individuals and organizations, including 5,326 active associate members. It maintains a skilled staff providing local consultant services; supplies publications of all types, including the monthly publication, *Recreation;* carries on research, and enjoys the confidence of recreation leaders and non-professionals throughout the entire world. The importance of its work is stressed frequently throughout this book.

OTHER SERVICE ORGANIZATIONS. The American Red

Cross, the Athletic Institute, the National Association of Settlements, Inc., and other organizations in the fields of child growth, mental hygiene, and social psychology are among the many service groups which contribute to the recreation movement.

SUMMARY

In the United States, the story of the growth of the play and recreation movement is an almost unbelievable one of extreme contrasts. Three-quarters of a century or so ago, a pile of sand was placed in the yard of a settlement house in Boston. Today, instead of occupying a backyard, the playgrounds have grown to the point where they are considered a vital part of city planning. Today, instead of being financially helpless, dependent upon the gifts of a few kindly supporters, the playground movement has progressed to the point where millions of dollars in public taxes are being voted for its upkeep and expansion. In other ways, too, the transformation has been just as marked. Originally meant to entertain little tots barely able to toddle, the recreation program now caters not only to young boys and girls but to men and women, and even to older people in a new trend promoted by gerontological principles. The gamut of age levels is run. A program originally intended for a few months of the summer now covers the entire year. A program which in the beginning included a few plays and games now has broadened to embrace a multitude of activities, including music, nature study, gardening, manual crafts, pageantry, clubs, camps, and many other areas that were once considered the province of the school and home. A program originally supervised by interested volunteers now is manned by competent and thoroughly trained workers. In these and other ways the play and recreation movement has developed until it is one of the most important social institutions in the United States at the present time—in fact, a rival of the home, school, and church in the building of young men and women, and in the preservation of wholesome standards of living.

SELECTED REFERENCES

DOELL, CHARLES F., and FITZGERALD, GERALD B. *A Brief History of Parks and Recreation in the United States.* Chicago: Athletic Institute, 1954. This is a comprehensive history of parks and recreation; also included is historical information regarding developments in hospital, industrial, and community center recreation, and in recreation activities conducted by the private or voluntary agencies.

DULLES, FOSTER RHEA. *America Learns To Play: A History of Popular Recreation—1607–1940.* New York: Appleton-Century-Crofts, Inc., 1940. A thorough analysis of the expansion of popular recreation in the United States from Colonial America to 1940 is detailed.

GABRIELSON, MILTON A. (ed.). *American Recreation Annual.* Vol. I. New York: American Recreation Society, Hoffman-Harris Publications, Inc., 1960. This recently initiated Annual includes an extensive treatment of recreation in this country. The several authors, covering a variety of subjects, indicate clearly the scope and the challenge embodied in the play movement and point out how recreation continues to play a more significant role in the daily life of the American people.

NEUMEYER, MARTIN H., and NEUMEYER, ESTHER S. *Leisure and Recreation.* 3d ed. New York: The Ronald Press Co., 1958. Chapter 3 in this work gives an excellent summary of the recreation movement in the United States.

RAINWATER, CLARENCE E. *The Play Movement in the United States.* Chicago: University of Chicago Press, 1922. This book, although out of print, represents a basic analysis of the early play movement in this country. Particularly important is the explanation of the stages, trends, and developments of the play movement from 1880 to 1920.

BUTLER, GEORGE D. *Introduction to Community Recreation.* 2d ed. New York: McGraw-Hill Book Co., Inc., 1959, Chap. 5.

COZENS, FREDERICK W., and STUMPF, FLORENCE. *Sports in American Life.* Chicago: University of Chicago Press, 1953.

DANFORD, H. G. *Recreation in the American Community.* New York: Harper & Bros., 1953.

MEYER, HAROLD D., and BRIGHTBILL, CHARLES K. *Community Recreation: A Guide to Its Organization.* Englewood Cliffs, N. J.: Prentice-Hall, Inc., 1956, Chap. 1.

RICE, EMMETT A., HUTCHINSON, JOHN L., and LEE, MABEL. *A Brief History of Physical Education.* 4th ed. New York: The Ronald Press Co., 1958.

Part II

FUNDAMENTALS OF PLAY AND RECREATION

4

Explanations of Play
and Recreation

Many attempts have been made to explain the fact that play is a part of man's behavior. The majority of these theories are more subject to criticism on grounds of narrowness or of incompleteness than of error. This perhaps is inevitable since play is both broad in its motivation and variable in its forms of expression. Moreover, play covers the life span of each individual and also is intimately woven into the culture patterns which constitute a major part of the environment through which it, in turn, is oriented. So varied and complex a phenomenon is not easily reduced to a brief and concise explanation.

Some of the original theories that have been advanced in explanation of play are now more or less outmoded. Yet these early theories caused much discussion of their authenticity and this, in turn, led to empirical research in order to arrive at a more scientific explanation of play. It is the purpose of this chapter not only to review the traditional theories of play but also to discuss some of the more recent research which may further contribute to the present understanding of the nature of play.

TRADITIONAL THEORIES OF PLAY

There are five traditional theories of play which merit review: the surplus energy theory, the recreation theory, the instinct-practice theory, the recapitulation theory, and the catharsis theory.

SURPLUS ENERGY THEORY. The surplus energy theory is

one of the oldest, simplest, and most widespread theories of play. According to this theory, play is "blowing off steam"; children play because they are so full of animal spirits, so overcharged with muscular energy, that they cannot keep still. Schiller, German poet and philosopher, expressed the idea clearly when he defined play as "the aimless expenditure of exuberant energy." Says Schiller in *Essays, Aesthetical and Philosophical,*

"When the lion is not tormented by hunger, and when no wild beast challenges him to fight, his unemployed energy creates an object for himself; full of ardor, he fills the re-echoing desert with his terrible roars and his exuberant force rejoices in itself, showing itself without an object. The insect flits about in the sunlight, and it is certainly not the cry of want that makes itself heard in the melodious song of the bird; there is undeniably freedom in these movements, though it is not emancipation from want in general, but from a determinate external necessity. The animal *works* when a privation is the motor of its activity, and it *plays* when the plenitude of force is this motor, when an exuberant life is excited to action."

That section of the theory which designates play as aimless is certainly open to criticism.

Hobhouse in *Mind and Evolution* says, "The singing of the birds or the play of the butterfly is no mere frivolity, but is serious courtship." Lehman and Witty hold the following point of view: "Undoubtedly much of what seems to be random or aimless movement in the animal world is in reality search for food and mate. One is not justified in designating an activity as an end in itself merely because no ulterior end is clearly evident."

In the surplus energy theory, it is contended that the playing animal has more energy than he needs for subsistence, reproduction, and defense. This he expresses in play. Often there is no opportunity for complete expression in pursuit of the serious purposes of life; hence an accumulation of reserve energy and strength results. This surplus energy is expended through the usual channels, not as work for serious life goals, but as play.

The theory contends that young animals, because they are protected and fed by parents, do not need their energies for self-preservation and are thus free to play at will; and children, being similarly free from economic pressure, do likewise. It is apparent, too, in other ways that activities are entered into with more zest when energy is abundant. The horse confined to the stall all winter is frolicsome and unruly when first let loose in the spring; the chained hound dog is all the more eager to hunt when it is freed; children shout and leap into the air when school is dismissed.

The surplus energy theory is not without truth and contributes importantly to those seeking to understand play. When the supply of energy becomes too low from long-continued exercise or the presence of infection, the customary recourse is to seek rest. The reaction to a stimulus when rested is different from that when the animal (or individual) is fatigued, and the organism is more apt to play when rested than when fatigued.

The argument raised against this point of view is that children who have the opportunity will usually play all day long every day of the week and are not willing to stop when night comes. They will play when they seemingly do not have energy to spare. They become so engrossed in their play that they forget fatigue and hunger and are entirely oblivious to dinner call and the passage of time. As they grow tired of one game, they enter into another with vigor.

An additional criticism of the surplus energy theory is that it fails to account for the *form* which play takes, i.e., for the fact that children possessed of energy like to play games but not to perform chores; the fact that play is universal over the world, yet differs from country to country; and the fact that play may be of a type that refreshes and re-creates.

The surplus energy theory was the first argument advanced for inserting athletics into colleges. It was contended that athletics were needed to use up the energies of students and prevent them from engaging in hazing, hair cutting, town-gown fights, and similar activities more or less characteristic of college life. This same point of view was also the first argument used to indicate the need for playgrounds—it was felt that ample chance to play would divert energies which would otherwise lead to juvenile delinquency.

Herbert Spencer's name has been associated with the surplus energy theory of play so often that his name is linked with Schiller in the Schiller-Spencer theory of play. Spencer had a much broader and more comprehensive conception of the nature of play, however, than is customarily accorded him.

In a chapter on the development of the nervous system Spencer explains that as fast as living nerve cells are torn down by their activity, they continually rebuild themselves and thus become again ready for action. With the renewed readiness to act comes also increased sensitiveness to stimulation, which is partially lost during fatigue. Spencer, however, repeatedly refers to instinct and to rivalry and the love of victory. Clearly, he does not make an excess of energy the sole motive leading to play; there is also an instinctive urge for playful activity. In addition there is a tendency to imitate; he points out that the forms of play of the young tend to take the forms of the adult activities of their own species, and refers to kittens simulating the catching of mice, and the play of girls with dolls resembling the work of women.

Spencer held that there is a close relationship between art and play and that art indeed is one form of play. Art and play, he felt, are similar in that neither subserves in any direct way the processes necessary to life. He further stated that play serves as a compensatory device through which satisfaction is obtained when the normal expression of natural impulses is impossible and in this he anticipated the work of many recent psychologists. In *The Principles of Psychology* he says "the love of conquest, so dominant in all creatures because it is so correlative of success in the struggle for existence, gets gratification from a victory in chess in the absence of ruder victories." Through a combat of wits in ordinary conversation, as another example, there runs the effort for mental supremacy, resulting in satisfaction of egoistic feelings which find at the moment no other sphere.

RECREATION THEORY. Play has been defined as an occupation engaged in for recreation, rather than for business or from necessity. Lord Kames, English philosopher, expressed this idea when he said, "Play is necessary for man in order to refresh himself after labor." Guts Muths, a German educator emphasized the recreative value of play as well as its value for development and training, and partly because of his influence, the recreation theory has always been popular in Germany. One of its strongest supporters was Moritz Lazarus of the University of Berlin, who urged people to "flee from empty idleness to active recreation in play."

The recreation theory is based on the obvious principle that a certain amount of rest and sleep is necessary, but beyond that a change to an active and interesting occupation is more restful than complete idleness.

Play revitalizes and restores the mentally and physically tired. As Lazarus puts it, "After work we require rest which accomplishes recuperation. But hardly ever does mere empty, inactive rest suffice for recuperation." The change of activity need not necessarily be to a widely different type—the mental worker may find rest and recreation in reading a story and the farm hand in baseball.

The recreation theory presents a valuable concept of the function of play although inadequate as a complete explanation of its nature. In one way the recreation theory is the opposite of the surplus energy theory; the latter looks upon play as a kind of activity by which those who have an excess of energy can get rid of it, while the former considers it a way in which those who have exhausted their energy can recuperate. These two points of view become reconciled by the fact that the individual may become fatigued locally by the type of activity he does during his workaday life, particularly by mental effort, but at the same time he may possess abundant energy throughout the general organism. He turns to play activity utilizing large areas of the neuromuscular system and as a result feels refreshed. School children, for instance, become weary of studying, but possess ample energy throughout the general organism, and when dismissed from school they often leap, run, and shout. After recess they return to their studies rested and relaxed because of the change in activities.

RELAXATION THEORY. G. T. W. Patrick, Professor of Philosophy at the University of Iowa, in his *The Psychology of Relaxation* (1916), sustained the recreation theory and offered the broadest explanation at that time. According to him, the common occupations of civilized life, especially among the intellectual classes, call for abstract reasoning, concentration of attention, and the use of the smallest muscles, such as those of the eyes and the fingers, in highly skilled activity—in writing, typing, needlework, and the manipulation of complex tools and machinery. Such activities have been acquired by the human race in comparatively recent times, are fatiguing, and seem likely to provoke nervous disorders. Mental powers in particular are subject to very rapid fatigue; one cannot exercise them long before demanding escape. This escape is found in age old activities which involve the big muscles and which demand but little abstract attention. This is why, says Patrick, professional men require shorter hours than laborers; why people get the most complete rest by going to the lakes, the forests, and the mountains, where they engage in hunting, fishing, canoeing, hiking, camping, and swimming—activities that remote ancestors pursued for an unknown number of generations. In children, the higher brain tracts are undeveloped and work in the sense of concentration, monotonous repetition, and the sustained use of small muscles is impossible. If they do anything, it must be primarily play; that is, their activity takes the form prescribed by brain patterns already developed, and these are racially old ones.

Patrick illustrated his theory by referring to popular sports: football, involving kicking, running, striking, plunging, and shock, is satisfying, and huge crowds turn out to witness it, vicariously fighting against the enemy as they sit in the stands. The same is true of boxing and wrestling. Attendance at these games furnishes to some degree an escape from an artificial life. They are like an echo from the remote past.

Patrick's observations regarding the nature of play activities are in general stimulating and provocative. Such a point of view is popular and timely today as a result of the nerve-racking hurry and rush of modern life and the monotonous grind which industry has forced upon its workers. In explaining the motivation of play in terms of "deep-rooted human instincts," "race habits," and a "racial memory," the theory is less satisfying. One soon seeks a definition of these terms that will square with proved, accepted psychological concepts.

The theory is correct in claiming that the so-called older race activities furnish relief and rest and relaxation after one has engaged in sedentary and small muscle activity. Big muscle coordinations are doubtless less fatiguing because they have been learned in childhood and have been practiced throughout life. The Patrick theory is inadequate, however, as an explanation of all of play responses; it does not account for the pleasure derived from mental activity and intellectual play; it applies primarily to adults, not children; it neglects the very important role which habit plays and, in general, bases its motivation of play upon an unproven premise.

INSTINCT-PRACTICE THEORY. The role of instinct as the motivating factor in life has played a large part in much of the older writings on play and culminated in the monumental work of Karl Groos. This Swiss scientist published in 1898 a book entitled *The Play of Animals*, followed a few years later by another entitled *The Play of Man*. These two volumes form the largest contribution to the theory of play yet made by any individual. Groos accomplished an enormous amount of work on the subject, both by study of all previous works on the theory of play and by study of literature on the play of savage tribes and of the children of civilized man. He gives a very complete and elaborate classification of all the varieties of play of animals and men. His writings have produced a profound effect on the minds of educators by showing to what an enormously wide range play extends, and its value to children, not only at the time of participation, but as training for later life.

On the theoretical side, Groos argued in favor of instinct as the motivating factor in play, and in connection with it he advanced two doctrines which were quite revolutionary at the time:

(1) Play is so important an element in the training of the higher animals and man that nature provides a long period of immaturity to give an opportunity for it. To quote his own words, "Animals cannot be said to play because they are young and frolicsome, but rather they have a period of youth in order to play." No one else, with the possible exception of a few of the most enthusiastic disciples of Froebel, has ever attributed to play such an important part in education as did Groos in the above statement.

(2) Play arises in each young individual from the appearance of certain very important instincts before he has serious need of them. This is the main difference in development between man and the higher animals on the one hand and the insects on the other and is the reason why man makes progress in his manner of living from one generation to another while the ants and wasps do not. Each insect is endowed with instincts that appear fully developed and ready for use just when they are needed, and as a consequence the insect never plays and is not capable of education. The kitten, on the other hand, plays at catching mice with a bit of wood or paper for a long time before the real act is required, and by so doing not only develops this particular element of skill, but a higher degree of intelligence as well. Play is necessary for the development of higher intelligence; for if human beings were provided with perfected instincts, as insects are, life would be automatic and there would be no such thing as education and no increase of ability or intelligence, either in the individual or the species.

Groos' contention that play is a preparation for adult activities applies in the case of animals and has considerable foundation in the case of primitive man, but its application to the civilized life of today has met with criticism. The child's impulses lead him to running, jumping, throwing, and striking, and the youth to hunting, fishing, swimming, and games like baseball and football. In what way, his critics ask, are these a precise and exact training for pursuits which civilized adulthood demands?

If it is assumed that Groos meant that the play of present-day children trains precisely and exactly for adult pursuits, then certainly his theory is in question. If, however, the point of view is taken that play leads to a mastery of the physical self and develops the coordinations which lead to general physical efficiency in adulthood, then this phase of the theory is sound enough. Play develops the basic coordinations which make possible the learning of the specialized movements necessary in modern adult economic pursuits.

If one is to assume, as Groos has, that the theory conceives of life as being lived during adulthood and interprets childhood as merely a preparation for it—that adult activities are serious and those of childhood are merely a sham or make-believe of real life activities—then the modern student must differ with this point of view. Child life and its play are quite as real and serious as the life of adulthood. Childhood is life, in just as real a sense as the workaday routine of later years.

Even though Groos's hypothesis of instinct motivation may not be generally accepted today, his colossal collection of observations of the play activities of animals and man still stands supreme in its field and has built for him an enduring monument. His work did much to hasten a realization of the social value of play and to focus attention on the important place of play in education in general.

RECAPITULATION THEORY. G. Stanley Hall was the most enthusiastic sponsor of the theory explaining play as the result of biological inheritance. He says, in *Youth*, "True play never practises what is phyletically new. . . . I regard play as the motor habits and spirit of the past of the race, persisting in the present, as rudimentary functions . . . akin to rudimentary organs. . . . In play every mood and movement is instinct with heredity. . . . Thus we rehearse the activities of our ancestors, back we know not how far, and repeat their life work. . . . This is why the heart of youth goes out into play as into nothing else, as if in it man remembered a lost paradise."

Hall, in his enthusiasm, went so far as to contend that the growing child passed through a series of stages which recapitulate the "culture epochs" in the development of the race. Thus the child lives, at certain ages, the animal, savage, nomad, agricultural, and tribal stages. During these periods he participates in activities characteristic of the serious pursuits which men practiced in the culture epoch he is recapitulating. Many educators of Hall's era, have attempted to build educational systems on this theory.

Why does the child relive these cultural periods? Hall would say because of instinct. But the question follows, why did not instinct lead individuals to pass through these periods before the race attained the cultural epochs in question? To this Hall would reply because the instinct arose during the course of the culture epoch. In this respect, Hall was a Lamarckian and assumed the inheritance of acquired characteristics, i.e., as skills were developed and cultural forms achieved, the capacity for them was passed on to the offspring. To Groos, on the other hand, instinct was the result of natural selection; in the struggle for existence those with certain drives or tendencies favorable for existence survived and had offspring possessing these drives and abilities.

Hall contended that if the child, in any particular stage of his rehearsal of the culture of the race, expressed his instinctive tendencies freely, the instincts became weakened and would not function so strongly in later life. Groos, on the other hand, held that the expression of an instinct through activity strengthened the capacity of the individual to function in this respect later in life.

Regarding the validity of the theory of recapitulation, it is agreed that the individual cannot separate himself entirely from the past because of the nature of his organic structure, the result of biological adaptation. Moreover, it is obvious that the individual in his social heritage, too, has access to the accumulation of previous cultures of mankind. Suffice it to say, however, that recapitulation of culture epochs is regarded as an invalid hypothesis and is without scientific support at present. August Weismann and a host of more recent scientists have proved quite conclusively that acquired characteristics are not inherited. Furthermore, the various primitive peoples throughout history have not progressed uniformly through distinct culture epochs as this theory assumes; some groups have never exhibited some of the epochs. Neither can it be shown experimentally that individuals live over the history of the race in this precise way. The great bulk of recent research shows that the types of play a child engages in depends primarily upon what the environment has offered him and upon the level of neuromuscular development he has attained.

Educationally, Hall's theory had the very beneficial effect of stimulating research in the interests of children of various ages.

CATHARSIS THEORY. The catharsis theory seems to have been first suggested by Aristotle and was sustained and developed respectively by Groos,[1] Carr[2] and Claparède.[3] The surplus energy theory contends that play is due to the accumulation of energy, and engaging in play consumes this energy. The theory of catharsis maintains that play is a safety valve for pent-up emotions. In the fighting play of children, for instance, emotions of anger are aroused but the fighting play gives adequate opportunity for expression, and through indulgence in it the emotions subside.

[1] Karl Groos, *Das Spiel, zwei vortrage Von Karl Groos* (Jena: G. Fischer, 1922. Part II. "Das Spiel Als Katharsis").
[2] H. H. Carr, *The Survival Value of Play*, Investigation of Department of Psychology and Education (Denver: University of Colorado, 1902).
[3] E. Claparède, *Psychologie de l'Enfant et Pédagogie Experimentale*, trans. M. Louch and H. Holman (New York: Longmans, Green & Co., Inc., 1911).

Fighting is a natural, spontaneous response to certain life situations but social taboos frequently prevent adequate expression of it. Since fighting in any satisfying form is often impossible in ordered society, anger, with resultant irritability, is frequently sustained. By turning to fighting types of play, a satisfying response is made possible, and the emotion subsides. Play thus has a cathartic effect, purging the individual of distressing emotions.

Aristotle confined his doctrine of "Catharsis of the Passions" to dramatic tragedy, maintaining that through tragedy the soul is freed from something that is injurious. Claparède, Carr, and Groos have developed and extended the point of view to show that play in general may serve as a cathartic. They pointed out that the instinct is not weakened or extinguished by the cathartic effect of play, but rather the emotion arising from the instinct is relieved. Claparède states that it relieves and soothes us, when we are angry, "to break a plate, to slam a door, or to flog an arm chair."

Another respect in which play provides a cathartic effect is in internal bodily changes which take place in the presence of a fighting situation. Glandular secretions such as adrenalin flow into the blood stream, making the individual a better fighting animal by alerting and preparing him for great muscular effort and conditioning his blood to clot more readily should he be wounded. If self-control is exercised and the accompanying emotions are inhibited, irritability results because of the changes in the organism which these secretions have produced. Engaging in strenuous fighting games serves as a substitute for actual fighting, and the organism is relieved.

In pointing out that emotions aroused in one situation can be relieved or can find expression by action in another situation, the catharsis theory anticipates and leads into the present-day concept of the compensatory nature of play, to be developed later.

SELF-EXPRESSION THEORY OF PLAY

In reviewing the traditional theories of play, it is obvious that there are certain inadequacies in each, particularly in accounting for all phases of play. Each theory advanced grew out of the inadequacies of the preceding, and each had some new scientific evidence to support it. Recent advances in psychology have superseded the basic assumptions of some of the older theories, and the developments in sociology and social psychology have brought new facts necessitating a shift of emphasis. The following explanation, The Self-Expression Theory, was first advanced in 1934 by Elmer D. Mitchell and Bernard S. Mason, leaders in sports, recreation, and camping, and is here refined and clarified, based upon newer interpretations. Later in this chapter there is also a presentation of the compensatory aspect of play, which is currently becoming more significant. To Mitchell and Mason, however, compensation is but an aspect of self-expression, not a separate entity.

In considering the human organism and its behavior there are a number of elemental, important facts which are basic in an understanding of play. *First, man is an active, dynamic creature.* Activity is the primary need of life. Nothing about man is more obvious or more elemental. There is no need for an explanation other than the fact that he is alive. This fact per se accounts largely for play: a desire for pleasure and hope of finding it is not necessary to stir people into activity—they are active in the first place. When one ceases thinking of the human organism as inert, needing some special incentive to coax it into action, it is not so necessary to account for play; all that is necessary is to determine why man engages in this or that particular form of play.

If the matter could rest with the tendency of man to be active, the surplus energy theory would be sufficient. However, something more is needed to account for the ways in which man plays individually and collectively. These factors must be considered together with the first factor in accounting for the form which play takes:

Second, the physiological and anatomical structure of the organism predisposes it to certain kinds of activity. The organism possesses certain mechanical possibilities of behavior. Man does not fly like the bird nor swim like the fish. Being put together structurally as he is and being alive, of course, he runs, jumps, throws, kicks, strikes, and turns somersaults. The play of animals varies as the structure varies. Structure varies with growth, and activities change accordingly; as soon as new capacities appear with changing structure in growth, the organism uses them. Play then is activity of that type for which the organism is physiologically and anatomically adapted.

Third, the physical fitness of the organism has an effect upon the type of activity it engages in. Abundant energy is a favorable condition for strenuous activity. True, children often participate in play when energy is too depleted for them to be benefited by it, but they feel themselves possessed of sufficient energy to satisfy their desires or they would not engage, and with the coming of weariness they change the activity or seek rest through sleep.

Fourth, the psychological inclinations of the individual predispose him toward certain types of activity. These inclinations are the result of physiological needs and of learned responses or habits and attitudes. Natural capacity or aptitude is also a determinant. Nothing is more certain than that one's habits and attitudes determine play activities to a very large extent. The nervous system is such that behavior responses of certain acquired patterns are constantly being called forth. Habits and attitudes are acquired through interaction with the social environment, with the result that the play forms of the group tend to become the individual's play habits. An individual's play patterns are quite generally in harmony with his social environment, and he tends to take on the customs and styles of play in vogue at any particular time. Furthermore, his play habits are determined by his physical environment, which offers certain opportunities for play.

In the light of the above discussion, play can be explained by the fact that the individual seeks self-expression. Being an animal with intellect and spirit, with the physiological and anatomical structure he has, with the degree of physical fitness he has, and with the psychological inclinations he has, all that is necessary to explain play is the fact that he seeks to live, to use his abilities, to express his personality. The chief need of man is life, self-expression. Play is activity which brings such satisfaction.

Man plays to feel the thrill of accomplishment. Man plays to achieve, to create, to conquer, to acquire, to impress, and to win approval. Thus he engages in activity that is on the level of his ability, activity in which he can succeed. If the attempted play of the child is too difficult for him, it loses its appeal as play and he tends to drop it. Play must bring some degree of success in accomplishment realized, whether in games, sports, artistic pursuits, or creative hobbies. In workaday life such success is not always forthcoming; in play one finds activity in which he has a feeling of mastery and success is reasonably assured.

When motives cannot be realized and desires satisfied by direct overt activity, the individual seeks compensatory satisfaction through imagination, either in imaginative play activity or in daydreaming and fantasy, or in vicarious adventure through reading, TV, and the theatre.

Play takes a great variety of forms. Individual differences are marked, depending upon variations in conditioning and in the situations in which individuals find themselves. In play one engages in activity which seems the natural and fitting thing to do considering the total set of circumstances at the moment.

With this brief statement of the self-expression theory in mind, an analysis is needed of the factors influencing man's inclination for the play activities in which he engages. The problem will be considered from the following angles: (1) the role of habit in play, (2) the role of social contact in the formation of play habits, (3) universal wishes, and (4) the compensatory aspect of play behavior.

ROLE OF HABIT IN PLAY. The traditional theories of play have offered a variety of explanations of why people play— why boys play baseball, hockey, and marbles, why they fly kites and dig caves; why girls play with dolls and make mud pies; why men play golf and gamble on horse races; why people daydream and engage in fantasy. Most of the older play theories would suggest instinct. That is, it was contended that man comes into the world with specific inborn impulses which predispose him to the particular types of activity he engages in during the play life. Granting the important role which unlearned responses play in animal life, the facts growing out of recent psychological research have led to a minimizing of the role of instinct, or inborn and unlearned drives, in human life and have forced a shift in thinking toward other types of motivation.

Nothing seems more certain than that play is activity resulting from motives or desires. What is the source of these motives? If not instinct, what is it?

Shortly after birth the motives growing out of physiological needs are complicated by acquired factors, that is, habits are formed, first in relation to the physiological needs, and then in relation to objects farther and farther removed from them. For the purposes of this discussion the important consideration is that *throughout life the individual is inclined toward those activities which are habitual to him.* *Attitudes* likewise arise as a result of social conditioning. An attitude is a positive or negative reaction to the total situation. It differs from habit in that habit refers to learned motor responses whereas attitudes are related to ideas and thinking and are conscious, emotional, and purposive. A certain way of striking the ball in tennis or swinging a golf club are examples of habits; a tendency to act in a friendly and courteous way toward one's opponents exemplifies an attitude.

Now these habits and attitudes constitute motives—they function as powerful drives to certain types of activity. A boy whose experience has conditioned him with habits and attitudes with respect to playing marbles is easily "touched off" by the sight of marbles, or by the suggestion of a friend that they play, or by the memory of the satisfaction derived in past play. The stimulus arouses this motive or desire, and play is engaged in for the purpose of satisfying it. So with the girl and her dolls, the housewife and her knitting, the man and his golf clubs. Since play is based on habits and attitudes, the play activities of an individual are more or less constant in type.

In habit is found the explanation of individual differences in play. While the fundamental pattern may be much the same, the range of individual differences in play is tremendous and obvious on every hand in any play group. Although heredity may account for one individual having certain capacities which another lacks, and although native physical ability may vary, people play at different activities largely because they have been conditioned differently— they possess different habits and attitudes, and thus they have different motives or desires.

The role of habit in play is conspicuous at every turn. Man likes to do what he can do well. Studies regarding the recreational activities of men and women of varying professions indicate that adults turn to activities in their leisure hours which are very similar to those they engage in during their workaday life: one would think that the lawyer might engage in aviation, horseback riding, and north woods canoeing, but as a matter of fact, the majority lecture, serve on committees, and argue in the smoking room of their clubs. The newspaper reporter reads, attempts to write stories, and dabbles in drama. The physical director engages in vigorous physical activity and watches athletic sports. The engineer tinkers with radios, electrical apparatus, automobiles, and building projects involving the use of tools. These types of professional men use the abilities they have and do the things in which they know they are proficient. In these activities they have a feeling of mastery and of sureness.

Learning a new activity often is irksome and unpleasant. The learning of play skills is frequently uninteresting and seems like drudgery, but once the accomplishment is perfected and the habits formed, the attendant activity is usually pleasurable. Many men refer to their first few weeks at golf as distasteful. But once the skills are perfected, the habits formed, and a feeling of mastery of the technique achieved, the game brings endless joy. So with the child learning to play a musical instrument—the practice hour may have all the aspects of drudgery. Unless some level of success is quickly achieved, the activity is dropped in favor of another. The feeling of mastery of the situation and the accompanying feeling of freedom are essential characteristics of play. Individual differences are as numerous as the individuals participating, owing to differences in experience.

Play progressively offers difficulties and obstacles that are within the powers of growing children to master. If they tried adult tasks and continually failed, as they would, they would lose all confidence. Play gives children miniature life with problems they can understand and with competition with their equals. As they master certain tasks and situations, they go on to more difficult ones until gradually their play merges into their life work.

It is evident that the form which play takes is dependent on the abilities the individual possesses, the skills attained, and the habits formed. Habits are developed in relation to the physiological needs and in relation to the social environment in which one moves. Out of habits and attitudes arise motives and desires. These are the drives which lead to play. The individual, being what he is and possessed of the motives and desires he has, seeks self-expression, seeks life.

ROLE OF SOCIAL CONTACT IN HABIT FORMATION. It has been suggested that play forms are largely learned responses and that play behavior of the organism may be regarded as habit or stimulus-response patterns. Since the play forms are the result mainly of conditioning, of social environment, it is important to look more carefully into the social process whereby the individual becomes conditioned to them.

No young and aspiring human being can live in any society without taking on, to a greater or less extent, the ways of that society. The group ways, whatever they are, tend to become the individual's ways. Folkways and mores become individual habits and attitudes. Through the tendency of the individual to imitate and his desire to get on, through many and various social controls which all groups employ, the conforming process goes on and all individuals are forced into patterns which make them act much alike. In this way the play activity of an individual is determined in the large before he is born by the play customs of the group into which he is born. From group play customs come individual play habits.

An illustration may be found in the play activities of European immigrants in this country. They bring with them the sports, dances, and crafts of the country in which they were born and raised. The English men take their games with them even into the hottest of climates; and English and South African students at American universities play at their own games of rugby and soccer without being attracted by the American games going on about them. German districts in this country strive to keep up their gymnastic exercises and the social spirit of the Turnverein. But the children of the immigrants, attending school, take on American play ways and are very seldom adherents of the play customs of the old country.

It will be noted that this point of view contrasts sharply with the older theories which placed emphasis on instinct as the determining factor in play behavior. Nevertheless, the factor of the inborn impulse cannot be ignored. The infant is born, according to John Dewey, with impulses, but these impulses are never primary in life: he is born into a society of adults as a dependent being, and from these adults he takes on human nature, forms habits through which the impulses express themselves in activity. To Dewey, then, the only factor that can be observed in conduct is learned responses. These habits themselves are not thought of by him as fixed and rigid but are constantly being reconstructed throughout life by the inborn impulses seeking more adequate expression. The impulses are mainly starting points for the taking on of skills and knowledge, but they continue to drive throughout life and lead to the constant reconstruction of habits when old habits fail to satisfy.

The point is made, therefore, that the play activity of the organism is the result both of pressure from within in the form of physiological urges and vague inborn impulses, and pressure from the social environment from which the individual acquires habits, attitudes, and sentiments. The latter is the significant factor in defining play forms: one's habits and attitudes predispose him to certain types of activity, and being alive and seeking self-expression, he engages in them and tends to repeat them as long as they bring satisfaction or pleasure.

Role of the Physical Environment. It is obvious that physical environment places certain limitations on the play activity of man and must be taken into the picture in understanding the play of any given folk. The child of the desert will not be likely to play at boating, nor could the child on the rocky seashore play at "sandstorm."

In cold regions like Norway and Sweden, skating, skiing, snowshoeing, tobogganing, and similar sports are favored by the people; and indoor gymnastics are more popular than competitive games. In temperate climates the vigorous out-of-door games of England and America are found. But in hot climates the leisurely pastimes are most evident along with the tendency to assume the simple role of spectators. For sustained effort, the temperate zone is the most favorable. Wherever the sea is found, water sports abound, such as swimming, rowing, skindiving, sailing and the water joust; and children rapidly learn to take part in them even at an extremely early age. Where stretches of sparsely settled land are found, such as in Finland, there is a predilection for long-distance running.

Now it appears from the discussion to date that both the

social and the physical environment are important factors in determining the play habits and attitudes of an individual.

ROLE OF UNIVERSAL WISHES. Since the motivation in play is thought of in terms of habits and attitudes, and since habits and attitudes exist in the individual man, does it follow that there are no universal motives or common desires of all mankind? A knowledge of which human motives, desires, and wants may be considered universal is extremely important to students and leaders of play.

One eminent sociologist, W. I. Thomas, has applied the term wishes to cover these universal wants of man. A classification of wishes is nothing more than a tabulation of those motives which appear to be present in some degree of intensity in all men wherever they are found. Although human wishes have a great variety of concrete forms, Thomas reduced them to four types which are universal and common to all mankind: the wishes for new experience, for security, for response, and for recognition. Two other wishes may be added: the wish for participation and for the esthetic.

The wish for new experience is illustrated by hunting, travel, reading tales of adventure, and scientific achievements; for security, by collecting hobbies, children's games in which a goal is a place of refuge, and by the comfort of sitting by the fireplace on a wintry night; for response, by family play, by mating and courtship, and by gifts; and for recognition by one's fellows, in the distinction that goes with stardom in sport, bravery in war, hazardous achievements, and fame acquired in art, music, literary effort, and drama.

A fifth wish, closely allied to response, but often given separate consideration, is the wish for participation. It is more than a gregarious inclination; it is the desire to belong and to contribute to an organization or movement. It is seen in the affiliation with clubs, lodges, and fraternities and in altruistic and patriotic devotion to causes.

Special consideration should be given to the wish for the esthetic or beautiful. A desire for the beautiful seems to be a characteristic of men the world around. No tribe or folk known anywhere in the world fails to show some conception of the beautiful and a desire to express it, as witnessed in their art achievements. Art forms of some type are found universally, although of widely varying type and degree of development. There is evidence of this wish in the decorations on the primitive's dagger and shield and the painting on his body, in his pottery and basketry, in his dancing and rituals. There is evidence in pictures and tapestries on the walls of homes, in the ceilings of the great cathedrals, and in the spectacle of the drama. Music—singing, orchestra concerts, grand opera—is another phase of it. The aesthetic sphere occupies such a large place in leisure-time pursuits that the desire for it, even though implicit in the other wishes, can well be differentiated from them and listed separately.

How do these wishes differ from instincts? In this very important respect: they are regarded as the result primarily of experience rather than as being fixed and inborn. They are considered to be universal throughout humankind and in this respect savor of a definition of instinct, but human life is much the same in fundamental pattern the world around, and experience through interaction with others gives rise to these types of desire. Is there no inborn basis for them? There must, of course, be some inborn basis—all behavior has some basis in original nature—but opinions vary as to the extent.

By way of review man is an organism with a characteristic structure, possessing certain physiological needs (sex, hunger, thirst, etc.) which constitute motives or desires. This organism is in contact with a physical environment and with a social environment. From these contacts, habits and attitudes are formed which also motivate conduct. These human motives can be classified into six categories of wishes which are common to all mankind: the desire for new experience, security, response, recognition, participation, and the aesthetic.

COMPENSATORY ASPECT OF PLAY. Man, in seeking self-expression, is frequently confronted with a situation in which the satisfaction cannot be obtained in the way he desires. His motive is blocked and thwarted. But desires will not be denied, and if expression is not found in one way, it must be in another. He is consequently forced either to drop the motive temporarily in favor of another or to seek compensatory satisfaction in other activities which he may relate to the desired activity in imagination. Or failing this, he may resort to fantasy and daydreaming for satisfaction.

The compensatory aspects of play have been referred to by a number of writers and some have set them forth as a theory of play in itself, but clearly all play behavior is not compensatory, and compensatory activity is clearly engaged in for the purpose of self-expression. The compensatory phase of play is therefore one aspect of the theory of self-expression. Spencer seems to have been the first to mention the compensatory aspect of the problem, and it was later expounded by Reaney, Robinson, Curti, and Murphy. It is given a conspicuous place in the thinking of present-day mental health experts.

It is contended that the child has a feeling of lack of freedom and power in a world of stronger playmates and adults, and that he finds escape from this feeling in make-believe play. Make-believe play thus brings compensatory satisfaction; it is a device which compensates for lack of opportunity to express the personality adequately within, usually, a restrictive environment. Conflicts arise in the life of the child in an adult world that imposes ways of behavior upon him which seem opposed to his desires and impulses. His impulsive nature leads him to do one thing and his desire to obey parents to do another. Hence the conflict! In games, he finds a way of expressing his impulses which is acceptable to adults and reasonably acceptable to himself.

The childish imitation of adult activities is directly compensatory. In doll play and the fondling of pets there is compensation for the desire to handle the baby; in mud pies, paper table sets, toy brooms, and the like, compensation for the desire to keep house.

A main tenet of mental health is based upon the fact that a person's psychological drives and desires seek overt expressions. They cannot be eliminated or destroyed. If denied, tensions result and a condition of unbalance within the organism exists. But, while these psychological drives and cravings cannot be repressed, their expression can be altered or transferred into other channels that, temporarily at least, will be found satisfying enough to keep the personality in a state of equilibrium. It will be recalled that the catharsis theory, of ancient vintage but the forerunner of the present point of view, indicated that in play one may reduce emotional pressures aroused in other situations. One may divert aggressive tendencies, for example, and through such sublimation drain off pressures that otherwise would result in tensions disturbing to mental well-being; instead of attacking a person, one attacks a ball with a bat or a playmate with a tackle. In play one is permitted a regression to more primitive tactics than the social conventions accept.

Although mankind is motivated by a wish for excitement, adventure, dangerous and thrilling experience, strenuous and daring adventure is denied in the day-by-day existence of life in the modern form. But the urge will not be denied. How, then, can the desire be satisfied? In two ways: (1) by aggressive overt action—by competitive sports and games, by roving and hiking, by creative play, by hunting and imitations of hunting; (2) by dreaming, reading, watching TV, attending moving pictures, and the like. In the world of fantasy the dreamer is no longer subordinate or imprisoned by taboos. In the "house of dreams," the motion picture offers a romantic and colorful world where in fancy one finds compensation for an hour or so from the monotony of everyday existence. The love wish particularly finds compensatory expression in many ways.

In a society where fighting is seldom possible, combative play offers compensation to pugnacious man; failing to find opportunity to participate in such activity, gratification may be found in a victory in bridge, in debate, or in imaginative play.

Robert Louis Stevenson, while confined to his home as an invalid, allowed his imagination to roam afield and produced *Treasure Island,* perhaps the greatest of the adventure tales for children. In imagination he achieved the life of adventure which in fact was denied him. Such flights of fancy are characteristic of people who because of handicaps are not able to find adequate self-expression in overt activity. The compensatory theory is the best answer to play of the imagination.

The knowledge that man seeks self-expression by means of compensatory behavior is essential to an adequate understanding of play. It is obvious, however, that much of the play of children is not related to conflicts. The carefree running, rollicking, and romping of children which constitutes so much of play may be regarded as natural and spontaneous expression. Much of the recreation of adults is compensatory for thwarted desires and aspirations in the pursuit of the serious ends of life, but certainly not all of adult play is engaged in for compensation.

ADVANTAGES OF THE SELF-EXPRESSION THEORY. The self-expression theory of play is more all-inclusive than any other in explaining the phenomenon of play. It presents a number of distinct advantages over the traditional theories; it adequately accounts for essential aspects of play behavior which were either ignored or misinterpreted by the traditional theories.

First, it emphasizes the conspicuous role of learned responses, of habits and attitudes, as the principal source of motivation in play, a point which none of the older theories maintained. In the surplus energy theory, the only motivation was an abundance of energy, while in the recreation theory the motivation was a physiological need for rest: both of these observations are only partial and do not strike at the heart of the problem. In the instinct-practice and the recapitulation theories the motivation was inborn instinct, but it is certain that such impulses can affect conduct only through the medium of learned responses, that is, habits and attitudes. In no two individuals could instinct produce exactly the same behavior because habits and attitudes differ.

Second, in emphasizing learned responses—habits and attitudes—as the source of motivation, the self-expression theory accounts for individual differences in play. If the recapitulation and instinct-practice theories were true, one would expect people of the same age stratification to play much alike, being motivated by the same instincts or living over the same epoch. As a matter of fact, differences from individual to individual are marked.

Third, the present theory accounts for the fact that activities distasteful in the beginning become play later on. On the instinct-practice premise, one would expect the activity which instinct impels to be fascinating in the beginning. As a matter of fact, it is when the individual has achieved some degree of mastery over skills and when habits are formed that behavior begins to function as play.

Fourth, the present theory accounts for the tendency of man to set goals of proficiency for himself in play activities by the fact that through social interaction he has come to consider these goals of value. He possesses a nervous system capable of focusing attention on objects of value, but objects come to have value, not because of an inborn or instinctive desire for them, but because of social experience.

Fifth, the theory of self-expression accounts for the fact that man courts thrilling and dangerous experiences and even risks his life in the pursuit of adventure. It substitutes for the pugnacious instinct which the older theories would say led him to take risks, the concept of a desire to achieve mastery over the forces of his environment and to gain social approval. These desires are more the result of life in society than of inborn impulse.

Sixth, the self-expression theory accounts for the creative type of play by substituting for the concept of a "creative instinct," the fact that an intelligent dynamic organism seeks adequate means of self-expression. There is no dodging the creative problem-solving capacity of mind nor the imaginative capacity. Through heredity some men possess more capacity for creative effort than others, hence more of a tendency toward such activity. Objects are conceived which are regarded as having value. Man, possessing the motive and the ability, seeks to achieve—he acts and creates. Having built, he experiences the joy of accomplishment, the thrill of achievement.

Seventh, the theory accounts for compensatory play by saying that it is the result of an effort to achieve self-expression when more adequate means seem impossible.

The objection may be raised that self-expression is obtained in all of life activity, work as well as play. Yes, certainly, and there are no specific play impulses or drives apart from the rest of life. The so-called serious pursuits of adult life consist of activities for self-maintenance, engaged under economic and social pressure—earning a living, building estates, caring for and protecting family, and so forth. One's motives or desires may be satisfied in this serious life, and if they all could conceivably be so satisfied, there would be no need for play or desire for it. But where is there a man or woman who attains full expression of his personality, full satisfaction of all of his desires in workaday life? Or where is there a child who attains such full expression in school?

Man seeks self-expression in all his life pursuits, both work and play. If in play, he cannot obtain satisfaction through overt activity, he resorts to fantasy and daydreaming. Children who are relieved of the struggle for self-maintenance find in play the medium for the satisfaction of the great majority of their motives. Indeed, to children play is the serious business of life.

OTHER EXPLANATIONS OF PLAY AND RECREATION

As in other areas of investigation, the explanation of play and recreation has recently undergone close scrutiny through research. Much of this work is clinical and experimental in character. Between 1920 and 1940 a considerable amount of research was done in the analysis of human play. Stuart H. Britt and Sidney Q. Janus (see Selected References) summarized these earlier attempts, critically reviewing the work of approximately 125 writers who published detailed research on the subject. They reviewed the theoretical approaches as well as the empirical studies completed in which researchers used observation, questionnaires, the play quiz, and experimental methods to study play in a variety of situations. It was concluded that play has taken an important place in the field of experimental social psychology.

Although this accelerated attack upon the analyses of play has not been continued since World War II, several attempts have been made to bring forth new ideas and relationships regarding the explanation of play. The subject has received some attention from psychiatrists who have attempted to explain play more technically, to direct the specific use of play situations as therapy for the mentally ill, and to investigate further the role of the psychiatrist in working with community leisure-time agencies.[4] Rolf Meyersohn's bibliography on the subject of leisure and play indicates the amount of attention the subject has had.[5] To introduce all of the concepts expressed in recent years would be difficult; therefore, the efforts of selected individuals and groups will be identified. Further study of the explanation of play is suggested in the selected references of this chapter.

PSYCHOANALYTIC APPROACH. Franz Alexander, in his psychoanalytic theory of play, emphasizes the fact that playful exercise of functional pleasure is not sufficient to explain play completely. He contends that play is a manifestation of surface excitation which is not needed for survival but which urges to some action, and that there is definitely a functional pleasure of gratification in the mastery

---

[4] Committee on Public Education, *The Psychiatrist's Interest in Leisure-Time Activities* (New York: Group For the Advancement of Psychiatry, 1958).

[5] E. Larabee and R. Meyersohn (eds.), *Mass Leisure* (Glencoe, Ill.: The Free Press, 1958), p. 389.

of an unsolved situation in play. Alexander points to the work of Walder and also to the clinical observations of Erikson which indicate that the content of children's play includes experimentation with not only external danger but also with inter-man conflicts (see Selected References). Alexander's theory is based on three principles:

1. The Stability Principle which pertains to the homeostatic viewpoint that leisure relieves stress in providing the periodic rest needed to rejuvenate the human physical and mental apparatus.
2. The Economy Principle which involves the advantage to the organism of a procedure arrived at by trial and error. Leisure allows for trial and error efforts that develop procedures which are available for periods of non-leisure. This is advantageous.
3. The Surplus Energy Principle which involves a theory of sexuality as a manifestation of surplus energy not needed for adaptive utilitarian (self-preservative) behavior. . . . Early erotic play for pleasure may later become connected with utilitarian functions. For example, curiosity, sense perception, and muscular control, though developed to perfection by simple play activity, can later become involved with sexual activity. In play, the solution of the problem is not imperative. In serious activity a solution is necessary.[6]

The urge to mastery was also emphasized by Freud. Although not expounding a specific theory of play, he pointed out that the child engages in repetitive activity (play) even in unpleasant experiences, because it permits him to achieve mastery over his environment. This mastery is seen by Freud to be one of the basic strivings of the child.

GENETIC APPROACH. Johan Huizinga, in his *Homo Ludens*, emphasizes the genetic aspect of play. He believes that play arises from instinctual need; it contains a serious element and is more than a mere physical phenomenon or

[6] F. Alexander, "A Contribution to the Theory of Play," *The Psychiatrist's Interests in Leisure-Time Activities* (New York: Group For the Advancement of Psychiatry, 1958), p. 376.

a psychological reflex. It is a significant function—there is some sense to it. Huizinga maintains that the elements of play exist in all aspects of culture and relates these elements to legal justice, music, and contests—even war; play is, he claims, involved in problem-solving in science as well as other basic elements of our culture. He points out that the "fun" element emphasizes the need for recognizing play as a concept in itself and that the experimental scientist avoids paying attention to the aesthetic or primary quality of play. Play is voluntary, executed within fixed limits of time and place according to accepted rules agreed upon by the players and is enjoyed by the players who are conscious of the fact that they are "playing" and not engaging in realistic behavior of ordinary life. Play, explains Huizinga, is separated from life in modern civilization—it is no longer a part of cultural activities but relegated only to sports and other specialized behavior patterns which are now more or less isolated from the essential fabric of everyday life. Huizinga emphasizes the fact that play is an integral part of life itself and to isolate it into specialized and regimented patterns, whether it be sports or bridge, destroys the true play spirit and the value of play to the individual and to society.

Play as Part of the Learning Process. The obvious relationship between play and motivation demands discussion of the motivational schemata of such workers as D. O. Hebb, a physiological psychologist, D. C. McClelland, a personality theorist who does extensive experimental work, and Jean Piaget, an imaginative thinker who until recently has not been concerned with experimental types of work (see Selected References). These writers agree generally on the common assumption that the living human being is by its very nature active; hence no external stimulus is necessary to "kick" the organism into action. The primary function of motivation, then, is direction. This concept of activity is not new—the *élan vital* of Descartes was essentially the same—the great difference being that there now seems to be neurological evidence confirming these notions.

Although these authorities consider play as a subsidiary issue, they explain it as part of the learning process. As the infant continues to develop after birth, he gradually reaches interestingly higher levels of ability, both motor and mental. The notion of how the subsequent learning develops differs with various researchers, but the baby begins to learn what actually makes up the world about him. Furthermore, his learning is interesting and often amusing. In adult terms, this learning is often a play form. As the infant matures into childhood and learns to speak and run about, the learning continues and is sought after because it is fun.

Since the child has not developed the cortical capacity necessary to do productive work—his attention span is not long enough—the comprehension of relationships is still inadequate. Consequently the child (1) possesses innate activity, (2) desires to learn through experience, since this has been fun in the past, and (3) cannot learn in an adult manner. The child is thus restricted to activity forms which offer simplicity and variety. These are adult-designed play forms. The fact that the child engages in them vigorously testifies to their attraction for him while at the same time the intensity of effort indicates that he is trying to apply himself completely to the immediate task—that of learning existing relationships. The child then learns only through activity he is able to perform. Piaget, in discussing the development of the psychological world of the infant, has included a theory of the nature of play which explains this approach in a more detailed manner. It is, more correctly, part of his total theory of mental growth.

Piaget considers the first year or so of life to be essentially characterized by dominance of sensorimotor activity. That is, the infant has a very small number of motor responses which he is able to make (many of them so stereotyped as to be regarded as a special class of responses—the reflexes) and a correspondingly small number of recognitions (discriminations) of environmental events. The very first stage in life is seen as being purely reflexive in nature. Consequently, at birth, the infant is considered to have no knowledge or intelligence and only a few basic patterns of response which Piaget calls "schema." The predominate schemas are sucking, grasping, and the like.

As the child develops after birth, he begins to learn new schemas (patterns of response). These might be splashing water in a tub, crawling, and making a certain noise when hungry. In all cases, the infant is forming an association between things in the environment and feelings, needs, drives, and curiosities within himself or, simply, he is learning. The formation of schemas is called assimilation.

This process of assimilation does not have to take place for every new situation, however, because some situations have very much in common with other situations. For example, if the infant learns to pull a toy auto towards him which is tied to a string, he will be able to draw close a balloon tied to a string. The reason is obvious and the process fundamental. The two situations have enough in common that the infant is able to grasp the basic similarity and act appropriately. The process of generalization of learned responses is called accommodation.

Piaget makes an important assumption about the schemata in the infant's repertoire. He says that the infant likes to exercise them and consequently he will repeat these schemas over and over again simply because he likes the achievement (or mastery) of completing a schema for its own sake.

Play is seen by Piaget as the exercising of old schemas so that objects in the environment become connected to the schemas or are such that the schemas themselves are mildly distorted. The mild distortion of these schemas has a ludic character for the infant; it is fun and leads to numerous repetitions. Another form of repetitive behavior is pure imitation, which differs from play in that the former focuses on objects or persons in the environment and subordinates the subjective schemas while in the latter the process is reversed. As a result, play is more fanciful since it depends primarily on purely autistic relationships.

It is obvious that as the child progresses he engages in

different play activities. This is seen as being the result of his maturation (permitting more events to be discriminated and responses made) and his experience (which accumulates a knowledge of relationships). The play forms go through three stages which reflect the ever-present transition. They are (1) the practice stage—in earliest infancy play is simply the practice of motor responses (schema), (2) the symbolic stage—the infant engages in activity (as described above) which has an internal reference point, and (3) the rules stage—where the demands of reality force the infant to give up forever those ludic forms which permit him to subordinate reality to himself. He finally achieves a state where his own body and self constitute objects in the environment and his play forms become reality oriented. From this point on, the existence of rules prevails.

BIOSOCIAL APPROACHES. Finally, the concept of motivation and its relation to play should be discussed in light of the biosocial approaches to the question in recent years. Gardner Murphy, in his explanation of motivation and personality, begins with the principle of inner constancy as formulated under the term homeostasis meaning a tendency to uniformity or stability in the normal body states of an organism. Since life processes occur within rather narrow limits of temperature, alkalinity, and acidity, the organism strives for constancy against the inconsistencies of the outside world. When the organism is out of balance, tension arises and there is activity to relieve this tension. Some tensions arise from within the organism, while others arise from psychic reaction to something outside the organism. Murphy concludes that all activity is traceable to tension. He says that tension is "need" for acting, and that tension, need, and motive are one and the same. The implication for play and recreation is that the organism pursues many courses of action, both conscious and unconscious, to orient itself, and that play is one type of behavior pattern which includes a variety of ways in which the organism may achieve the balance it constantly seeks. Further implications of this explanation of play behavior emphasize the constant attempt of the individual to maintain balance through reduction of tensions, which take the form of basic needs in specific situations in life. Charles C. Cowell, of Purdue University, relates some of these needs as expressed by goal- and satisfaction-seeking behavior of adolescents and outlines how the specific needs of these individuals may be met through planned play, recreation, and physical education programs (see Selected References). Finally, it is of greatest importance that the play leader understand the fundamental motives, drives, and needs that impel people to act in order to help them to express themselves and to achieve the balance and adjustment they seek.

SUMMARY

The present-day knowledge and understanding of the function of play and recreation is admittedly somewhat limited. The theories and explanations of play as described in this chapter represent attempts to clarify the question for the play leader. The older theories of play help to give a sound background of the early thinking about play. The recent theories deal more with the direct causes of human behavior, taking into account self-expression as well as the primary causes of physiological, psychological, and environmental factors that motivate the individual's action.

Certainly there remains much to be done to supplement the present knowledge about the subject of human play. The course of action is quite clear for the future. First, there is a need for the controlled observation of the play of animals (to replace anecdotal and impressionistic descriptions of animal behavior) and of the effect of environment on the play habits of animals. This information, it is hoped, would offer significant ideas for the increased understanding of play behavior in man. Second, there is a great need to subject currently accepted interpretations of human play and recreation to direct test in order to add to the present knowledge of the subject and to formulate explanations in more objective terms. This leads up to the subject of defining play and recreation and differentiating them from work—the task of the next chapter.

SELECTED REFERENCES

BEACH, FRANK A. "Current Concepts of Play in Animals," *The American Naturalist*, LXXIX, 785 (November-December, 1945), 523. A significant summary comment is presented regarding the conclusions resulting from experimental work with the play of animals.

BRITT, STUART H., and JANUS, SIDNEY Q. "Toward a Social Psychology of Human Play," *Journal of Social Psychology*, XIII (May, 1941), 351–84. The authors examine the major theoretical studies and empirical investigations of play, summarize and evaluate them, and suggest problems for further investigation regarding the theories of play. A comprehensive bibliography of writings on play is also included.

MURPHY, GARDNER. *Personality: A Biosocial Approach to Origins and Structure.* New York: Harper & Bros., 1947. An excellent and thorough discussion of motivation, basic to the study of the theories of play, is presented in Chapter 5, "The Elementary Biology of Motivation," and in Chapter 6, "The Biology of Motive Patterns."

ALEXANDER, FRANZ. "A Contribution to the Theory of Play," *The Psychoanalytic Quarterly*, XXVII, 2 (1958), 175–95.

BOGARDUS, EMORY S. *Fundamentals of Social Psychology.* New York: Appleton-Century-Crofts, Inc., 1950, Part I.

Committee on Public Education. *The Psychiatrist's Interest in Leisure-Time Activities*, Report No. 39. New York: Group for the Advancement of Psychiatry, 1958.

COWELL, CHARLES C. *Scientific Foundations of Physical Education.* New York: Harper & Bros., 1953, Chap. 3.

ERIKSON, ERIK H. "Studies in the Interpretation of Play," *Genetic Psychological Monographs*, XXII (1940), 563–564.

FREUD, S. *Beyond the Pleasure Principle.* New York: Liveright Publishing Corp., 1950.

GROOS, KARL. *The Play of Man.* New York: D. Appleton & Co., 1901.

HEBB, DONALD O. *The Organization of Behavior, A Neuropsychological Theory.* New York: John Wiley & Sons, Inc., 1949, Chaps. 8 and 9.

HUIZINGA, JOHAN. *Homo Ludens—A Study of the Play-Element in Culture.* Boston: The Beacon Press, 1955.

LARABEE, ERIC, and MEYERSOHN, ROLF (eds.). *Mass Leisure.* Glencoe, Ill.: The Free Press, 1958, p. 389 (Bibliography on leisure).

McCLELLAND, DAVID C. *Personality.* New York: Holt, Rinehart & Winston, Inc., 1951, Part IV.

NASH, JAY B. *Philosophy of Recreation and Leisure.* St. Louis: The C. V. Mosby Co., 1953, Chaps. 5 and 6.

PATRICK, GEORGE THURMAN WHITE. *The Psychology of Relaxation.* Boston: Houghton Mifflin Co., 1916.

PIAGET, JEAN. *Play, Dreams, and Imitation in Childhood.* New York: W. W. Norton & Co., 1952.

————. *The Moral Judgment of the Child.* Glencoe, Ill.: The Free Press, 1948.

ROBBINS, FLORENCE G. *The Sociology of Play, Recreation, and Leisure Time.* Dubuque, Iowa: William C. Brown Co., 1955, Chap. 3.

ROBINSON, EDWARD S. "The Compensatory Function of Make-Believe Play," *Psychological Review*, XXVII, 6 (November, 1920), 429–39.

SHIVERS, JAY S. *An Analysis of Various Theories of Recreation.* Unpublished Doctor's thesis, University of Wisconsin, 1958.

SPENCER, HERBERT. *Principles of Psychology.* New York: D. Appleton & Co., 1873.

WALDER, ROBERT. "The Psychoanalytic Theory of Play," *The Psychoanalytic Quarterly*, II (1933), 208–24.

5

Definitions and Characteristics of Play and Recreation

For many years people have attempted to define the complex human behavior patterns generally referred to as play. Further, there are differences of opinion about the meaning of *work, leisure, drudgery, recreation,* and similar terms. This chapter proposes to examine these terms as defined by leading social scientists and others who have studied play, to analyze the opinions held, and to indicate specific concepts which will aid communication in discussions of play and related patterns of human behavior. The essential characteristics of play, the play of adults, the aim of play, play as work, and other factors relating to play and recreation in present-day living are discussed.

MEANINGS OF PLAY AND RECREATION

The simple word play reveals complexity as one tries to analyze its meaning. Play to one person may mean the romping and shouting of children on the school ground; to another it may correspond to an afternoon of golf; to another it may suggest a boy's experiments with the homemade radio set; and to still another it may indicate the very highest form of intellectual achievement as found in literature, science, and art. Thorndike said that most of the disputes about the service of play hark back to a vagueness in defining what play is to be taken to mean. To this disagreement on the meaning of play add the differences of opinion regarding the connotation of the word recreation, which has more recently come into common use, and some rather pointed questions of definition are raised. The following definitions of play and recreation illustrate the broad variations in meanings given these words:

PLAY.

Schiller: The aimless expenditure of exuberant energy.

Guts Muths: The natural exercise and recreation of body and mind.

Froebel: The natural unfolding of the germinal leaves of childhood.

Lazarus: Play is activity which is in itself free, aimless, amusing, or diverting.

Hall: The motor habits and spirit of the past persisting in the present.

Groos: Instinctive practice, without serious intent, of activities that will later be essential to life.

Lee: Instinctive activity, looking toward an ideal.

Dewey: Activities not consciously performed for the sake of any result beyond themselves.

Gulick: What we do because we want to do it.

Stern: Play is voluntary, self-sufficient activity.

Patrick: Those human activities which are free and spontaneous and which are pursued for their own sake alone. Interest in them is self-sustaining, and they are not continued under any internal or external compulsion.

Rainwater: Play is a mode of behavior, either individual or collective, involving pleasurable activity of any kind, not undertaken for the sake of a reward beyond itself and performed during any age period of the individual.

Curti: Highly motivated activity which, as free from conflicts, is usually, though not always, pleasurable.

Pangburn: Activity carried on for its own sake.

Dulles: An instinctive form of self-expression and emotional escape valve. . . .

Slavson: Play and recreation . . . are leisure-time activities . . . motivated by pleasure and serve as diversions from the more pressing and serious occupations of daily living.

Nash: Any act other than such survival activities as eating and sleeping which carries its own drive or any act in which an individual enters of his own volition, without feeling, in any way, outer compulsion.

Dictionary of Education: Any pleasurable activity carried on for its own sake, without reference to ulterior purpose or future satisfactions.

Mitchell: Play is self-expression for its own sake.

Huizinga: Play is more than a mere physiological phenomenon or a psychological reflex. . . . It is a significant function—that is to say there is some sense to it. In play there is something "at play" which transcends the immediate needs of life and imparts meaning to the action.

Piaget: Play is a symbolical manifestation . . . it is a sensory-motor exercise, regulated and essentially social, and symbolic—especially with infants after the second year.[1]

RECREATION.

Butler: Recreation may be considered as any form of leisure-time experience or activity in which an individual engages from choice because of the enjoyment and satisfaction which it brings directly to him.

Neumeyer: Recreation is . . . any activity, either individual or collective, pursued during one's leisure time. Being relatively free and pleasurable it has its own appeal.

Meyer and Brightbill: Recreation is activity voluntarily engaged in during leisure time and primarily motivated by the satisfaction or pleasure derived from it.

Fitzgerald: Recreation is the natural expression during leisure of human interests seeking satisfaction.

One who studies these definitions observes the radical differences of opinion apparent in the theories of play and those of recreation; at the same time, however, one can see gradual progress toward a common understanding accompanying the growing knowledge of the subjects. As previously mentioned, early studies of play have been supplemented by a considerable number of studies in social psychology undertaken since 1920. A number of modern scientists, including Beach, Britt, and Janus (see Selected References), maintain that the present disagreement regarding the definition of play stems from lack of essential data and that further empirical research will lead to significant results in understanding the play of both man and animals.

The present differences of opinion are, then, differences

[1] For a documented summary of definitions of play by various scientists see S. H. Britt and S. Q. Janus, "Toward a Social Psychology of Human Play," listed in Selected References for this chapter.

in point of view. The oldest definitions, as found in the dictionaries of forty to fifty years ago, attempted to define play in terms of certain specific activities which were aimless, frivolous, and seemingly barren of any useful results. In a vague way it was recognized that play might possess some usefulness as indicated in the old proverb, "All work and no play makes Jack a dull boy." But on the whole, play was considered a waste of time; and work, which produced something of consequence, was touted as the great goal of education. Play was held to be the antithesis of work, an impassable barrier separated the two.

The attitude towards play has changed to the point today that work and play are not considered antithetical but instead are considered so much alike that they often overlap and it is hard to tell the difference between the two. No longer is the term play defined by certain specific activities, but, on the contrary, it is defined as an attitude of mind which may pervade any given human activity. It is recognized that play to one person may at the same time be work to another, and vice versa.

Likewise, the attitude has changed with the times in regard to the meaning of the word recreation. During the early part of the play movement the word recreation grew out of the implication that the industrial worker would recreate or restore the balance of the organism, more or less depleted by work, through participation in satisfying leisure-time activities. While play was still employed to describe certain early developments of the play movement (e.g., playground), the term recreation gradually grew in use and acceptance. Today recreation is generally used to describe broadly the entire field of activities engaged in during leisure time. Play has grown to have a restricted meaning, still retaining its traditional reference to growth and maturation and still used to describe specific behavior patterns long classified as play; but it does not describe the total concept of the recreative activities of people during leisure time. Recreation and play are often used interchangeably; some authors now refer to play as a phase of recreation. It is only a matter of interpretation, then, as to what these words mean.

In the discussions following the scope of the meaning of these words is evident from the frame of reference in which the words are used. The word play is considered synonymous with recreation in those instances where this word seems to be most appropriate and meaningful to describe all of man's recreative activities; at other times, the word play is used in its more traditional and restricted sense, implying that it is only a phase of recreation. Both words, play and recreation are often used together for emphasis, mainly to assure that the broadest meaning of the text is imparted to the reader.

These efforts at clarification suggest that concepts in the recreation profession are changing rapidly and that the profession is seeking to develop a language more consistent with that of related social science disciplines and at the same time is seeking to develop more descriptive terminologies which will be clearly recognized and understood by the general public.

CHARACTERISTICS OF PLAY AND RECREATION

While leading educators are not yet in full accord as to the meaning of play or what should be included in the concept and, therefore, are not in agreement as to its value in education, they do agree more closely on a few fundamental points:

1. Play is activity; it is not idleness, but is in contrast with it. Loafing and dawdling are not play, but a cessation of activity because of lack of interest in it, indicating a loss of the play spirit.
2. Play is not limited to any particular form of activity; it may be neuromuscular, sensory, mental, or a combination of all three.
3. The value of play in education is in proportion to its power to interest the player, absorb his attention, and arouse him to enthusiastic and persistent activity.

4. Whether an activity is play or not depends on the attitude of mind of the doer toward the thing he is doing. It follows that there is no particular activity, be it baseball, fishing, or playing with dolls, that is always necessarily play; neither can an activity be mentioned that may not under some conditions be play. Some activities, such as games and sports, are usually play, but we can never be sure that a certain activity is play for a certain person unless we know his mental attitude towards it while he is actually engaged in it. What is play one day may be drudgery another day, for mental attitudes change with conditions.

5. There is general accord in regarding the play spirit as an attitude of mind, but there is not so full an agreement as to the nature of this attitude. Mainly, the essential characteristic of play is a satisfaction in the activity itself. If some external compulsion is necessary to continue the activity, then the activity is no longer considered play.

PLAY OF ADULTS. There can be no basis for the belief that the adult does not play, whichever of the definitions of play is preferred. He at times expends surplus energy aimlessly (Schiller); he engages with joy in racially old activities (Hall); he carries on actions for amusement or diversion (Webster); he engages in activity for no other reason than that it is pleasurable; he seeks self-expression and turns to play to obtain it. The play of the adult differs from that of the child because he has greater abilities than the child in some directions and lesser abilities in others: he has lost some of the impulsiveness of childhood, but his aims are more complex and remote; he has less capacity for vigorous physical exercise and therefore is more inclined to accept recreation of a quieter type.

In summing up this differentiation, while the child's play is a skill-perfecting process, the adult's recreation is more the exercise of perfected skills. The adult is inclined to be satisfied with skills already developed and is more reconciled to his inabilities and shortcomings. As Joseph Lee so aptly puts it, "Play to the child is growth—the gaining of life; to the adult it is recreation—the renewal of life."

GOALS OF PLAY. The presence of an aim or goal gives meaning to an activity. It is this goal that gives play value to activities, and the measure of the play value is found in the intensity with which the goal is sought.

Man is by nature a goal-seeking creature. The goal may not always be a conscious one; indeed it may be hidden so that the individual cannot state it or the observer easily identify it. For example, some of the spontaneous activity of children may not have a conscious or explicit aim, in that the child is motivated primarily by the physiological need for activity and just romps and frolics about or engages in spontaneous tussling. But such momentary expenditure of energy is soon turned into purposeful activity. The young child may run just to be running, but soon he runs to catch someone or to get to first base. He spends most of his time in experimental activities, in collecting and constructing things, and in playing games, all of which have obvious aims.

Children often loaf and dawdle at their tasks but seldom at their play. They take the goals of their play seriously, and that is why they put the best of their ability into it. The enthusiasm of play, aroused as these goals are sought and accomplished, gives play the superior educational value it possesses. Only to the adult who engages in languid types of activity to pass away his leisure time does play lack the serious aim it has in the child's life.

To contend that play is lacking in aim, therefore, is to ignore its fundamental nature. A question more worthy of consideration is whether play can have an aim beyond that involved in the activity itself.

Groos claimed that while play may have an aim, it is a fictitious one, like that of a kitten that plays with a leaf as if it were a mouse, or a girl who flirts with her male acquaintances; as soon as it becomes real, as when the kitten chases a mouse, or the girl falls in love, the activity ceases to be play and becomes real life. Several students of play strongly object to this view, claiming that the play of children is real life and that play can achieve for them results beyond the play itself.

John Dewey and others hold a point of view similar to that of Groos but with a slight distinction, saying that play has an aim within itself as when a boy aims to hit a ball or tag another boy, but if the aim extends beyond the game and looks toward a material result, as when a boy sticks to football practice to earn a sweater, it is no longer pure play. This is an important distinction. When the participant has an interest in the activity for its own sake and is not participating for the sake of a remote goal, he has a direct interest in the activity. Such activity is pure play, and some would limit the word play to activity of this direct interest type. When he has an interest beyond the activity, such as the desire for a football sweater, then his interest in the activity is indirect, his interest being in the remote goal.

It does not necessarily follow that play is eliminated from those activities of the indirect interest type, that is, activities engaged in to obtain remote goals. Individuals are constantly setting remote goals in all activities of life, in play as in others. In play activity, boys and girls constantly set goals of perfection upon which their eyes are fixed and their minds are set, even though some of these cannot be attained for months or years. They will undergo unpleasant activity if necessary to attain these ends, but the disliked activity is less distasteful than it would be without the coveted end, and often what would be drudgery becomes interesting because it means progress toward the goal. Although the activity now is unpleasant, it is leading to the ultimate satisfaction of goals; progress brings satisfaction and happiness. Happiness is not obtained by immediate pleasure; it comes from sensing progress toward the ultimate satisfaction of goals or ends which one has set.

There usually is an end beyond the satisfaction obtained from the immediate participation in play, especially in the play of youth. A boy plays football not only because of the joy it brings today, but because he has his mind fixed on a level of perfection in the sport he hopes to attain in the tomorrow—perhaps on the goal of playing on a favorite college team several years hence. There is of course an end within the activity itself, but there is also an end beyond the immediate activity. Activity takes on far-reaching educational significance only when the real interest is a remote goal.

The tendency of youth to set goals for the development of proficiency is at the root of the difference, referred to earlier in this chapter, between the play of youth and the recreation of adults. It is this tendency to set goals for themselves that makes of children's play a skill-perfecting process, and it is the absence of such goals that often makes of adult recreation merely a performance by skills already developed. It is the setting of goals that makes of children's play a forward-reaching, growth-producing process, as contrasted to the somewhat constricted nature of the recreation of adults who often have become resigned to their present level of proficiency.

This goal-setting gives to the play leader a potent educational tool which he will do well to utilize. The wise leader aims to do more than bring joy in the immediate activity: he strives to assist and to inspire his players to set goals of proficiency for themselves, knowing that in so doing he is releasing a dynamo of energy in the pursuit of those goals. The player himself must set these goals, however, and he will strive for them in proportion to how strongly he himself wants to reach them. Education and play, then, merge so that the line between the two becomes difficult to draw.

When a remote goal is set and the individual's mind becomes focused upon it, he calculates the steps he must take to attain it. The remote goal is often forbidding as it is contemplated, and it is only as intermediate goals are visualized that the goal seems attainable. Leaders can do much to assist children in laying out the intermediate steps which must be taken, showing them at each stage of progress what the next step is and how it may be attained.

A goal need not necessarily be a material one though a material end may serve to intensify the interest in the activity. If the interest is only in the material reward, however, the activity to attain it will probably not be play. One learns in proportion to the interest in the activity itself. A case in point is the use of honors and awards. The end very often is merely getting the badge, and, if this is the case, the process, so far as mastering the activity is concerned, is of insignificant educational importance to the individual. But, on the other hand, the award may serve to start him in the activity which in itself may soon become interesting, as in the case of the boy who first takes up knot-tying only as a means of earning a badge and soon develops a fondness for knot-tying itself. His direct interest then shifts from the award to the activity. Honors and awards as ends or incentives, then, are educationally acceptable to the extent that this shift takes place.

One can play baseball as a means of earning a living, and it may still be play; that is, the mere presence of the pay check in the situation does not necessarily destroy the play value. The situation is materially altered, however, by the fact that baseball in this case is the means of subsistence. The constant realization of this fact may take away much of the spirit of freedom, because the player knows that he must play well or serious consequences will result. It is conceivable, however, that in the course of his daily games, the player experiences as much joy and thrill as in his former carefree sand-lot days.

People do have aims beyond the immediate activity in practically all play—the boy has an aim in becoming a better tennis player, the girl of becoming a skilled equestrienne, the woman of crocheting more efficiently. There may be a material reward for the activity, as a football sweater, and it may serve to intensify the interest in the play rather than to destroy the play value. And, again, there may be a money reward and still the activity may have all the aspects of play, which leads to the question, "Can play function as work?"

PLAY AS WORK. It is generally agreed that when an activity is of itself attractive enough to make one want to do it, it is play. Much that one does to earn a living may be play at times. Whether an activity is play, work, or drudgery depends upon one's attitude toward the effort expended on the activity.

The distinction between work and play is largely based on the nature of the respective rewards and the time of their realization. Play is activity for its own sake; work is activity for some extrinsic consideration, yet play and work can overlap, or play can at once be work when one's attitude toward an activity reaches this point. There is no essential difference in the form or outward appearance of work and play; the difference is in the spirit with which each is undertaken. When the satisfaction one gets out of an activity is sufficient reward for keeping it up, then there is play. If, however, it is necessary to have some external reward before one will engage in an activity, that is work.

That the same activity may be either play or work is illustrated by the classic experience of Tom Sawyer. When his aunt ordered him to paint the fence, Tom dreaded it as work; however, he fooled the boys into thinking it was great fun, and they brought him their jackknives and tops to get the privilege of painting a few boards. More modern cases in point are easy to find. It seems like work to dig a ditch; yet this is fun to the professor excavating for ancient relics. Boys who would groan at running on errands will think it great sport to engage in a footrace. Again, playing tennis may be thrilling and compelling throughout the afternoon, but late in the fifth set, with weary legs and the score hopelessly favoring the opponent, one will long for the showers and home.

Proportionately as the feeling of pleasure is strong or feeble, a given activity will be play or work. Some activities usually give pleasure to everyone, and therefore it is safe to call them play activities. This is true of most of the activities of childhood. However, while certain activities are not universally liked, they may afford great play value to certain individuals who have a special talent for them.

There are several factors which may affect our attitude toward any given effort and which may cause us to regard some activities as work or drudgery and others as play.

First, an awareness of what kind of consequences are apt to result from the activity affects one's attitude toward it. In our efforts to earn a living, defeat or failure is often tragic; we are aware of the seriousness of the consequences. In play, however, there are no serious consequences. The tennis player, for instance, can throw himself into the game with every atom of will and ounce of power, can play his heart out in an effort to win, so long as he stays within the rules of the game, knowing all the time the result, whether victory or defeat, will have no vital or enduring effect upon his life. If it were a real business duel of importance, defeat would mean a setback in the attainment of lifelong ambitions for self and family. But not so in play. The awareness of serious consequences, then, may make some activities appear as work whereas they might otherwise be play.

Second, the probability of success is conducive to the play attitude. In play, an individual constructs his activities so as to keep them closely adapted to his abilities, with the result that success is a frequent achievement and failure more infrequent. A game can be adapted to the person or people engaging in it, whereas in work people must adapt to the task. Play thus has a greater flexibility than work. To the extent that the situation offers the probability of frequent success and a rather constant feeling of security, the play attitude prevails.

Third, suspense in a situation is a factor conducive to a play attitude. In play there is always a large element of suspense which keeps the activity going and makes it interesting. When the suspense is relieved, the activity starts over again, and the cycle goes on and on. For instance, in games when the goal is made or point scored, the routine starts again, and a new situation involving suspense begins. The repetition is thus rhythmic in nature.

Fourth, effort involving routine conformance to a definitely organized pattern with little opportunity for imagination is usually unconducive to the play attitude. The more opportunity for imagination and spontaneity, the greater the chance for self-expression, which is an integral part of play.

Fifth, long-continued repetition of the same activity is not conducive to a play attitude. The human organism needs change, craves new stimuli, fresh experiences. Spontaneous impulsive action is usually accompanied by the play attitude; long-continued repetition of the same response, by the work attitude.

Sixth, effort in which motives and desires are satisfied directly and immediately is apt to appeal to us as play. In earning a living, human motives are often thwarted and satisfaction postponed. The slowness of attainment is annoying and disappointments are many. Such effort is conducive to the work attitude. In play there is a feeling of mastery; one strikes directly at opponents, and satisfaction of desires comes quickly. There is also a freedom from conflict, and there is a wholeness to the game that does not exist in one's continued efforts to earn a living; each game is a sufficient whole, and when it is over, it is over. The immediacy with which desires are satisfied in effort is a factor favorable to a play attitude.

There are three attitudes of mind toward effort which are defined as follows:

Drudgery is effort from which there seems no adequate reward other than mere drab existence, no adequate satisfaction of any motive. There is neither fun in doing the activity nor reward afterwards which seems adequate to compensate for the monotonous effort. A drudge is someone who seems to toil unceasingly without hope of satisfying recompense. Society can combat the conditions of drudgery by offering more leisure-time opportunities to the worker, especially to the worker performing the lowest menial tasks where the scope of responsibility is limited and where there is no chance for experiment with individual initiative.

Work is effort performed for rewards or satisfactions which are outside of or in addition to the activity. In work, the reward comes in the future in the form of a pay check, perhaps, or an attractive, well-mowed lawn, or an essential article for the household. The reward is apart from the activity and is postponed until the activity is completed. Modern guidance in education should aid the child in his quest to discover his natural bent and capabilities. If the proper life-long occupation is discovered, the individual has his best chance of finding enjoyment as well as material gain. The rewards will then be immediate as well as remote.

Play is effort in which the satisfactions are in, and a part of, the activity itself. The goals are immediate, and they are accomplishable. It is effort scaled down to capacity of the performer, so as to provide a balance of success and failure possibilities, with the result that there is always hope of achievement. Play is its own reward, and no other inducement is needed. Play is self-expression for its own sake.

Society should increase the individual's appreciation of play so that he can make the most of his leisure time, so that he may energize and recreate himself through play and recreation.

None of the above factors in themselves classify an activity as work or play or drudgery. They are merely factors which are apt to affect our attitude toward the effort. It is impossible to determine whether an activity is work or play by any kind of objective criteria—future rewards, pay check, honors and awards, reputation, or what not; no one knows but the participant himself. It depends upon what is going on in his own mind.

In all walks of life, then, whether in school, in daily labor, in business or in the professions, there are differing attitudes an individual can take toward effort. At one pole is drudgery, in between is work, and at the other pole is play. Play and work overlap, and if one can succeed in fusing the play spirit with daily work, one is doubly rewarded, in that one not only enjoys the activity immediately but will also receive the future recompense.

SUMMARY

Play was once looked upon as a curious and unimportant feature of child life. Now it is considered a factor in education and a very important one. With this change of viewpoint has come a change in the definition of play, which now encompasses a wider range of activities. At first only aimless activities were classed as play; then activities with a fictitious or make-believe purpose were added; later a real and serious aim was conceded as a possibility in play, but always with the provision that the object to be accomplished lies within the activity and is a part of it, rather than a remote object of value. The modern concept of play stresses its educational significance and allows the presence of the play spirit even in work.

The term recreation is sometimes used synonymously with play; however, play is the effort expended in these activities. Also, recreation has outgrown its earlier connotation which connected it with the play of adults and implied a more passive and less serious or purposeful type of activity. Although many definitions and concepts of recreation persist, and with justification, in this volume recreation is applied in a broader connotation, i.e., the leisure activities of adults as well as children; all types of activities, active as well as passive, sought by both children or adults for personal expression. Thus the meaning of recreation has become more inclusive—it encompasses the meanings of play in general and in addition describes a community service as well as a new profession.

With a play spirit in his work and a capacity for recreating himself when away from his work, the individual should have a good start toward being a contented, contributive citizen. He will be a citizen to whom there even may be some drudgery in life, to be sure, but at the same time, this drudgery will be willingly undergone for the sake of the larger compensations that his work and his leisure time are holding forth to him.

SELECTED REFERENCES

The following two sources provide summaries of approaches made in more recent years by various individuals in order to develop scientific information regarding play, including a definition of it.

BEACH, FRANK A. "Current Concepts of Play in Animals," *The American Naturalist*, LXXIX, 785 (November-December, 1945), 523.

BRITT, STUART H., and JANUS, SIDNEY Q. "Toward A Social Psychology of Human Play," *Journal of Social Psychology*, XIII (May, 1941), 351–58.

SESSOMS, HANSON D. *A Glossary of Selected Public Recreation Terms.* Raleigh, N.C.: North Carolina Recreation Commission, 1956. This publication includes definitions of terminologies in the park and recreation field, including definitions of play, recreation, and other basic terms.

6

Classification by Motor Movements

Play denotes innumerable games, sports, dances, participation in musical activities, arts and crafts, dramatics and similar forms of expression, both mental and physical. By classifying these activities an understanding of the objectives accomplished by participation in particular types of play may be gained. On the basis of specific games or activities classification would be confusing and impractical. Play activities are best understood classified in three ways: first, according to physical movements involved, a procedure followed in this chapter; second, according to the interests of participants, a method taken up in the chapter following; and third, according to play forms, the classification of which follows in turn. It should also be noted that play movements in this chapter refer to fundamental physical movements of the body, in contrast to the modern play movement appearing in previous chapters which refers to the growth and development of play and recreation activities throughout the world during the past one hundred years.

EARLY CLASSIFICATIONS OF PLAY ACTIVITIES

Many classifications of games and activities have been made, some based on age levels, some on materials used, some on organization, some on movements required, some on interests, some on psychological drives involved.

The following selected classifications from early writers in the field show the variety of classifications which have been used.

Guts Muths

A. Movement plays.
B. Rest plays.

Types of plays under the above two classes:

1. Plays of observation and sensory judgment, e.g., ball games (A) and puzzle games (B).
2. Plays of attention.
3. Memory plays (B only).
4. Plays of wit and imagination.
5. Rational plays (B only).
6. Plays of taste (B only).

Froebel

A. Games of imitation.
B. Games of bodily exercise.
C. Games of the senses.

Spencer

A. Sensory and movement plays.
B. Games, or play by rule.
C. Artistic-aesthetic play.

Lazarus

A. Chance play.
B. Intellectual play.
C. Exercise play.
D. Ideal play.

Groos

A. Experimental play, leading to self-control.
1. Sensory practice.
2. Motor practice.
3. Practice of higher psychic facilities.
B. Plays involving relationships of living beings with each other.
1. Combat play.
2. Love play.
3. Imitative play.
4. Social play.

G. E. Johnson

A. Games which conserve biological and physiological growth.
B. Games which perfect the body.
C. Games which develop individualistic virtues.
D. Games which develop the individual in social relationships.

C. W. Hetherington

A. Mimetics.
B. Story plays.
C. Rhythmical activities.
D. Hunting games.
E. Relay races.
F. Stunts.
G. Athletic games.
H. Individual athletic events.

KINDS OF PLAY ACTIVITIES

Play activities are naturally divided into three main groups: motor, sensory, and intellectual. Motor play may be illustrated, primarily, by running, jumping, climbing, or throwing; sensory play by watching a gymnastic exhibition, a game, or a movie; intellectual play by listening to an interesting lecture, taking part in a debate, or playing cards.

This three-fold division of play activities seems simple enough at first, but it is not so simple as it seems. It is not easy to name an example of purely motor, sensory, or intellectual play. The typical motor plays of running, jumping, and climbing, involve along with the motor activity much exercise of the senses—sight, hearing, and touch; also, much exercise of the intellect—attention, memory, imagination, reason, and judgment. To get full enjoyment of a ball game or a picture show—typical sensory plays—one must sit up, turn head and eyes here and there and focus the eyes, and all this is muscular rather than sensory. Even intellectual play involves a small amount of motor activity and a large amount of sensory activity.

All bodily movements are first divided into two groups: fundamental and accessory. Fundamental movements are those that employ the big muscles of the trunk and limbs, e.g., running, swimming and dancing; whereas talking, playing a violin, and operating a typewriter employ accessory movements. The former are called fundamental because they are older in racial history, are found in animals as well as in man, and because they involve muscles whose mass is so great that their activity controls the amount of food and of oxygen needed and of waste to be eliminated, and therefore controls indirectly the activity and development of the heart, lungs, breathing muscles, digestive system, and other organs necessary to life, health, and vigor. The accessory movements are of more recent origin, as shown by their absence in animals, and by their appearing later in the life of each individual child. Further, the accessory movements are too small to have any significant influence on the heart action or other vital processes of the body as a whole.

FUNDAMENTAL MOVEMENTS IN PLAY

From the standpoint of the player, the fundamental movements involved in play, as first pointed out by Gulick, form two divisions: movement of the player's own body and movement of other bodies; the first is called locomotion and the second, handling objects. Locomotion is accomplished mainly by the lower limbs, with the arms and trunk used incidentally; handling objects is performed mainly by the hands and arms, with the trunk and lower limbs used incidentally.

LOCOMOTION. Motor play includes seven distinct forms of locomotion: *creeping, walking, running, dancing, jumping, climbing,* and *swimming and diving,* and, in some cases, locomotion with the use of a vehicle. There are several variations of walking and running, such as skating, skiing, snowshoeing, and walking on stilts—locomotion, that is, with an apparatus attached to the shoe.

Locomotion with the use of a vehicle also belongs here when it involves considerable motor activity, which it does in the case of sleds, bicycles, scooters, rowboats, canoes, swings, and teeters, but not in the case of trains, steamboats, airplanes, trolley cars, and automobiles, for in these the activity is chiefly sensory. There are in all ten forms of locomotion.

Creeping. Creeping is a crude form of quadrupedal locomotion, usually done on hands and knees. It is an important stage in the neuromuscular development of the young child but is of less importance after walking is mastered, and is seldom used in later play activity as such. However, sitting, kneeling on the knees, and similar positions continue to be important movements made by children during the pre-school and early elementary school years.

Walking. Walking is usually learned after creeping, and in civilized times is by far the most important, since civilized man scarcely uses the other forms except in his sports. The widespread use of the automobile, as well as the accessibility of rapid, convenient forms of public transportation, has eliminated much of the necessity for walking; people have also learned to live by a time schedule which does not allow sufficient time to walk from one place to another. And even children are unable to walk any considerable distance because of the danger involved in crossing streets having fast-moving vehicular traffic. Since walking is not used to any large extent in our common plays and games, it has been necessary to stimulate interest in it through games such as golf, but even here the electric cart to transport golfers from hole to hole is becoming more popular. In all fitness programs, walking is being stressed considerably and people are reminded that short recreation hikes and walks are healthful and can be incorporated in the daily routine of life.

Strolling is a leisurely, languid type of walk, taken as if to pass the time rather than to go to any place; it is too mild to call the heart and lungs into vigorous action, but is useful for invalids and convalescents. Standing still for a long time, which of necessity is required of surgeons, bank tellers, and soldiers at attention, for example, is a practice that is harmful to the feet, the strain without movement blocking the circulation. Even the slow, languid walk usually seen on the streets causes a circulation of blood in the feet, and helps to prevent foot trouble.

Hiking is walking of the more vigorous, hustling type; the term is applied especially to long steady walks, several miles in extent. Hiking is moderate exercise, affording outdoor recreation for many who are not equal to the demands of the usual athletic sports; it is rather mild for men and boys of athletic habit but even for them it is good if the tempo is speeded up and the course leads uphill and down, for it develops an endurance that games of short duration fail to give.

Running. Running differs from walking in that it leaves the body unsupported for a part of the time, each step being a spring into the air, while in walking the body is supported all the time by one limb or the other. Running is the most rapid form of locomotion in man, and as such was of daily use to primitive man. Now, like climbing, it has practically passed out of use as an activity of civilized life except as it is preserved in play. But running is the most universal of motor play activities and is probably the most valuable of them all, developing as it does not only the lower limbs but the trunk, arms, and vital organs.

A slow run is called a jog; but when a runner goes at top speed, expending considerable strength and wind, it is called a dash or a sprint. Hurdling is running and jumping over obstacles called hurdles. The hurdles are of standard height and placed at standard distances, so that an athlete can learn to space his steps.

Foot racing is now done on smooth cinder tracks which favor the fastest pace. The ancient Greek athletes, on the other hand, ran their races in soft sand wearing armor. The change to the cinder paths followed the invention of the stop-watch. So long as races were without any instrument for timing, the only incentive was to beat the opponent, but with the establishment of records of so many seconds for a race of a designated length there came an interest in faster time, and hence, in better tracks and in light wearing apparel.

Dancing. Dancing consists of rhythmic bodily movements combined with a succession of steps and taken to accompany certain types of music. The separate steps are usually simple and easy to learn, such as touchsteps, glides, turns, and simple walking steps; these are combined into groups of which there are an indefinite number, such as the skip, polka, two-step, waltz, galop, schottische, mazurka, pirouette, and pas de basque. Certain lively and vivacious dances are known as clogs, jigs, or lilts, and include almost continuous hopping or jumping combined with other movements; minuets are dignified and slow.

The most popular and satisfactory dances for small children are the song plays, in which the steps are easy (usually skipping), and the children sing to accompany the movements. "Did You Ever See a Lassie," "The Muffin Man," and "The Farmer in the Dell" are familiar examples. Much valuable dancing material has been found in the *tribal* and *folk dances* of various tribes, races, and nationalities. The artistic types of dancing include the ballet, natural dancing, and other interpretive and expressionistic forms generally referred to as the modern dance.

Jumping. Jumping is springing into the air from one or both feet. To jump is the same as to leap; it is a general term, including several varieties. If the jumper springs from one foot and alights on the other, it is a step; if he alights on the foot from which he sprang, it is a hop: these are the most common of the special forms. A hurdle-jump is a form of step, so taken as to pass over the hurdle most easily, without striking it. A high jump is taken to find how great a height can be passed over by the body; a broad jump to find how great a horizontal distance can be reached; a rope jump is a jump taken to allow a swinging rope to pass beneath the feet.

A common modification of jumping is vaulting, in which the hands and arms are used to aid the lower limps. The hands may (1) be placed on a stationary object, such as a bar, fence, or special apparatus, (2) grasp a suspended rope or pole, (3) hold a pole which is used in vaulting at the end of a run.

A number of stunts usually classed together under the name of tumbling or acrobatics may also be considered as modifications of jumping. The simplest is rolling, where, starting with a spring from the feet, the body is flexed to approach the form of a wheel and one or more revolutions are made across the floor; the backward roll being the reverse of the forward roll. When the roll is preceded by a spring into the air, head and arms first, going from that start into a roll, it is called a dive, which may be made for height or for horizontal distance. When the same movement as a dive is quickly followed by a complete revolution of the body, as in a roll, but before the body reaches the floor, it is called a somersault or flip; this is taken forward or backward. Headsprings, handsprings, and snap-ups or kips are other acrobatic stunts of this class. This whole group calls for exceptional strength and coordination of muscles. In more recent years, tumbling and acrobatic stunt routines have been developed with mechanical aids such as the trampoline.

Climbing. Civilized man has gradually done away with the ageless activity of climbing by first inventing ladders, then stairs, and finally the elevator and the escalator, so that this form of locomotion, like running, persists almost only in play.

Climbing means mounting or descending slowly and laboriously, using hands or feet, or both. It has been found that climbing vertically requires thirteen times as much energy as moving the same distance horizontally; this shows how strenuous an activity it is. The term is also used to refer to locomotion horizontally as in progressing on the horizontal ladder in the gymnasium or hand over hand on a rope suspended over a stream as in army maneuvers.

Climbing is a very popular play activity with most children. Ladders are climbed with both hands and feet and with each of these alone; ropes and poles with hands and feet and hands alone. (Such apparatus is needed on every playground.) Climbing trees and climbing hills and mountains are the most natural forms and are the most popular where the opportunities exist. Where they do not, the outdoor gymnasium is the best substitute. Climbing is included in many achievement tests.

An important group of play activities that may be considered as a modified form of climbing consists of exercises on bars, rings, horses, bucks, and other kinds of heavy apparatus. The body is supported by the arms in many of these exercises, swinging from one position to another and combining the swings with vaults and movements closely resembling those of tumbling. Wonderful feats of strength and skill are performed on the heavy apparatus, and many favor its more general use, on the ground that locomotion by the lower limbs only leaves the upper part of the body with too little development for health and vigor. The bars, rings, and horse are found in every fully equipped gymnasium.

The forms of climbing most often used in athletic contests are rope climbing and chinning the bar. The latter consists of lifting the body repeatedly by the arms until the chin is above the bar, to see how many times this performance can be done in succession without touching the floor with the feet.

Swimming and Diving. Swimming includes several forms of locomotion on or through the water. The breast stroke and the similar movement on the back are close imitations of the swimming of the frog; the scissors-kick is a modification of the frog kick used when the swimmer is on his side. Other forms of swimming use the four limbs in alternation, after the manner of quadrupeds as they walk, run, or swim. The dog paddle is the simplest, imitating closely the manner in which horses and dogs swim. The side stroke is made in the same manner while lying on the side, or the alternate leg movements may be replaced by the scissors-kick, which is more effective. The overarm is like the side stroke except that the upper arm is lifted out of the water and carried forward beyond the head while it is in the air, then dipped and used to propel the body. The alternate overarm is like the single overarm but taken alternately right and left with a roll of the body from side to side; the trudgen is very similar, the scissors-kick being narrowed or replaced by a single leg-thrash. The crawl has the alternate arm stroke with much less rolling from side to side; the face is immersed most of the time, the breath being expelled under water and inhaled at regular intervals as the head turns to one side. The back stroke is an inverted crawl. The leg and arm action is the same but it is unnecessary to turn the head and tilt the chin when breathing.

Diving is entering the water head first by a spring from a supporting object. The simplest form is the plunge, which is made to gain distance without much regard to form; in other dives the diver is expected to enter the water with little splashing. The main types are the front and back dives, with or without a run. These may be done in straight, pike, or tuck formation. There are also several variations, including somersaults and twists. Interest in swimming has been stimulated by skin diving and the use of mechanical devices such as the snorkel and underwater diving devices known as the scuba, or self-contained underwater breathing apparatus.

Swimming and lifesaving techniques have been constantly improved over the years through the efforts of the American Red Cross, which awards insignia for skill in a group of movements such as swimming, floating, treading water, towing a person, breaking holds, removing outer clothing while in deep water, and the more recent back pressure arm-lift method of artificial respiration.

With Apparatus or Vehicles. Ice and roller skating, skiing, snowshoeing, and walking on stilts are modifications of walking that make very attractive substitutes under certain environmental conditions. Coasting, bicycling, riding scooters, and the like, and horseback riding are forms of locomotion in which the body is carried but which nevertheless provide considerable exercise. The use of rowboats, canoes, and sailboats is one of the chief attractions of summer camps and resorts. Swings, teeters, and giant-strides are popular items of equipment on most playgrounds.

HANDLING OBJECTS. The bodily movements involved in handling objects are throwing, catching, striking, swinging, pushing, pulling, lifting, carrying, and others.

Throwing. Throwing is moving an object so swiftly while it is held in the hand that it will travel through the air for some distance upon releasing it. Here is another example of a complex movement developed to a high degree in earlier times and now persisting only in our play. It is an important exercise for bodily development, involving the grasping movement of the hand, a swing of the arm and shoulder, a twist of the trunk and hips, and a push from the rear foot. There is perhaps no single exercise more enjoyed by players. Strength is developed by throwing for distance, as in contests with a baseball or basketball; skill by throwing at a mark, as in target throws and throwing for goal in basketball. Skilled players learn to curve the ball in different directions as in baseball, and to impart English (or spin) on the ball as in basketball.

Tossing is a variety of throwing used by the pitcher in softball, also in bowling and some other sports; the arm is swung far back in preparation and then swiftly downward and forward, releasing the object after the arm has gone well forward. Pitching quoits involves the same style of motion. In serving tennis, one hand tosses the ball directly overhead, in preparation for striking it with the racket.

Putting is a variation of throwing used in handling heavy objects, and especially in putting the shot in athletic competition. Here the shot is held close in front of the shoulder and then pushed directly forward and upward by an extension of the joints of the arm instead of using a swinging movement. Slinging is throwing by means of a sling, which is an implement made of an oblong piece of leather or fabric to hold the missile and two cords by which it is swung around the head to give it momentum. Casting is a form of throwing used in fishing for trout and bass, the bait with the line attached being thrown a considerable distance by a swing of the fishing rod, which unwinds the line from a reel attached to the rod. Bait and fly casting have developed as popular sports; game activities such as skish have developed from them.

Catching. Catching is stopping a ball or other missile and grasping it with the hand. It may be done with one or both hands; in baseball one hand is protected by a glove or mitt, which also aids the player in holding the ball. In lacrosse the ball is thrown and caught with the crosse, which is a loosely strung racket with a long handle. Bean bags are used with young children to help in perfecting the coordination. The most difficult part seems to be to train the eye to make accurate judgments as to the path an object is following and where it will go.

Striking and Swinging. Striking is used in boxing, fencing, and in military combat, where a sword or bayonet is used; more often still in games of ball. In handball the ball is hit with the hand, often protected by a glove; in football it is struck with the foot, with the tip of the shoe in a drop-kick and a dribble, and with the instep in punting; in other games with some kind of a swinging implement such as a bat, racket, crosse, club, or mallet. English (spin) is often imparted to the ball by a racket to divert it sharply from its original course in order to confuse an opponent in games such as squash or tennis.

Pushing and Pulling. Pushing and pulling are seen in the *tussling* play of children, in wrestling and related combats, and in *rowing* and *paddling.* Pushing is found also in football; pulling in handling a sled. These activities are often brought in incidentally in connection with all kinds of motor play rather than in particular games. The same is true of *lifting* and *carrying.*

SENSORY AND INTELLECTUAL ACTIVITY IN MOTOR PLAY

It was pointed out earlier that motor play involves much sensory activity. Now that the details of the motor activity have been discussed, it is well to recap this point. The use of the eye and the cultivation of muscular sense involved in walking and running, especially in the cross-country variety, indicate how motor activity trains the senses. The jumper, springing to full height or distance and watching the place to alight illustrates again the training of the eye in coordination with the limbs. Yet it is in throwing, catching, and striking that eye training and muscular sense training reach their maximum. Hearing and touch also receive valuable training in active play. This sensory training is not only an important factor in the judging of distance in game situations but is also valuable as safety education and in general life situations.

It would be absurd to claim that motor play does not involve intellectual activity. What could be better training in quick and accurate thinking than a baseball game? There must be thinking in the midst of active, rapidly shifting situations calling for choice; and the successful player must be accurate and quick in making his decisions and implementing his reactions. The good player gets the situation accurately in mind while there is a moment of pause, and then, when the ball is in motion, he knows the facts on which a decision must be made instantly. If he fails to grasp the situation, he bungles the play; if he is slow in thinking, opponents get the start of him. On the other hand, what can be better training in painstaking and careful thinking than the planning of the strategy of a football game or the careful observation of the weak points of an opponent in tennis and planning how to take advantage of them?

Boxing, football, and all such games are commonly referred to in intellectual circles as competitions in strength only, when in reality they require quite as intense activity of senses and intellect as of muscle—success depending even more on a quick eye and a clear head than on strength or endurance. All the active games and sports, always classified as motor types of play, are in fact well-balanced combinations of motor, sensory, and intellectual activity, with just enough emotional excitement to make them enjoyable and beneficial. It should be also pointed out that certain types of play activities such as music, drama, the dance, art, and the like are considered by many to be mainly mental activities but in reality they involve considerable physical coordination, and also neuromuscular and emotional control.

SUMMARY

Although man has developed a more complex, refined civilization over the past two thousand years, the fundamental play movements have remained relatively the same. Man still must move and exercise his body to maintain its minimum fitness for living; basic skills must be learned and exercised for man to become efficient in the use of his body. Since modern life has become so mechanized, the practice of these fundamental movements has been substantially reduced. Walking, running, jumping, and similar movements are performed in directed activities such as sports or substitute calisthenics, or they are done little at all: they are no longer a major part of daily living.

This change in the mode of living points to the great need in modern life for motivating individuals to participate in some form of activity which involves the practice of fundamental play movements. As our society has changed, the interests of people have been diverted to more sedentary pursuits, and the need for the physical maintenance of the body is largely ignored. Chapter 7 deals with the study of basic motives which compel people to engage in play activities and the importance of the play leader's understanding of these motives in order to stimulate people to participate in a wide range of activities involving considerable use of the fundamental play movements.

SELECTED REFERENCES

BROER, MARION R. *Efficiency of Human Movement.* Philadelphia: W. B. Saunders Co., 1960. In addition to general explanations of mechanical laws, this text (pp. 85–196) shows clearly how basic movements, such as walking, running, hopping, climbing, throwing, striking, and others, underlie our everyday play, work, and many other types of physical activities.

MOREHOUSE, LAURENCE E., and COOPER, JOHN M. *Kinesiology.* St. Louis: The C. V. Mosby Co., 1950. Chapters 13 through 22 include a technical explanation of the basic body movements, relating them to both sports skills and physical movements in daily life.

SCOTT, M. GLADYS. *The Analysis of Human Motion: A Textbook in Kinesiology.* New York: F. S. Crofts & Co., 1946. Part III of this text gives a clear analysis of activities, including movements of locomotion and manipulative skills; special consideration is given to the relationship between fundamental movements and selected sports and between home and occupational activities.

BRECKENRIDGE, MARIAN E., and VINCENT, E. LEE. *Child Development— Physical and Psychologic Growth Through the Years.* Philadelphia: W. B. Saunders Co., 1955. See Chapter 8 and Bibliography, pages 443–70.

WELLS, KATHARINE F. "Underlying Principles of Basic Motor Movement," *Kinesiology.* Part III. Philadelphia: W. B. Saunders Co., 1960.

7

Classification by Motives and Interests

The last chapter gave an account of fundamental play movements, classified according to the parts of the organism that are involved. Emphasis was laid on the wide range of play activities and the well-balanced training given by the so-called motor plays. No attention was given to the motives and interests of the players, but rather to the bodily movements involved. The play leader, however, depends on interest to stimulate activity, and so he is concerned with play motives. The motives of the players determine the character of the play and form the basis for its classification into very important types.

MOTIVES IN PLAY

According to the traditional play theories, which now appear somewhat incomplete, the motives which impel people to play arise from instincts which have come from the struggle for existence in the remote past. Groos listed eight major instincts to account for the main motives that man has in playing.

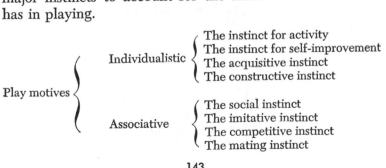

Play motives
— Individualistic
  - The instinct for activity
  - The instinct for self-improvement
  - The acquisitive instinct
  - The constructive instinct
— Associative
  - The social instinct
  - The imitative instinct
  - The competitive instinct
  - The mating instinct

Groos was of course not alone in positing a system of instincts to account for human behavior. Many others have prepared similar classifications, among them James, Angell, McDougall, Thorndike, and Drever.

It was pointed out in Chapter 4 that there were six universal types of motives (or wishes, as sociologists have also called them), each having a variety of concrete forms. It should be again pointed out, however, that there is general recognition of the difficulty encountered when one attempts to define motives. Actually motives are drives that have been modified through learning; the complexity of human motivation cannot be reduced to any simple scheme of a few dominant motives. Habits, attitudes, and purposes—all forms of human behavior—also function as springs of human action. The term motive is a convenient and brief description of a complex, socially learned pattern of behavior. A motive may be simple or it may represent the concept of a group of motives, interrelated in varying degrees. With this frame of reference, it is possible to analyze the interests included under motives (or wishes) and gain an understanding of their particular application to the scope of play.

New experience
$\begin{cases} \text{Fighting} \\ \text{Hunting} \\ \text{Curiosity} \\ \text{Roving} \\ \text{Speed} \\ \text{Creativeness} \end{cases}$

Security
$\begin{cases} \text{Flight and Avoidance of Danger} \\ \text{Acquisition} \\ \text{Imitation (from fear of social disapproval)} \\ \text{Religion} \end{cases}$

Response
$\begin{cases} \text{Sociability} \\ \text{Courtship and Mating} \\ \text{Parental love} \\ \text{Boon Friendship} \\ \text{Altruism} \end{cases}$

Recognition	⎧ Desire for victory ⎪ Desire for proficiency ⎨ Desire to lead ⎪ Showiness ⎩ Desire for undying fame

Participation	⎰ Desire for membership in groups ⎱ Desire for affiliation with causes

Aesthetic	⎧ Desire for beauty in color ⎪ Desire for beauty in form ⎨ Desire for beauty in sound ⎪ Desire for beauty in motion ⎩ Desire for rhythm

PLAY INTERESTS OF INDIVIDUALS

With the shift from the vague concept of pure inborn impulse to socially acquired behavior patterns as the basis of motivation, instinct has been superseded by cravings or urges or wishes. Wishes, as has been explained, refer to the universal desires of men, to those things which men everywhere want. Interests are individual matters. However, the specific interests of individuals although varying in detail fall under certain types which can be classified. The wishes are classifications of desires or motives which all men possess. A knowledge of universal motives is extremely important to play leaders, in that it forms a basis on which programs of activities may be built.

NEW EXPERIENCE. Life is activity. The primary need is the need to be doing because man is a dynamic, driving individual. He does not sit patiently and wait for a stimulus to come and set him into motion; he goes forth searching and seeking excitement. Complete quiescence is intolerable. Monotony or ennui appears to man as the very opposite of life, and most often he seeks to escape it. The constant need is for new experience, for change. Man seeks adventure, new adventure, high adventure. He seeks motion, change, thrill, danger. Risks mean excitement. Life is driving, advancing, pursuing, attacking.

Fighting. Life is struggle. Fighting patterns appear on every hand in life: They are seen in the gang fights of adolescents, in duels and feuds, in the verbal battle of adulthood, in economic struggles against one's business enemies, and in the intellectual battles of scientists and philosophers. Man fights not only with fists and feet; he hurls missiles in the form of tomahawks, arrows, bullets, and bombs; he swings clubs in the form of sticks, spears, and bayonets. In the absence of actual fighting situations for self-preservation, man's missiles take the form of snowballs, baseballs, footballs, tennis balls, discus, shot, javelin, playing cards, jibes or profane words, and his clubs the form of baseball bats, cricket paddles, tennis rackets, hockey sticks, and golf clubs. The fighting arts are among man's most precious possessions.

One of the most conspicuous of the concrete forms in which the fighting drive expresses itself is pursuit and capture. The essential essence of the fighting wish is this drive toward one's foe and the pursuit of him if he fails to fight and seeks safety in flight. It appears in countless play and competitive sport patterns.

In organized society the more elemental, random, and informal methods of fighting tend to give way to definite fighting patterns, and in civilized society the desire for physical fighting finds expression largely through the medium of competitive sports and play forms. Practically all competitive sports are of the fighting type, with the objective of defeating one's opponents. The fighting drive furnishes the motivation which largely accounts for the popularity of the long array of competitive sports. A play leader anywhere can obtain a ready response from any group by the use of competition forms in which a we-group is pitted against a they-group. So deep-seated is the fighting drive that in intense situations in competitive sports the taboos which society has inculcated in the form of rules and standards of sportsmanship are often discarded, anger flames up, and the players resort to the more elemental forms of fighting.

Hunting. Man is not only a fighting animal, but he is a hunting animal. In fact the two lines of activity are very

similar in nature; some feel that hunting is more fundamental even than fighting. Common observation reveals
the conspicuous role which hunting plays in human activity.
Consider the appeal of fishing: children quite generally long
for it and seem never happier than when perched on a bank
of a muddy stream with a bamboo pole; a countless army of
sportsmen spend more money each year than their check-
books can well afford to take them to the fishing waters;
more rods and reels are manufactured in the United States
each year than tennis rackets. The amount of money spent
for fishing equipment in 1955 amounted to approximately
$793,000,000, which exceeded by far the amount spent for
baseball, football, basketball, and boxing goods combined;
total expenditures of twenty-five million persons who fished
and hunted, including travel, equipment, licenses, and other
expenses, were approximately three billion dollars.

The weapons of hunting and their use hold a widespread
appeal. The deer-hunting season sees an army of armed
men advancing bushward, and it is no uncommon thing for
many men to lose their lives, so eager are they to shoot at
any moving object in the woods which might by chance be
a deer. Guns, bows and arrows, darts, jackknives, and blow-
guns hold an appeal to children and to quite a few adults
which is all out of proportion to their use in modern life.

If fighting patterns are conspicuous in competitive games,
hunting patterns are equally easy to note. Hide and seek
games, pursuit and capture games, and hidden object games
are illustrations.

Curiosity.   Closely akin to the hunting urge is curiosity.
It too leads to hunting and searching. Anyone who has
been around children cannot fail to be familiar with their
seemingly boundless curiosity. They are relentless in their
questioning. Their curiosity leads to the exploration of
woods, fields, caves, and deserted buildings; to hunting for
natural objects, rocks of peculiar formation, wildflowers,
birds, even curios, antiques.

Children and adolescent boys and girls transported to
camp in the woods often display a desire that will not be

denied to explore the new world, and they seek the acquaintance of those who know the secrets of the woods to answer their queries. This thirst for knowledge seems so great at times as to be unquenchable.

Curiosity also manifests itself in reading, in solving puzzles, and in scientific research. It is one of the major factors which send scientists forth in their search for facts.

The desire for new experience and particularly that aspect of it we call curiosity is seen in the drive that sends adult explorers into the remote corners of the world, by foot, canoe, pack mule, or airplane—often at great risk to their lives. Many explorers have commented on the fact that curiosity as to what lies beyond the next mountain range is the urge that leads them on and on, when common sense tells them that lack of food and time should turn them back.

Roving. Wanderlust seems to grip everyone at times, and seasonally at least to impel people to move away from familiar surroundings and follow the open trail. Hiking parties of boys and girls are seen along the roads, canoeing parties strike into the unknown bush, and an army of auto tourists start their annual trek across the country with the coming of spring. The periodic appeal of roving and the grip of the wanderlust seem quite universal and the lack of opportunity to satisfy it in a modern world of insistent duties leads to restlessness. If it cannot be experienced in fact, it is indulged in in fancy.

The craving for new experience and for change is a constant drive which sends folk on to travel; the desire to escape the here and now and search for a there and then that is more satisfying is, seasonally at least, a compelling urge in all mankind.

Speed. Structurally man is constructed for movement, and throughout much of his existence, survival depended upon the rapidity with which he could move. The archaic ends of pursuit and escape no longer need to be served, but swift movement remains pleasurable in itself. Speed is needed in hunting and fighting forms of play activity, but entirely aside from any other ends it may serve, there is a craving for it for its own sake. It is seen in the joy which comes in coasting, skating and skiing, in horse racing, in speed boating and fast sailing, in motoring and flying. It is a thrilling form which the urge for new experience and adventure takes.

Creativeness. The craving for new experience appears again in the desire to construct, to build, to create. It is inherent in the block building of children, in the hut and shack building of boys, in the doll dressmaking and the cake-making of girls; in the arts and crafts, the pewter, silver, copper, and leather crafts; in story writing and composing poetry in adults. This creative urge, this longing to express the personality through fashioning that which is new is given little opportunity for realization in modern life. The desire to build and construct is so compelling and irresistible, particularly to youth, that it offers play leaders an excellent motive around which programs of outstanding educational and recreational merit can be built.

Vicarious New Experience. To all who are young and aspiring, the here and the now seems inadequate. All of us regardless of age are impelled by a longing at times for another world, a world replete with new experience, with romance, color, and picturesqueness, which in our own little corner of the world is denied us. The routine of life, the social taboos and inhibitions irk and irritate us. New experience and the keenness of living it implies seems at times not to be our lot.

In the realm of imagination, however, there is another world. A person can watch a movie, read a story, or attend an athletic contest, and vicariously experience a life that in reality is not his. The movie brings to him the world of his dreams, a romantic world of love and color and fighting. Vicariously for an hour or two he lives this life of romance. He pictures himself in the hero's role and fights his cause with him, battles with him as he struggles against impossible odds, and woos with him as he seeks his love. The house of dreams takes the onlooker to the north woods with its Indians, the plains with its cowboys, the South Sea islands with their romance and allurement, the homes of the rich with their luxury, the underworld with its battling gangsters, the wild free life where taboos and gossiping neighbors are no bother. So when new experience and change is denied in actual life, it may be experienced vicariously in the theatre. Man, in his imagination, may defy the inhibitions, fetters, and annoyances that envelop him in his world of reality.

The same is true in reading and storytelling. The question is frequently asked why reading, which is a recently acquired art in the history of the human race and involves the higher nerve centers that become quickly fatigued, is so fascinating. It seems too obvious to mention that it is not the physical act of reading, involving the use of eyes and the connecting nerve tracts, that makes reading satisfying; it is the content of what is read. What is the content of a good part of the novels and stories of the world's literature? Fighting and love making. Through the medium of stories the reader vicariously achieves new experience and response.

When the realities of life do not bring the satisfactions that are craved, there is often resort to daydreaming. This is a world of the imagination in which heroic deeds may be performed, great honors won, great speeches made, and works of art created. This world of reverie and make-believe is temporarily satisfying but should not become a refuge to avoid facing life's realities.

The crowd in the stands at athletic contests enjoys vicarious experience in watching their heroes perform. The spectator at the football games fights the cause with his team; he leans and pushes in the same direction as they hit the line; he shouts and glories in their victory, he experiences the sorrow and chagrin of defeat. The more combative the type of game, the more elements it has in it to satisfy the fighting aspect of the wish for new experience, the more popular it is. Whatever may be said regarding the value of participation as opposed to spectatorism, the fact still remains that there is such a decided satisfaction in watching combative contests that they are the occasion of holidays and festive occasions of oustanding importance.

Man, then, is eager for new experience and all that it implies, and when he fails to find it in actual experience, he seeks it vicariously. The thing to do is to strike at life problems directly and seek satifaction through actual achievement, but man often finds this impossible; so he does what seems to be the next best thing.

SECURITY. The desire for new experience, as has been discussed, is cmotionally related to anger and tends to invite danger and even death. It implies motion, risks, social irresponsibility, and a disregard for social customs and mores. The desire for security, on the other hand, is based upon fear and the avoidance of danger. Timidity and flight are aspects of it. It causes the individual to be cautious, conservative, regular in habits, and to act in accordance with socially acceptable standards.

Perhaps the most outstanding characteristic of the youthful years of life is the longing for new experience. Where does youth stand in respect to security? The desire to be safe is as firmly implanted in young people as in older: children are timid, but they feel protected by adults. That is, youth takes his security for granted; the presence of adults in whom he has confidence insures it, puts his mind at ease regarding it. But it is the primary concern, the ever-present worry of middle age. The business of youth is to take on experience; the business of adults is to see that no harm comes as a result of it. Age stratification in society throws new experience into the spotlight at the youthful levels and fades it out in favor of security in mature levels.

Among the ways in which the wish for security manifests itself are flight, acquisitiveness, imitation, and religion.

Flight. People do not stand inert in the presence of what they perceive to be of immediate and destructive danger, unless they are paralyzed with fear. If the opposing force cannot be fought with some hope of success, the individual flees. People are afraid of different things depending on what they have learned to fear, but all men retreat from and avoid what they perceive as immediately destructive. Flight is the basis of many games. It is found in tag games, hide and seek games, pursuit and capture games in general. And when the child flees from danger in these games, he runs until his "heart is in his mouth." The drive to seek safety is a tremendous force upon which play leaders can build.

Acquisitiveness. The desire for safety leads to the accumulation of property, to taking out of insurance, building estates. It is at the basis of the desire for ownership. The tendency manifests itself in children's play in the collection of toys, in stamp collections, butterfly collections, and the like. Other factors enter into the motivation behind these collections but acquisitiveness may nevertheless be regarded as a manifestation of the drive for security.

Imitation. Everyone is engaged in the business of taking on an endless chain of behavior patterns which make people act alike, eat alike, dress alike, talk alike, and play alike. This is a chief factor in the uniformizing process which society employs. Habits are acquired by trial and error, but more often by borrowing them, that is, imitating others. Imitation characterizes all age stratifications of society, but if it is strong in adulthood, it is far stronger in youth. To "get on" in a group and to be secure in one's group relationships, one must live in reasonably close conformity to the group customs. Imitation is a process by which such conformity is achieved and thus appears as a means to security.

Imitation would lead to stagnation in the evolution of games, were it not for the fact, discussed in Chapter 1, that man cannot imitate exactly. In this way a gradual evolution goes on from generation to generation. Now and then a leader produces an invention which leads to sudden change. The new way is then imitated, and becomes the vogue.

Imitation appears in the make-believe games and the dramatic games in which the children mimic the idiosyncrasies of the types they are portraying. It is seen also in folk dancing and rhythmic games in which a direct effort is made to imitate the movements of the leader who is setting the pattern.

Religion. Among primitive peoples magic and religion were devices for securing the help of the supernatural for the protection of the tribe. They were devices for safety. The belief in the supernatural owes its beginning in part to fear and to the shock of death, although illusions and dreams caused the primitive mind to believe in a life after death and that through these mediums the dead come back to them. In magic the supernatural being was coerced through various acts of ritual. In religion which appears later in cultural evolution, the attitude toward the Divine Being changed from propitiation mainly to reverence and awe. Whatever the method the chief object was security, and even today security is one of the major motives in religious observance—security in this world and hereafter.

RESPONSE. The craving for response is the love desire, the desire not for the acclaim of the crowd or the public at large but for the affection of the few who are close and dear to us. It manifests itself in companionship, courtship and mating, parental love, boon friendship and altruism. Homesickness and loneliness are manifestations of it. It leads to sociability and the making of friends. It is a craving for close intimate response. Devotion and self-sacrifice are aspects of it.

In play life, the satisfying of the desire for response appears in calling and visiting, conversation, parties and picnics, the doll play of children, boys' gangs, mating play, social dancing, and mother-love play. Most sociable gatherings involving both sexes are mainly for the purpose of bringing together possible mates, whatever the avowed or announced purpose of the gathering may be.

The deep-seated aspect of the desire for response involving the love of mother for child and child for mother affects tremendously the type of play of young children. These mother and child play activities must not continue too long, however, and mothers should assist children in breaking away for the sake of the child's independent personality. Aspects of mother-love play are seen in children in the imitative plays in which they play the roles of mother and children, and in all of the doll play activities.

RECOGNITION. The wish for recognition manifests itself in the desire for victory, proficiency, leadership, showiness, and undying fame. The plaudits of the crowd are sweet music to human ears. Actors frequently prize applause almost as much as salary checks. Athletes can never sever from consciousness the spectators in the stand, and while in the heat of contest they may be unaware of the roar of approval from the bleachers, they court it nevertheless, and the will to fame is a constant incentive to their efforts.

Public approval, fame, and social immortality—memory in the minds of the public—are among the most coveted of human goods. Recognition is sought through showiness of dress, automobiles and palatial homes, mannerisms and grandstand playing. Social climbing is an aspect of it. It is evidenced in the ambition of artists and authors, in efforts to amass huge fortunes and to create business empires, in politicians striving for high office. In play it is shown in the eagerness of children to win honors and awards in the organizations to which they belong, to win athletic letters and trophy cups, to win the personal praise of leaders and coaches. It is behind the desire of many for high academic grades in school. It is an incentive in the hazardous undertakings of boys—and of men in war and exploration. The desire for recognition is the will to power.

Praise and recognition are not only strongly desired, but they are needed for the development of the individual's self-assurance and poise. The desire for recognition is not a drive which expresses itself in the development of any particular type of play; rather it manifests itself in any and all types of play. It also appears in play groups in the desire to lead, to be elected to the captaincy of a team or presidency of a club, for example.

PARTICIPATION. Participation is not a mere wish for sociability, but relates to the desire to belong to some organization or movement larger than oneself. It manifests itself in (1) joining organizations, and (2) affiliation with causes.

There are those who have a desire to join many organizations, a type commonly referred to as "joiners." Not all people wish to belong to a large number of organizations, but practically all normal individuals want to belong to some organization and to feel that their personality counts in some group.

The desire for participation also has to do with the tendency of people to affiliate themselves with a cause or a movement. Many people affiliate themselves with a religious cause, to the extent that it becomes a dominant drive in life; some identify themselves with a moral cause and devote a lifetime of energy to its promotion. Social and economic issues such as socialism and communism, the rights of laboring men, and child welfare become ardent causes to some, to the extent frequently that they are willing to sacrifice their lives for them. Nationalism, often called patriotism, is a cause to many, and in time of war it flames up to religious intensity and leads to the willing sacrifice of life.

Causes have all the aspects of play or recreation. They grip and impel to such an extent that their devotees would rather promote them than do anything else. They absorb much of leisure time and give opportunity for emotional release and intense satisfaction. Crusaders for such causes are often so absorbed that they have little time for, or interest in, less serious pursuits. It has been said that the frivolities of present-day American youth, to the extent that they can be said to exist, can be accounted for in part by the absence of a nation-wide cause which grips the imagination and claims ardent devotion. Youth particularly is given to causes owing to its idealistic tendencies so much so that propagandists leading causes look to youth for their supporters.

While the desire for participation does not lead to the development of any precise kinds of play, it is nevertheless of particular interest to play leaders engaged in organizing clubs and teams. Group leaders utilize this tendency to organize youth for the solving of social problems and remedying social evils. Debating, arguing, and abstract discussion are typical activities growing out of interest in causes.

AESTHETIC. The desire for the aesthetic relates to beauty in color, form, sound, and motion. Most of us are sensitive to our surroundings. Beauty cheers and ugliness offends. The love for the aesthetic is expressed in dress, in home surroundings, in lawns and flowers, in singing, music, painting, arts and craft work, in poetry, in movies and dramatics, in ceremonials and rituals. Much of the interest in nature is tied up with the appreciation of its beauties. In ancient Greece the beauty of body was sought and developed and was the ideal symbolized in poetry and sculpture.

Religion is a widespread source of aesthetic satisfaction. However religion is viewed, it is recreational in that it takes the worshipper away for a while to another world that is restful, beautiful, and inspiring. Theology is intellectual play, but in religious services ritual is used to furnish satisfaction for aesthetic sentiments.

While the desire for the aesthetic is universal, some cultures have developed it far more than others. In America, the material phases of our culture have been developed to the point where they are far in advance of the non-material. The cultural lag in respect to the aesthetic is still conspicuous. This has resulted in serious maladjustments and is at the root of many of our social problems.

The aesthetic and all that it implies is an important phase of a well-balanced play and recreational program. There should be no let-down in the continued development and promotion of physical play, but in addition to it there is a distinct need for more aggressive leadership in the nonphysical sphere. Play is spiritual as well as physical. Those activities which administer to the spirit should become more abundantly available.

Rhythm. Mere sound by itself has little interest to man; the factor that turns music and poetry into something pleasing to the senses of man is rhythm. The term rhythm has other connotations; it has been used in recent years to describe the total dance experience offered to children. Whether procured through the ear, the eye, or through touch, rhythm is appealing. It is rhythm of motion which makes dancing so compelling. In a sense, it is rhythm of form which makes drawing, sculpture, and pottery satisfying to us. Rhythm is intimately associated with that which we conceive to be beautiful; the desire for the aesthetic is in no small respect a desire for rhythm.

Man has a tendency to perform physical movements in general in rhythmic routine. Herbert Spencer maintained that there is a law beyond the sphere of man which accounts for rhythm—a universal law of rhythm of motion. He pointed out that it appears in the swinging of the pendulum, the pennant in the breeze, the swaying of leaves on a tree, the waving of grain in the field, the ripples of the stream, the vibration of the bow string, the changes in the atmosphere, the motion of heat, light, sound, electricity, in waves and tides, in day and night, the return of seasons, in the pulse beat, the regular periodic need for food and rest, the waves of emotional reaction, the annual migration of birds, birth, marriage and death, waves of crime, waves of public opinion, waves of style, social cycles as seen in the rise and fall of cultures and nations. Social movements seem to go in a cycle of advances and pauses. Man being a part of the universe is regulated by the law, as seen in his movements. Havelock Ellis suggests the same point of view in saying that the significance of dancing lies in the fact that it is part of a general rhythm that is not only expressive of life itself but of the entire universe.

Rhythm is pronounced in walking, in music, in marching, and in dancing. Whenever music is heard, there is a tendency to accompany it with rhythmic motion, if not in the movement of the entire body as in dancing, in the tapping of feet, the drumming of hands, the nodding of the head.

Rhythm leads to economy of effort; the worker's movements soon take on a rhythmic swing and repetition, and unnecessary movements are eliminated. Rhythm, too, is restful and relaxing. Primitives paddled their war canoes to rhythmic beat and children in camps today sing rhythmic songs to accompany the stroke in the canoes; the Volga boatman's song carries a rhythmic swing so symbolic of the pulling motion that even an unimaginative listener pictures in his mind the straining boatman. Marching songs accompany the hikers' rhythmic steps. Through the use of rhythm in this way, man's work becomes less arduous.

Rhythmic movement on the part of a group leads to a feeling of oneness and unity, and an exhilaration of spirit; thus the primitives danced before taking the warpath for the psychological effect produced. The rhythm of marching steps moves the army with a feeling of unity.

The fact that rhythmic movement is less fatiguing than other types of movement makes dancing and similar rhythmic response a particularly efficient means of physical exercise. Dancing is doubtless one of the oldest of human arts and is the most restful and relaxing type of exercise that man can engage in today.

Dancing has been said to be the most popular single type of play with girls and has occupied a much larger place in their play program than in that of boys. This is not owing to any lack of interest in the part of boys in rhythm but rather to the fact that boys in the United States have been conditioned to look upon dancing as effeminate. Yet many of the most warlike tribes and nations have considered dancing as the prerogative of the male rather than the female sex. The Spartans, who made war their vocation and even slept by their arms, gave much attention to dancing in the training of their youth. The Pyrrhic dance was considered in ancient times as a very necessary part in the training of the warrior. Today, one can turn to the European nations and find that men are star performers in many of the traditional folk festivals and dances.

SUMMARY

It is important that the play leader understand the principles underlying motives or drives which have been modified through learning. It is difficult to explain play interests as being rooted in instincts, since instincts cannot be clearly identified. It must be pointed out too that motives describe relatively complex forms of behavior—they do not singularly impel the individual to action, but rather describe how his acquired drives and mechanisms operate. Habits, attitudes, and purposes also function as springs of human action and must be considered in understanding why and how people develop interests in certain play and recreation activities. Play leaders, teachers, recreation administrators, and others working with people in leisure-time activities should study the fundamental wishes of man; they should understand the universal desire for recognition, for new experience, and other types of human needs and then help individuals develop interests in desirable activities of their own choice. No other area of understanding is more important than understanding why people develop specific behavior patterns and interests in various types of activities. With such insights, the play leader can best carry out his mission as an educator and can help each individual to develop his own personality through worthwhile, leisure-time activities, thus contributing to the individual's happiness as well as to his effectiveness as a citizen in a free democratic society.

SELECTED REFERENCES

McCLELLAND, DAVID C. (ed.). *Studies in Motivation.* New York: Appleton-Century-Crofts, Inc., 1955. These selected readings include basic information relating to the biological and social origins of motives and values, and how motives and values affect human behavior and expression.

NASH, JAY B. *Philosophy of Recreation and Leisure.* St. Louis: The C. V. Mosby Co., 1953. The relationships between play, work, and leisure are shown; man's fundamental drive to engage in activity, his need to belong to a group, and to express himself in a variety of ways is explained.

BORST, EVELYNE, and MITCHELL, ELMER D. *Social Games For Recreation.* 2d ed. New York: The Ronald Press Co., 1959.

DONNELLY, RICHARD J., HELMS, WILLIAM G., and MITCHELL, ELMER D. *Active Games and Contests.* 2d ed. New York: The Ronald Press Co., 1958.

GROOS, K. *The Play of Man.* New York: D. Appleton & Co., 1901.

8

Classification by
Patterns of Organization

Play activities were classified in Chapter 6 according
to the fundamental motor movements involved when engaging in them. Chapter 7, just preceding, classified motives
significant to the development of play interests. The
present chapter deals with the classification of play activities according to their form—that is, the general pattern of
organization they follow, the attitudes of the players, and
the types of activities involved. In general, there are two
main groupings: competitive and non-competitive.

NATURE OF COMPETITIVE PLAY

As compared to other types of play, competitive games
and contests involve a much greater degree of organization.
They require rules and demand strict obedience to them.
This factor necessitates competent officiating. Games are
not successful or popular unless such needs are provided for.

The varieties of competitive play are almost endless, but
they all fall easily into two well-defined groups: contests and
games. Contests may be exemplified by foot racing and
competition in jumping; games by dodgeball and basketball.
The main distinction is this: contests are calculated to test a
player's separate abilities, one by one; while games test
many coordinated abilities along with "generalship" in
choosing the right thing to do to meet any emergency.

For the purpose of determining the separate abilities of
the players, there are events to test all the main lines of
physical ability: short runs to test speed, long runs to test

endurance, high and broad jumps and vaulting to test different types of agility, shot and discus to test strength and skill, ad infinitum. Any trial of ability may be called a test, but in order to have a contest there must be opponents.

Games are competitions that are full of unexpected situations, strategy, and deception. It is a part of the game to outwit the opponents, also to interfere with their plans and plays as much as possible. In order to make the game the most satisfactory to all concerned there must, of course, be some rules placing a limit on the kinds of interference and deception a pitcher, for instance, might use; and there are restricting rules in the interests of safety as in football.

Bowling and golf have the aspects of a contest because interference by an opponent is not permitted. However, the game element appears to a limited degree because there are varying situations and the player must make choices. For example, in golf he must make a choice as to the type of shot he will try to make and also the particular club to use. Horseshoe pitching, quoits, curling, and bowling-on-the-green offer very little chance for interference with one's opponents, but since some opportunity is offered, they are also classified as games resembling contests.

The only example in current literature of any extensive use of the word *game* to designate any other than competitive plays is found in the books of play for small children, in which the rhythmic and dramatic plays suited to the period of early childhood are sometimes called "singing games" and "dramatic games." Since, strictly, the term *game* applies only where there is a struggle for supremacy, confusion will be avoided if the more general term *play* is used for simple activities of children that are non-competitive.

Now that contests and games have been defined, what is meant by the term *sport,* which is so commonly used? Sport is a general and all-inclusive term, including hunting, fishing, skating, and swimming, which may or may not be competitive, as well as horseracing, track and field, base-

ball, football, and the other activities which have been
classed under contests and games. The term athletic sports
(or athletics) refers to competitive physical activities involving accepted rules of play and a system of scoring for
determining winners from among two or more contesting
individuals or teams.

As distinguished from games and sports, which are
primarily competitive and recreative, the term gymnastics
refers to exercises for the purpose of developing strength
and control of the body. A varied program of gymnastics
is used in modern programs of physical fitness, especially
for development of the upper part of the body and for
special corrective and therapeutic exercises.

KINDS OF CONTESTS

CONTESTS BETWEEN INDIVIDUALS. Primarily, a contest is
a comparison of ability between individuals. This was the
earliest form of competitive play, described in the oldest
myths and legends of prehistoric times, long before there
were any games.

Track and field events, swimming, and gymnastics are the
outstanding examples of sports in which highly organized
contests are held. Their outcome determines championships. The athletic competition of the early Greeks was on
a championship basis. Each city had local contests to find
who was champion of the city in the various events, and as
early as 776 B.C. national contests were held at Olympia.
Starting with running only, the list of events was gradually
lengthened to include jumping, throwing (discus and
javelin), wrestling, and other events such as chariot racing,
not common today.

In modern times the championship plan of conducting
athletic contests was revived by the British; it was brought
to America about 1850, when the city clubs forming the
Amateur Athletic Union began active promotion of track
and field sports; and finally it culminated in a revival of the
International Olympic Festivals, the first of which was held

in Athens in 1896. Another series of festivals has since been held in the Far East. Others include the Bolivarian Games and the Pan-American Games. In these modern festivals a much wider range of events is run off than in the ancient ones, and several games are included.

Participation Plans. The principal fault of the championship plan of conducting contests is its tendency to encourage extreme specialization and its failure to stimulate any but the few best athletes to practice or compete. The Greeks recognized the first of these defects and devised the *pentathlon,* a combination of five events, to counteract it. In modern championships the same idea is carried out in several ways. The reorganized Olympic Festival holds a pentathlon and a decathlon, the latter consisting of ten events; the YMCA holds a hexathlon (six events). The hexathlon is applied to three types of activity: indoor, outdoor, and aquatic.

In the Greek Olympic games, and even today in some European circles, only one place was awarded in each event. In the United States an effort has been made to encourage those individuals who feel that they do not have the ability to win an event, by selecting more than one place. First and second places were therefore selected, then third place, later fourth, and today in intercollegiate competition five or more places are frequently selected.

Another application of the same idea is to divide the players into groups depending upon athletic ability and to conduct separate programs of competition for each group. Sometimes chronological age is used as the basis of grouping, sometimes weight, sometimes height; most frequently today the method is a combination of age, weight, and height.

A third plan to encourage participation is to handicap the more expert players by requiring them to overcome advantages given to opponents of lesser ability. Expert golf players are handicapped when playing men of lesser ability; bowlers, too, are equalized through the medium of handicap leagues.

The extent of competition is increased in some cases by having what is called a qualifying round to select the contestants for the meet from a larger number, and sometimes there is a consolation series of contests for those who lose out in the first round.

Among the students of a school or college who do not succeed in "making the team," individuals representing classes, fraternities, and other groups compete for intramural championships.

Achievement Tests. Also, to encourage wider participation, and to motivate individual interest, several plans of tests have been devised. In these tests, each individual must pass a certain standard in a selected list of events to get a badge or certificate. Separate tests are provided for boys and girls and for the different age levels. Among the best known of these tests are the Athletic Badge Tests of the National Recreation Association, and the more recent test standards established by the American Association for Health, Physical Education, and Recreation. In reality, a test is a form of contest, in which the player competes against an imaginary opponent in the form of an arbitrary standard of proficiency or against his own previous record in the attempt to better it.

CONTEST BETWEEN GROUPS. Another device to encourage participation in competitive play is the group contest, which compares groups—teams, schools, colleges, cities, and nations—instead of individuals. The comparison has been made in three different ways.

The first and theoretically the simplest way is to have the two groups come together and compete directly, as in the familiar "Tug-of-War." Unfortunately, there are very few of the common athletic abilities that can be tested between groups in the simple way in which the ability to pull is tested in "Tug-of-War" and so this method is practically of little value.

A second method for comparing abilities of groups is to have individual contests and combine the results to give group scores. The oldest and simplest way to do this is to give points to those who win first, second, and third places, usually 5 for first, 3 for second, 1 for third, then to add the points made by the group. When events are used in which there is a scoring table—contests in which there are weight classes—a fairer way is to add the points made by every contestant in the group.

The relay race is the third form of group competition. It is a form of contest especially adapted to running and swimming. The runners of a group take part in turn, each starting just as the preceding runner finishes, with the object of seeing which group can finish first. The official form of track for relay races is the round or oval track, but in less formal races with large groups the organization can be handled more conveniently in a shuttle form, the first, third, fifth, and other odd runners taking a straight course in one direction and the second, fourth, and other even runners going in the reverse direction. The file type of relay has also become popular, particularly for conditioning purposes. Each player runs to a turning line and back to his place to touch off the next runner in his file.

Relay races used for more formal competition are being more and more standardized, just like other contests, but there is at the same time also a tendency to vary them greatly in informal activity. To make them still more interesting, novelties are introduced at intervals of the run, consisting of all kinds of simple exercises that the runner must stop and perform before he finishes, also various types of locomotion.

KINDS OF GAMES

Games are best divided, according to the general age period to which they are naturally adapted, into elementary games, combats, and team games.

ELEMENTARY GAMES. In elementary games the competition is largely individualistic, and the organization comparatively simple. Some of them are modified forms of the more complex team games, modified to suit children, such as "Newcomb," "Rotation," and "Captain Ball"; but most of them are running, dodging, and chasing games, played without balls or other equipment. There are two main groups: one where the play centers in getting possession of a home, base, or goal; and the other having chasing and tagging as the chief points of interest. Dozens of these games, named and described independently in books of play, are found on careful examination to be no more than slight variations from a few well-marked types.

GOAL GAMES. There are two kinds of goal games, quite different in idea and manner of play. In the first kind each goal is held by one player and there are almost goals enough for all, but there is always at least one player without a goal; all effort and interest centers in avoiding being the one left out. The games differ only in the dramatic setting and in the way provided that one may get possession of a goal. In the simplest form only two players are active at once. The one who is "It" chooses someone else who has to do something that takes him away from his goal, and then it is a game of wits and speed to see which of the two will reach the vacant place first. "Come with Me" and "Good Morning" are games of this kind; another popular one is the old "Beater Goes Round." In "Pussy Wants a Corner" the players slyly trade goals while the one who is "It" is a safe distance away, and he gets a goal as they become more careless; in "Squirrels in Trees," "The First of May," "Changing Seats," "Stage Coach," and several others there is a signal of some kind when all must exchange goals, giving the player who has no goal a chance to seize one. In one type, like "Huntsman," "Going to Jerusalem," and "Merry Go Round" all the players have to leave their goals to take part in some required activity, and then at a signal all rush for goals.

The second type of goal games is made up of a few games of "Hide and Seek." There is a single goal used in common by all the players. The interest of the game centers in the hiding and hunting to find the hidden players, and in the race to touch the goal when one is seen or tries to get in free. The choosing of the one to be "It" by the use of counting-out rhymes adds to the interest.

TAG GAMES. Most tag games are dramatizations of hunting or warfare. Tag signifies capture. It is usually done by touching a player, in a few instances by hitting him with a thrown ball or bean bag, and in a few instances by seizing and holding him until he is tagged or slapped three times. In some tag games there are goals, which here are places of safety.

Tag games vary greatly in the amount of activity involved. In general, the simpler ones are least active and the vigor increases with the complexity of the play. A few have features that permit players to be just as active or as inactive as they choose, and this fits them for mixed groups where there is wide variety in the strength, skill, and endurance of the players, as at picnics, play days, and in the recess play at rural or ungraded schools. The best way to classify tag games is to begin with the simplest and take up in order the added features that make them more complex and more vigorous. There are four varieties of tag games that are entirely individualistic, and two types of games in which cooperation is a factor.

1. The simplest tag games such as "Hunt the Fox" and "Squirrel and Nut" have only two players active at once, the others merely standing or sitting and looking on. One of the two is the chaser, and the other is the runner who tries to escape being tagged. When the chaser tags the runner, or if he does not succeed in doing so and the leader thinks the play has gone far enough, another chaser and runner are chosen and the game begins again. In some games of this kind, features are introduced that let the other players have some part in the activity, as in "Cat and Rat," "Bull in the Ring," and "Fox and Chickens"; or there may be more than one runner, as in "Cat and Mice."

2. The next group of games is made slightly more complex and active, the play being continuous without the interference of the leader, by having the winner or loser in the chase choose a player to take the place of the one who re-

tires. Most of these are played in ring formation; the list is rather long, with "Drop the Handkerchief," "Exchange Tag," and "Have You Seen My Sheep?" the most familiar ones.

3. The third group, including "Fox and Squirrel" and "Three Deep," usually has only one chaser and one runner, but the instant the runner is tagged he becomes chaser, and the player he is to chase can become free and make another player take his place at any time, the way of doing this being varied in the different games. This feature keeps everyone on the alert, as any player is likely to be tagged at once if he fails to pay attention.

4. Games of the fourth class differ from those of the third in that any player may be tagged, instead of one particular player. There is usually some way to avoid capture, differing in each game: sometimes it consists in staying in a safety zone, as in "King's Land" and "Duck on the Rock"; sometimes in assuming some posture or position, as in "Statue Tag," or "Hang Tag"; or touching some kind of substance or object, as in "Wood Tag" and "Tree Tag."

5. Thus far the games have been strictly individual games, but now we come to the beginning of team play, with the players who have been tagged joining the chaser and helping to tag all the others. This group includes about twenty games, the most familiar being "Pom Pom Pull Away," "Hill Dill," and "Black Tom." Many differ from these only in the dramatic features; a few like "Fisherman," "Looby Loo," and "Trades" have a little more team play.

6. The final group, of the type of "Prisoner's Base," is made up of tag games of the strictly team kind, the players no longer being satisfied to join the opponents as soon as they are tagged but instead being prisoners of their captors until their teammates are able to release them. These games are very complex and very vigorous. They are not so popular as they once were, younger players liking the simpler games better and the older ones preferring the modern ball games.

PERSONAL COMBATS. Combats are games rather than contests when analyzed, even though they take place between individual players rather than between groups. They include boxing, wrestling, fencing, and minor varieties of each such as "Hand Wrestle," "Indian Wrestle," "Badger Pull," "Wand Pull," "Chicken Fight," and several others. They are very popular with boys of adolescent age and provide very good vigorous exercise.

TEAM GAMES. The team games that have won most popularity among players in recent years are all ball games. The use of the ball, in addition to all such interesting activities as running, jumping, dodging, etc., involves throwing, catching, and striking, and the most intense sensory and intellectual activity, and this no doubt accounts for the popularity of ball games of all kinds. There are three fundamental types of ball games, quite distinct in their nature and origin: *baseball, tennis,* and *football.* In many respects basketball and hockey are also of the football type; for they are played on a rectangular field with a goal at each end, and the play is centered upon the securing of a goal. However, because they differ considerably in important details from football, they are often considered as distinct types of games.

Baseball Games. These combine throwing, catching, and striking with the goal and tag elements of the elementary games. They are of English origin (cricket and rounders) but the English and American forms have come to differ considerably. Baseball is distinctly modern, its most rapid development having occurred since the Civil War.

After a great many attempts to devise or find a baseball game of a form simpler than the regular professional game and suitable for girls and children, softball has come into popular use. "Long Ball," "German Bat Ball," and "One Old Cat," long used as introductory games, have gone out of favor and the softball game has taken their place.

Tennis Games. These can be traced back to the tenth century, when they were played by the nobility in the castles of Central Europe. They were indoor games, played in a court with walls on all sides. Lawn tennis was invented by an English army officer in 1875. It was standardized within a few years and has since become popular the world over. Badminton is a form of tennis played extensively in more recent years. Racquets and squash are popular among wealthy social clubs in many countries. Handball and its English variety, Fives, are also popular games of the tennis type; the Spanish play a form called pelota known in some countries as jai alai and the Italians another variety named pallone.

The most popular game of the tennis type that has been devised in recent years is volleyball. It is the only one of the group adapted to use with large numbers and is popular with players of both sexes.

The games of the tennis type are also played in singles form, but inasmuch as they are often played with two or more partners assisting each other in teamplay, they are classed as team games.

Football Games. This type uses a rectangular field with a goal at each end, usually consisting of two upright posts and a cross-bar. Football games were once played in Western Europe by teams representing walled towns, the goals being the gates of the towns or fortresses, and the field, the country between. The game had few rules, and there was no limit to the number of players or the manner of their selection. This crude game was taken up by the English schools of the last century, standardized, and sets of rules agreed upon. In this way the two types of football— rugby and association—were developed, and in a similar way field hockey, ice hockey, and polo grew up in certain schools and athletic clubs. American college football and basketball are of more recent origin, the former being developed around 1880 and the latter in the 90's.

MENTAL COMPETITION. There are a number of games which are based primarily upon mental competition. Conspicuous among these are the well-known games of chess, checkers, cribbage, dominoes, and the many varieties of card games, such as bridge, poker, etc. The games of this type are also closely allied to social play, as they are used for entertainment at many social gatherings.

FORMS OF NONCOMPETITIVE PLAY

The forms of non-competitive play are almost endless in number. They subdivide into so many highly specialized activities that it is impossible to give more than general attention to them here. Many of them are pursued individually in an unorganized manner, and so are more within the realm of the individual's own self-direction. Consequently, they are not so fully the responsibility of the school or community play program as are the activities that need organized direction. The non-competitive forms of play are classified and discussed under the nine general headings that follows.

HUNTING PLAY. Actual hunting is a socially acceptable form of behavior, which is not the case in actual fighting. Actual hunting takes the following forms:

Shooting	*Angling*	*Spearing*
with guns	still fishing	in rapids
with bow and arrow	bait casting	through ice
with slings	fly casting	harpooning
with blow guns	trolling	

Trapping
with arresting traps, such as nooses, mechanical jaws, mesh, or nets
with inclosing traps, such as pitfalls and door traps
with killing traps, such as weightfalls

The weapons of actual hunting can also be used competitively in contests, as in riflery, trap shooting, and target and field archery.

A very popular form of hunting in recreational activity is that type which involves no intent to kill, as in hunting with field glasses and cameras. It also takes the form of hunting for non-moving objects such as wild flowers, trees, nature objects in general, and curios.

Intellectual play involves hunting, as in hunting for words in crossword puzzles, for parts in jigsaw puzzles, in hunting for facts, in scientific effort.

CURIOSITY PLAY. Curiosity is a factor in many play activities—in fact in all play activities when taken up for the first time. Curiosity is a particular conspicuous drive, however, in play of the following types: exploration, nature lore, mental games, reading, puzzle-solving, and experimenting with apparatus.

ROVING PLAY. Roving includes all those activities which involve movement across some considerable amount of space: hiking, back-packing, trek-carting, pack-muling, horseback riding, gypsy hiking with team and wagon, dog teaming, bicycling, automobiling and hitchhiking, paddling and portaging, sailing, motorboating, flying and gliding.

CREATIVE PLAY. The desire for creativeness opens a vast sphere to the play leader and an extremely valuable one both from the educational and recreational standpoints. Creative effort in play life divides into two general fields: (1) creative effort using material objects as in the arts and crafts, and (2) effort in the non-material sphere such as composing poetry and music. A selected suggestive list illustrating the scope of the possibilities in play programs is shown on page 173.

The tendency in creative activity today is to incorporate a project with other activities or with the life situation of the individual at the moment, rather than just to make things for the sake of making them. To illustrate: the making of archery tackle is an accompanying feature of archery as a sport, and similarly, the art of fly-tying is linked with the sport of fishing. Photography accompanies travel. Bird lore and animal life tie in with hiking and canoeing. When thus related to other activities, the activity takes on new meaning. In connection with dramatics, there is scenery and costume making; with music there is the study of simple and primitive instruments; and with nature lore, there are endless opportunities for creative projects.

Creative effort utilizing material objects

Arts and crafts

Basketry
Batik-dyeing, tie-dyeing
Beading
Block printing: linoleum, wood
Bookbinding
Candle-dipping
Caning and seat-weaving
Cement craft
China-painting
Cord-tying
Crocheting
Decorating ready-made
articles
Embroidering
Etching
Feather craft
Glue craft
Jewelry-making
Leather craft
Mask-making: modeling, casting, papier-mâché
Metal crafts: brass, copper, pewter, silver, and wrought iron
Modeling in clay
Needlework
Paper-folding
Plastic-relief-painting
Pottery
Raffia
Rug-making
Sketching
Soap carving
Spinning
Stenciling
Tin work
Wax craft
Weaving: hand loom, foot power, cord, and braid
Wood carving
Woodworking: airplanes, kites, boats, ship models, paddles, boomerangs, toys, furniture

Woodcraft

Ash baskets
Bows, arrows, targets
Bridges and towers
Buckskin: making buckskin clothing
Caches
Camp knicknacks: noggins from burls, paper knives, brooms, rakes, willow beds, candlesticks, war clubs, coat hangers
Drums
Dugouts and rafts
Firecraft: fire-building, cranes, hangers and claws, rustic grills
Gourds
Horn craft
Hunting-knife making
Peace pipes
Pine-needle craft
Rawhide craft: rattles, parfleche cases, and pouches
Rope and twine from bark
Rustic furniture: stools, log benches, chairs, and tables
Shelter-building: bough lean-tos, bark shelters, tepees and wigwams, slab camps, log lean-tos, log cabins
Totem poles: miniature, large, snow
Whittling

Experimental

Radio
Television
Chemistry
Scooters and automobiles
Model airplanes and space objects

Creative effort utilizing nonmaterial subject matter

Dramatic skits, composing of   Poetry, composing of
Music, composing of   Stories, composing of

VICARIOUS PLAY. When direct participation in the above kinds of play activity, growing out of the desire for adventure and new experience, is impossible, people participate in them vicariously through the medium of make-believe play, reading, moving pictures, drama, listening to the radio or recordings, and daydreaming and reverie.

IMITATIVE PLAY. The learning of all games involves imitation, and the imitating of expert players goes on constantly in all forms of play. Most of coaching is based upon demonstration, observation, and imitation, or experimentation. There are certain types of play, however, which are primarily imitative: free play, simple imitation, story plays, rhythmic plays, and mimetic exercises.

Free Play. Individual children and small groups regularly use the swings, teeters, sand piles, giant-stride, or small play implements such as jumping ropes, bean bags, or balls. A certain amount of organization and supervision is always needed in free play, to provide for rotation in the use of the equipment. At home, tricycles, scooters, and toy autos are favorites.

Kinesthetic pleasure in movement is probably the outstanding feature of free, informal play. Recreative swimming is one example. Other examples are the carefree participation in throwing and catching a ball, in shooting baskets, and in trying stunts. The imitative element is strong, as the participant is usually conscious of the proper form in the activity and is trying to approximate it.

Simple Imitation. The whole group acts in unison in imitation of the teacher or some leader. "Follow the Leader" is the most familiar example. The interest that small children have in direct imitation of someone else is reinforced by the variety and novelty of the movements and by the chance to be leader some of the time. There are only a few variations of this type of play, for it does not make much appeal to older children, and dramatic imitation suits the younger ones better.

Story Plays. Story plays illustrate dramatic imitation. The players make believe they are doing something they have seen, experienced, or learned about, everything being omitted from the story but certain physical activities chosen by the leader. The leader sets the example by performing the movements to a certain extent, but his most important duty is to stimulate the imagination of the players by mentioning the things to be done in their turn, and by making comments about them that will arouse enthusiasm and at the same time dictate the form of movement without seeming to do so. However, to make corrections, as in a gymnastic lesson, at once spoils the play and brings it down to the level of a drill, for it destroys the make-believe, which is the soul of the play. The popularity of story plays among game leaders has waned with the increasing emphasis upon rhythmic play.

Song Plays and Folk Dances. These forms of play are imitative in nature. They involve rhythm, music, sociability, and interaction with the opposite sex. The dramatic or make-believe is an added attraction.

Song plays and folk dances often involve dramatizing the habits and mannerisms of people, as in "Did You Ever See a Lassie?", the movements characteristic of earlier occupations, as in "The Shoemaker" and "The Weaving Dance"; or the features of courtship as in "The Villagers," "The Unique," and in "Coming Through the Rye." As was noted in Chapter 1 these plays and dances are remnants of once serious religious rituals, which have long since lost their original significance and are pursued as play.

Mimetic Exercises. Devices are utilized to teach large classes the correct form in gymnastics and in the standard track and field events, such as putting the shot and the crouching start for sprinting. Today the fundamental movements in many games and contests are taught in classes by means of mimetic exercises in mass instruction; the crawl stroke in swimming, the arch shot in basketball, punting in football, the service stroke in tennis, and the club swing in golf are examples. The correct movement is shown and a trained leader stands before the class and leads in the movements. Squad leaders, who themselves are expert performers in the sport being taught by mass instruction, intermingle with the class, giving help to those whose form needs correction, as well as praising the efforts of those who are performing faultlessly.

ACQUISITIVE PLAY. Acquisition in play life takes the form chiefly of collections—postage stamps, coins, match folders, tobacco cans, nature cards, autographs of famous people, pictures of athletes and movie actors, butterflies, arrow heads, and so on without end. Adults are similarly given to collections centering around some hobby, such as guns, antiques, Indian curios, books, and stamps. Nature lore and woodcraft leaders utilize this collecting interest extensively in teaching their subjective matter, urging children to collect nature specimens.

SOCIAL PLAY. The simplest type of play involving the desire for response is conversation, as seen in the casual gatherings of children, and in making calls on the part of adults. Parties, picnics, banquets, and outings are for purposes of sociability and response.

The various club movements, although primarily concerned with certain purposes like scouting, church work, civic progress, outing recreation, music, also are fostered by the desire for a congenial group to meet together in sociability.

Athletic contests and games furnish opportunity for sociability along with the training in physique and in emotional adjustment. The play day is a form of athletic get-together between schools in which the competitive aspect is de-emphasized and in which there is more opportunity for sociability than in the traditional type of interscholastic meets.

The most common courtship and mating **plays** among the

western nations are social dancing and similar plays in which the main feature of interest is a division of the group into couples, so as to provide companionship with one of the other sex. Social dancing is popular year in and year out and, although the type of dancing changes from time to time, dancing continues as a most enjoyable type of recreation. There is a decided satisfaction in the rhythm of dancing, yet the fact that people usually dance in couples shows the prominence of the craving for response.

AESTHETIC PLAY. The appreciation of the aesthetic manifests itself in: (1) music—in listening, participating, and composing; (2) art—painting, sketching, sculpturing, crafts, and photography—through both observation and creative effort; (3) religion, as seen in ritual and worship; (4) nature appreciation; (5) dramatics, pageantry, and club and lodge ritual; (6) literature, both reading and composing, and (7) rhythmic play. Rhythmic play appears in children's song plays and in the various dances the outward forms and characteristics of which were described in Chapter 5.

The possibilities of accomplishment and appreciation of each of these seven forms of aesthetic play are so great that each of them would require a whole book for adequate treatment. Those individuals familiar with them, particularly if they possess special talent, are fortunate because the aesthetic type of play permits lifelong participation and enduring satisfactions.

SUMMARY

People have different capacities, abilities and dispositions to engage in different kinds of play and recreation activities. The more aggressive are stimulated by individual and dual sports, or by contests and games between groups; this has led to extensive participation and nation-wide interest in tennis, football, basketball, baseball, and other competitive sports so characteristic of American culture. Noncompetitive play includes a myriad of personal, unorganized patterns of play that allow for the individual's expression through such activities as hunting and roving, creative play, social play, and appreciation of the aesthetic.

SELECTED REFERENCES

BANCROFT, JESSIE H. *Games.* New York: The Macmillan Co., 1948.

BORST, EVELYNE, and MITCHELL, ELMER D. *Social Games for Recreation.* 2d ed. New York: The Ronald Press Co., 1959.

COX, DORIS, and WARREN, BARBARA. *Creative Hands—An Introduction to Craft Techniques.* New York: John Wiley & Sons, Inc., 1951.

DEMARCHE, EDYTHE and DAVID. *Handbook of Co-Ed Teen Activities.* New York: Association Press, 1958.

DONNELLY, RICHARD J., HELMS, WILLIAM G., and MITCHELL, ELMER D. *Active Games and Contests.* 2d ed. New York: The Ronald Press Co., 1958.

HINDMAN, DARWIN A. *Complete Book of Games and Stunts.* Englewood Cliffs, N. J.: Prentice-Hall, Inc., 1956.

LEONARD, CHARLES. *Recreation Through Music.* New York: The Ronald Press Co., 1952.

SIKS, GERALDINE B. *Creative Dramatics, An Art for Children.* New York: Harper & Bros., 1958.

VINAL, WILLIAM G. *Nature Recreation.* Boston: American Humane Education Association, 1954.

9

Age and Sex
Influences Upon Play

While Comenius, Rousseau, Pestalozzi, Froebel, Herbart, and others of the older educationists emphasized that educational principles should be based on child nature, it was not until the advent of recent scientific methodology that the nature of the child became the object of thoroughgoing study. The appearance of Wilhelm Preyer's *Soul of the Child* in 1882 marks the beginning of the modern child-study movement. This lead was quickly followed by the works of Sully, Shinn, Baldwin, Major, and Moore. Later a long array of scientists and educators gave their attention to the matter of childhood, among them G. Stanley Hall, James, Dewey, Thorndike, Binet, Stern, Bagley, Terman, Claparède, Kilpatrick, Bode, Buehler, Koffka, Gesell, and others.

Child study is regarded today as a major phase of the science of psychology, and psychological and sociological literature abounds with treatises on the subject. Many books popularize the results of research for the use of parents. Special attention is being given to the gifted, the deficient, and the delinquent child. The White House Conferences on Child Health and Protection evidence the importance with which the subject is regarded.

As a result of this study of child life a number of interesting and significant facts regarding the characteristics of the different age stratifications of children have been brought to light. Children are not only smaller than adults, but the body has altogether different proportions in the child; children have less ability than adults in some lines and more in others; they have different likes and dislikes; their interests are not at all the same as the interests of adults, and they have a wholly different outlook upon life. Of special interest to us at this time is the fact that every normal life consists of several rather well-marked stages, of which adulthood is only one, and that the things that appeal most to a person in one stage of life may mean little or nothing at all to the same person when he arrives at another stage.

EFFECT OF INDIVIDUAL DIFFERENCES

Before approaching the play characteristics of the different age periods, it must be thoroughly understood that individual differences in interests are enormous and, as a result, play behavior varies tremendously as one goes from individual to individual through a group. Practical workers in the field of recreation and camping are quick to point out the wide range of individual interests. The recent scientific studies of play behavior show emphatically that individual differences in any given age group are so striking and characteristic that they seem to be of more importance than differences between age groups. It is impossible to say, therefore, that in any particular age group—say 8 to 12 years of age—certain definite play activities are to be used which will meet the needs of all or even the majority of the participants.

Earlier writers were much inclined to break up the prematurity years of life into age periods and recommend definite lists of games as the ones particularly adapted for each period. While it may be possible to show that certain types of activity may be more characteristic of certain age levels than of others, it is safe to say that no activity will prove interesting and satisfying to all individuals in any age group, for the reason that there is such a wide variation in physical and mental growth and in interests growing out of varying experience.

Recent years have placed the emphasis more on continuity

of interests than on periodicity. It has been found that no given play activity is limited to any one age period; while it may be a major interest in one period, it had its beginnings in the preceding period and carries over into the next, and also that some activities, such as reading for pleasure, and throwing and catching, are characteristic of the play of young people from 8½ to 22 years of age. Hedley S. Dimock's significant studies of adolescence (see Selected References) also indicate clearly that constancy rather than shifting characterizes the activities of boys throughout adolescent years. In only one activity did a sudden increment appear, that of driving a car, which is readily explainable by the increased physical size of the person, making it appear that he is old enough to meet the stipulations of law. This factor of constancy is indicated in a study by Harold E. Jones, in which the University of California Interest Record was administered to boys beginning with the sixth grade. The study clearly disclosed that there was a continuous decline after the seventh grade in early childhood interests such as collecting and marbles, and these interests were generally replaced by the more mature interests of youth. Similar conclusions were also reached by Karl C. Garrison. He points out in *Growth and Development* that although interests and habits do change with age, the play interests of early childhood actually provided the basis for possible expansion so as to embrace more distant experiences. Thus a child who displays an interest in Indians, even though this be only an experience gained from moving pictures, has already acquired a focal point for the development of further knowledge of the life and activities of Indians of the past as well as the present. The job of the play leader or teacher is to find ways of connecting worthwhile information and skills with existing interests.

Manifestly, periodicity exists in physiological growth, and concurrent with such growth, increments take place in physical strength and motor ability. A knowledge of these period characteristics is essential to the practical play leader. In respect to interests and activities, however, continuity is now regarded as more characteristic than periodicity. While some changes in types of activities preferred are apparent, the more significant observation is that in the case of most activities, they tend to continue but are engaged in in a different way or in a different form, or with perhaps different degrees of intensity, and with different levels of proficiency and organization. The difference is thus mainly a qualitative one.

Classifications of play activities according to chronological age are a useful tool if regarded as suggestive rather than conclusive and binding. Modern informed play leaders, while taking full cognizance of the implications of periodicity of growth, are inclined to substitute for the concept of fixed periodicity of interests that of continuity and to pace the play activities with the growth and development of the individuals in the group.

PLAY PERIODS OF LIFE

The transition of each individual from one period of life to another is gradual and partial, his interests developing slowly with experience and his body changing proportionately with growth. There are also exceptions and variations in the order of development when various individuals are compared; for example, most children walk before they talk, but in some cases this order is reversed.

Another reason why there is not full agreement upon the stages of life is that they have been studied from different points of view. Some have studied the growth in height and weight; some have studied intellectual growth, and others the development of the emotions. Most scholars divide human life into five or six periods, but some go so far as to describe ten; on the other hand, a few writers recognize but two.

The time of transition about which there is most complete agreement is puberty, which occurs in girls of the civilized races between the ages of 11 and 13, and in boys, between 12 and 15. This age period is the dividing line between childhood and adolescence. It has been recognized from early times and has been known to savage races, who make it a time of rites and ceremonies admitting the youth to certain formal privileges, such as hunting and accompanying warriors to battle. Marked changes in physical traits occur at this time.

For practical reasons, directors of recreation divide the years of childhood into several periods. The years from infancy to six include the pre-school group. Of the pre-school group, most public playgrounds and play programs include supervised play for only the 4– to 6-year-old's, who are usually accommodated in special areas called tot lots or pre-school areas. The second major period is referred to as later childhood, which is usually divided for purposes of play supervision into midgets—6– to 8-year-old's; intermediates—9– to 12-year-olds; juniors—12– to 14-year-old's; and seniors—15– to 18-year-old's.

Playgrounds connected with schools are necessarily influenced, in their methods of arranging play groups, by the divisions found in the school. It was the general custom for a long time to divide the twelve grades of school life into three periods of four years each: the primary school, the grammar school, and the high school. This is a rather artificial division because it is based on the nature of the subjects to be taught, rather than upon the nature of the child. A later plan groups the first six grades together to form an elementary school and divides the next six grades into two equal periods, known as the junior and senior high schools.

Some individuals complete the stage of growth and development that belong in the period of adolescence by the time they finish high school; some others, especially boys, are still immature during the greater part of college age. There is a wide range of difference in the time of attaining maturity. In the educated classes in Europe and the United States the stages of growth appear to be lengthened and maturity postponed, with the result that adolescence often persists until the age of twenty and sometimes even later.

Making a combination, therefore, of the plans of grouping used in the summer playgrounds and in the educational system, one finds six play periods of life which play leaders need to study:

1. from birth to six years, early childhood;
2. from six to twelve, late childhood;
3. from twelve to fifteen, early adolescence;
4. from fifteen to eighteen, late adolescence;
5. from eighteen to sixty-five, maturity;
6. from sixty-five on, older adults.

EARLY CHILDHOOD (BIRTH TO 6 YEARS). Probably no other period of the life span has been so extensively studied as the period of infancy and early childhood. From what is now known of these years it can be said that in no other period of life, not even in adolescence with its sudden eruptions, does such rapid change take place in the behavior of the organism. The result is that these early years cannot be regarded as a period in themselves, but rather as many periods, demarked not by years, but by months and even weeks.

First Year. At the age of four weeks the self-activity of the infant consists largely of turning the head from side to side; light possesses an appeal and the head will turn to follow it. Sociability already begins to express itself and the baby will stare long and intently at any face that is held close to him.

At sixteen weeks, physical activity is rather constant during waking hours, involving grasping whatever is within reach, clapping the hands, rolling, and kicking. Light still fascinates, and bright colors, particularly yellow and orange, are soothing. The baby becomes talkative, and self-demanding in respect to attention from people other than mother.

Twenty-eight weeks finds the child sitting up, kicking with vigor, extending his legs, and handling his feet. He is fascinated by moving objects and likes swinging toys. The appeal of rhythm becomes apparent and he enjoys being bounced. Sociability is further extended and he responds to more than one person at a time, but is shy of strangers.

At forty weeks, the baby begins to cruise by rolling and creeping, and being led by both hands. The one-year-old creeps with animation and stands, but seems to find his greatest joy in handling and throwing; he loves toys that can be thrown. Sociability reaches a climax, and he increasingly seeks the attention of others. He enjoys being chased and hides behind furniture to be hunted. He throws objects to have them given back to him.

Second Year.   At fifteen months the child handles everything, and at eighteen months, being secure on his feet, becomes an avid furniture mover. He begins to climb and loves to explore. Music fascinates him and he responds to its rhythm by keeping time to it, by running, whirling, and bouncing up and down. He has a sense of ownership, not only in respect to himself but others, and loves to fetch things.

The two-year-old has a longer interest span, and there is a greater continuity to his activities. He runs errands, waits on people, and plays at keeping house. He finds in whirling objects a particular fascination. He demands longer walks, and his curiosity leads him off the beaten path to explore. Books interest him and his interest in music becomes intensified. He understands property rights and gets into less trouble from handling other people's property. He is not ready for group activity yet but prefers a single playmate.

Third Year.   A strong sense of ownership begins to manifest itself at two and one-half years and the child guards his possessions. His behavior becomes characterized by ritualism and he sees to it that life goes on around him in routine fashion. He knows where things belong and puts them there; he rebels if furniture is shifted. He becomes more independent and less affectionate. He very much wants people around him but his lack of social adjustment makes it difficult to handle them successfully. He is much given to snatching and grabbing.

At three, the child enters an imaginative world. He prefers child companions to adults, loves to go to other children's houses, and when alone plays with an imaginary playmate. Sex differences begin to appear. His curiosity leads to an endless string of questions. It is time for a tricycle and a gym with ladders, teeters and a swing, all of which will find enthusiastic use.

Fourth Year. The four-year-old is a truly social being. He is less inclined to create a playmate in imagination but wants real-life children around him and seeks children rather than adults. He is ready for group activity, even if not too successful in it, owing to his bossy, boasting tendencies. His sense of family and home is strong, and father and mother are quoted as authority. He craves admiration and approval for the results of his efforts. He dramatizes the situation of both things and people around him. He is beginning to understand rules.

Fifth Year. At five years the child has become a little man. His adjustment is good. He deals less in pure imagination and begins to face reality. He has definite ideas as to what he wants and sets goals for himself. He has moved out of the home in social comprehension and is ready for community experience. His postural control is in general good, although he lacks refinement in manual coordination, which may become apparent in his efforts at throwing.

LATER CHILDHOOD (6 TO 12 YEARS). *Primary Grades.* The primary school teaches the 3 R's—the elemental tools of knowledge. In the same way, this is the period when the child should gain the fundamental skills of physical activity —the 3 R's of later sports and recreation, so to speak. All kinds of exercise are almost equally interesting, as the special aptitudes have not yet begun to develop. The experience is a foundational one, so all children alike should receive it.

The outstanding characteristic of this period (6–8) is the wide scope and variety of activities engaged in. In later periods the number of activities grows less and less. Childhood is the period of exploration and experimentation. The drive for new experience and all that it implies is boundless in intensity. Curiosity is paramount. All of the world is new and challenging, and all normal children go forth adventuring to see what it is like. They seek to test themselves in the activity of the world—hence the tendency toward many activities, both physical and mental, and the great versatility of interests.

This stage of childhood has as its achievement objective the sense of industry or the development of the sense of duty and accomplishment. Learning how to do things and to do them well is an important step at this stage of personality development.

Imitation is still a major characteristic of play: boys are much given to playing cowboy, Indian, air or space pilot, soldier, and teacher, and girls to playing with dolls, playing house and school, and dressing up like adults. Toy play of the younger period gradually goes out. Children are much inclined to give the objects they handle a symbolic meaning which is in keeping with their make-believe tendencies at these ages.

This is the period when tag games and games of hiding and finding have their greatest popularity. Just running and romping may be satisfying enough at times, and means of locomotion are much loved, such as roller skating and coasting. Big-muscle activities involving pleasurable movements are sought, and those involving rhythm, such as skipping a rope, are popular. Singing and rhythmic ring games are much engaged in, particularly by girls.

Reading and drawing absorb interest, and creative effort involving attempts at construction is in evidence, with the tools of construction of particular appeal.

Middle Grades. In the later years (9 to 12 years), group games of low organization are loved, and team games, particularly baseball, basketball, and football, are exceedingly popular, although played more informally than in later periods.

Much has been said about these being the individualistic

years, but the evidence does not show that children of this period are any less social in their play than in later periods. Indeed, solitary play is very seldom seen. Their more limited social experience, as compared to later periods, may lead to the quarreling and self-assertive arguing so often seen in these years, with the result that they may appear more individualistic. This would indicate lack of social conditioning, rather than individualistic or unsocial tendency, and it is out of such give-and-take that the increased effectiveness as group and team participants of later years develops.

A tendency of this period which might be called individualistic, although not unsocial or solitary, is the love of activities involving a high level of individual skill and the drive to develop such skills. Activities of the self-testing and individual competition type are popular; examples are found in such play as marbles, wrestling, climbing, running, roller skating, and rope skipping. Although not cooperative in the team sense they are none the less seldom participated in alone by preference, and social consciousness is evidenced by the very desire to display individual skill in them. This period of later childhood is important as a time for acquiring muscular control. Great perfection of muscular coordination is not yet possible, but this is the time when practice must begin if special and unusual skill is to be obtained.

EARLY ADOLESCENCE (12 TO 15 YEARS.) The junior high school offers general courses in its academic curriculum, such as general history and basic science, with the purpose of presenting introductory work for later, more specialized courses. In the same way, this is the period in which there is an introduction of team play in various games for both boys and girls, without any thought as yet of specialization or of mastering intricate patterns of strategy.

Adolescence is the period of life when sex characteristics are developing and when the body in its growth gradually takes on the size and form that belong to men and women. Puberty is the name given to the time when adolescence begins. Marked and relatively sudden changes take place in the adolescent's growth in height, weight, and strength. While development in motor ability slows down at the time when the spurt in weight and height first begins, it is increased substantially during the postpubescent period of most rapid growth in height and weight.

Play behavior shows no sudden or marked change during this period. Imitative or make-believe play, declining through later years of childhood, is now of little importance; romping, hide-and-seek, simple tag games, and similar activities have now passed out of the picture completely. There are distinct changes in reading interests and in the types of movies, music, television, and radio programs enjoyed.

Self-testing play and individual contests still continue, but tend to take the more standardized form of track and field sports. Baseball and football, which were characteristic of the younger period in an informal and "scrub" form, now tend to become more highly organized. Basketball becomes exceedingly popular and shows the greatest increase in participation of any game. The adolescent years show an increasing tendency to travel as chronological age advances, with the result that the circle of activity expands farther and farther from home. At this age sports and games, outdoor activities, and learning to drive a car are most interesting to girls as well as boys; girls are also very interested in self-improvement, social activities, and participation in group organizations.

In general there is a decrease in the number of activities participated in, a fact that remains true throughout the entire adolescent period. It is important that the physical activity program in this period should be generalized in nature, providing every boy and every girl with the opportunity to participate in many activities. Continued exposure to a broad range of activities is paramount, as well as exposure to all the skills within each activity. For that reason, in his team activities, the boy should acquire experience in all the positions on the team, rather than begin to specialize immediately in any one. In addition to the absorbing team games, there should also be training in leisure-time activities that have a recreation or hobby value, such as those activities conducted in recreation centers or voluntary, youth-serving agencies.

For these reasons, the wisdom of interscholastic competition on the junior high school level is open to question. Not only does it deprive the young athlete of the opportunity to browse around and find his interests in the various sports and various positions, but early specialization is gained at the expense of general all-round ability. A comprehensive intramural program, on the other hand, makes for versatility and also greatly enlarges the numbers of potential players and leaders for the senior high school and college programs.

At this age, the liability to overstrain in the excitement of varsity competition and in the zeal for victory is greater than in the case of older high school boys, for the junior high school period is one of rapid growth and liability to exhaustion under long-sustained effort. Furthermore, in games of physical contact, competition between junior high school boys is dangerous because boys vary so much in size at this age. A suitable classification plan is necessary. The value of all activities engaged in by children should be carefully evaluated by specific methods and be in direct relationship to their many needs during any one period of development as well as to their needs in later life.

Much has been written in years past to the effect that adolescence is a time of crises, with marked changes taking place in religious and moral thinking, in moods and interests, and in personality factors. Recent research indicates quite the opposite. In these factors, as in play behavior, continuity is more characteristic than periodicity. Changes do take place during adolescence in the moral and religious and in the personality spheres, but they occur gradually, being the result of the influence of social and economic factors from without rather than of changes from within the person himself.

LATER ADOLESCENCE (15 TO 18 YEARS). In the senior high school the preferences of the pupils are given precedence. The high school assumes that the child has been taught the common elements of life, and now he is allowed a chance to discover and develop his special aptitudes and powers. This is made possible through allowing a varied program of studies with the chance for the pupil to explore many fields and find where his talents lie. The time has now come when specialized aptitudes in sports begin to develop, and the student selects favorite pursuits and plays them intensively. Moreover, he is eager and ready to apply himself to the mastery of the intricacies of complex team play.

Although interest in track and field sports, with emphasis on individual superiority, is still a prominent factor, it is still further stimulated now by group competition, in which players win scores for their team as well as for themselves. The desire for individual recognition and the tendency to push one's self forward means that there is danger of players overdoing under stress of championships contested before a partisan crowd. The danger here is in the direction of too long-continued effort rather than too severe exertion; for example, football, with its supreme efforts of strength alternated with periods of rest, unless overdone, is not so apt to be productive of harm as long-distance running and such games as basketball, where the practice is both strenuous and long-continued. To avoid impairing the health from physical overexertion, games of the basketball type are played in quarters instead of halves, and runs over one mile have been omitted from high school meets.

High school girls have about the same tendency to strive for individual superiority and to develop a spirit of loyalty and cooperation as do high school boys. Girls are subject to the same dangers of injury as the boys, and they are even more liable to overdo and suffer injury under stress of competition. Schools should require physical examinations for all students. This provides an added safeguard to students engaging in athletic competition.

MATURITY (18 TO 65 YEARS). These years, which include the time of college life, are the years of greatest physical efficiency and hardihood. The possibilities of bodily development in strength, speed, skill, and endurance are so far beyond the attainments of the average man and woman that the exhibitions given by athletic teams and individual athletes attract a larger number of spectators than any other type of display. The interest of communities in their own teams has its advantages, because it stimulates the interest of the public in such forms of play and helps to finance broader play programs.

There is a marked tendency at this time of life, even though the possibilities of development are so great, to forego all active recreation and engage only in amusements of passive character. During college life and in business and professional life later, interest in the various problems of the individual and the community tends to keep people from engaging in any active recreation; loss of health and efficiency follow. The promotion of wholesome play is the most promising preventive; those who become heartily absorbed in active sports in high school and college form a habit that will stimulate them to continue wholesome recreations rather than to slump into those of the passive type.

OLDER ADULTS (65 YEARS ON). Except for children under ten, the group of people over sixty-five is the fastest growing age group in our population. In 1959 there were approximately fifteen million of these older people in the United States, or approximately one in every ten persons, with an anticipated increase of over 400,000 per year. This lengthening span of human life, long considered a basic accomplishment of modern medicine, has in itself raised new social problems. So important have these problems become that the field of gerontology (the scientific study of the phenomena of old age) is now well established.

The years after sixty-five are indicated by definite traits which are characteristic of later maturity. Four major traits, among others, are most obvious: (1) declining energy which modifies behavior in everyday life; (2) changes in personal appearance, which are different with each individual but are inevitable and affect people in different ways; (3) onset of disability—slowing of reaction time, inability to see well, arthritis, rheumatism, and other ailments which are characteristic of older adults; and (4) loss of earlier adult roles—the inevitable decline in the importance of the role of older adult in the family, the retirement from work, and the loss of status and importance formerly held by the adult as a worker. The medical profession has recognized the need for special treatment for the diseases and physical difficulties of the older adult; from this has grown the specialty of medicine known as geriatrics.

Among older adults, women are hardier than men; there are ten women of sixty-five to every nine men, and half of the older women and one-third of the men are single, widowed, or divorced. This means that this age group is more alone than the rest of the adult population. Most older people—seven out of ten—live in their own homes; two out of ten live with relatives; only one out of ten is in an institution, hotel, rooming house, or nursing home.

As a group, there is great need during the years after sixty-five for individuals to engage in activities that give them status and mark them as useful and needed in their immediate family and in the community. In this respect they often find community service work very interesting and rewarding. Also, there is a need for spiritual expression and many find great solace in the activities of the church or similar religious or cultural groups. Older adults thoroughly enjoy companionship and social relations with others of their own age to pass away the many hours of leisure available to them. They wish companionship and enjoy mixed parties and gatherings that provide opportunities for social play. Perhaps most of all there is a need for self-expression—a desire to have facilities and opportunities to develop a hobby and a place to develop projects which reflect their ideas, abilities, and interests. If physical abilities allow, older people are avid readers and enjoy attending literary-type activities.

Perhaps of major concern to older adults is health and the ability to move about comfortably. In this regard it is important to note that they wish to maintain good physical vigor and adjust their physical activities in accordance with their condition. Moderation is the answer. For the man or woman who has not exercised vigorously for years, moderation would mean mild exercises; for one who has been more vigorous, it would mean playing golf, doubles tennis, swimming, hiking, and other physical activities commensurate with his strength and abilities. Such physical activity is an antidote to fatigue, and, if not overdone, brings exhilaration and recuperation. For the older person, neither too much exercise nor too much rest is the answer.

Special recreation programs for older adults are being conducted by public as well as private agencies throughout the country. Further reference to these programs and the activities of older adults is made in Chapter 20.

EFFECT OF SEX DIFFERENCES

It goes without saying that there are many differences in the behavior of the two sexes which must be considered in play leadership. These differences are due primarily to two factors: (1) difference in physiological structure and function, (2) difference in social conditioning.

In considering the physiological differences, one is impressed immediately with differences in the skeletal framework of the two sexes. The bones of the female are not only lighter, but the greater width of the pelvis gives the thigh bones an obliquity which affects the running ability of the girl and makes it impossible for her to compete against male standards. Even at birth there are differences in bodily development between the sexes, boys on the average being taller, heavier, and larger about the chest. Boys continue to be taller and heavier until the age period from eleven to fourteen, when girls become taller and heavier than boys of the same age. The prepubertal acceleration in growth occurs a year earlier in girls than in boys, and boys continue to grow in height later than do girls.

Numerous measurements have been taken to discover other differences between boys and girls. Generally, boys exceed girls in weight; during adolescence girls have a higher pulse rate than boys, and there is a significant difference favoring the boys in relative strength of grip, speed of running, height of jumping, distance of throwing a ball, and length of broad jump. There are differences in the rate of metabolism between the two sexes, the male possessing a metabolic level approximately 10 per cent higher than the female. This is a conditioning factor favoring greater activity and aggressiveness. There are functional differences in the female, not only in respect to the obvious reproductive functions of menstruation, pregnancy, and lactation, but also in respect to the ability to store up energy and withstand cold and pain. The female is held to possess a greater general constitutional vitality.

The glandular make-up of the sexes is also different. The endocrine glands and thyroid and adrenal glands function to a great extent in the female causing a higher output of nervous energy and a smaller production of physical energy.

These physiological differences are not sufficient, however, to account for the behavior differences between the sexes, and when compared to social conditioning, are a minor factor. That the differences in conduct between the sexes is more the result of social than of biological inheritance is illustrated in the changes which have taken place since women have had the opportunity to participate in activities outside of the home. Girls are participating more and more in the activities which have been regarded in the past as the peculiar sphere of boys. The girl of today has taken to athletics and outdoor sports with eagerness since the taboos have been removed.

Current research and thought indicate that men and women in their inborn intellectual and social capacities are much closer together than has been generally assumed in the past. Women are more observant of small details, less interested in things, and more interested in people and their feelings, less given to pursuing, capturing and fighting, and more given to nursing, comforting, and relieving pain. The main differences are that women show less variability, greater affectability, and greater primitiveness. These differences are small, however, and the striking thing is not the differences between the sexes but the individual differences within each sex.

Even though the behavior differences of the two sexes are largely the result of tradition and education, they are none the less real. There is a marked difference in the way in which the activities are played. Boys are more given to competitive games than girls and play them with more of a driving, winning spirit. Organized play activity in general is more characteristic of boy behavior than girl. Games requiring a high degree of muscular skill are more frequently preferred by boys than girls. Girls are more conservative and sedentary in their play behavior.

Both boys and girls are interested in creative effort but boys are more given to constructing large projects and girls to smaller and more delicate things; girls are somewhat more interested in decorating the project than in its mechanical construction. Both boys and girls make collections and while both collect stamps, birds' eggs, marbles, and autographs, girls' collections of nature objects show more of an indication toward mosses, butterflies, and colorful things, and less toward the boys' favorites namely, leaves, rock specimens, animals' teeth, live frogs, lizards, and the like. Girls collect handkerchiefs, samples of soap, perfume, toilet articles, and art books.

From the teaching standpoint these differences do not need to be taken into account up to the time of entering school. Until then boys and girls are so nearly alike in ability and interest that they can easily be led to play and enjoy the same activities.

ELEMENTARY SCHOOL AGE. The exact time when the separation of boys and girls in their play should take place varies in different cases; some groups grow apart in their abilities and interests as much as two years earlier than others. The influence of the teacher has something to do with this. Some teachers who are experts in teaching rhythmic plays are able to maintain the interests of the boys in folk dances and clog dances through the elementary grades and into junior high school, and some teachers are more successful than others in enlisting the interest of girls in track and field sports and ball play. It is wiser, however, to pay attention to the natural interests of the players than to expend too much effort in leading children away from their natural bent in these matters.

Just before the end of the elementary school, at the age of eleven or twelve, some girls reach the age of puberty, at which time they begin to grow more rapidly than before. As a matter of fact, in the fifth and sixth grades the boys usually excel the girls in strength and skill just enough to make competition between them on the same plane unsatisfactory. At some point, therefore, between the end of the third grade and the end of the sixth, separation of the sexes in competitive play seems advisable.

JUNIOR HIGH SCHOOL AGE. Not so much because of difference in the kind of activity they like but because of differences in physical capacity and differences in the way they play, it seems best to separate boys and girls at this time in practically all active games. Boys play more vigorously and roughly and seek opportunity to match their strength against their equals. Girls particularly enjoy social dancing beginning with the thirteenth year, while boys do not develop this interest to a marked degree until about the sixteenth year. Girls play baseball but in a less vigorous and driving way. Basketball for girls likewise must be modified since they are not capable of as much continuous running as boys. Volleyball also should be modified and when both boys and girls are playing together the girls' rules should be used. Track and field events and athletic tests are popular with girls of this period, but it goes without saying that they should compete against standards of their own. Girls should have play fields of their own, separate from those used by the boys. Camping, hiking, nature lore, and woodcraft are major interests of girls of this period.

It is good social training to have the sexes play together part of the time during this age period, but such a situation calls for a thoroughly competent teacher with good judgment, and necessitates a program limited to less strenuous games. In the interest of social education, also, the two sexes should be brought together as much as possible in the non-physical types of recreation, such as dramatics, music, handicraft, social dancing, and sociable functions.

SENIOR HIGH SCHOOL AGE. From the time of early adolescence onward, girls excel in dancing, while boys keep gaining in general athletic ability. It follows that, with the exception of a certain few recreative forms of activity, such as tennis, badminton, archery, bowling, golf, swimming, and dancing, the plays of the two sexes must be separate.

For practically all organized sports, modified rules to meet the needs of women are prepared by the Women's Athletic Committee of the American Association for Health, Physical Education, and Recreation. When boys and girls play together in a sport, it is imperative that the girls' rules be followed.

Interscholastic competition for girls in athletic sports, once frowned upon, is now favored within strict limitations. The present thought is that interschool games and contests are advisable provided the strain of intense competition is eliminated and a variety of sports is utilized rather than concentration on one or two. It is considered essential that girls' teams be coached by women, and the games handled by women officials. Approved practice holds that girls' teams should not play in any event at which admission is charged, or play prior to or following a boys' event. Overnight trips are considered unwise. Rather than scheduling a single event, the trend is toward sports days in which representative teams from the competing schools play in several events on the same day, and since everyone is kept busy in actual play, there is no large spectator group. Such sports days using representative teams are rapidly replacing play days in which all available students play on improvised "color teams."

The gymnastic program for girls differs from that of boys and all activities are modified to meet the needs and capacities of girls. The classic formal systems differentiated between exercises suitable for men and women, and such differentiation is still essential in a well-conducted gymnasium program.

College and Maturity. The play interests of the later high school period are usually carried over into college and sometimes maturity. After high school, however, men are more prone to keep up their active play than women, and the result is that men develop their strength correspondingly greater than women. The average college girl is able to practice outdoor recreative sports with profit, but she frequently neglects this chance for exercise; however, the women's physical activity programs of colleges have become so efficient and are presented so attractively that an ever increasing percentage of girls is participating.

Women of college age participate mostly in basketball, volleyball, tennis, badminton, field hockey, softball, golf, soccer, speedball, fieldball, fencing, bowling, swimming, canoeing, rowing, riding, and folk dancing. Track and field events, gymnastic movements, tumbling, and pyramid building are also used. Much popularity surrounds such less strenuous activities as deck tennis, clock golf, table tennis, tetherball, and dart throwing.

There is a marked tendency on the college level to bring both sexes together for recreational activity. Hikes, outdoor recreational meets, and informal social gatherings are very common. Many colleges have social and recreational organizations for graduate students. When mixed groups are together the active games and sports which are used must of course be determined by the women's ability: volleyball, tennis, table tennis, golf, badminton, swimming, skating and softball are the most commonly used.

The play activities of the two sexes are probably more similar in interest during maturity than at any time except early childhood. The school play program should familiarize boys and girls with the type of games and sports they will need in later life. Busy men and women, who must snatch their exercise while they may, and who are not in the physical condition necessary to take part in rugged competition with safety and comfort, must look to the milder recreations as their proper field of play. This does not mean that they must lose their interest in the more strenuous sports but they should be willing to enjoy them vicariously by watching the performances of younger players.

Throughout history, the loyalty of women has been bound up with the home, rather than with the larger group organizations, such as the tribe or state. As a result girls were lacking in qualities of cooperation and loyalty which are prerequisites to team play. Once they were permitted to do so, they entered into athletics and vigorous sports with enthusiasm, with the result that there has been a marked improvement in the cooperation, loyalty, and sportsmanship of women players.

Not only has there been a change in the attitudes of women players but a marked development in the physiques of young women during recent years. Statistics accumulated in measuring the physiques of students entering college show that girls of this group are from an inch and a quarter to two inches taller today than they were thirty years ago. This increase is probably due to better nutrition, improved medical care, and to a general increase in physical activities which characterizes their freedom in our present-day social pattern.

SUMMARY

Play interests and needs vary with age. In designating six distinct play periods, attention is directed toward recognition of play activities that are characteristic during development throughout the life span. Although one may generalize and point out needs and interests during each play period, it is a significant fact that, due to individual differences, interests in activities often persist after an individual passes through a particular period. In planning activities, then, it is important to be aware of the factors pertinent to meeting interests and needs during any one play period and at the same time recognize the importance of continuity of activities between periods. A successful and effective play and recreation program is the result of careful consideration of the overall needs of each group as well as the careful analysis of individual needs within and among the different age groups.

There is a greater similarity than difference in the play interests of the two sexes. Many play activities are engaged in by both sexes with equal frequency but, of course, there is a difference in the way the activities are played. Differences are to be noted in the greater tendency among boys than girls toward the more vigorous active games, toward organized and competitive games, and those requiring muscular skill. These differences are due to differences in physiological structure and function and to differences in social conditioning. Girls entered into strenuous play as soon as the taboos were lifted.

SELECTED REFERENCES

Each of the following references contains basic information, relating to growth and development, which is fundamental to a broad understanding of the effect and the role of play and recreation in the development of the individual in present-day society.

BIRREN, JAMES E. (ed.). *Handbook of Aging and the Individual—Psychological and Biological Aspects.* Chicago: University of Chicago Press, 1959, Chap. 10.

BRECKENRIDGE, MARIAN E., and VINCENT, E. LEE. *Child Development.*

Philadelphia: W. B. Saunders Co., 1955, Chap. 6.

CROW, LESTER D., and CROW, ALICE. *Adolescent Development and Adjustment.* New York: McGraw-Hill Book Co., Inc., 1956.

ERIKSON, ERIK H. *Childhood and Society.* New York: W. W. Norton & Co., Inc., 1950, Chap. 6.

GARRISON, KARL C. *Growth and Development.* New York: Longmans, Green & Co., Inc., 1959, Chap. 13.

GESELL, ARNOLD L., ILG, FRANCES L., and AMES, LOUISE B. *Youth, The Years From Ten to Sixteen.* New York: Harper & Bros., 1956, Chap. 16.

GESELL, ARNOLD L., ILG, FRANCES L. *Child Development—An Introduction To The Study of Human Growth.* New York: Harper & Bros., 1949.

KEPLER, HAZEL. *The Child and His Play.* New York: Funk & Wagnalls Co., 1952. The author explains a wide variety of recreation activities for children and relates in nontechnical language and by practical suggestions how these activities may be most beneficial and interesting to children at various age levels.

DIMOCK, HEDLEY S. *Rediscovering the Adolescent.* New York: Association Press, 1941.

WILLIAMS, ARTHUR. *Recreation for the Aging.* New York: Association Press, 1953.

Part III

SIGNIFICANCE OF
PLAY AND RECREATION

10

Need for Recreation
in Modern Life

Many very significant changes, far-reaching in their effects, have taken place in recent years and have resulted in serious social maladjustments. So swiftly have these pathological social conditions occurred that the remedial measures of society have lagged far behind. Among other things these changes have projected into startlingly bold relief the need for an immediate and extensive development of a well-rounded play and recreation program for the whole United States, regardless of age, sex, location, or social stratification.

Fortunately, far-sighted vision has kept the recreation movement well abreast of social needs, even though much remains to be done, as the problem is ever-expanding and ever-varying. Today, the recreation leader needs no longer to argue for the introduction of a program—this has been accomplished. His present responsibility is to make the best use of the facilities and programs. Even so, to meet this new responsibility, he himself should understand the basic educational, social, and economic needs out of which today's impressive recreation movement was brought into being. He is thereby better fortified to meet his pressing tasks. In short, the field of recreation offers new opportunities that seem without limit when the increasing hours of leisure are envisioned.

Many of the points raised in this chapter are elaborated upon elsewhere in the book. This treatment is an introductory one to provide orientation to the subject matter in its broader aspects and in its total functioning.

ENVIRONMENTAL AND SOCIAL CHANGES

A general survey of man's physical activities previous to the present era of civilization shows that he was an active person. In the remote past, members of both the upper and lower classes of society were forced into all-round physical development: the lower classes tilled the soil, erected buildings under the direction of their superiors, dug canals, built roads, manned boats, and served in the military when drafted; the upper classes were constantly engaged in supervising all work, which was done out-of-doors, and led military and trade expeditions. There was no escape for a man, whether of the one class or the other; the very stage of civilization demanded an active life spent in a wide variety of employments.

Later types of civilization until very recently have also made the same demands on individuals. The pioneer settlers in America fought with Indians, felled trees, cleared land, and dug stumps; they depended solely upon their own efforts to sustain their entire existence. In the household duties, the women made their own bread, churned their own butter, fashioned all the clothing, and so on. The whole family was called upon to contribute to the problems of everyday living. Moreover, the children walked to school, to town, to the picnic grounds, to the river or lake— they always walked when it was a matter of a few miles. Whatever trade was pursued was learned fully, pursuing all aspects of the trade or occupation. Each individual tradesman could not escape the physical development that these varied activities demanded.

SPECIALIZATION OF WORK

Today the all-round craftsman has given way to the laborer who contributes but one small item to the final product of the industry; to the supervisor who uses the telephone, telegraph, messenger boys, charts, and diagrams; to the housewife who disposes of nearly all forms of physical work by means of electrical appliances and of ready-made articles of food for the table and garments to wear. The very devices that are termed labor-saving must be recognized at the same time in some way as body-weakening. In this age of intense specialization the opportunity for all-round work that will contribute to the development of the big muscles of the body has quite disappeared. There has been an appalling emigration from the country to the city. In the city there has been an evolution from the handy-man to the specialized man. The type of the specialist's work can be seen in the automobile assembly room, where the worker stands by a moving track tightening one particular bolt as one machine after another passes slowly on to the next specialist.

So it is true that, until the present generation, physical exercise had been provided by the type of work in which man was engaged. And children had family chores, which have largely disappeared. Even walking to school or to a party, perhaps, is now giving way to riding in the family car, the school bus, or the taxicab.

It can be seen that, whereas the past gave man a well-balanced physical development, the present has robbed him of it. Modern civilization, however, through the invention of so many time-saving devices, has provided one thing that the past could not give—leisure time. It is during the leisure time that the body must be trained in the wholesome activity that one's occupation denies.

Science, in all its advances, has tended from a medical standpoint to prolong life, and to make it less harsh from the standpoint of material welfare; but science has tended also to encourage the physical degeneration of the individual. The present conditions that it has produced, compared with those of the past, refute all arguments against physical education, supervised play, and recreation; rather, they emphasize the immediate and future need of them. And leisure, which science has granted, is needed for the physical upkeep of the individual.

STULTIFYING EFFECTS OF INDUSTRIALIZATION. The degree
of industrialization in society today affords only one-sided
physical development and exercise and play and recreation
are needed to supply generalized use of the muscles in a
normal way. Moreover, specialized labor does not command the interest of the worker as does general work.
There are several reasons why interest is apt to be lacking
in the modern mode of work: (1) the monotony of repetition
in piece work; (2) the lack of opportunity for expression of
the creative; (3) the lack of opportunity for sociability; and
(4) the strain of the modern tempo in industry.

Monotony. Modern industry from the worker's standpoint is built upon concentration upon an unvarying task,
suppression of variation, and the subordination of personality. The net result is monotony. Hour after hour and
day after day the same small seemingly meaningless task is
repeated. Monotony is the very opposite of life. It makes
of man an inanimate machine and he is so constituted that
he rebels against repetition and seeks new experience and
adventure. It has been asserted that mentally retarded individuals do many tasks in industry and on the farm more
methodically than normal individuals—the plodding, slow-
thinking can endure the monotony cheerfully, but normal
men cannot.

Lack of Creative Effort. The pewter smith in the old
days made his article completely from the time he first
handled the rough pewter until the polished, finished article
was sold. The design was his, and he put into it all the
beauty and artistry at his command; he placed it before the
customer with a distinct feeling of pride in the thought that
no one in the community could do it as well. Much of the
same thing is seen among the Southwest Indian and Mexican
craftsmen today. In a craft culture the desire for creative
effort is satisfied. Who makes the modern automobile? No
one in particular but many, many individuals. Who de-
rives the satisfaction of having created it? No one. So another human aspiration, the creative, is not served by modern industry.

Dubin gives the following succinct description of the industrial worker's lack of interest in his every-day tasks: "The industrial workers' world is one in which work and the workplace are not central life interests for a vast majority. In particular, work is not a central life interest for industrial workers when we study the informal group experiences and the general social experiences that have some affective value for them. Industrial man seems to perceive his life history as having its center outside of work for his intimate human relationships and for his feelings of enjoyment, happiness, and worth." [1]

Lack of Sociability in Work. Not only did the craft worker find interest in his work, but he did his work at home with the good wife close at hand to drop a pleasant word at times and the children admiringly watch him fashion the raw material into the finished product. Then, too, he had time to gossip as he worked. His customer would discuss the topics of the day with him, and, as a result, both assumed the position of casual philosophers and students of literature. There was a certain pleasantness about the work that gave relaxation to offset the weariness naturally brought on by twelve and sixteen hours of daily work. It was somewhat of a leisurely business; the working man mixed his work, play, and conversational efforts thoroughly in the day's routine. Today, however, his machinery is noisy, conversation of any length is not tolerated in the necessity of speeding up the output, and the result is that the man is isolated while he works.

Strain in Modern Life. It is realized that long-continued concentration on a task and the resulting monotony soon terminate in nervous exhaustion. This strain has been recognized almost universally in recent years.

Not only has strain entered into work but also into every activity of the day. The modern individual is forced to maintain a tremendous pace. Everything is speeded up: his work, his lunch hour, his pastimes, and even his time for

[1] Robert Dubin, "Industrial Worker's Worlds," *Social Problems*, III, 3 (January, 1956), pp. 131-42.

sleep. The cross-country trip by horse and carriage or oxen has given way to the mile-a-minute train; the walk or the drive with the horse and buggy, to the high-powered automobile; the airplane has now supplanted both of these, with the commercial jet airplane now a reality. The speeding-up process together with that of specialization make daily life one of minutely cooperative affairs, one of many appointments that must be kept punctually. The net result is hurry.

The laborer leaves the close confinement and monotony of his specialized work, dodges the traffic of buses and automobiles, finds his recreation in television, perhaps, or in a speeding auto ride, and sleeps to the accompaniment of shrill whistles and horns and the grating of gears. The child finds himself shut up in a schoolroom, his activity curbed, with restlessness and tension prominent factors of his daily existence.

Industrial unrest is not economic but spiritual, not physical but moral. It is the revolt of man who sees life slipping away from him without his having lived, who sees wishes unfulfilled and aspirations unattained and unattainable. There are two alternatives in solution—strike at the industrial system and change it to something more satisfying to human interests or make life challenging in its fullest extent to men in the margin outside of work. It is to the cultivation of life in this margin that the modern recreation movement is dedicated.

INCREASE IN DELINQUENCY. Life will not be denied, and, when socially acceptable living fails to bring opportunity for the satisfaction of basic drives and desires, individuals tend to turn to antisocial ways. Crime is in a large part a compensatory device when other forms of satisfying amusement are not forthcoming.

Probably the first argument advanced for the introduction of playgrounds was that they would help to reduce the rapidly growing amount of juvenile delinquency. In order to prove this contention, a number of studies were undertaken. As early as 1907, Allen T. Burns, a social worker, made such a survey in Chicago, concluding: "To provide a probation district with adequate play facilities is coincident with a reduction of delinquency of from 28 per cent to 70 per cent, or 44 per cent as an average." The obvious conclusion drawn was that delinquency in this situation was largely a matter of inadequate play facilities and leadership.

These early studies and later investigations showed dramatically that in specific situations juvenile delinquency rates dropped markedly with the provision of well-supervised, well-equipped playgrounds, community centers, and similar general recreation operations. The National Recreation Association has, from time to time, published testimonials from local police officials, juvenile authorities, and other leaders indicating that recreation services are a potent force in the prevention of juvenile delinquency.

The cause of the tremendous increase in juvenile delinquency has not been definitely determined. It has been a difficult problem to solve. The U.S. Children's Bureau, after extensive research and an analysis of the prevention attempts, came to these conclusions:

1. No panacea for preventing or reducing juvenile delinquency has been discovered.
2. Certain measures by themselves, such as counseling, recreation service, psychiatric service, and group work service, have been unable to appreciably reduce delinquency.
3. A start has been made toward identifying the kinds of measures that are likely to lessen delinquent acts of particular types of children.

The answer lies in careful research that will indicate more clearly what the various community services can each contribute to meet the overall problem of delinquency. Sheldon and Eleanor Glueck, in their intensive study *Unraveling Juvenile Delinquency,* have contributed much to the analysis of the causes of delinquency. They detail the factors causing delinquency, the traits of the delinquent child, and the approach to the problem through improved home conditions, changes in school curriculums, increased positive influences in the community, and further research. Lander has made further contribution to the methodology of studying juvenile delinquency. He refers to juvenile delinquency as being caused by social disintegration. Adult as well as juvenile delinquency is thus caused by emotional insecurity, social inadequacy, apathy, confusion, and cultural conflict.

While the effect of recreation on delinquency cannot be accurately determined, the studies to date seem to indicate that recreation does have a desirable effect on lessening antisocial activity. Delinquency areas seem to be paralleled by a lack of play opportunities. The inference is that much juvenile crime is simply the bursting out in some form or other of the child's inherent desire for action. The more this action is repressed or undirected, the more extreme the outburst. Stealing, breaking windows, defying the "cop," and the like are the perversions which the child's inherent love for activity brings about in congested districts without playgrounds. The directed playground transfers, for example, the juvenile's ambition from stealing apples from the corner grocer to an ambition to be a member of the team. "Bill has been so busy stealing bases this summer he has not had time to steal anything else and has not been seen in our court," one juvenile judge is reported to have remarked.

Optimism is another keynote of the play situation. The child who is stealing, or gambling, or doing things he knows are forbidden, is not particularly happy or contented; he is always worried and afraid of punishment. On the playground, however, the child is free to express himself without any restraints save those of the rules of fair play. He is more apt to become a happy child, developing in a normal way and having an optimistic outlook on life.

Juvenile delinquency has many causes and requires a coordinated attack at both the local and national level. Recreation is one of the major community services that will, with other community services, help to bring about a solution to the problem. Park Commissioner Robert Moses of New York City emphasizes this coordinated approach:

What can we do affirmatively for youth? Speaking for the Park Department, we can build and operate facilities for health recreation and athletic competition where the need is greatest. This may not be the sole answer to the youth problem, but it surely is one of them. I do not for a moment minimize the contribution to be made by doctors, welfare agencies, police, and courts to the task of providing, under difficult urban conditions, a normal and happy childhood for all who can enjoy it. Above all, there is no substitute for good parents, good homes, and helpful church, religious, and school influences. All the efforts of all concerned will be needed, and we should therefore dissipate none of our energies in petty differences over method and procedure.[2]

INCREASE IN MENTAL ILLNESS. Contemporary life seems to produce many types of mental disturbances. Labor in industry is frequently under conditions which are unhygienic, filled with noises, nerve-racking vibrations, dust, odors, and stale indoor air. These factors put a strain upon mental equilibrium and physical resistance. Sedentary habits of students, intellectual workers, and business men likewise tend to result in an unfavorable condition of the organism. Industrial work and much of economic effort in general today is unsatisfying to the wants of man, and when motives are unsatisfied, irritability and an unfavorable mental condition are apt to result. The feeling of security which is one of the main bulwarks of mental health is often denied with recurring unemployment, seasonal and cyclical, the tendency of large corporations to relocate personnel in various branch cities, and ever-expanding technological advances in automation reducing the need for human hands.

Nervous disorders and disturbances of mentality are on the increase to an alarming degree. In the quarter of a century between the years of 1909 and 1934, there was a 100 per cent increase in the number of mentally ill cared for in hospitals and sanitariums. Today the mentally ill constitute about half of all patients in the hospitals of the United States and 50 to 60 per cent of all patients who consult doctors.

Menninger emphasizes the fact that play and recreation activities should occupy an important role not only in the treatment but also the prevention of mental illness.

[2] Address of the Park Commissioner, New York City, 1954.

For years they have used recreation in the treatment of the mentally ill. Hobbies, crafts, and occupational therapy proved extremely beneficial in restoring these men and women to health. Having found these methods helpful in treating the ill, psychiatrists feel confident that recreational activities—the *right* recreational activities—can play a large part in preventing mental illness, in maintaining good health, and in promoting a sense of well-being in all of us.[3]

The methods employed through play and recreation activities in the prevention and treatment of mental illness are discussed further in Chapter 12.

PUBLIC AWARENESS OF NEW RESPONSIBILITIES

There is a well-awakened consciousness on the part of the general public of the disrupting changes that have taken place, both environmentally and socially, in recent years. This awareness carries over to many community needs and accompanying responsibilities, among them those particularly concerned with health, safety, alleviations of congested space, assimilation of diverse population elements, and economic considerations. The societal developments that accompany this awareness are treated in the paragraphs which follow.

HEALTH NEEDS AND SERVICES. The schools have long offered exercise in the form of plays and games, athletics, gymnastics, and rhythmic activity. Too, they have often required a physical examination to determine whether or not the pupil is in good health. More recently the schools have regarded it as their function to teach proper health habits to the entire group under their supervision. The present point of view in respect to health education in the school is discussed in more detail in the next chapter.

Statistical studies of the results of the examinations in connection with the draft during the first World War, World War II, the Korean War, and the present Selective Service Act are often misleading. The specific population groups drafted, the techniques used for examination, and the basic

[3] William C. Menninger, *Enjoying Leisure Time* (Chicago: Science Research Associates, Inc., 1950), p. 4.

standards for rejection have differed and comparisons are rather difficult. It is estimated that in 1917, 33⅓ per cent of the males 17 to 31 years of age examined for military service were rejected; in 1940, of two million men examined, over 40 per cent were found unqualified for general military service. The examinations in World War II, however, were much more exacting regarding defects of the eyes, ears, and teeth, as well as those resulting from malnutrition. Chest examinations employed X-rays; and emotional instability was newly listed as a cause for rejection. Among the men rejected there was and still is widespread prevalence of poor posture and physical defects leading to poor body mechanics. Many of America's young men are simply not physically fit for rigorous activity and give evidence of the great need for a more vigorous health and physical education program in all grades of the schools.

The question of how many children in the United States are handicapped is difficult to determine. At one time the term "handicapped" referred mainly to those with orthopedic defects. Today there are included children who are handicapped by many other similar diseases or defects. One thing is sure—that the statistical estimates indicate clearly how formidable is the country's social burden in regard to rendering adequate services to such handicapped individuals. Many public and private schools are now providing special educational programs to help these handicapped children to adjust themselves to normal living. Significant progress has been made in special education for the blind, the hard-of-hearing, and those afflicted with cerebral palsy and other handicaps. Also, many camps and special municipal recreation programs are conducted for handicapped children.

Particular progress is being made with children having orthopedic defects. Exercise therapy is being instituted in the public schools in many communities. That play and recreation activities can be utilized to improve these conditions is becoming increasingly apparent as experimentation goes on. Various contests and games of kicking, running, reaching and stretching, and various rhythmic plays are being used for deformities by imaginative orthopedic leaders. These informal play activities, carefully alternated with specific therapeutic exercises, motivate the patient and bring joy and zest into the treatment and at the same time develop recreation skills the patient will practice in everyday life. Archery, bait casting, bowling, and other less strenuous activities are being prescribed for shoulders, spines, and chests which need attention. In general, play-motivated exercise helps develop the body in a normal way.

SAFETY EDUCATION. Modern city life has brought with it many hazards which jeopardize the safety of the individuals on every hand. With the speeding-up of methods of transportation, the unalert pedestrian is seldom safe on congested streets. The traffic toll is constantly mounting. Industry presents similar hazards. At the end of 1932, the average number of accidental deaths per year was set at 95,000 and although an all-time high of 101,513 accidental deaths was reported in 1941, the figure was 90,000 in 1954. The total of accidental deaths in 1957 was 95,000; of these 38,500 were caused by automobile accidents; in addition, the 9,600,000 injured and sustaining temporary total disability or permanent impairment must be considered. The total cost of all accidents to the nation in 1957 reached the staggering figure of almost twelve billion dollars. The spectre of accident hangs constantly over the heads of children and is a leading cause of their death. Death rates of children from one to fifteen years of age have been reduced substantially during the past ten years, yet 10,991 children of this age group were killed in accidents during 1957. Recent records also show that accidents claimed three times as many lives in the five-to-fourteen-year group as cancer, the second leading cause of death, and seven times as many as congenital malformations or pneumonia, the third and fourth leading causes.

The responsibility of the school and play leader in respect to safety goes beyond supplying of safe apparatus and adequate leadership in supervising play; it includes education in safety and the development of physical capacity to the fullest possible extent for all students. The efforts of all school grades from the kindergarten through high school, including all departments and all teachers, have been enlisted in the modern program of safety education. It is a correlated and cooperative program which reaches out beyond the school into the home and enlists the support of all community service agencies. The following principles indicate the scope of a modern school safety program.

1. The numerous dangers inherent in our modern way of life make safety education an essential part of the school curriculum.

2. A safety program should serve the general purposes of education—the development of individual potentialities and the promotion of democratic behavior.

3. All teachers, administrators, and other staff members should be responsible for safety education, which should permeate the entire school program, and their own attitudes and habits should exemplify the best safety practices.

4. By providing day-by-day experiences in safe living, the program should help the child develop desirable habits and attitudes that will serve him throughout life. It should teach him not only to live safely in his present environment but to meet emergencies as they occur and to solve the safety problems that arise with new situations.

5. Safety education should be positive rather than negative; it should foster wholesome reactions, not instill fear and develop timidity. The teacher must make sure, however, that the child does not confuse courage with foolhardiness.

6. Safety education should develop social awareness and social responsibility.

7. The program should stress the most pertinent problems of the group, but no one area of safety should receive undue emphasis at the expense of others.

8. Although the school should develop its own safety program, outside agencies should be encouraged to supplement it, and an attempt should be made to coordinate the

efforts of all who participate in educating the child for safe living—teachers, parents, and other interested members of the community.[4]

Statistics seem to indicate that the efforts in safety education which were started in 1924 have borne results. According to the 1955 reports of the National Safety Council, the death rate for children between the ages of 5-9 years declined 61 per cent, and the rate for children 10-14 years dropped 39 per cent; during 1955, however, the death rate for youth 15-19 years increased 14 per cent and the rate for those 20-24 years increased 31 per cent. As a result of this evidence an additional emphasis has come into the safety education movement, that of driver education for students of high school age. Driver education courses for both students and instructors are being aggressively promoted, with considerable subsidization by state departments of education, foundations and automobile agencies.

URBAN AND RURAL PLAY SPACE. Modern cities, with space congested in every possible way, have found the matter of play spaces a grave problem. Left to themselves, the children would have no place to play except in the streets and alleys, and the danger from automobiles practically excludes the former. Some cities have had to close certain streets to traffic at special hours that they might be used for children's play; and roofs of buildings have been used for playground purposes. Because of this condition artificial play spaces needed to be created—the modern playgrounds—and economy demands that these spaces be carefully allotted to the various sections of the city in order that all may benefit.

As will be pointed out in Chapter 16, the modern city is being more carefully designed according to a city master plan providing physical facilities. Playgrounds and open

---

[4] *Safety Education for Teachers: A Guide for College Safety Education* (Washington, D.C.: American Association of Teachers Colleges, The National Commission on Safety Education, National Education Association, 1947), Part II, pp. 66-7. For a curriculum in school safety, see Florio and Stafford, *Safety Education*, pp. 38-50.

places for recreation are being constructed in conjunction with parks, schools, and other facilities directly related to providing leisure-time services. At the same time, new subdivisions are being planned according to zoning patterns that prevent neighborhood deterioration and spreading of slums.

Even, however, under a well-developed master plan for recreation, the playground does not leave the child close to his doorstep, but for certain types of play takes him several blocks from home and away from the guidance of parents. This necessitates the provision of qualified play supervision; otherwise the playground will not be given the maximum amount of use, the larger children monopolizing the space to the exclusion of the smaller ones.

To conserve the use of these precious play areas and get the most use out of them, it has been necessary to invent space-economizing games, such as softball and volleyball, and also to have the children organized so that every possible bit of ground is utilized in some form of activity. Their physical activity must be organized and made attractive by play leaders with winning personalities. The playground must have magnetic force, and must be run on a self-governing principle, as the attendance is purely voluntary.

There is always much hue and cry about the need for play in the cities; but, when one mentions the rural community, the answer is nearly always that the country children have plenty of play space and also receive the healthful exercise of daily chores. While it is true that the conditions of the city make the need for play stand out more strikingly, there are also many sound reasons why the play center should have a prominent place in the rural locality.

Today, urban and rural life are much more alike than in previous years. Many people live in rural areas and commute to their work in large urban centers. Children now more often than not attend a consolidated school, a trend which is especially evident in the Midwest areas. In Illinois, for example, there were over twelve thousand school districts in the state in 1938; at the present time there are approximately sixteen hundred districts. The consolidated school has also become a community center and has brought new opportunities for learning and social life not only to children but to adults. With television, telephone, and modern household conveniences in the home, modern farm machinery reducing labor in the fields, specialized farming changing the work routine of the farmer, and the distance to urban areas reduced by automobile and airplane travel, rural life is greatly changed from that of twenty years ago.

With all of these changes, one still cannot overlook the recreation needs in certain rural areas. There are still areas where, as in former years, children have a place to play but have no one with whom to play, and the result is a lack of opportunity for a well-rounded social development. Also, the social institutions such as local 4-H clubs and agricultural organizations, the closeness to nature and the outdoors, and the social heritage of the past give the agricultural areas a distinct rural character.

As noted in Chapter 15, it is helpful to have the necessary legislation for people in rural areas to develop recreation areas and facilities through organized tax-supported county and similar recreation programs. Also, the Extension Division of the United States Department of Agriculture has provided many rural residents recreation services through its functions on the county and local basis. The 4-H clubs, Future Farmers of America, Parent-Teacher groups, the Grange, and many other organizations give a great deal of attention to the provision of recreation and leisure-time educational programs.

AMERICANIZATION. All forms of play are most useful in our country in Americanizing our great influx of aliens, both children and adults. Foreigners come to this country with different habits so deeply rooted that one finds traces of them even after they have been settled in the United States for several generations. It is not sufficient to teach them how to handle the English language; the appeal to the intellect alone often leaves them cold, unresponsive, shy. Play, instead, touches the emotions of these aliens and makes them a part of the social group, teammates in the common cause of happiness, good will, or victory, as the case may be, and breaks down the antipathies more quickly than can anything else.

Play affords a common meeting ground where people of any heritage can find an interest. The athletic teams in this country, whether school or professional, are made up of players of practically every national background. Even newcomers who have never played the way we do, readily take to our sports if at all encouraged. Social centers use play and recreation to attract the foreigner, and often by gaining his confidence find him quite willing to exhibit his native dances and games. This, in turn, enriches our American culture.

ECONOMIC ASPECTS OF RECREATION. Wherever man is more contented and interested in progress, there is a saving of energy and elimination of waste, and, hence, a better product. The betterment of social conditions is reflected immediately in an improvement of the economic.

To illustrate: when the delinquent boy is given a chance to accommodate his burst of energy in the activities of the playground he is also made an economic asset. This is true from two points of view: first, there is saved the cost of penalizing him for his delinquency, that of keeping truant officers and of paying upkeep for juvenile courts and of juvenile reform institutions; second, there is a new valuation that must be placed on him as he changes from the irresponsible gangster. True, it does cost money to run the playgrounds. It has been found, however, that the cost is very slight in comparison with the other alternatives.

The schools have found that the healthy child makes faster progress than the child who is subnormal in physique. Many of the pupils who fail in studies belong to the latter class, and this is especially true of the student who must repeat a full semester's work. In the sense that play makes a positive contribution to health, it must be counted as an economic factor in helping to reduce the enormous amount of money that is being spent on "repeaters."

Effect upon Industrial Output. The industries have come to consider play in the economic valuation of their workers for utilitarian as well as benevolent reasons. Wherever there are efficiency experts in factories it is found that they also advocate recreation programs for the workers. Early programs in industrial recreation were limited in scope. Since World War II, however, many corporations have changed to a direct approach in meeting the leisure-time needs of industrial workers.

The attitude of many large corporations has been somewhat different. They have attacked the problem of employee leisure head on. They have provided all sorts of sports facilities, music clubs, theater groups, and bowling leagues. IBM has its own golf courses for its employees. Bell and Howell has baseball fields lighted for night games. Ford's River Rouge plant has an indoor shooting range, tennis courts, baseball diamonds (nine of them) and horseshoe pits. Corning Glass has its own museum, visiting repertory theater, and changing exhibitions, in addition to automatic bowling alleys, basketball courts, and dancing classes.

Business is not sentimental about the new leisure. "Many of these off-the-job or after-hours activities," the head of employee relations for General Motors has said, "have not only a therapeutic value, but can actually sharpen or increase employees' skills." And the President of Bell and Howell has said, "Everyone in the organization gains from a well-planned recreational program."[5]

Short play recesses during the working day increase the efficiency of the workers. Inasmuch as play is conducive to good health, it is also advantageous from the standpoint of reducing the worker's days of sickness. Then, again, workers who are well contented do not job jump—one of the biggest savings to the corporation and possibly the biggest reason why it favors broad recreation programs. A big economic loss is involved in breaking in new workers: the output is temporarily less than normal, a trained instructor must spare valuable time, and wear and tear on expensive machinery is considerably greater when operated by a beginner. For these reasons industries, seeking cities in which

⁵ Russell Lynes, "Time On Our Hands," *Harper's Magazine*, CCXVII, 1928, (July, 1958), pp. 34-9.

to locate, invariably ask what recreational facilities the municipality is able to offer.

INCREASE IN COMMERCIAL VENTURES. The research student of recreation will be interested in another area that has economic significance. Sports have become big business in the United States. A vast amount of money is expended annually upon sporting equipment and facilities. The same is true of touring, travel, and camping. The money spent on movies and other forms of commercial recreation add to this picture, which, in its totality, means expenditures of billions of dollars. It becomes apparent, therefore, that recreation assumes the proportions of one of America's largest industries. Moreover, the tax income to the government from sporting events and other forms of entertainment totals many millions. These funds are available to the government, whether local, state, or national, as the case may be, for public use.

NEED FOR EDUCATION FOR LEISURE

The working day has been shortened from ten hours to eight hours, and, often, six; the working week was shortened from six days to five and one-half days and then to five days. The six-hour day and the five-day week in themselves mean leisure time to an extent we would never have believed possible a few years ago. But, if our leading social thinkers are to be believed, the end has not yet been reached. They are holding forth the prospect of still more spare time for the future and are maintaining that this will be necessary if the available work is to be evenly divided among the available workers.

Man, throughout history, has always prized leisure and has longed for it. Whenever he has tried to conceive of an ideal state of existence he has always dreamed of many free hours when he could follow the dictates of his pleasure. In Plato's *Republic*, in Sir Thomas More's *Utopia*, in George Bernard Shaw's *Back to Methuselah*, in H. G. Wells' *A Modern Utopia*, the happy and contented citizens are pictured as having many hours free from work and compulsory activities. It would seem that mankind, with leisure provided in such plenitude as never before, had at last found Utopia. But perversely, now that man has this leisure, he is not sure that he wants it—at least not in such abundance. The sad truth in the present situation is that people do not know what to do with their free time now that they have obtained it.

This is not the first time that people have had leisure at their disposal. The ancient Greeks had this possession. It was, however, the leisure of a privileged class and was made possible by the work of a downtrodden slave class. Rome also had leisure for a select group of citizens at the expense of slaves and of spoils from its many provinces. Today, however, machinery has replaced the slavery of previous ages and has placed free time at the disposal of all men instead of a privileged few. This, while democratic, makes the problem a stupendous one.

USE OF LEISURE. In general there are two ways to use leisure. The one is the way of Greece in its Golden Age. Freedom from want and liberty of time were used to produce a great culture of art, literature, and philosophy that remains as a heritage to all time. Some writers of today predict that America will use its newly-born leisure in the same way to raise the level of refinement, happiness, and culture of its people. Most writers however are not so optimistic and instead see a menace confronting us. To them, America is headed in the opposite direction—namely, the way of Rome in its decline. Then leisure meant idleness, doles, free entertainments, license, and corruption. Such a prospect is, to say the least, a pessimistic one. It is nevertheless a possibility as the titles of current articles and books on the subject would indicate.

It is not difficult to see why the men and women and even children of today are bewildered by the leisure which has been thrust upon them so unexpectedly. To the worker of the old ten-hour day and six-day week, recreation simply meant rest for a tired body and weary spirit. When, later, he found himself with two extra hours a day upon his hands and an extra half day to boot, he found the answer in new devices which were fostered to entertain him—movies, automobiles, radios, professional sports, and others with which we are all familiar. He had no resources within himself for the art of self-entertainment and for a while had need of none, for commercial recreations were offered him and with prosperous times he had the means to pay for them. But he may have reduced resources to pay for this recreation and may have found that there is a limit to the satisfaction offered by strictly passive amusement. More often, he wishes to *do* for himself—to achieve in reality and not vicariously. Man is skill-hungry by nature and it is much better to educate men in skills for self-active leisure hours than to attempt to amuse them in their leisure.

In seeking a solution it is assumed that there is promise in leisure—that leisure offers a hope and not a threat. In taking this stand there is no attempt to try to prophesy. It is not known which way leisure is going to take us—whether to new heights of happiness and attainment or to the road that spells ruin for ourselves and our civilization. The answer lies in the years ahead but the responsibility lies in the course that society chooses to take today. Society can utilize education—education for leisure. Communities can add to their schools a fourth R—namely Recreation.

One cannot escape being pessimistic about the possibilities of the uses of leisure by the present generation of older people. With leisure thrust upon them so suddenly and so generously, it is only to be expected that they would not know how best to use their spare time nor does the generation just growing into manhood and womanhood, for the reason that the schools have also failed to prepare them. But, for the youngsters still with many years of schooling ahead of them, there will be no excuse for permitting them to face life similarly unequipped to use their free hours happily and profitably.

Despite this unpreparedness, the period of pessimism in leisure need not necessarily be prolonged. It is possible for adults to acquire an interest in physical, educational, and cultural hobbies, although it must be admitted that with age there is more inertia to overcome. Nevertheless these interests are possible to the adult and for this reason it has become a vital necessity that adult education for leisure hours be provided.

SCHOOL RECREATION PROGRAM. The greatest hope, however, lies in the education of children. Just where does the school stand in regard to education for leisure? Before the present century it ignored it. Then, largely at the students' insistence, it recognized such extracurricular activities as athletics, orchestras, dramatic and debating clubs. At first the main emphasis was centered on keeping the children busy for the moment according to the interests that appealed at the particular time. But this in itself was not enough. Many a football and baseball player graduated from school and, after the zest of competition was over, rather envied a less athletic individual who knew how to play tennis, who enjoyed hiking, or who could dive and swim. In similar fashion, the boy who tooted loudly on the bass horn in the school band wished afterwards that he had also learned to strum a ukulele or to sing. In short, the team or group activities, valuable as they were for the immediate period, provided little opportunity for participation after school days were over.

The schools have now come to realize this shortcoming, and recent years have witnessed an additional emphasis in the school recreational program. Today, the student finds encouragement and opportunity to swim, to play tennis, volleyball, golf, handball, and other games that he can use in middle age as well as in youth. Reading and literature as attributes to a rich recreational life are being stressed with particular emphasis on the enjoyment and appreciation that come from being taken into the inner dwelling of the world's greatest minds, rather than from the standpoint of the mechanical details of grammar and punctuation. Dramatics, music, and art also have untold possibilities of recreational value and are therefore being taught from that angle. And so on through the handicrafts which will form foundations for hobbies for those skilled with their hands; and so on to student clubs, which will be a training for those who enjoy the arts of sociability and conversation. In general, the school is tending to place less emphasis upon rapidly outdated subject information and more upon life craft. The old method of homework is being supplanted by challenging hobbies.

With the inclusion of recreation into the school curriculum, education indeed becomes a life-long process. There is no reason why education should cease with formal schooling. It should, to the contrary, persist informally and unceasingly as long as hobbies can give new meaning to the physical, intellectual, aesthetic, inventive, and social arts.

YOUTH ORGANIZATIONS AND SUMMER CAMPS. The recreational-educational organizations for youth are making a distinct contribution to the education for leisure. Their many varied activities develop interests which will mean enduring hobbies and which will lead to a richer and fuller life.

The summer camp looks upon its function in education largely as a preparation for leisure. Its skills are not those for the earning of a living but for the enjoyment of life. Those who learn to love nature and find enjoyment in the woods, and those who know woodcraft and canoeing have a world open to them throughout life that others do not have. So also with respect to horseback riding, sailboating, dancing, handicraft, artscraft, and countless other activities which camps embody in their programs.

When one takes a long view of life, it is probably true that the most enduring form of play is that which grows out of the imagination. Anything which develops the scope of the imagination is preparation for leisure hours. To the extent that the summer camp capitalizes upon its opportunities and conducts a varied challenging program rich with compelling and imaginative activities, it is making an educational contribution of first magnitude.

SUMMARY

From the past with its asceticism exalting the mind at the expense of the body, with its scholasticism emphasizing the intellect, and with its Puritanism worshipping other-worldliness, there has been a swing of the pendulum back toward the physical, and particularly, in play. For the changes in the manner of living since the Industrial Revolution have resulted in conditions which in many ways are not as conducive to health and development as the outdoor life. This has resulted in an increasing awarness of the necessity of developing a leisure-time program of healthful and muscle-building activity. The modern play and recreation movement is, therefore, regarded as providing physical activity which develops and conserves neuromuscular and organic power, which aids in mental health and in programs for the handicapped, and which is closely associated with the modern programs of school health and safety education.

There is also the need of satisfying human interests. From the standpoint of interests, motives, desires, and satisfactions, modern man has been likened to a caveman living in a crowded city. It is a far cry from the running, striking, throwing, hunting, and fighting life for which nature has fitted man, from the adventuresome life to which he is predisposed, to the endlessly monotonous movements of modern life. Those attending the tools of industry merely exist while working; restlessness results and is obvious on every hand. Laborers are not usually aware of the source of their irritation, but they are vaguely conscious that somehow life is unsatisfying. They may leave one factory and go to the next; they may strike for shorter hours and higher wages. But these changes when they occur give only momentary respites from the working treadmill which nullifies their hopes. School children in many industrial areas are faced with very much the same situation. They may find school life uninviting and look forward to the time when they can escape school and enter industry only to find industry defeating to their life purposes.

Closely associated with physical and emotional health and with the satisfaction of normal self-expression and achievement is the value inherent in wholesome play as a preventive of delinquency and crime. The prevention of the harmful types of play and recreation by the substitution of compelling, fascinating, socially approved activity is conspicuous among the objectives of the recreation movement. The increasing amount of leisure-time accentuates the magnitude of this particular problem and the need for education for the use of leisure time.

Education for the healthful, enjoyable, constructive, and creative use of leisure has become one of the most pressing social problems of today. The programs of education for leisure, when summed up, are proceeding along three lines: first, the provision of facilities and full opportunities to those now in need of wholesome recreation; second, the refinement of recreation interests already formed through such media as adult education and improved standards for the theater, sports, reading, radio, television, arts and crafts, and hobbies of many types; third, a conscious, constructive attitude toward recreation so that the children now growing up may be interested in and provided with the types of recreation that will be useful to them throughout life.

Summing up the economic aspects of the recreation movement to society, these points stand out: decreased juvenile delinquency, fewer institutions to provide for this problem, decreased shiftlessness, poverty, crime; and, from the positive point of view, increased employment, industrial output, and support for the institutions of social improvement and progress. The economic value to the nation as a whole is shown by the cumulative benefits to the separate communities.

Lastly, in brief, there are these further needs which play and recreation help to serve. There is, for example, the need to provide play space in congested cities, planning these in advance as much as possible while costs are still not prohibitive, and also the need for obtaining the maximum use of these areas through experienced direction. The rural recreation needs also demand attention and many social-educational-recreational groups have grown up to meet this situation. In assimilating aliens, too, the play and recreation movement has made, and is still making, a most important contribution. In recreation there is a common level of understanding, of interests; there is an intermingling of foreign cultures with the native American, and there is universal recognition of performance and talent on the basis of merit. A modern leisure-time program thereby enriches everyday living for all groups of America's vast heterogeneous population.

SELECTED REFERENCES

CHAPMAN, FREDERICK M. *Recreation Activities for the Handicapped.* New York: The Ronald Press Co., 1960. This is a thorough description of types of recreation activities which may be utilized in a hospital setting or in recreation for the handicapped. Included also are suggestions regarding the use of recreation activities with different types of patients, and how recreation activities may be integrated into the total treatment program.

DIEHL, HAROLD S., and THOMSON, STEWARD C. *Textbook of Healthful Living.* New York: McGraw-Hill Book Co., Inc., 1960. Chapters 4 and 11, as well as various other sections of this text, explain clearly the value and importance of play and recreation in maintaining basic physical fitness and sound mental health.

NASH, JAY B. *Philosophy of Recreation and Leisure.* St. Louis: The C. V. Mosby Co., 1953. The importance of education for leisure and the need for recreation in modern life are explained. See especially Chapter 15.

FLORIO, AURELIO E., and STAFFORD, GEORGE T. *Safety Education.* New York: McGraw-Hill Book Co., Inc., 1956, Chap. 14.

GLUECK, SHELDON, and GLUECK, ELEANOR. *Delinquents in the Making.* New York: Harper & Bros., 1952.

————. *Unraveling Juvenile Delinquency.* New York: The Commonwealth Fund, 1950, 284–89.

HUNT, VALERIE V. *Recreation for the Handicapped.* Englewood Cliffs, N. J.: Prentice-Hall, Inc., 1955.

JONES, ANNA M. *Leisure Time Education.* New York: Harper & Bros., 1946.

LANDER, B. *Toward Understanding of Juvenile Delinquency: A Study of 8,464 Cases of Juvenile Delinquency in Baltimore.* New York: Columbia University Press, 1954.

LARABEE, ERIC, and MEYERSOHN, ROLF (eds.). *Mass Leisure.* Glencoe, Ill.: The Free Press, 1958.

LESSER, ARTHUR, and HUNT, ELEANOR. "The Nation's Handicapped Children," *American Journal of Public Health*, XLIV (February, 1954), 166.

MENNINGER, WILLIAM C. *Enjoying Leisure Time*. Chicago: Science Research Association, Inc., 1950.

National Recreation Association. *A Positive Force For Juvenile Decency*. New York: National Recreation Association (June, 1954), 1–8.

————. *Recreation: A Guide to Books on Recreation*. New York: National Recreation Association, 1958–59. Published annually.

National Safety Council. *Accident Facts*. Chicago: National Safety Council, 1958.

SOULE, GEORGE. *Time For Living*. New York: The Viking Press, Inc., 1955.

FILM.

Town and Country. (20 min.). 16 mm. Sound. Color. Athletic Institute, Merchandise Mart, Room 805, Chicago, Ill.

11

Physical Benefits
of Play and Recreation

Good health is the physical condition that man has always desired and for which they pray. Such a condition implies completeness and soundness of body, and this means the absence of disease and infection, and the normal functioning of every organ.

William James is the source of the phrase, "Simply to live and breathe should be a delight." The individual with an abundance of vigorous health has a decided advantage in everyday life. With sound health there is resistance against disease, abundant energy for a strenuous life, and reserve force to meet emergencies when they arise.

In a recent survey, there was virtually unanimous sentiment among medical and health officers regarding the basic value of exercise for both preventive and therapeutic purposes. At the same time in order to attain maximum value from exercise, it must be keyed to age, sex, physical condition, and individual reactions to activity; the periodic medical examination is considered to be an integral part of any exercise program.

Health implies more than absence of disease. It indicates adequate organic condition as well as wholesome interests, habits, and attitudes which enable one to maintain sound emotional balance and to function effectively and live happily. Health should mean strength and stamina to carry on one's work, family and community responsibilities, and one's recreations with a maximum of joy and efficiency and a minimum of fatigue.

The maintenance of good health has commanded more attention from the nation and each separate community and family in recent years. Great educational compaigns have been undertaken to instruct everyone in personal and public hygiene. Emphasis has been laid on the preventive side, that is, to build up the body, to increase its vital resistance, and to establish wholesome conditions of environment. The schools have been increasing the time for physical education training, introducing new types of activities, examining the pupils to discover defects that might lead to serious complications later, prescribing remedial measures in cases where improvement is possible, and educating the entire student body in the principles of healthful living. Today, all communities have their public health departments which are on the watch for epidemics, on the alert to isolate any case of contagious disease as soon as discovered and to locate and stamp out the source. This source may be in the water, milk, or food supply; it may be from impure air; or it may be from crowded housing conditions. The basic health of the community is looked upon as an economic problem, just as industry is interested financially in the working power of each individual citizen.

Every effort must be made to conserve human life. This point is a fundamental principle in the philosophy of the people of the free world. That the efforts of the health movement to conserve it have borne fruitful and far-reaching results can be proven with a wealth of statistics. In the eighteenth century the expectation of life in England and America was between thirty-five and forty years. Owing to the battle against disease and the health education movement, the total population of the United States has doubled during the first half of the twentieth century and the number of persons over sixty-five has quadrupled. The increase in life expectancy at birth has risen from 49 years in 1900 to over 70 years at the present time. The five diseases which were the great killers in the past century— tuberculosis, diphtheria, typhoid fever, infant diarrhea, and pneumonia—are minor medical problems today. Deaths from pneumonia and tuberculosis combined have declined about 90 per cent in the past twenty years. The major killers today are heart disease, cancer, and kidney disease. Among persons under twenty-four years of age, cancer is rated the major cause of death from disease; among those over twenty-four, heart disease is the number one killer with over a million deaths a year, and cancer is the second greatest cause of death. Nervous disorders are also on the increase and cause many physical and emotional disorders. These statistics have relevance to the material that follows in this chapter.

The recreation movement with its advocacy of the inherent need of childhood to play, its education of children in health, its emphasis upon activity for all, and its fascinating, compelling program which constantly beckons adults away from the sedentary life and nervous strain of work, is doing much to advance the cause of health. At various times during the growth of the movement different emphasis was put upon how people might best obtain the physical exercise required to maintain maximum health. These ideas and relationships about physical exercise and play are now reviewed briefly.

PLAY AND OTHER KINDS OF EXERCISE

There have always been arguments concerning the relative values of different types of exercise, such as play and sports, manual labor, military drill, and gymnastics, each at various times favored most. In the paragraphs that follow these values will be evaluated in the light of today's needs.

PLAY AND MANUAL LABOR. In pioneer days children were taught to do useful things about the home and to help in caring for the domestic animals. Labor of this kind occupied much of their time and gave them a certain amount of physical exercise. As has been pointed out in a former chapter, there is no opportunity in modern life, and especially in town and city life, for any such occupations for children; besides, it is doubtful if any kind of labor that a child might have can do nearly as much for him as his spontaneous play.

Labor is usually simple and monotonous, instead of being varied and progressive. The work required of the child in school puts a strain on his powers of attention and other activities of his nervous system; a strain so great that it must be offset by play after school hours, rather than by still more work. If labor under a task master were the best exercise for physical development, slaves and convicts would be the best physical specimens in the world; instead we go to competitive sports to see the finest physiques.

PLAY AND MILITARY DRILL. During war, and immediately following, there is a wave of enthusiasm over military training as the best means of improving the physique of boys and young men. This form of exercise has several points in its favor. The work is usually done out-of-doors; it tends to induce erect posture; it is not so severe as some competitive sports; groups can be taught routines that make an impressive appearance in public: the result is that men who spend a few weeks in training in the army camps show a wonderful improvement in physical condition. The improvement is owing largely to a complete change in the manner of living. The men have plenty of good food, several hours of vigorous exercise in the open air every day, outdoor sleep and plenty of it, the best of medical service, and good opportunity for competitive sports.

To substitute military training for physical education in a school situation, however, is another matter. The advantages of complete military control are not present in the school situation. Students receive only a limited amount of exercise in their military drill and the program is not inclusive enough to meet total fitness needs of growing boys. Military training has as its objective the training of men and women for duties associated with war; and, with the present emphasis on mechanized and atomic war, the program tends to be more of a technical training than a physical training, so that military training must be supplemented with fitness and conditioning activities specifically designed to prepare individuals to meet the exigencies of war conditions.

PLAY AND GYMNASTICS. Gymnastics has different meanings in different parts of the world. A. D. Munrow, an English writer, defines gymnastics as artificial and systematized forms of exercise designed to produce particular effects on the body. In the elaboration of his definition, Munrow includes most of the Swedish gymnastics and some of the basic technique practices for modern dance. In the United States, to some gymnastics means exercise in which every move is performed more or less under the direction of an instructor; to others it is a combination of exercises which are predominantly formal in nature, involving calisthenics and similar exercises.

The controversy of gymnastics versus recreation and sports activities has been argued for many generations. It is claimed for gymnastics that the pupils get exactly the training they need, for the reason that the work is planned and conducted with an eye to the best interests of the class; also that the training is scientific, exact, and that lessons are designed with great care while play is apt to become one-sided, subject to individual whim, and wasteful of time. Those who favor only games and sports in the physical education program are equally vociferous. They contend that systematic gymnastic exercises violate the normal inclinations of the individual toward natural movement, and that few pupils like these activities as a steady program or participate in them for the joy of doing them.

The time has come to realize that both gymnastics as well as play, games, and sports have a place in modern physical education and recreation. Gymnastic activities are invaluable in the practice of modern exercise therapy; also, special types of exercise are often necessary to prepare for military service, where mass exercises are necessary, or for the physical requirements necessary in certain types of work. Many adults are participating in calisthenics. Often this is the most convenient type of exercise for them because of the lack of space and facilities. Then, too, they have learned calisthenic and gymnastic exercises from instructors who were careful to combine these activities with rhythmic activities and games. On the other hand, it is obvious that games and sports activities should not be entirely abandoned in favor of a restricted gymnastics program. The fundamental need in physical education is to instill a life-long interest in physical activities through a well-rounded program. Gymnastics and games and sports are complementary—each is a part of a scientific, well-planned physical education and recreation program.

PLAY AND PHYSICAL EDUCATION

From the standpoint of growth and development, the play and recreation movement is closely allied to physical education. Physical education, a phase of total education, helps prepare all children and youth to be responsible, productive citizens in society. Since physical education is interested in the development of the whole man, it is not unappreciative of its opportunities for the development of mental health and social education. Its primary concern, however, is big-muscle activity which stimulates organic health and muscular development. Objectives for physical education have been formulated throughout the years to meet the changing needs of society. Those recommended by an important national joint committee follow:

1. To develop and maintain maximum physical efficiency

A physically efficient person enjoys sound functioning of the bodily processes, is free of remediable defects, and possesses such qualities as strength, endurance, quick reaction, speed, a sense of balance, agility, good posture and efficient body mechanics. He employs these qualities according to his age and physical condition, maintaining a balance of activity, rest, work, and recreation. A person who has defects that cannot be corrected learns to adjust and compensate for his infirmities and develops his capabilities in order to live a happy, useful life.

2. To develop useful physical skills

A skillful person is proficient in many fundamental skills, such as walking, dodging, gauging moving objects, and lifting, which are

essential to living safely and successfully. He has abilities in a variety
of activities, such as, swimming, other individual and team sports,
and dancing, which contribute to physical and social efficiency at
each stage of life. Young people, particularly, find status and a sense
of belonging with their contemporaries when they are skillful in physical activities that are valued by the group.

3. To act in socially useful ways

A socially mature person works for the common good, respects the
personalities of his fellows and acts in a sportsmanlike manner. He
manages his emotions satisfactorily even in intense situations; he is
courageous and resourceful. He finds socially acceptable outlets for
feelings and aggressions which sometimes build up under the pressures of living. Games, sports, and other physical education activities that are often stimulating and emotionally charged, help the
individual develop social maturity. Understanding and capable leadership is essential in making the most of these opportunities. A
socially adequate person enjoys, contributes to, and is at ease in a
variety of wholesome social situations. Coeducational sports, dancing, swimming and similar activities provide learning experiences that
help the individual develop these social qualities.

4. To enjoy wholesome physical recreation

A person who has acquired a fund of recreational interests, knowledge, appreciation, and skills will include, in daily living, activities
that are creative, relaxing, or stimulating.[1]

PLAY AND HEALTH

Play is one of the chief contributing agents to the attainment of effective health. Heredity has a very important
role in the development of the individual; a balanced diet,
opportunities for engaging in activities in fresh air and
sunlight in safe, pleasant surroundings, and adequate rest
are necessary. Preventive hygiene must be practiced to
ward off disease and remove defects. Basically, however,
growth is enhanced by exercise and movement of the body
—it is activity which stimulates the organism and creates a
favorable condition for its development. In the remainder

[1] Joint Committee Report, *Physical Education—An Interpretation* (Washington, D.C.: Society of State Directors of Health, Physical Education, and
Recreation, and the American Association for Health, Physical Education,
and Recreation, 1952), pp. 3-4.

of this chapter, the values associated with physical play and sports will be discussed in more detail.

PLAY AND ORGANIC HEALTH. One of the chief reasons why the spontaneous plays of childhood and the games and sports of youth are effective for developing physical condition is that they involve chiefly those fundamental movements of the body that are natural and performed easily. They are progressive, and the child uses his natural capacities as they appear in growth, building them up into complex acts such as walking, running, jumping, throwing and climbing, just as quickly as the growth of the organism prepares the way. Opportunities must be made available for children at the various age levels to participate in a wide variety of plays, games, and sports activities. And it is logical that gymnastic activities, carefully chosen for the development of the child at various age levels, form a supplementary part of a well-balanced program of physical education.

Big-muscle activity stimulates growth, and consequently play is an absolute essential to the growing child. While the development of the muscles in general is a condition favorable to health, the development of the muscles of the trunk is of particular importance. The abdominal muscles must be well developed and in good condition for the maintenance of upright posture and for holding the internal organs in their proper place.

Physical exercise is commonly thought of as contributing primarily to the development of the muscles, but a still more significant complementary contribution, however, is to the development and general health of the organs of the body. Exercise is the best known means for such development.

A convincing indication in this direction is to be found in the Report of the Joint Committee on Health Problems in Education of the National Education Association and the American Medical Association of 1924. Although revised and elaborated upon in the Joint Reports of 1941 and 1948, the content of the following list of items remains essentially the same.

1. Circulation is increased throughout the entire body or through the part exercised. This circulatory activity increases carriage of food to the tissues, removal of wastes, distribution of the endocrine secretions, and equalization of the water and heat content of the body.

2. Big-muscle activity increases the demand for oxygen, and thus causes an increased respiratory activity, with the resulting increase in the rate of oxygenation of the blood, increased rate of elimination of the carbon dioxide, and increased oxygen supply to the tissues. This increased respiratory activity is the result of the demands made by the exercise; and deep breathing without the bodily exercise will not have the same results. During increased activity the respiratory apparatus naturally responds by frequent and deep respirations.

3. Exercise stimulates the excretory system and increases the elimination of waste through kidneys, lungs, intestines, and skin.

4. Digestion is improved and assimilation is accelerated by exercise. Digestion is not only a chemical but a muscular process. If the musculature of the alimentary canal is flaccid, digestion is retarded and impeded. Peristaltic movements are more vigorous when the muscle tone of the alimentary canal is good. Exercise is essential in keeping the muscles in good condition. The constipation resulting from sedentary life is in large part due to inadequate muscular activity.

5. Big-muscle activity stimulates growth and for the growing child is absolutely essential.

6. The heart is strengthened by the exercise of the skeletal muscles of the body. The best known way in which some types of weak heart can be made strong is by gradual and increasing amount of physical work of the skeletal muscles. Exercise for the person with a weak heart should be arranged by skilled specialists; it should not be prescribed by any untrained person.

7. The muscles of the body are directly developed by physical activity. This is of great importance for health as re-

gards the muscles of the trunk; the abdominal muscles must be in good condition for the maintenance of the upright posture which is necessary for the best position and functioning of the abdominal and pelvic organs.

8. Rational exercise results in increased neural activity, and in neuromuscular control, which develops skill, accuracy, endurance, agility and strength.[2]

It is evident that exercise has a beneficial affect on (1) the heart and circulatory system, (2) the respiratory system, (3) the digestive system, (4) the excretory system, and (5) the nervous system. There is constant interaction between all these systems in exercise stress; also, research indicates that the effects of exercise are directly related to the type and amount of activity as well as the vigor with which the individual participates. Informal play, engaged in at irregular intervals and causing limited stress on the organism, will have only a limited effect upon improving organic condition. The amount of exercise required to produce a healthy organic condition is being constantly studied and the results as obtained are made available to recreation leaders and physical educators.

Heart and Circulatory System. Muscular power and cardiac muscle power are developed jointly by exercise. Stroke volume, a measure of cardiac efficiency and power, increases with training. The size of the heart is directly related to the general development of the muscles of the body and is somewhat affected by the type and amount of physical activity engaged in. The efficiency of the heart is increased by physical exercise. The heart of the trained person pumps a greater volume per minute, empties itself more completely, and has greater output per beat than that of the untrained person. The pulse rate of the trained person is also slower during exertion than that of non-active

[2] Thomas D. Wood, *Health Education.* A Report of the Joint Committee on Health Problems in Education of the National Education Association and the American Medical Association. Chicago National Education Association and the American Medical Association, 1924 (rev. 1941 and 1948).

individuals; it also returns to normal much more quickly and is slower during periods of rest.

Numerous studies of pulse rate among trained athletes and men not in condition show that a lower pulse rate is associated with the former. Exercises such as weight lifting do not develop the heart muscles and lower the pulse rate to the same extent as sports which demand sustained running and endurance.

Exercise stimulates in general the circulatory system. When muscles are active certain chemical changes take place: the muscle fuel is expended and must be restored or replaced by glucose brought by the blood stream. In vigorous exercise lactic acid is created and must be reduced by oxidation or removed through the excretory organs. Both of these responses are vitally dependent upon blood flow. In strenuous exertion such as running, the tissues are crying for oxygen and the heart works frantically to supply it. In stimulating the circulatory system, exercise is instrumental in causing the oxygen and nutriment to be carried to the tissues of the system, the lactic acid, carbon dioxide, and other wastes to be removed, and the endocrine secretions in long sustained efforts to be transported to organs where they are needed.

The best known way in which some types of physiologically inefficient hearts can be strengthened is by gradually increasing the amount of physical exercise the individual takes. The person with a weak heart of such a type that it can be strengthened in this way must increase the amount of exercise slowly, however, and should be under the constant supervision of a skilled specialist. Exercise of the strenuous and gruelling type must be carefully regulated during the periods of most rapid growth. Following sickness it is also exceedingly important that exercise be increased gradually.

Respiratory System. Exercise increases the demand for oxygen which in turn is also the reason for increased circulation and heart rate. The increase in the oxygen during exercise is a quantitative change and a measure of capacity.

The qualitative change during rest (lowered heart rate, larger stroke volume) indicating greater oxygen difference between the arteries and veins is one measure of efficiency. This is a vital aspect of the biological man, and the effect of exercise upon these relationships is of greatest importance.

The increased rapidity and depth of breathing during exercise is the result of the condition of the organism created by the exercise, the respiratory mechanism responding with deep respirations to meet the demands. Deep breathing while not exercising will not produce the same changes as natural breathing during exercise.

It is in the period of youth that exercise makes its greatest contribution to the development of the respiratory system. Exercise in adulthood, however, maintains the breathing mechanism in good condition and increases ventilation. A large, well-developed chest often leads to the supposition that the respiratory system is efficient, but this is not necessarily the case. A person with a well-developed chest may have poor mobility and pulmonary ventilation. Proper exercise, regularly taken, is the best known means for the efficient development of the respiratory system.

Digestive System. Mild exercise is thought to materially aid the normal functioning of the digestive system through increased circulation of blood in the alimentary canal and the increase of digestive juices. In addition, mild exercise also increases peristaltic action, but it is clear that moderate to severe exercises temporarily inhibit both the flow of gastric juice and peristaltic action. Good muscular tone is essential to vigorous and efficient peristalsis and aids the mechanical factors of digestion.

Excretory System. Efficient elimination is a factor of primary importance in the attainment of good health and the capacity for continuous and efficient work. Lack of energy and ambition, general sluggishness, headaches, and muscular aches may result from poor elimination from the intestines, kidneys, and lungs. Regular vigorous exercise is beneficial to intestinal elimination through the general circulatory response to exercise with the added response of muscle tone development. Exercise involves muscular massage of the visceral area which is a stimulus to the entire organic system—respiration, circulation, kidneys, sweat glands, water components of the body, and endocrine glands, all of which serve to maintain good elimination processes.

The functioning of the kidneys is temporarily stopped the moment a person begins strenuous exercise, and they secrete very little during the period of extreme activity owing to the fact that the surplus water in the body is needed for perspiration. After exercise perfectly normal and healthy kidneys frequently throw off albumen and an excessive amount of acid. This condition is not to be considered alarming but rather as the normal reaction after strenuous play. In common with all internal organs the kidneys are toned up and invigorated by regular exercise.

Nervous System. Just as the various organs and muscles of the body are stimulated by exercise, so the nervous system is directly stimulated by the biological and chemical reactions that occur. Important as these biological and related effects are, the neural changes brought about by physical play and exercise are also of significant importance. The changes are evident in (1) the area of motor reflexes or reaction and the release and satisfaction gained through the development and performance of neuromuscular skill; (2) the improvement of emotional tone—stimulation of the body to actions as opposed to lack of action or inertia; and (3) the psycho-intellectual benefits of play as the result of heightened sensory perception and its general effect on the higher centers of the nervous system. Menninger and others have referred to the value of physical activities as one way of releasing emotional energy and securing much-needed recognition or compensation for lack of adjustment in other areas of life. The mental and emotional releases found in physical play, both immediate and projected, are receiving increasing attention and are referred to more fully in other chapters.

Individual Consideration. Regardless of age or sex, moderate and regular physical exercise is decidedly beneficial and necessary to good health which every normal person so much desires. It benefits directly or indirectly all organs of the body, tones up the organism in general, and makes possible strenuous and efficient effort in the pursuit of one's life aims. Care should be taken, however, in selecting the proper exercise. Individual differences in the capacity for exercise vary tremendously, and the normal beneficial results of exercise may be destroyed by activity which is too strenuous or not suitable for the individual. Older people often make the mistake of endeavoring to continue the sports of their younger days or of attempting to compete in activities in which they are not conditioned to participate. Outdoor exercise in contact with sunshine and fresh air is much to be preferred to indoor activities from the standpoint of general health.

PLAY AND RELAXATION. A study of the mounting increase of nervous diseases will reveal at the same time the inability to relax. Rest and relaxation should be planned at times to balance the demands that activity has made upon the muscular and nervous systems. There are alternating periods of effort and rest in play and there is rhythm in exercise itself which is restful. It is also true that play activities help to relieve mental strain by change of occupation and attention.

A knowledge of many leisure-time activities, while helpful, does not necessarily mean that the individual will be able to relax—he needs special education along this line. Unfortunately, the recreation leader of today is not prepared to instruct the adult of tomorrow how to overcome unnecessary tension, when to be quiescent, how to recover quickest from muscular fatigue, or, in particular, how best to overcome chronic nervous fatigue and the pessimism which invariably accompanies it. The need now is for research and investigation in this neglected field. An understanding of relaxation and its applications should be included in teacher-education preparation and become a part of each individual's equipment in health knowledge.

PLAY AND GRACE OF MOVEMENT. Play is natural, free, and balanced exercise. It develops grace of movement. Grace is art, wherever found. The ball player exemplifies high art when he catches and throws a ball, every movement expressing grace and conservation of effort. The master musician makes himself a part of a great melody, just as the great actor holds us spellbound with his portrayal of a character. In the same way the slouching cowboy may make us wonder at his horsemanship or the untrained street urchin delight us with the dancing of a jig. Grace is essentially dependent on mastery of an art to the point where details do not demand attention and to the point where there is absolute confidence in one's ability; qualities exhibited when both the acrobat balances on a wire, and the gracious hostess receives her guests.

Since grace can be acquired, there is another reason why every child should play. The timid child, looking on while others dance, may at first be awkward when persuaded to join in the play, but with mastery over the elements of the dance the self-consciousness fades away and he is soon absorbed in the spontaneous fun of the group. Play movements must be practiced in childhood or a graceful command of them will be difficult to attain. The asset of grace contributes to mental hygiene by the assurance and self-confidence it instills in the individual.

NEW EMPHASIS ON PHYSICAL FITNESS

Much experimental work has been done within the past several years regarding physical fitness. Universities, the Armed Forces, and other groups have established physical fitness laboratories employing physical educators, physiologists, medical doctors, and other specialized personnel to study the effects of exercise. As a result, many concepts of exercise have been changed and new knowledges about play and exercise and its effects upon the body are being discovered.

Physical fitness has been defined in different ways. Karpovich points out the difficulty of defining physical fitness:

> Strictly speaking, physical fitness means that a person possessing it meets certain physical requirements. These requirements may be anatomical (structural), physiological (functional), or both. Anatomical fitness may require a person to be able to withstand certain temperatures or altitudes or able to perform specific physical tasks involving muscular effort. A person may be perfectly fit to meet some of these requirements and yet be unfit for others. A person physically fit in all respects does not exist. A grown-up person who is fit to be a jockey will never become a champion heavy weight lifter.[3]

It is generally agreed, however, that a person is fit for a particular kind of activity when he can accomplish it with reasonable efficiency, without undue fatigue, and with rapid recovery from the effects of the exertion. It is also agreed that there is continuous gradation from the most fit individual at one extreme to the least fit at the other extreme, and that most types of stress require varying degrees of anatomical, physiological, and psychological fitness.

DEVELOPMENTS IN OBJECTIVE TESTING. Current thinking and research in physical education have resulted in the classification of the basic elements of physical fitness, and specific tests have been designed to measure these elements to determine the degree of a person's fitness at a given time under specific conditions. These measures of fitness are called physical fitness tests. Some tests can measure quantitatively the differences between the fit and unfit. Certain fundamental physiological adaptations common to fitness for all kinds of exertion can be distinguished from the particular skill essential for the successful performance of different physical activities. T. K. Cureton in *Physical Fitness Appraisal and Guidance* indicates that there are

---

[3] P. V. Karpovich, *Physiology of Muscular Activity* (Philadelphia: W. B. Saunders Co., 1959), p. 262.

three approaches for objective testing of physical fitness, apart from diagnosis of disease. These are appraisal of physique, organic capacity, and motor fitness.

Physique, or appearance, is characterized by healthy and robust appearance; apparent muscular development; good posture displaying ease, alertness and poise; good proportions of bone, muscle, and fat; normal bones, joints, and muscles; and good size for age and sex. Organic capacity, or organic health, is affected by the conditions of the systems: heart and circulatory, respiratory, digestive, excretory, and nervous systems. Motor fitness includes balance, flexibility, agility, strength, power, and endurance.

ANALYSIS OF PHYSICAL ACTIVITIES. As previously pointed out, the degree of physical fitness depends to a great extent on the type and amount of activity in which the individual participates from time to time. Laboratory tests have resulted in accurate measurement of the energy cost of a wide variety of activities. The energy cost of bicycle riding, running, walking, skiing, football, and many other games and sports has been calculated; also studied have been the energy cost of housework, climbing stairs, snow shoveling, and many other tasks of everyday living. This knowledge, useful to the physical educator in formulating many types of activity programs for physical education, is also helpful to the general public is seeking advice on the type of activities meeting individual needs. This type of information is outlined in the following chart as a guide to rating the contribution of various activities to fitness items.

Important as regular physical activities of the gymnasium and playfield are, it is also important that people realize the possibilities of improving physical fitness through informal activities in everyday life. People may engage in a wide variety of fitness activities in the home, office, and in other informal settings. Such specific exercises, as well as information on diet, rest, relaxation, and other matters are all related to the goal of total fitness. The individual may, in dressing and undressing, walking, standing, climbing stairs, and in many other physical acts of daily life, perform these

RATING OF SPORTS [4]

H—high; M—medium; L—low referring to contribution to fitness items

Sport	En-dur-ance	Agil-ity	Strength			Age Range Recommended
			Leg	Abdo-men	Arm and Shoulder	
Archery	L	L	L	M	H	All ages
Badminton						
Singles-Doubles	H–M	H	H	M	M	Singles under 50
Basketball	H	H	H	L	L	Under 30
Baseball (hard)	M	H	H	M	M	Under 45
Bicycling	M	L	H	L	L	All ages
Bowling	L	L	M	L	M	All ages
Boxing	H	H	H	H	H	Not recom-mended
Canoeing and Rowing						
Recreational	M	L	M	M	H	All ages
Competitive	H	L	H	M	H	Under 30
Field Hockey	H	H	H	M	M	Under 30
Football	H	H	H	H	H	Under 30
Golf	L	L	M	L	L	All ages
Handball						
Singles-Doubles	H–M	H	H	M	H	Singles under 45
Heavy Apparatus						
Tumbling	L	H	H–M	H	H	Under 45
Hiking	M	L	H	L	L	All ages
Horseshoes	L	L	L	L	M	All ages
Judo	H	H	H	H	H	Under 30
Lifesaving	H	M	H	H	H	Under 45
Skating						
Speed	H	M	H	M	L	Under 45
Figure	M	H	H	L	L	All ages
Skiing	H	H	H	M	M	Under 45
Soccer	H	H	H	M	L	Under 45
Softball	L	H	M	M	M	Under 50
Swimming						
Recreational	M	L	M	L	M	All ages
Competitive	H	M	H	M	H	Under 30
Table Tennis	L	M	M	L	L	All ages
Tennis						
Singles-Doubles	H–M	H	H	M	M	Singles under 45
Touch Football	H	H	H	M	M	Under 30
Track						
Distance	H	L	H	M	M	Under 45
Jumps	L	H	H	H	M	Under 45
Sprints	M	M	H	M	M	Under 45
Weights	L	M	H	M	H	Under 45
Volleyball	L	M	M	L	M	All ages
Wrestling	H	H	H	H	H	Under 30

[4] Courtesy of A. H. Steinhaus, from *How To Keep Fit And Like It*, p. 70.

activities in such a way as to keep the body alert and strengthen the muscles to the extent that they would be helpful in maintaining total fitness.

The need for fitness programs is being emphasized from the federal to the local level. President Eisenhower on July 2, 1956, called a Conference on Youth Fitness; in September, 1956, approximately one hundred delegates met in Washington, D. C., to consider the problem of the fitness of American youth; a second meeting was held in 1958. The recommendation to step up fitness activities in all walks of life has started a vigorous campaign throughout the United States under the direction of the President's Council on Youth Fitness; then, too, state-wide meetings and local meetings have initiated interest in the problem of improving the fitness of the American people.

The need for developing a minimum fitness for living through a regular program of exercise and play is urgent. A minimum physical fitness is required to enable individuals at various stages of life to perform routine tasks of day-to-day life without undue exhaustion and have sufficient reserve strength and vitality to be able to meet emergency situations efficiently. Building basic physical condition and a reserve for emergency needs is predicated upon the principle of overload and crest load. Overload is generally confined to exercises of strength and phenomena of the muscular system; crest load is an endurance factor which implies stress upon the organic system. Each forces the system to work in a deficit balance and will, if continued, result in exhaustion. Continued practice of specific exercises results in raising the level of exhaustion and adds to the reserve potential of the organism. This is the essence of training and physical fitness. Thus proper exercise, in proportionate amounts and performed regularly, will raise the fitness level of the individual to the point where he becomes most efficient in performing daily tasks without undue fatigue and in maintaining a potential fitness that will allow him to develop a high degree of fitness if the life situation so demands.

In a world where children walk less, do few chores, and engage in limited physical activities and adults are becoming more sedentary as a result of automation and other physical changes in our environment, the need for active, vigorous exercise, play, and physical recreation is more important than ever before to the health and welfare of our people.

SUMMARY

Much has been learned about the benefits of physical exercise and play in recent years. Perhaps the most significant fact is that experimental research has confirmed the basic values of physical exercise for the individual and has reinforced the long-discussed reciprocal relationships that exist between the physical condition of the body and the effectiveness of the nervous system and the individual's capacity to react to maintain a homeostatic condition. The importance of physical exercise to organic development as well as muscular development has become recognized; so, too, have the effects of invigorating, enjoyable play activity from the standpoint of mental hygiene. Furthermore, research has revealed many fallacies about exercise and has added much to the understanding of the effects of specific types of exercise upon the organs and the efficient functioning of the body.

The conduct of physical education programs in the schools and the development of informal play and physical exercise programs should be based upon a scientific analysis of the effect of these activities upon the individual. The basic elements of physical fitness are well defined and are measurable. The fitness status of the individual may be accurately determined within reasonable limits. It is the task of the recreation leader to utilize scientific information to promote activities that are beneficial and conducive to the development of total fitness for living. These activities must motivate people to participate regularly—of their own volition—in physical activities of sufficient intensity to maintain a minimum level of fitness. At the same time these exercises must also involve some play and recreation to allow for self-expression and emotional release to help meet the needs, interests, and desires of people.

SELECTED REFERENCES

CURETON, THOMAS K. *Physical Fitness Appraisal and Guidance.* St. Louis: The C. V. Mosby Co., 1947. This is a fundamental professional textbook in physical fitness including a definition of physical fitness, the principles of health and fitness guidance, descriptions of modern techniques of measuring physical fitness, basic measures of physical fitness, and other information necessary for the approach to the scientific study and analysis of physical fitness.

DUNBAR, FLANDERS. *Mind and Body: Psychosomatic Medicine.* New York: Random House, 1947. This work includes an introduction to methods and practices in psychosomatic research. The author uses case studies to indicate in lay terms the influences of, and relationships between, the psyche and certain bodily symptoms or physical illnesses.

KARPOVICH, PETER V. *The Physiology of Muscular Activity.* Philadelphia: W. B. Saunders Co., 1959. This is a guide to the scientific basis of the physiology of exercise. A concise analysis is given the relationship between the principles of the physiology of exercise to physical education and to health and fitness in present-day life. See especially pages 93–123.

STEINHAUS, ARTHUR H. *How to Keep Fit and Like It.* Chicago: The Dartnell Corp., 1957. This is a very practical and usable reference to fitness. Based upon sound scientific research, this book includes specific exercises and procedures the lay person may follow in everyday life to achieve and maintain physical fitness in modern living.

BAUER, WILLIAM W., and HEIN, FRED V. *Exercise and Health, A Point of View.* Chicago: American Medical Association, 1958.

COWELL, CHARLES C. *Scientific Foundations of Physical Education.* New York: Harper & Bros., 1953.

Exercise and Fitness: A Collection of Papers Presented at the Colloquium on Exercise and Fitness. Sponsored by the University of Illinois and the Athletic Institute. Chicago: Athletic Institute, 1960.

JACKSON, C. O. (ed.). *Report on the Governor's Conference on Youth Fitness.* Champaign, Ill.: University of Illinois, 1957.

JACOBSON, EDMUND. *You Must Relax.* New York: McGraw-Hill Book Co., Inc., 1957. Offers a detailed discussion of the subject of relaxation.

JOHNSON, WARREN R. (ed.). *The Science and Medicine of Exercise and Sports.* New York: Harper & Bros., 1960.

JOKL, ERNST. *The Clinical Physiology of Physical Fitness and Rehabilitation.* Springfield, Ill.: Charles C Thomas, Publishers, 1958.

Joint Committee Report. *Physical Education—An Interpretation.* Washington, D.C.: Society of State Directors of Health, Physical Education, and Recreation, and the American Association for Health, Physical Education, and Recreation, 1952.

MOREHOUSE, LAURENCE E., and MILLER, AUGUSTUS T. *Physiology of Exercise.* St. Louis: The C. V. Mosby Co., 1959.

MUNROW, A. D. *Pure and Applied Gymnastics.* London: Edward Arnold, Ltd., 1957.

National Safety Council. *Accident Facts.* Chicago: National Safety Council, 1958.

The President's Council on Youth Fitness. *Fitness of American Youth.* Washington, D.C.: U. S. Government Printing Office, 1956.

RATHBONE, JOSEPHINE L. *Teach Yourself to Relax.* Englewood Cliffs, N. J.: Prentice-Hall, Inc., 1957.

WOLFFE, JOSEPH B. "Future Basic Research Relating Physical Education to Sports Medicine," *59th Annual Proceedings, The College Physical Education Association* (1956), 115–25.

12

Mental Benefits From Play and Recreation

People have ever held to the idea that the body is the servant of the mind. This thought was expressed by Plato centuries ago: "gymnastics for the body and music for the soul . . . but the teachers of both have in view chiefly the improvement of the soul." Bridging the gap to modern times, Rousseau is found expressing a similar opinion: "If you wish to cultivate intelligence, cultivate the powers it should rule. . . . Exercise the body continually. . . . Let the pupil be a man in vigor and soon he will become one in reason." Today this idea of the relation of mind and body still prevails. Such statements as "sound mind in sound body," and "the body the temple of the mind" are familiar today.

The notion of the body as subordinate is based on the ancient dualism which held that mind and body are separate entities. Man has risen to his high plane of superiority over the animal world and over many of the forces of nature through his intellect. Today's struggle between men is mental rather than physical. Because of these things, man has largely come to place more importance on his mental development.

PHYSICAL AND MENTAL GROWTH

Mental growth goes hand in hand with bodily growth. Just so long as the body is growing, physical exercise in the form of play should be pursued, for the mental in man is built upon a physical foundation, and the more solid this foundation, the more promising is the outlook for favorable mental growth. After maturity, play is still needed, not so much to educate as to recreate.

The human organism must be regarded as a unit, and anything that contributes to its physical well-being tends to enhance its psychological well-being. This view is universally supported in the field of psychology and education today. One of the chief bases of mental health is an abundance of vigorous play. Play aids bodily health, and bodily health is a contributing factor to mental health.

The results of studies on the degree of relationship which exists between mental development and the various aspects of physical growth have been somewhat conflicting. Early investigators reported positive relationships between advanced growth and mental development; however, more recent studies indicate that close relationships of mental and physical growth do not necessarily occur. For example, Terman, in his *Genetic Studies of Genius*, concluded that gifted children were taller and heavier than the average. Witty's study of gifted children showed that they are not physical weaklings but, rather, tend to be average in physical development and health. Finally, Jones more recently found little relationship between physical defects and intelligence level. Thorpe, in his writings, also came to the conclusion that such structural characteristics as height and weight are correlated only slightly with intelligence.

This type of disagreement, of course, does not disprove the fact that play and physical activity are directly related to total fitness, including the improvement of general mental health. Such a conclusion is pointed out by Bauer and Hein. Also, the increasing evidence of the importance of recreation therapy, recently emphasized by many in the field, has been demonstrated by work at the Menninger Clinic and in other clinical settings and has been described by Wolffe, Layman, and others.

Breckenridge and Vincent point out very logically the need for clarification of exactly what is involved in the consideration of the interrelationship of mental and physical growth:

> Perhaps some of the confusion in the evidence lies in the misunderstanding as to whether we are talking about sheer intelligence or about the way intelligence functions. That physical condition, short of brain or nerve damage, has little to do with native intelligence is probably true. Promoting physical growth will probably not increase inherent intellectual capacity. In this sense they are not interrelated. However, the manner in which the native intelligence functions, being dependent upon attentiveness, concentration, self-confidence, and aggressive attack upon problems, is unquestionably related to physical well-being. Physical well-being, then, affects and is affected by the individual's psychological condition; also, the individual's ability to make effective use of his intellectual and cognitive capacities.[1]

With adults the relationship between mental and physical fitness appears to be quite evident. Disorders of the body may produce various mental illnesses; and good mental health requires physical activities.

Play hobbies have therapeutic value by taking attention away from subjective worries about self and focusing on interesting objective pursuits. Play in this way acts as a balance wheel for the normal personality, thus contributing to a stable outlook on life and everyday problems.

The normal individual, when mentally fatigued from long concentrated study, also depends upon his body to furnish pleasurable exercise that will freshen his whole system again and restore his mental vigor. Man, so to speak, when his mental tower has crumbled, may seek to repair with physical masonry. Mental activities and bodily activities are only two aspects of the same thing—the life of the organism. Well-integrated they serve to stimulate and to relax the child as well as the adult, thus contributing to the solid foundation of man's well-being.

PLAY AND BODY CONTROL

It has long been assumed that there is a relation between the intelligence of an animal and the length of its infancy.

[1] M. E. Breckenridge and E. L. Vincent, *Child Development* (Philadelphia: W. B. Saunders Co., 1955), p. 26.

With the lower forms of animals all the bodily powers spring into full maturity without long practice or training. Their activities change but little from one generation to another, and their hereditary tendencies are practically fixed and rigid. Man, possessing the highest animal intelligence, undergoes the longest period of infancy. While the chicken is born with a definite instinct to get food by picking up small round things in its mouth, and the cat by pouncing on small moving objects, the infant of the human species relies on learned responses for survival and must to be trained in a multitude of functions which are a part of adult life. He is born, not with a complete set of powers, but rather with a plastic nature which has an immense teachability.

Nature has provided for the child's first education by endowing him with the tendency to be active, which is a primary and ever-present fact in life. This self-activity of the infant is his play, an outlet in which he expresses himself as earnestly and fully as the master workman does in any of the higher arts. The first steps in the child's education should be in the direction of his natural impulses and interests. Play changes concurrently with the child's growth and his mental outlook takes on a different aspect—in the words of Froebel: "the plays of children are the germinal leaves of all the later life." The scheme of education today aims to direct the play so that it gradually blends itself into work as the child's mentality grows stronger.

The nervous system consists in general of the two great clusters of nerve centers, the brain and the spinal cord. Through it muscular and glandular control is achieved; and through it the individual obtains knowledge of the outside world and is made aware of the various states of his own being, that of physical exhaustion, for instance. The nervous system is the most complex structure of man, and, of all organs, the least is known about it. Part of its control over the body is an involuntary one, such as over the various vital organs; but much of its activity, the so-called voluntary actions, is accompanied by an awareness, a consciousness.

Bodily and motor control must be achieved before the higher brain centers can be freed for more abstract thinking. The more actions that can be made automatic and involuntary, the more time and energy are correspondingly left free to meet the complex problems of adult life. For example, the child must practice the different movements of walking over and over again, with his attention concentrated on the accomplishment. Only after considerable effort are they learned. Later, however, attention no longer need be given to the bringing of all these movements into action. Mental energy is thus conserved for other use, so with the other physical movements connected with everyday living. The order of development of bodily control and perfecting of coordinations proceed, in general, along the lines indicated below.

EARLY CHILDHOOD. During the first few years the infant practices the mechanics of the ordinary movements of life (those needed every day), such as kicking, reaching, holding, sitting, crawling, standing, and walking. Included also are the vocal coordinations needed to produce speech. No one of these accomplishments is an easy one. The same movement must be repeated over and over again with attention fixed closely on the process of doing it. These actions after many repetitions become automatic— performed without conscious attention to the process. In early childhood the more difficult bodily movements of running, jumping, throwing, climbing, and handwork, in turn, are practiced, and the process of making them automatic is begun. The plays of the child are lessons in learning to control these fundamental bodily coordinations. The child in his play freely copies actions he sees, and in this way his motor development proceeds economically along the lines which tradition and custom mark out as being the most useful and valuable.

These efforts of the child in mastering everyday movements demand practically all the nervous energy that he has to spare. They compose his serious business in life. As these fundamental movements become habitual the child is freed from the necessity of giving conscious attention to them and is at liberty to turn his attention and interest to other things.

LATER CHILDHOOD. The period of later childhood is one of great motor activity. Rejoicing in his newly-found control over the body, the child responds in action to the many sensations that come from this mysterious world about him. The preceding habitual activities are not only perfected but tried out in combination with each other. The newer complex acts involve concerted actions of many muscles throughout the various parts of the body and, therefore, bring different parts of the nervous system into concerted action also. Considerable coordination of nerve center and muscle is necessary to perform these acts with ease.

All the while, too, experiments are being made with the finer, more specialized muscles of the body; and the corresponding nerve centers are going through their process of development. The stunts of the playground (somersaults, chinning, balancing, etc.), the throwing, catching, and batting of a ball (involving reactions of time and distance), along with wrestling and boxing, swimming, dancing, shooting with bow and with the sling, marbles, kite-flying, whittling, miniature housekeeping, collecting, and handcrafts, all testify to the child's perfecting his motor possibilities.

In this new type of physical skill the advantage of having developed automatic movements in the preceding years is present, for the child now has time and energy to spare in planning results apart from the activity itself; his higher brain centers are free to concentrate apart from the actual directions of movements. This is seen in the entrance of competition and strategy into his plays, which now have rules to be observed and fall under the classification of games; it is also demonstrated in the new enjoyments in intellectual games such as checkers and cards.

The more complicated muscular movements of later childhood, while largely made automatic, are not so to the extent that the more fundamental everyday movements are. However, adults are agile and graceful in relation to the extent that they have practiced these movements in youth, and this is also the case with their ability to move quickly in emergencies. This period of later childhood is the time to develop the finer motor and sensory adjustments.

ADOLESCENCE. When the period of adolescence is reached it is evident that play has little more to build up the physical direction of the body. The everyday movements of adult life have been made automatic and the occasional ones needed for emergency or to enjoy certain types of recreation have been made readily adjustable. The play activities of this period clearly show the liberation of the higher nerve centers from gross muscle activities, for the movements have no end in themselves, being utilized for individual and team success in situations that approximate adult life—for athletics contain the elements of cooperation, specialization, and competition that are such prominent factors in the business and professional life of today.

How fully the individual has mastered his body at this time and gained mental freedom, is demonstrated in the fact that less time is needed for his active play life, and that the remainder of his time can be devoted to his studies and to the development of delicate physical skills. Except for perfecting physical coordinations and relating them to more complex mental situations, there is little need for the ordinary individual to develop outstanding athletic skill. This is the province of the athlete. Even he reaches the peak of his efficiency in early maturity.

MATURITY. When the state of maturity is finally reached, the individual finds his play has gradually changed from being what once was his most serious business in life. One half-hour to one hour a day now suffices in the way of active exercise. This does not mean that this exercise—now a recreation—is unimportant to the nervous system. Modern civilization, with its many demands in the way of finer and specialized muscular and nerve coordinations, has thrown the burden of work on the higher areas of the brain, the ones that can only be exercised with considerable direction and expediture of nervous energy. Such work involves tiring effort involving sustained attention, analysis, reason, will, choice, and inhibition.

PLAY AND MENTAL RELAXATION

The nervous system becomes fatigued following sustained effort or worry. Fatigue comes when the tissues cannot throw off the waste products of combustion as fast as they are accumulated. An important factor in relieving fatigue is change. The best place to turn for relaxation is to the activities which can be performed without a great deal of conscious direction—the exercises that involve the big muscles and related nerve centers. The school boy, tired from his study, goes out to the playground during recess and returns invigorated; the tired factory hand, instead of sitting down for complete rest during his noon hour, joins in games like softball and quoits, and starts afresh when the afternoon whistle blows. The change of attention gives rest to the tired parts of the nervous system. The child, if unrestrained, will change to a different activity when the one at hand has become monotonous. He finds his attention diverted by the variety of games in which he indulges. The adult, however, must deliberately take his attention away from his ordinary routine duties and center it on an interesting occupation such as hunting, fishing, or some sport. The change is all the more valuable when it brings big muscles into use. Big muscles coordinate without much voluntary effort. Then, too, big-muscle exercise quickens the heart action, and the increased blood supply brings nourishing food to the run-down nervous tissues and helps to carry away the waste products.

The people who have enjoyed play in their childhood and youth are the more fortunate ones as regards the capacity for self-entertainment. Their play spirit remains with them, and proves an effective antidote for worry and despondency. But the play spirit cannot be ignored until adulthood and then suddenly discovered. The play movement thus has a distinct function to perform in educating for leisure by providing familiarity with a wide variety of interests and skills which will act as balancing factors later in life.

PLAY AND MENTAL HEALTH

At many points in these pages indirect reference has been made to the relationship between play and mental well-being. Of such significance is the contribution of play in the development and maintenance of mental health, of such importance in the therapeutic treatment of the mentally ill, that a knowledge of the elements of this relationship is altogether essential. It is doubtful if any of the manifold contributions of play in other areas of human life, even its contribution in physical development, exceed that to mental health.

DEVELOPMENT OF SELF-CONCEPT.   At the vortex of mental health are two concepts which when understood explain the whirl of activity rotating around them. The first of these is that a person's self-concept is a vital factor determining his behavior. At early years the child begins to form an image of himself as he considers himself to be; not a mere physical image, but an image of the kind of person he feels himself to be. This image is socially acquired, for the chief means one has of arriving at it is observing how others react to him and by comparing himself with others. This concept of self becomes incorporated in his personality and then becomes a factor in affecting the kind of person he becomes— it goes a long way in determining his actions. For example, a person who pictures himself as being inadequate or inferior may often become loud, boastful, and obnoxiously forward in his actions, his actions being a screen behind which he hides his sense of insufficiency. The feeling of inadequacy may be justified, and again it may be purely imaginary, stemming from early childhood experiences, but it is none the less real in affecting his conduct. The records are replete with examples of individuals with unusual ability who feel themselves to be insufficient, and therefore fail. Many outstanding athletes are unable to perform up to their capacity for this reason, and some of the great names in professional baseball in their rookie days needed assistance to help them alter their self-image. Examples can be drawn from all walks of life. Such people are simply unable to mobilize their powers.

It is doubtful if any factor can be singled out which affects conduct to a greater degree, or that is more basically related to mental health, than a person's self-concept. The child's play life is one of the major mediums through which this image evolves, and, hence, intelligently supervised play becomes a major medium in reconstructing negative and distorted images into more healthful ones.

The first concepts of self derive from the home. If a child lives in a home where his personality is respected and his opinions and acts are treated with consideration, he should grow up comparatively free from doubts and anxieties. If, however, he is continually admonished, the child evolves an image of himself as bad, unworthy, and weak. In addition to his family, if other adults—his teachers, his recreation leaders—continue the practice of playing up negatives, the individual's self-image of weakness and unworthiness is heightened further.

Achievement of success in some activity or other is a contributing factor to a positive and healthy self-image, and to correcting a negative, crippling one. Even in normal or healthy personalities, success is essential to the maintenance of emotional balance. Now it is the important and perpetual function of play to provide opportunity for achievement which may be denied in other areas of life. The adult who finds success coming slowly in his work, his goals remote and the achievement of them far off, turns to play where success is accomplishable and immediate. A lift to sagging spirits is thus found. The child who encounters negative responses in home and school, with a resultant image of inadequacy, may in his play life find achievement, prestige, superior attainment to alter his self-image. Conversely, however, his play may contribute to his notion of inferiority, with the result that his image of inadequacy may be thrown into even sharper focus. With these facts in mind, the wise play leader will keep his approach consistently positive, will point up successes and commendable efforts, and will minimize the importance of unavoidable failures, realizing that all the time he is adding positive line and color to the child's image of himself. Moreover, he will make available a wide range of types of activities so as to provide opportunity for success to each individual, regardless of what his inclinations or physical limitations may be.

The wise leader will also understand that social acceptance is essential to an adequate self-image. Status is necessary, a feeling that one's personality counts for something in some group. The child's play groups provide this, and the alert leader helps to achieve it for each child.

In short, the person, child or adult, is fortunate who has a deep and consuming interest in his work and achieves a sense of importance and success therefrom. Even greater value accrues from strong and all-absorbing interests outside his work, which produce feelings of success and a sense of worth. Fortunate, too, is the individual, child or adult, who first finds love and security in his home life, for emotional balance and a wholesome concept of self are dependent on successful adjustments with those who mean most to us.

EXPRESSION OF DRIVES AND NEEDS. The second basic concept at the center of mental health is that man's psychological drives and needs must find expression. There are basic drives or urges common to all men in varying degrees of intensity, and, in addition, there are drives peculiar to each individual resulting from his talents, experiences, and set purposes. If mental health is to be maintained, these strivings must find expression in behavior which adequately satisfies them. Fortunately, however, when direct expression is denied or undesirable, a redirection or sublimation of the drives may be possible so as to provide a reasonably acceptable outlet. It is in this area of the redirection of cravings that play makes one of its greatest contributions.

Much of society's energies are directed toward repressing these drives and strivings, with the result that a conflict exists between society and the individual. The school and the home inculcate repressive ideas. The mores demand repression; and law, religion, education reinforce the demand. At the same time, the cravings will not be denied. The result is tensions and conflicts within. Against the background of society's "thou shalt not's," too frequently one's effort to express his cravings lead to guilt feelings and fears of social rejection. One of the main functions of play is to provide outlets for human strivings and cravings which will satisfy the individual and at the same time be acceptable to society. A brief discussion of human desires, their expression, and the means of redirection and sublimation, will illustrate this point.

The deep-seated aggressive tendency in men if uncontrolled would lead to a chaotic state in society. From infancy on up through the various age groups, aggressiveness is restrained and rechanneled by means of plays and games. Combative sports, especially of the body-contact type, and to a lesser extent vigorous games without contact, serve as sublimations for aggressiveness. Vicarious experience in witnessing such games may help when participation is impossible. Society sanctions behavior in these games which it would not tolerate in everyday living. Such games thus provide a satisfactory outlet without guilt feelings and without the danger of social rejection. They thus serve a useful purpose in maintaining mental health.

Regression is another tendency which finds expression in play. By this is meant the inclination in adults to return to childish methods of expression, a tendency present in almost all adults, but stronger in some than others. To many, maturity is but a role they are playing, in which they represent something they are not. The respectability and propriety, the reserved demeanor and well-bred restraint are but a veil, a make-up that must be worn to make them acceptable. At heart, they crave the freedom, the lack of restraint, and the irresponsibility of childhood. The veil is thin and easily ripped off and must be constantly guarded lest status and friends be lost.

One of recreation's salient contributions to happiness and to mental health is that it gives adults an approved way of "acting like kids" again. Men shout and laugh loudly, argue and tussle, run around, cavort, clown, and otherwise act like preadolescents. They attend conventions and home-coming football games and act in a way uncharacteristic of their age. It is well known among social recreation leaders that childhood singing games will on occasion be played by adults with unrestrained, childish delight. In active games they "kick up their heels" to the amazement of their children. All this surprising activity, "at their age," is a regression to childhood. In recreation and play, situations are created where it is socially acceptable to express urges that in other than play situations would be socially taboo. Approved as it is, there are no guilt feelings. Pent-up urges thus find outlets, tensions are relieved, and the personality is healthier as a result. Herein rests one of play's most valuable gifts to mental well-being.

It is probably true that no other human urge or craving encounters more rigid restrictions than that of sex, and it is doubtless true also that the conflicts that it engenders, first elaborated by Freud, lead to more devastating tensions and more keenly felt convictions of guilt than any other. Redirection and sublimation of this drive is particularly important. An analysis of recreational patterns reveals that no small percentage of them are engaged in to achieve sex expression in acceptable forms. All mixed social activities such as dances, parties, and picnics are of this type. Sex emphasis in stories, novels, and the theatre offer sublimation.

The need for change must find expression, and for many that expression can be found only in play. Whether a pupil in school or an adult worker, play brings relief from monotony. The longing for speed or movement through space again can be satisfied for many only through play and recreation.

It should be clear that play is a major channel through which man redirects his urges and cravings and thereby achieves a state of emotional balance that otherwise would be impossible. Were it not for this function of play, life would be found exceedingly difficult, the tensions immeasurably increased. The compensatory aspect of play is thus one of its most significant and valuable phases. Mental health finds in play a preventive and remedial instrument without equal.

It thus appears that there are four levels of expression of human drives and yearnings. First is the direct expression of the drive by the precise type of action the drive impels. More often than not this is impossible in an ordered society and in refined surroundings. Second is sublimated expression, a redirection of the drive into action that is reasonably satisfying to the individual and acceptable to society. Third is vicarious satisfaction, through watching or reading about actions by others and affiliating oneself with the situation. Fourth is fantasy, imagining oneself doing the things that in practice are denied. These are all valuable, but they are desirable and satisfying in the order listed. When one is impossible, one makes the next best choice. A word of caution is needed regarding fantasy, however. Fantasy serves a valuable function in emotional release, but carried to an extreme is dangerous. Rather than allowing imaginative play to satisfy, it is always better to try to bring the desired achievement into actuality in some acceptable form. Sublimation or redirection is much to be preferred.

PLAY AND EXPANDING THE RANGE OF EXPERIENCE

While the child is exercising in active pursuits of spontaneous nature, it is not only his muscles and their motor centers of control that are being developed: he is acquiring intellectual interests, he is forming moral attitudes, and he is becoming more and more a social being. This intellectual life will now be studied, first from the aspect of his direct experiences and sensations, and later from the relation that these bear to his more abstract processes of thinking.

KNOWLEDGE OF ENVIRONMENT. The universal urges of self-activity and of curiosity lead the infant on in his investigations. He soon learns to manipulate the objects within reach, to test their possibilities of taste, and to drop them to the floor to hear their rattle. Brightly-colored objects and moving objects prove fascinating. Later, when he masters the arts of creeping and walking in turn, he widens his range of experiences. He sees animals, birds, trees, and other wonders of nature, and man-made creations such as airplanes and automobiles. He hears strange noises and learns to associate them with their respective sources. This is his proper education. His first perceptions must deal with concrete things, because he can think of something abstract only by forced attention and with difficulty. Later, the playground and school furnish him with new materials for investigation. If he is fortunate, he will be able to hike and to travel and thus widen still further the boundaries of his environment.

During the period of infancy the child's pleasure is found directly in sensory stimuli that he is receiving. He has no remote interests in mind when he plays. But these impressions are necessary in that they are retained in memory and form the basic materials used in imagining and reasoning and as these capacities develop they gradually become factors in his play, and introduce enjoyment of ends remote from the direct enjoyment of the stimuli in themselves.

The child should be encouraged in this experimentation, for out of it can grow a well-trained capacity of observation as regards the practical interests of life, and a clearness of perception that will serve to stimulate the workings of his intellectual powers. Play forces the child into contact with the environment and therefore into learning; through it, he becomes more objective and observant.

Play is to the child what travel is to the adult. Of play in this connection and of its importance to the child, Froebel wrote, "It is through play that he comes to know the physical qualities of the objects that surround him, their motion, action, and reaction upon each other, and the relation of these phenomena to himself." More recently, Luther Burbank has pleaded that children be allowed their natural heritage. In *The Training of the Human Plant* Burbank said, "Every child should have mud pies, grasshoppers, water-bugs, tadpoles, frogs, mud turtles, elderberries, wild strawberries, acorns, chestnuts, trees to climb, brooks to wade in, water lilies, woodchucks, bats, bees, butterflies, various animals to pet, hay fields, pine cones, rocks to roll, sand, snakes, huckleberries, and hornets; and any child who has been deprived of these has been deprived of the best part of his education." These things, which prove delightful to growing boys and girls, have largely disappeared from their life, except in so far as organized play provides them.

ASSOCIATION WITH OTHERS. Knowledge of one's physical environment, including one's relation to it, is not the only type of information to be amassed during the years of infancy, childhood, and youth. Impressions are gained from the experiences and thoughts of other people with whom one comes in contact.

The big step in this direction is made at the close of infancy when the child learns to vocalize—speech brings in more rapid and certain communication than the cries and signs by which he formerly attempted to convey meanings. Now, he can get ideas from his parents and other children and add to his own store of information by finding out about their experiences. This is a quicker way of learning things than trying everything out himself, and the child's education now grows by leaps and bounds. His play group has a tremendous effect in the development of his personality. The play group is a primary group, and it is in the close, intimate face-to-face contacts of primary relationships that human nature is most affected and the social heritage is transmitted. Next to the home, the play group has greater potentialities in broadening the child's mental sphere than any other type of relationship in the life of the average child.

When children meet in spontaneous play, they throw off self-consciousness, artificiality, and restraint, and are shown

in their true personalities. Their associates can then judge
them for their real worth. In no way can one learn better
about human nature than actually to contact it. Play is
social and furnishes this opportunity; and as the games
grow in complexity and demand more rules, the better the
chance to observe whether a person is honest, whether he
is loyal, whether he acts well in the emergencies, and
whether he persists under reverses.

The failure to mix sociably with one's fellow beings often
is the reason so many brilliant students fail in the actual
work of their profession. Some brilliant students cannot
teach successfully, some others cannot fill executive positions because they do not understand how to handle other
personalities. It is certain that a person, if he is to be successful in business life, must have more than an encyclopedic
accumulation of facts. He must know how to meet and
deal with people.

ADJUSTMENTS TO PRACTICAL SITUATIONS. Everyday life is
much different from that of the classroom. Different types
of judgment and reaction are required in each case. The
scholar in his research can think calmly and deliberately and
defer his action; but when he attempts to become a man of
practical affairs he finds himself in a world which is complex, changing, and confusing, and which demands close
attention and quick adjustment on his part. That our
modern education has come to recognize this double need in
training is demonstrated by the increased emphasis being
given to extracurricular activities, such as play, athletics,
club work, dramatics, music, debating, and many others, in
which the participant must be a doer as well as a thinker.
If, on the one hand, overemphasis of abstract study produces
the impractical dreamer, on the other hand, overindulgence
in a life of action produces a person who is incapable of
fully enjoying the subtler aspects of life, those involving
aesthetic appreciation and which bring culture, refinement,
and repose.

Play and recreation give a progressive education in adjustments that approximate the practical life of adults. The

child gradually becomes able to master increasingly difficult situations: first, to control his bodily movement in itself; then, with this bodily control, to imitate persons and things, and later to imitate creations of his imagination; then to use his new physical skill to some desired end that involves rivalry with other playmates or that involves the manipulation of objects or of bodies other than his own; finally, to make the still more difficult adjustment found in the team game, in which he must make instantaneous choice between several courses of action, complicated by the restrictions of rules and unexpected moves on the part of opponents. Here, the player must keep his mind concentrated on the progress of the game, be alert for opportunities, and follow the rules. The emergencies come and decisions must be quickly made and acted upon. No other situation of youth can more closely resemble adult life unless it would be premature entrance into adult life.

Competitive life is a succession of games. One who is trained in games is apt to be a quick thinker and interpreter in the midst of the present-day, kaleidoscopic life of moving persons and things. The person trained in such judgments and reactions will not have identical situations facing him throughout life; but his mind will be the more adaptable for having had this kind of experience. This training for life need not necessarily be in athletics; the student finds much the same type of experience in serving on the school newspaper, perhaps, or in holding student office, playing in the school band, or acting as manager for athletic teams or other organizations. Students who are prominent in school activities are usually prominent afterwards in their community life.

PLAY AND FORMAL EDUCATION

The previous paragraphs have emphasized the first-hand information that a person gathers through his own experiences and those in connection with other people of his acquaintance. Play proves to be the child's first teacher in this respect. It absorbs the child's whole interest and relates doing and feeling to learning.

If left to himself in his play the child learns through trial and error, and also through imitation of the ways of others whom he admires and whose ways seem successful and satisfying. But one cannot rely upon these natural methods of education alone; direct means of inculcation equips the child for life. This shaping pressure is of two types, informal and formal. Examples of the former are found in the Indian father teaching his son to make a bow and arrow or the present-day mother teaching her daughter how to cook. This is education, but it is casual, irregular, and unsystematic, and, while it met the needs of the early life of the race, such apprenticeship falls far short of an adequate preparation for the complex life of today. The boy would not get very far in law or medicine, for instance, by mere association with those engaged in these professions. He must begin early and build a careful foundation. This calls for the formal type of education we see in schools.

The formal education is one of books, formulas, and symbols, as opposed to real persons, things, and happenings. The child's mind has much difficulty in grasping the more abstract meanings of life—but as this is overcome it can be readily seen that he has added a distinct asset to his equipment for life. Through the help of teachers and books he can transport himself beyond the realms of his immediate environment and live in a world of thought with people and customs that belong to other lands and to other ages—he can know of things that neither he nor his playmates could otherwise experience and discuss with one another.

Valuable as abstract knowledge is and as increasingly valuable as it becomes in the child's life as he matures, it would be largely meaningless unless accompanied by practical experience as well. Just as the progress of civilization today is built up out of the cumulative experiences of the many peoples who have lived in ages before us, so the higher mental advancement of the individual is shaped by his previous store of experience. Many experiences are the raw products upon which later experience is constructed and reconstructed throughout life.

A child who has many clear and vivid impressions is prepared to visualize the more abstract lessons of the school-room—when he reads a book there will be pictures presented to him as he goes along. After he has seen a thing, he can the better understand references to it, just as the person who has traveled always has an intimate interest in the places he has seen. Abstract teaching material can always be enlivened by reference to actual events within the bounds of ordinary understanding.

Actual experience then is the basis of abstract thought. Observations such as the falling apple and steam in the tea kettle led to the discoveries of the law of gravitation and of the steam engine. Many new inventions have been devised upon these discoveries in turn, but the fundamental basis is one borrowed from another's experience; it was around this experience that the abstract theory was built.

Every new experience that the child can gain has an influence on his later life. One's present thoughts and actions are largely the outcome of antecedent acts or impressions. Many of these occurrences, apparently submerged below the level of conscious memory, are apt to resurrect themselves at any time. The importance of environment upon our early lives is bound up in this truth. The play life, which is the natural life in the tender years of child-hood, is a means of acquiring varied experiences. The wider the range of concrete experiences in developing manhood and womanhood, the greater the power for clear image-making, for judgments, and for correct anticipation of the consequences of action; and, as result, the more effective the intellect in maturity.

This, then, is the proper order of education: from the concrete to the abstract; from the spontaneous, motor, and emotional life, to the reflective and symbolized life. Action and feeling should precede thought in the earlier emphasis of education. Motor play and sensory play should therefore precede intellectual play, and intellectual play should precede intellectual work.

A study of this order will show that next to actual experience in working out a thing for himself, a person can become most interested in—and find most meaning in—information that comes through the media of storytelling, radio, motion pictures, television, and picture books, where the mind is helped to form a picture almost as clear as if the objects were actually present. Reading, too, can be made so entertaining as to be play; and many people, whose lives are barren in many ways, enrich their outlook by this vicarious means. In general, the information gathered from formal education has play interest accordingly or not as it resembles things in actual life. Interest in abstract things will not come until the child has accumulated sufficient facts from which to generalize.

SUMMARY

Play is the child's exploration world. In his play he undergoes a learning process. From infancy on, play gives him the opportunity to be venturesome on his own. He is a fledgling trying out his wings. He is removed from oversolicitous protection. In his adventuresome activities he learns to control his bodily movements without conscious effort and to make them subject to his will. The child progressively masters more difficult coordinations in turn and then subjects his newly gained motor control to consciously directed courses of action as they arise in his game experiences with other children. This is the first stage of his mental growth. The great educators of all time have recognized this play value.

Play, in addition to developing neuromuscular control, also offers a wide range of experiences. Concomitant with these experiences, the child learns from other children—through exchange he shares his own knowledge with the others. Each child thereby gains a wider perspective of life. His play adventures constantly take him farther from his home surroundings and include a wider circle of playmates. He learns from his expanding environment and his associates accordingly. He also gains an understanding of the temperaments and personalities of others.

This is nature's first-hand information. It is concrete; it is practical. Such a training provides rich experiences which help give meaning to more abstract learning later and translate academic knowledge into effective action. Knowledge is then applied to life instead of being merely knowledge for its own sake. Play experiences thus afford a basis for the higher mental processes.

Education cannot approach the child from the same standpoint it does the adult. The child looks at the world from an entirely different outlook and judges in the light of an impoverished experience. The facts he possesses have meaning largely in their isolated selves. It should be realized that all the study and application given to real life or to subjects having much in common with real life therefore will provide a larger understanding of it; whereas abstract and unenlivened school work will be of use only to those who happen to specialize along one particular line. From concrete general experience there can be gained some benefit for all lines of mental endeavor; but exclusively abstract specialized study exercises and develops a narrow and restricted ability. This is the reason why our schools and universities demand general cultural courses before allowing specialization. All individuals alike need the former; only the few whose special aptitudes and talents are appealed to will derive particular benefit from the latter.

With adults, play and recreation have the therapeutic value of change. Subjected to the demands and restrictions of his work-a-day life, an individual can turn in free time to something he wants to do on his own. In change of activity, particularly to a type in which he is skillful, he finds recreative satisfaction. In his recreation he can take chances without endangering his livelihood, can exercise his skills, can relive some of his youthful experiences, can regain some of his youthful spirit. From this standpoint, play and recreation have important mental value, on the one hand, in building up healthy personalities and, on the other hand, in rehabilitating sick personalities. Recreation offers many sublimations when real life denies self-expression or creativity.

The adult man or woman, with fully developed powers, needing play and recreation more as a relaxation, has undergone a marked transformation from the infant who started life with merely physical wants and desires, and even then lacked voluntary power of control over them. The developed product of civilization shows a being who, although still motivated by basic needs and emotions, uses his intellect in setting goals for himself and predicting the consequences of his actions, and also relies upon his reason and abstract thinking to assist him toward intelligent goals. His aesthetic appreciations have been developed and refined. Ideally, his broad social experience will have contributed to the appreciation of the ideals in human conduct. The sentiments of justice, truth, religion, friendship, and loyalty will be personified for him and invested with living beauty.

SELECTED REFERENCES

DAVIS, JOHN E. *Clinical Applications of Recreation Therapy.* Springfield, Ill.: Charles C Thomas, Publishers, 1952. The author illustrates the practical application of recreation therapy as it is being developed as adjunctive therapy within the framework of modern psychiatric practice.

JONES, HAROLD E. "The Environment and Mental Development," *Manual of Child Psychology,* ed. LEONARD CARMICHAEL. New York: John Wiley & Sons, Inc., 1954, 631–96. Included in this work is an extensive analysis of the effect of schooling, social class, social experiences, physical condition, racio-cultural influences, family relationships and other environmental factors upon mental development. A bibliography gives many references to further investigation of the relationship between environment and mental development.

LAYMAN, EMMA MCCLOY. *Mental Health Through Physical Education and Recreation.* Minneapolis: Burgess Publishing Co., 1955. The entire book is devoted to showing the various relationships between physical education, recreation, and mental health. In Chapter 12 the author discusses the physical, as well as the intellectual benefits of play and the role of play in personality diagnosis and therapy.

MARTIN, WILLIAM E., and STENDLER, CELIA B. *Child Behavior and Development.* New York: Harcourt, Brace and Co., 1959, Chaps. 4 and 5. This is an excellent all-round reference to child development and the effect of environmental influences upon the individual's mental and social development.

BAUER, W. W., and HEIN, F. V. *Exercise and Health, A Point of View.* Chicago: American Medical Association, 1958, p. 2.

COWELL, CHARLES C. "The Interrelatedness of Development," *American Academy of Physical Education, No. 6* (1958), 122–31.

HURLOCK, ELIZABETH B. *Child Development.* New York: McGraw-Hill Book Co., Inc., 1956, Chap. 10.

JERSILD, ARTHUR T. *Child Psychology.* Englewood Cliffs, N. J.: Prentice-Hall, Inc., 1954, Chaps. 16, 18.

JONES, H. E. "Environmental Influence on Mental Development," *Manual of Child Psychology,* ed. L. CARMICHAEL. New York: John Wiley & Sons, Inc., 1946.

LATARJET, A. "Physical Education, Athletics, and Mental Hygiene," *Journal of Health and Physical Education,* III (November, 1932), 26.

LAWTHER, JOHN D. *The Psychology of Coaching.* Englewood Cliffs, N. J.: Prentice-Hall, Inc., 1951.

LAYMAN, EMMA McCLOY. *Mental Health Through Physical Education and Recreation.* Minneapolis: Burgess Publishing Co., 1955, pp. 342–79.

PIAGET, JEAN. *Play, Dreams, and Imitation of Childhood.* New York: W. W. Norton & Co., Inc., 1951.

SHUTTLEWORTH, F. K. "The Physical and Mental Growth of Boys and Girls Aged Six to Nineteen," *Monographs of the Society for Research in Child Development,* IV, 3 (1939).

SLAVSON, SAMUEL R. *Recreation and the Total Personality.* New York: Association Press, 1946.

TERMAN, L. M. *Genetic Studies of Genius.* Vol. I. Stanford, Calif.: University of California Press, 1925, p. 5.

———. *The Gifted Child Grows Up.* Vol. IV. Stanford, Calif.: Stanford University Press, 1947.

THOMPSON, G. C. *Child Psychology, Growth Trends, and Adjustments.* Boston: Houghton Mifflin Co., 1952.

THORPE, L. P. *Child Psychology and Development.* New York: The Ronald Press Co., 1955, pp. 178–83.

WITTY, P. "A Genetic Study of Fifty Gifted Children," *The Thirty-Ninth Yearbook of the National Society for the Study of Education,* Vol. I. (1940).

WOLFFE, J. B. *Recreation, Medicine and the Humanities.* Chapel Hill, N.C.: University of North Carolina, 1957.

13

Social Learning Through Play and Recreation

The previous chapters have discussed the physical and mental benefits of play and recreation; now attention will be given to their educational contributions as they relate to social experience. One of the chief goals of education is the training of the kind of person whose conduct is consistently acceptable socially or, in common parlance, one who has good character. The contribution that play and recreation may make to such social learning is the subject matter of this chapter.

The value of play in the development of character qualities has long been recognized by foremost educators. In ancient times, Plato, Aristotle, and Quintilian expressed their convictions on the social value of play; and later Locke, Basedow, Guts Muths, and others also credited play with offering potential moral strength. In 1840, Thomas Arnold, an English headmaster at Rugby, introduced play and athletics, with special emphasis upon team games, into his school curriculum as subjects regarded even more importantly for their moral values than for health and recreation. This has since been followed by other English schools. In the United States, schools, particularly private schools, place great stress on athletics for its character-building potentialities. Leading educators have stressed the value of play from the kindergarten on as a dynamic force in shaping the character of the growing child.

278

NATURE OF CHARACTER

There is considerable disagreement as to the nature of character and how it may be engendered in children. The terms personality and character have often been used synonymously. Generally speaking, the habits and attitudes of an individual, taken together and integrated, constitute character. The term refers to a person's tendency or predisposition to react in characteristic ways toward life situations. Conduct is the result of overt acts and is thus the objective phase of character. Personality, which includes the sum total of an individual's traits, is a more inclusive term than character, with the latter being one of its components; character refers more specifically to an individual's behavior relating to laws, customs, and moral standards.

Vernon Jones contends that character is not necessarily to be considered as corresponding to morality and ethical behavior, because morality implies conformity, which may represent simply the line of least resistance in various situations. On the other hand, Emma M. Layman defines character as that aspect of personality which is appraised on the basis of moral and ethical standards, thus involving value judgments. (See Selected References.)

Character, in a more restricted sense, consists primarily of habits and attitudes involving standards of right or wrong. These attitudes are the individual counterparts of the mores which are the social customs or folkways the group considers indispensable and of particular importance to its welfare, and which all are expected to follow. The mores constitute the group's moral standard. An individual determines rightness, as we shall see presently, not only by reference to the group's moral standards but by a consideration of the consequences of his conduct. Conduct, then, which, more than other types, is considered as evidence of character, is activity which involves standards of morality and rightness.

Qualities of character are frequently referred to by such words as loyalty, courage, honesty, thoughtfulness, etc.

These are said to be traits of character. In a sense, however, loyalty is an abstraction. One cannot be loyal in general but only in relation to specific situations. In the experience of an individual there may be hundreds of specific responses, each differing more or less from the others, all of which involve some type or degree of loyalty. Man expresses thought mainly through words. To speak accurately and precisely, however, one should have a separate word for each of the responses involving loyalty. Since that is impossible the word loyalty as used refers to a number of specific action patterns which are characterized by having a common element designated by the term loyalty. Character traits are convenient words, then, to represent groups of experiences having certain obvious attributes in common and, hence, fall under one heading.

In talking with children, however, one cannot speak of honesty or sportsmanship or any other trait with any assurance that it has meaning to them unless the terms are associated with specific experiences which they have had.

CRITERIA OF MORALITY

As a result of conflicting philosophies of morality in the United States today, the development of a methodology for character education is very difficult, and the situation exceedingly complicated.

In the following paragraphs three points of view regarding morality will be canvassed briefly: (1) right for right's sake, (2) social standards, (3) consideration of consequences.

MORAL LAW. To Kant "two things fill the spirit with ever new and increasing wonder and awe . . . the starry heavens above and the moral law within." The moral law within determines rightness. What is the source of this moral law? It is other-worldly, not conceived by mortal man in this mundane world, but superimposed by a Divine Being. Since the Divine Being has imposed this universal law of right upon the world, man is in duty bound to follow it. This is Kant's famous categorical imperative: the obligation to do one's duty regardless of the results. Not only has this absolute law been laid down with the resultant duty of man to follow it, but there has been placed within the human breast a monitor, that greatest of wonders to Kant—the human conscience—to guide man in following the law. Nothing in this world can account for the conviction that each must act from a sense of duty and duty alone.

Character education, according to this point of view, consists of developing in men attitudes and sentiments in conformity with the moral code laid down by religion so completely that men will act in accordance with them regardless of consequences.

SOCIAL STANDARDS. Whenever people live together for any length of time, they develop folkways or group customs. When these ways are evaluated by the group and some of them are found to be indispensable to its welfare, there is the rise of mores. Since the mores constitute the moral standards of the group and are considered indispensable to its welfare, all societies take pains to see that all conform to them and employ various devices to secure or enforce this conformity.

The mores are held to be right by the group. They constitute the only standard of rightness and morality the rank and file of the group knows. They are not necessarily other-worldly, superimposed on the group by a Divine Being, but are the result of experience and are supported by years of tradition.

Now, since society by one scheme or another enforces conformity to the mores, there is a case of might makes right. The individual is relatively helpless, and the group is powerful. To get on, he must conform. In time he comes to think the mores are right and helps to force others to conform. Might of this type always has been an important factor in leading people to believe certain actions or goals to be right, whether or no they agree to the dictates of human conscience.

Most of character education today is built upon the

acceptance of social standards as the criteria of right and moral conduct and the inculcation of them in youth. If the youth can be so trained that he will react in socially acceptable ways, he is thought of as having good character and the task of character education has been adequately performed.

DESIRABLE CONSEQUENCES. In most of the experiences of life it seems obvious that action in conformity to the social standards is the desirable and right thing to do. However, it may easily happen in certain situations that conduct in conformity to social standards may be immoral. Obviously then, the social standards as a criterion of morality do not always apply to all the situations of life. The reason lies in the fact that action in accordance with the mores may at times have undesirable consequences. Suppose, for example, that one is confronted with a situation involving telling the truth and one is strongly tempted to tell a lie. Two courses lie open—which should be followed? At this point a moral situation arises. Morality starts with a conflict of desires. The foundation of a moral life lies in the ability to choose.

When the social standards do not seem to apply to the situation, the other course open is to anticipate the probable consequences of the contemplated acts and proceed in such a way as to insure the maximum of desirable consequences. In such a situation one must act out of consideration not only for his own desires but also for the desires of others.

Character education consists of developing in youth habits and attitudes of living in conformity with the socially accepted standards so long as such conduct seems to insure desirable consequences to everyone concerned, but when conflict arises and such conformity does not seem to promise these desirable results, youth should be able to act in such a way as to insure them, even if such action is in opposition to the standards.

The end, therefore, in character education is to develop in the individual a philosophy of life free from conflicting standards. Such a philosophy seems attainable only when the approach in education is such as to help him to develop attitudes which will safeguard desirable consequences for everyone with whom he is associated and will lead to the richest possible attainment of satisfied needs for all.

LEVELS OF CHARACTER DEVELOPMENT

Character is primarily based upon emotions, in that attitudes always have an emotional connection. Man's conduct is more dependent upon feeling than upon thought. The worth of any activity in the promotion of moral qualities is determined chiefly by the opportunity it affords for the development of attitudes, and by the nature of the emotions it arouses.

The way in which moral training is best applied will vary according to the child's age and experience. Many writers have traced the order of character development from infancy to maturity. While it may be difficult to show experimentally that children pass through definite stages, there is evident a general sequence of development as the child grows into society.

CHILDHOOD. The very young child is a creature of impulse, dominated by emotions, with little, if any, capacity to reason. He has no sense of right or wrong. He learns that certain acts have pleasant results while others produce pain or discomfort, and in this way his conduct becomes somewhat regulated.

As the child develops he profits by his experience with the physical environment and understands the consequences of bumps, burns, and falls, and he finds, too, that there is an additional factor in the environment—that of his parents and teachers. He finds that he must satisfy an adult world. He is too young to understand the adult standards and he does not question them. His actions please or displease others as well as himself. To his own immediate satisfaction or pain in the act, he learns that there is an added set of consequences—the praise or reproof of his elders, as the case may be. It is from this fact that praise and censure derive their importance in moral training. Undesirable acts should be followed by an impressive evidence of disapproval, and what is fully as important, though more frequently neglected, desirable acts should be suitably commended. As the development of the self expands, the child strives independently to succeed. He goes through a process of trying himself out and testing himself in a great variety of situations.

ADOLESCENCE. As the years of adolescence approach, and the child's capacity to rationalize increases, the discipline of mere restraint and coerced obedience must be gradually modified. He is no longer interested in a certain type of conduct merely because parents and teachers or adult-imposed codes say it is desirable; he insists on knowing why, that is, what consequences result from it that make it desirable. His increasing fund of knowledge of consequences makes him increasingly able to foretell the future results of his present actions, and he seeks an increased independent control of his own conduct. If unexplained discipline is too long enforced, either the child's independent spirit will be broken or he will rebel; in which case he is forced to face life with no adequate moral training and will have to find out the consequences of acts by the dangerous trial-and-error method.

As the growing child moves out from the home and affiliates with groups of his own age, still another set of consequences of conduct appear to him. To his own gratification and to the satisfaction of adult approval, there is added now a satisfaction in the larger social approval of his own circle of associates. The individual now wants a share in setting the standards of conduct by which he shall abide; and when they are set, he desires praise for conforming to them. His conduct now becomes regulated by the approval and disapproval of the group, and the leader or teacher can best regulate the conduct of the individual through wise supervision of the group. The disapproval of one's own group is a much more powerful influence than adult disapproval.

MATURITY. With approaching maturity the man or woman takes his conduct into his own hands. He has passed through the socializing stages of adult regulation and group regulation, and now he becomes a self-governing individual. His background of social experience, his memory of the results of past actions, both immediate and remote, make it possible for him to foretell for himself the probable results of conduct. The gang law is no longer sufficient; he has become a law unto himself.

This recognition of standards even higher than that of the group means that the individual may have to act contrary to the will of the group if he is to be true to himself and is to safeguard the desired consequences of conduct. In short he has established for himself a philosophy of life which is based on the point of view that no act is right unless it leads to desirable results in the richest possible fulfillment of satisfied needs for everyone. This is the end and aim of character education. The personal attitudes and values which are reached in late adolescence do not become a fixed and rigid standard that regulates conduct throughout life— they are constantly changing with added experience. As Dewey so aptly puts it, education is the "constant reconstruction of experience," and education is a lifelong process.

PROCESSES OF CHARACTER EDUCATION

No one can live in a group for any length of time without having his character affected. Just living with people and interacting with them is bound to affect conduct. But while character is the inevitable result of interaction, it must be remembered that, qualitatively, there are various kinds of character: the gangster has character as well as the pastor. The point upon which there can be no assurance is that desirable character will result from social interaction.

There are four main processes by which society alters and shapes human character, each of which will be discussed in turn, namely, imitation, suggestion, instruction, and control.

PROCESS OF IMITATION. The preceding chapters have stressed the fact that man is an imitative creature. He is so constituted that he takes on from others the ways he admires. Habits and attitudes are acquired by trial and error, but they are also acquired by borrowing from others. Much imitation is unconscious, and people take on the ways of others unknowingly. Again, in many circumstances, they imitate deliberately and consciously.

Through imitation boys and girls take on the ways of the play group. This play group is a primary group and, next to the family, is the most potent factor in affecting conduct. Its ways and attitudes, good or bad, moral or immoral, social or antisocial, tend to become the ways of the individual members. Play groups are manifestly more potent in determining attitudes and habits than the formal environment of the schoolroom.

The set of values which the family holds is usually very different from that which exists in the gang. The child adopts both and acts according to one or the other depending upon which group he is in at the moment. These conflicting standards exist in his personality without his being conscious of the conflict until adolescent years when he attempts to develop a philosophy of life for himself. Leaders can do much to assist him in straightening out these conflicts.

Hero worship is an especially potent force in affecting character. By hero worship is meant an emulation that strives to imitate some admired character in a spirit of loyal enthusiasm. Youths are constantly seeking models who picture for them the ideal life they hope to attain. Whether the leader is aware of it or not, he is constantly a model to many of his followers. The very fact that he holds a certain attitude or habit adds prestige and authority to the attitude. The fact that he acts in a certain way becomes proof sufficient that it is the thing to do. This places a distinct challenge on the shoulders of the play leader or coach. His opportunity and responsibility in respect to personality guidance are ever present. No one, however skillful he may be in his specialties and however gifted he may be as a leader, has a place in a play organization unless he, himself, can display a personal example that is acceptable as a model for youth.

PROCESS OF SUGGESTION. By suggestion is meant the process of communicating an idea from one individual to another, whether the idea is accepted critically or uncritically. Children are particularly susceptible to suggestion, and the remarks and comments of their play associates and particularly of leaders are thus implanted in their minds. Three factors determine the effectiveness of the suggestion. First, there is the prestige of the source of the suggestion. The respected leader holding a position of high esteem is able through suggestion to influence his follower tremendously. Second is the duration and repetition of the suggestion. When a positive suggestion comes over and over again from a play leader, it tends to penetrate. In the third place, the volume of the suggestion enhances its effectiveness. In one sense this is closely related to duration and repetition, but the volume of a suggestion may come from its intensity as well as from its repetition. However, the more enduring effect upon behavior comes from continuous stimuli, of low order intensity and high order frequency. Innumerable small suggestions continuously provided can count for more than one dramatically powerful impact.

An indication of the effectiveness of suggestion in influencing behavior is clearly seen in advertising, for much of advertising is nothing more or less than suggestion. That advertising pays is proof that suggestion works. The radio and television commercial repeats the product name over and over and over; the singing commercial with its catchy ditty provides rhythmic repetition, and through its very monotony it gains in suggestive power. The play or group leader who would alter behavior patterns will do well to keep in mind the importance of the repetitive attack.

If strong, aggressive, vivacious leaders of play who occupy a position of unquestioned prestige and popularity among boys and girls suggest frequently and forcefully the desirability of certain types of action, it will unquestionably have some effect in shaping attitudes. For this suggestion to be most effective, however, it should not be divorced from activity and handled in academic fashion; it should come in the course of activity which presents the possibility of immediate action upon the suggestion, or if not immediately, in the very near future.

PROCESS OF INSTRUCTION. Adults are not willing to leave the social education of their children to the natural and unplanned process of imitation and suggestion. Through affection for them and fear of consequences, they deliberately try to inculcate in children the attitudes and sentiments which they desire them to hold. The development of right attitudes is one of the primary goals of education, if not the most important. Children will receive training in morality from some source, and it is folly to leave the development of moral judgment to chance information or to trial and error. The question is not one of whether or not the child is to be instructed in morality, but rather how the instruction is best given.

Direct and Indirect Methods. Some educators favor the plan of special classes in ethics or morality in the school curriculum, in which the various character traits are defined, discussed, and interpreted. The use of such definite classes which deal exclusively with character and morality constitute what is called direct moral instruction.

The Sunday school relies primarily upon discussion and preaching for the development of character. The Boy Scout program presents a series of character qualities in its law saying that a Scout is trustworthy, loyal, helpful, friendly, courteous, kind, obedient, cheerful, thrifty, brave, clean, and reverent; boys learn them and repeat them, they are discussed, and it is assumed they put them into practice. The educators who support the use of direct moral instruction in the school hold that it affords an opportunity for thorough-going systematic presentation of moral qualities.

Other educators, however, feel that moral education can best be carried on in connection with the regular school courses and in connection with activity in general instead of in special classes in ethics. This point of view maintains that since the habits and attitudes which constitute character are attained through conduct, the most effective place for such education is in connection with situations calling for moral living. Since such situations arise in all classes in the curriculum, all teachers are confronted with the necessity of teaching morality incidentally in connection with these courses. This method is called indirect or incidental moral instruction.

Discussion of the qualities of character—trustworthiness, loyalty, helpfulness, etc.—has a place in social education, but it cannot be handled totally in an abstract way in dealing with children; these words take on meaning and become understandable to youth only as they are related to definite experience. One cannot teach honesty effectively except in situations calling for honesty, and such situations might appear in arithmetic, shop work, history, civics, handcraft, baseball, or other activities of the school and club, and in all of the activities of life. And so with all traits. Every teacher on the staff has constant opportunities for moral instruction and every teacher shares in the responsibility. In the social give-and-take of play situations an unexcelled opportunity is offered to play leaders.

Laws of Learning. The same laws of learning apply in character education as in any other phase of education. Character education in common with all education is governed by (1) the law of readiness or interest on the part of the individual himself, (2) the law of exercise or practice, and (3) the law of effect.

According to the law of readiness the child must want the desirable habit or attitude. It cannot be forced upon him by adult authority, discipline, or extrinsic incentives. When he wants the right, is interested in acquiring right habits, he is in a state of readiness to learn and acts accordingly. This leads to the second law—practice and exercise. Moral habits and attitudes are acquired through practice—precise practice. The boy on the football field learns sportsmanship only through wanting to be sportsmanlike and practicing sportsmanship.

It is only through practice that moral lessons are learned, just as it is only through practice that one learns to swim or play golf. Information helps, but it is in doing the act that learning takes place. Neumann puts it as follows:

> Character is essentially a matter of action, the habitual performance of certain kinds of deeds rather than others, and the only genuine way of learning how to do these deeds is to do them, just as the only way to learn tennis is to play it. Nobody really understands what "responsibility" means until he has been entrusted with a task that has succeeded or has failed because of him. So with respect to "service," "generosity" and all the other possible terms of the moral vocabulary; any genuine comprehension of them, as Aristotle pointed out, first requires practice in the deeds themselves. . . .
>
> Pupils take to activity so much more readily than they do to the relatively passive business of listening or reading. They are eager to engage in athletics, to run a school paper, to dance, to act plays, to build, to do dozens of things impossible for those who merely sit at a desk, study, and recite. One of the richest veins of education has been tapped in recent years by turning these energies to account.[1]

This leads to the third law: not only must the child practice the right but he must practice with satisfaction. William H. Kilpatrick, the renowned educator, once said: "What the children think and feel as they act is probably the largest factor in determining what traits shall go into their character." To a certain extent, the learning of moral habits is thus beyond the control of play leaders and teachers, but in the course of situations calling for moral conduct on the play field or in the class room, leaders can call the child's attention to the need for a change in his ways, and then can give him an opportunity to practice the desired quality in such a way that it will bring satisfaction. Leaders can also help a child see the situation in its entirety and to consider the remote as well as the immediate consequences.

Conduct leads to habits and thus to character. Since the

[1] H. Neumann, *Education for Moral Growth* (New York: D. Appleton & Co., 1923), pp. 191-92.

character is slightly different because of the new habits, the conduct is different. This new type of conduct leads to new habits and thus to a further change in character, and so the process goes on. The laws of learning being what they are, the leader or teacher must begin in character education with conduct—with activity, rather than preaching, academic instruction, and abstract discussion.

If an activity is to offer character-building opportunities it must be interesting to the child and his participation must bring satisfaction. The activity, then, must give the child an opportunity to choose and experience the consequences, as well as follow dicta passively; it must offer opportunity for self-direction.

Concomitant Learnings. The recreation leader is constantly finding opportunities for moral instruction in situations which call for immediate application on the part of the players. The direct learnings in play are the skills in the game that is being played, and the moral learnings are the concomitants. One can run the whole gamut of so-called character traits and find very few that do not represent possible concomitant learnings in a week of play activity. The need is that the leader should constantly analyze the situation for possible desirable concomitant learnings and emphasize them at every possible turn. Right here rests the greatest weakness in the use of play as a definite means to character education: the leader or teacher becomes so engrossed with the game or subject matter itself that often he fails to take advantage of the opportunities for moral education. Character instruction is as much the duty of the leader as teaching skills.

The possible concomitant learnings which may result from a single contest, such as the high jump, will indicate the analysis that may be made for any game or contest. In high jumping the player may learn among other things to be considerate of others by putting the bar up after knocking it down, by avoiding undue delay in taking his turn, by jumping in proper turn, and so on.

The concomitants which may successfully be taught vary

with the age and development of the child. In general, they may be divided into three main types according to the order of their appearance and development, as follows:

1. The individualistic qualities, or those pertaining to personal conduct independent of others.
2. The social qualities, or those which are concerned with the individual as a member of a group.
3. The civic qualities, or those involving the attitude of the individual toward organized society.

The individualistic qualities involve those necessary for the success of the individual in competition and life. They are most primitive in the race and likewise appear first in the child. Proper control and direction are needed if the desirable qualities of this type are to be fostered and the undesirable ones discouraged. Without direction the development of the individualistic qualities is apt to produce a self-centered person who is unmindful of the welfare of others. Wise direction in home, school, and playground is needed to temper this extreme individualism. Types of individualistic conduct are represented by the following traits: courage, ingenuity, initiative, decision, perseverance, determination, self-reliance, self-control, self-restraint, thoroughness, aggressiveness, ambition, enthusiasm, reliability, and resourcefulness.

The social qualities are those which provide for proper relationships between the child and his associates, and which include the simple moral virtues of the home and other primary groups. They begin to develop as soon as the first playmate enters the child's life. Even the engaging in elementary games means that the child is subjecting himself to a social discipline. He must comply with the rules of the game (a social institution) and he must make himself agreeable if he is to be a popular playmate. The concomitant learnings of the social type are represented by the following words which taken together are often spoken of in the world of play as sportsmanship: kindness, unselfishness, friendliness, truthfulness, justice, honesty, thoughtfulness, courtesy, helpfulness, tolerance, sociability, and cheerfulness.

The civic qualities are those which deal with organized society and its institutions. These qualities parallel the social qualities very closely, but do not develop until later. It is not until after the child has been taught his social obligations to a group in which the members are immediately present with him, that he can be taught a correct attitude towards the more complex, remoter groups of society. An ability to think in the abstract is required, for the youth must become loyal to ideals. The society of which he now realizes himself to be a part is larger than his own immediate environment. Therefore, he must visualize it and account for his relations to it. The civic qualities include loyalty, cooperation, obedience, and service.

Means of Learning Through Recreation Groups. Of the various methods employed in character education, five are of most interest to recreation leaders: (1) games, contests, and play projects, (2) discussion, (3) individual counseling, (4) storytelling and dramatizing, and (5) mottoes.

Games, Contests, and Play Projects. Habits and attitudes are the result primarily of activity. Stories and books are valuable in building ideas and practicing moral judgment, but it is in actual practice in life situations that social learning is finally achieved. (See Humphrey, Selected References.)

It thus appears that the greatest opportunity comes to play and club leaders through guidance during the course of games, contests, and club and school projects such as found in the handcrafts, woodcraft, nature lore, publishing the school or club paper, rehearsing a play, and participating in community enterprises and civic service. Applying the points brought out in the discussion earlier in the chapter, the following suggestions should be kept in mind, if the play is to result in the greatest possible accomplishment in social education:

1. List the probable concomitant learnings.
2. Bring satisfaction by praising and commending the desirable moral act.
3. Bring annoyance by condemning the socially undesirable act.
4. Enforce the rules promptly, surely, impartially.
5. Point out at every turn the destructive consequences of the bad act; the desirable consequences of the good. The player may learn by trial and error, but the business of education is to substitute instruction for this blundering, time-consuming process and to prevent the frequently disastrous results of trial-and-error learning in the moral field.
6. Emphasize the broader, more remote, and far-reaching consequences of the good and bad act as well as the immediate. Winning at any cost may appear as an immediate and very desirable result, but it fails to take into consideration all of the consequences which appear when a larger view is taken.
7. Study the effect of the games on the individual players.

Leaders are so often engrossed with winning that they fail to observe the social effects of the game on individual players. These outcomes should be studied if effective character guidance is to result. For instance, it may be found in observing a game that:

1. A player constantly attempts to star at the expense of good team play (a factor often evaluated by coaches in terms of the winning efficiency of the team rather than in terms of the effect on the individual's character).
2. A player takes the hard knocks of the game with courage and self-control.
3. A player assumes leadership in supporting high standards of sportsmanship.
4. A player refuses to recognize and give credit for a good play on the part of the opposing team.
5. A player is timid and self-conscious in the presence of the crowd.
6. A player consistently breaks a rule when he finds he can "get away with it."
7. Certain players clique together in team play in an effort to make an unpopular member of the team "look bad."

8. Certain players change their attitude toward people of another race through constant association with them on the team.
9. A player flares up in anger when fouls are called on him.
10. A player becomes sullen and morose in defeat.
11. A player abandons poor living habits which lessen his effectiveness for the good of the team.

Discussion. Preaching has been the tool upon which traditional character education has relied. Reference has been made at many points in the foregoing pages to the relative ineffectiveness of words in influencing behavior as compared to activity. It should not be assumed, however, that language is useless as a means of acquiring experience, or that a child must actually perform an action in order to learn its significance. The importance of the phrase "learning by doing" can be exaggerated. The animal learns only by doing, but the human being can profit by the experience of others and of past generations.

In the case of young children, verbal teaching is ineffectual unless based upon responses in specific situations. Having had experience, discussion may be distinctly beneficial in helping the child to relate the common elements in situations which seem to him to have nothing in common. Occasional discussions on the part of an athletic team or play group may serve to classify seemingly unrelated types of experience as undesirable or desirable behavior in the minds of the players. The leader, however, must draw his material out of the definite experience of the group or the discussion will be ineffectual. He must use many stories and illustrations which deal with situations similar to those the group has recently experienced. In other words, discussion must supplement activity, never replace it, in social education.

Individual Counseling. When an individual child differs in behavior in some significant way from the rest of the group, the individual approach to character education is indicated. The following are examples familiar to many games leaders: the shy and backward child who does not participate; the player who is unduly selfish; the player who persists in grandstand playing; the child who is oversensitive and moody; the child with capacity but who accomplishes little; the bullying and quarrelsome child; the child with temper tantrums; the daydreaming and introverted child; the child who has no regard for equipment or property rights; the child who because of lack of physical ability or confidence hangs on the edge of activities.

In such cases as these the game leader will have to work with the deficient individual constantly and will have to seek sympathetically to help him toward a more desirable adjustment. In difficult cases the leader may need to secure the assistance of the psychologist, the psychiatrist, or the social worker.

Storytelling and Dramatizing.   Of all the ways in which the spoken word may be used to influence behavior, the story is the most effective. It is not activity, but it is the next thing to it. In his imagination the listener experiences the situation. He sees himself in the hero's role. It is as if it were he who accomplished the heroic act—who was loyal to a friend, obedient to orders, kind when there was provocation to be cruel. When a similar situation arises the listener has, in a more real sense than we are apt to realize, "been there before." A good storyteller not only has the capacity to entertain, but he possesses an outstandingly effective device for education. Storytelling is a skill every recreation leader should strive to master.

Great care should be taken in selecting a story which portrays vividly the lesson desired and which at the same time has a compelling and intriguing plot to carry it on. Once the story is selected, care must be taken to let it teach the lesson, to tell it as interestingly as possible and with no thought of moral instruction while telling it. If the lesson can be taught by the story at all, the plot will do it. To moralize at the end all too often destroys the effect.

Dramatics constitute a medium even more effective than storytelling in social education. The listener pictures himself in the desirable roles in a good drama just as he does in listening to a story. Participation in dramatics also is a valuable means of character education. Children learn to play the role of desirable characters and to project the sound of disapproval when there is a portrayal of undesirable traits. Owing to the small number of people involved and the time consumed in producing an effective play, dramatization is not as convenient a tool for everyday use by play and club leaders as storytelling.

Mottoes. The force of suggestion in influencing behavior has previously been discussed. The motto suggests to us a moral principle, a way of acting, and its repetition through sign and spoken word acts upon us in much the same way as the advertiser's cleverly turned phrases.

There has been, however, a confidence in the capacity of maxims or mottoes to influence conduct which is all out of proportion to the facts. Children, and adults, for that matter, arrive at a true general conception only through experiencing a number of particular instances. The motto has meaning only as it refers to concrete examples or individual instances which the child has recently experienced or is experiencing. Properly handled, mottoes do have effect and can be made a very worth-while tool. They are so easy to grasp and to use, however, that leaders are apt to depend upon them without full realization of their limitations.

Problem of Transfer. Although it is generally granted that in the course of games, desirable moral attitudes are developed, can there be assurance that these attitudes will shift to other phases of life and result in desirable behavior? Will sportsmanship on the baseball field transfer to the business world and result in ethical conduct?

Although recent research indicates that learning does not transfer to the extent that was once thought, the assertion has frequently been made that there is no transfer of moral attitudes from play and athletics to the activities of one's larger life. That such transfer can take place becomes clear in reviewing the following points already mentioned in other connections earlier in the chapter.

First, moral habits are learned in specific situations, and a habit learned in one situation may be expected to function in another situation only to the extent that the second situation has elements like those in the first. The fact that specific learnings transfer only to very similar situations would be discouraging to the play leader interested in social education, were it not for a second process.

Second, if two experiences involving the same social situation are analyzed for the child he may learn the common elements in the two and attach the same trait to them. The child may think of obedience to the rules as one thing and obedience to the law as something else, but if the common elements are pointed out to him and he grasps the similarity, there is a possibility of transfer. The pointing out of the common elements in varying situations leads the child to generalize them, and with growing maturity, to intellectualize the process. In this way moral attitudes learned in specific situations in play are transferable to other situations. Very obviously such transfer will not take place without guidance on the part of leaders, teachers, or parents.

It must be remembered that socially undesirable attitudes learned in play may transfer by this process as well as the desirable ones. To the extent that there are identical elements, antisocial practices may carry over and transfer to other spheres of life.

It is too much to expect the play leader alone to integrate the desirable moral learnings in games with the rest of life. The cooperation of the entire faculty is necessary. The history teacher can easily associate the chivalry of the knights with sportsmanship in athletics; the civics teacher can show that service to the state is essentially the same in principle as sacrifice for the team and the school; and so with all subjects in the curriculum.

PROCESS OF CONTROL. Society everywhere utilizes certain means of social control to protect its standards and enforce conformity. Reference has already been made to some of these, such as instruction, discussion, and persuasion. When these methods do not result in the desired behavior, other means are sometimes employed: rewards and punishment.

Rewards. At first glance the use of rewards for right conduct appears to be both unnecessary and undesirable, if not actually defeating of purpose. If what is meant is a material reward available to the person after he acts in a certain way, then this verdict may be justified. An analysis of the concept, however, reveals the fact that praise is after all a form of reward, and there is no more useful and valuable device in personality guidance than this. It is particularly important that praise should accompany all commendable acts on the part of children. It helps to stamp in the desirability of the act and leads to the awareness that pleasant consequences ensue from so acting. In the learning process activity must be accompanied by satisfaction. It is the *continuousness* of such praise and recognition that bears fruit in permanent attitudes, just as it is the repetitiveness of suggestion that leads to action.

The difference between material rewards and praise rests not so much in the fact that one is material and of tangible value and the other not, but in the fact that the one is usually offered before action starts, while the other comes along afterward as a natural and often unanticipated consequence. Badges, pins, and buttons in children's organizations and the playground point systems offering points for sportsmanship and approved conduct fall under the category of material rewards. In a certain sense using material rewards is purchasing right conduct, which of course is socially undesirable. It can be said that there may be the same danger in using praise, but obviously here the individual is more apt to participate in the activity for its own sake and praise just comes along afterward. If honors and awards can be used in this incidental way there would be no objection, but, when they are publicized and held before children before the activity starts, the chances are that the attainment of them will, to many, become the end.

Punishment. Since satisfaction must accompany the right if learning is to take place, it would seem to follow that annoyance should accompany the wrong. Certainly the individual must come to know as early as possible in his experience that wrong conduct has undesirable consequences.

There are two types of punishment employed by society, whether it be a state, a club, or a team. The first is the legal, imposed by law or by authorities; the second is the extra-legal, applied informally by the members of the group itself.

Disciplinary action on the part of a leader partakes of the legal type, in that it carries the impact of authority. Such action in its extreme form may involve penalties. The use of penalties should be the last resort. A leader who is admired and liked will find actual punishment seldom necessary. In serious matters of undesirable conduct, a quiet sympathetic talk between the leader and offender, in which the consequences of the act are made clear and the emphasis is placed on right conduct, is usually all that is needed. What the offender needs is help, sympathetic help. Such a kind, sympathetic, friendly relationship is the best means of control—punishment then is seldom necessary, and advice is sought and cheerfully received.

The second type of punishment, the extra-legal, is applied constantly in all types of groups and among all ages, for people do express disapproval in various ways when the conduct of one of their associates is not in keeping with the group's accepted standards. Such group pressure is effective, often more so than that of the leader, because people will often sacrifice status with the leader rather than with their associates. The offender rectifies his ways because he feels he must get along. Informal types of group pressure are often more desirable than action by the leader, in that they originate with a person's equals. On the other hand, careful guidance may often be necessary, particularly with children, because the efforts of children may result in a gang-up against the offender with cruel and harmful results. Rather than lending support to the group through silence, the leader may need to give vocal support to the victim.

PLAY AND CITIZENSHIP

Throughout history play has adapted itself to the national ideal, becoming a reflection of it, and a means of advancing it. From ancient Greece and Sparta, through ancient Rome, and on through the Renaissance, play has been a mirror of the national culture, and an instrument for promoting the national design. The same is true in the present period.

There are, in general, two opposing philosophies of government. The one, totalitarianism, exalts the state; the second, democracy, exalts the individual. Both utilize physical exercise and recreation activities for their needs— the former, consciously, because it grasps this chance to build up its nation in physique, and at the same time to make its subjects submissive, disciplined, machine-like, and carefully indoctrinated; the latter, unconsciously, because in following the ideals of freedom, it allows free choice in its activities, which means that the program followed is in keeping with the desires and wishes of its people. Autocratic nations have been impressively successful in making their educational system, in which recreation and physical training take a very important part, serve the national aims. One must recognize the apparent perfection of this militaristic type of educational training, particularly, when it is backed up with the moral philosophy of duty for duty's sake, accompanied by a subsequent development of a blind, fierce loyalty for, and desire to serve, the state. Such a system, throughout the history of the world, has been influential in creating nations and groups of nations which are controlled by a few or one individual and present a constant threat to peace.

Rulers have had a way throughout history of utilizing play as a means of inculcating in youth their own ideas and dogmas. Children's clubs in all countries are used quite generally as a means for instilling a nationalistic attitude and are utilized by political parties as a medium for spreading their own particular doctrines. Youth is gullible, impressionable, and easily swayed, and once convinced is a dynamo of energy for the advancement of the cause.

EVIDENCE OF DEMOCRATIC CONDUCT. The capacity for democratic living is not an inherited gift of a child born in a democracy. Contact with adults who hold democratic citizenship is not enough—children need experience as democratic citizens themselves in a society geared to their capacities. The play group, the club, the athletic team offer the possibility for that experience. Whether these groups are democratic or autocratic depends largely upon the point of view of their leadership.

Democracy is an attitude of mind. Its very essence is a thorough-going, sincere respect for persons—a regard for persons that holds them of greater worth than physical equipment, than property, than profits, than favorite play activities. It regards the play group and its activities merely as means to an end, that end being the person. It is a faith in human possibilities. Without this attitude on the part of the group leader, there is little chance of running a democratic group. Given this attitude, there is no probability of the play leader riding roughshod over the players, no probability of his forcing players into activities without regard to their aims and interests, no probability of worshipping game victory over human personality.

The following may be considered "inch marks" on the foot-rule of democratic play in recreation group, club or team. If the group is democratic, there is evidence of:

1. A sincere interest in, and respect for, everyone on the part of the leader, irrespective of their ability or value to the group.
2. Mutual confidence among all members of the group, leaders and members alike.
3. The right of self-expression, of freedom for everyone to criticize constructively the group's procedures.

4. The tendency on the part of all members to accept others as equals, regardless of race, religion, or economic status.
5. The delegation of responsibility to members to the extent of their capacities.
6. The lack of many rules, restraints, and rigid controls; lack of fear of those in authority.
7. Participation in the formulation of rules by those expected to live by them.
8. Participation in the planning of programs and making decisions on the part of the members.
9. Strong intrinsic motivations rather than those arising from coercions and administrative authority.
10. Initiative on the part of members.
11. Free group discussions and frequent meetings of leaders and members.
12. The use by those in authority of the terms "we" and "our" instead of "I" and "mine."

SHARING IN DECISION-MAKING. Democracy implies a certain amount of self-regulation and self-direction, and it goes without saying that children do not possess the experience, the judgment, and the information to regulate themselves fully and completely. Neither does the non-swimmer possess the ability to swim, but he is not told he cannot go near the water. Rather, he is initiated and, with careful instruction and all possible safeguards, he is taught to swim. It is no more sensible to set up a régime of democracy and expect children to achieve satisfactory results without guidance than it would be to throw the non-swimmers into water over their heads and expect them to swim a crawl stroke to shore.

The ability to make choices is a fundamental requisite for successful living in a democratic state. Children learn to make choices only by making them, not by having them made for them. In the democratic group or club, everyone shares in the making of decisions, or more correctly, everyone who has a stake in the matter.

The opportunity for putting democratic practices into operation varies with the nature of the group. The athletic team may have few compared to the club with more varied programs, and the club few compared with the camp which is a miniature isolated society. But the principles apply whatever the situation, and the leader with the democratic attitude will utilize the opportunities wherever he finds them.

ATTITUDE OF SERVICE. Education begins in the home, but it cannot remain there long. The child soon moves out to the street and the alley where neighborhood children make their contribution. Later he enters the school, affiliates with the gang, and moves in enlarging, widening circles. His loyalties are first tied up with the home, then with the neighborhood group, the school, the city; his loyalties are related to larger and more scattered groups. In the end he conceives of the full meaning of the state and his loyalty is to it. The role of the citizen becomes understandable to him, and, if his education has been adequate, he strives to play the role.

Citizenship involves service to the state. This service is not limited to the military type nor performed only in time of war; but in his everyday life, as needs arise, the good citizen owes an allegiance and a service to his country in the solving of its problems.

Recreational-educational organizations for children attempt to utilize play in the development of this attitude of service. The Boy Scouts, for instance, foster the ideal of serving the community through community good turns such as regulating traffic, distributing literature for the Community Chest campaign, and clearing alleys in the spring clean-up drive. The Girl Scouts and Camp Fire Girls do likewise. Two points of view are behind this service activity on the part of these organizations. First, the citizenship attitudes are taught through activity—the ideal of service is acquired primarily through serving. Second, citizenship does not begin at twenty-one, when the franchise becomes available. Children are citizens in as real a sense as are adults and owe their obligation of service to their country within the limitations of their capacities.

BREADTH OF VISION. Patriotism is loyalty to place, whereas nationalism is loyalty to culture. That a certain amount of nationalistic emotion is desirable and necessary goes without saying—no national group could long survive or retain unity without it. Too much nationalism or worship of the country's culture, however, leads to provincialism and narrowness of vision, shutting out the contribution of foreign cultures.

Play groups do much to overcome provincialism. Children who play on the playground with children from foreign countries find that the latter are quite human, likable, often having some different qualities which all American children might do well to acquire. The school athletic team which has members of many nationalistic groups on it contributes to race tolerance and the breadth of vision which is the essence of democracy. The YWCA and YMCA have clear-cut objectives in this direction. Likewise the social settlement house is based upon the philosophy that all foreign-born neighborhoods in our large cities have something to offer in the way of culture.

Democracy depends upon the development of common interests and the sensing of a common life among all elements of the population. The social aim of education is to develop children with the ability to enter into a wide variety of interests; in short, to regard all things human as part of themselves.

SUMMARY

Individuals learn and develop behavior patterns through their experiences. Traditional formal education includes the fundamental body of knowledge one must learn to survive in present-day society. But this formal education does not extensively teach one how to get along with others, nor to exercise positive behavior through activities which develop good character and other positive personality traits. Obviously, much character education and other social learning does take place in well-directed formal education.

But it is also obvious that all social learning cannot take place through the formal education processes alone. It is here that the play and recreation of children, youth, and adults provides a process through which desirable moral and social behavior may be learned. Carefully directed activities in sports, drama, music, dance, and many informal recreation activities provide situations in which individuals, under social pressure, must react. As this reaction takes place, the parent, the teacher, the play leader, the counselor, and others can help an individual choose desirable patterns of social behavior which develop lifelong habits leading to high moral standards, personal expression, and the development of desirable personality traits. It is through practice that conduct may be observed and that habits leading to positive character may be developed.

Play and recreation activities, coordinated with sound formal education, may contribute much to help the individual to understand himself as well as others and to develop the high moral standards, the civic responsibility, and the attitude toward others that is so necessary to meet the greatest challenge of the world today—that of man learning how to live in peace with his fellow man.

SELECTED REFERENCES

JONES, VERNON. "Character Development in Children—An Objective Approach," *Manual of Child Psychology*, ed. Leonard Carmichael. New York: John Wiley and Sons, Inc., 1954, pp. 781–832. The main psychological problems involved in character development and evidence or clues toward their solution are reviewed. An intensive bibliography is included.

LAYMAN, EMMA McCLOY. *Mental Health Through Physical Education.* Minneapolis: Burgess Publishing Co., 1955. Chapter 9 contains a discussion of the principles and procedures for developing a character education program through physical education and recreation activities.

NEUMEYER, MARTIN H., and NEUMEYER, ESTHER S. *Leisure and Recreation.* New York: The Ronald Press Co., 1958. Chapters 6, 9, and 10 are devoted to a summary analysis of the various phases or social processes of the social environment. Particular emphasis is given to showing how play and recreation provide desirable avenues for personality growth and opportunities for the individual to learn to adjust in the complex phases of group living.

ROBBINS, FLORENCE G. *The Sociology of Play, Recreation, and Leisure Time.* Dubuque, Iowa: William C. Brown Co., 1955. Along with an analysis of how play, recreation, and leisure-time activities are promoted in various settings, the author explains how these activities may integrate learnings, skills, and interests from many areas of the individual's cultural and social world.

BOWER, WILLIAM C. *Moral and Spiritual Values in Education.* Lexington: University of Kentucky Press, 1952, Chap. 13.

BRECKENRIDGE, MARIAN E., and VINCENT E. LEE. *Child Development— Physical and Psychologic Growth Through the Years.* Philadelphia: W. B. Saunders Co., 1955, Chaps. 12, 13 and 14.

COWELL, CHARLES C. *Scientific Foundations of Physical Education.* New York: Harper & Bros., 1953, Chap. 6.

DOTY, RICHARD S. *The Character Dimension of Camping.* New York: Association Press, 1960.

Education Policies Commission. *Moral and Spiritual Values in the Public Schools.* Washington, D.C.: National Education Association and the American Association of School Administrators, 1951.

HUMPHREY, JAMES H. *Elementary School Physical Education, with Emphasis Upon Its Integration in Other Curriculum Areas.* New York: Harper & Bros., 1958. Chapter 9 suggests methods of integrating play and physical education with other school subjects.

McCLOY, C. H. "Character Building through Physical Education," *The Research Quarterly,* I (October, 1930), 41–59.

SHAFFER, LAURANCE FREDERIC, and SHOHEN, EDWARD JOSEPH. *The Psychology of Adjustment.* Boston: Houghton Mifflin Co., 1956.

SHAW, F. J., and ORT, R. S. *Personal Adjustment in the American Culture.* New York: Harper & Bros., 1953. See especially pages 244–51 for a discussion of the value of play groups in preparing children and youth for adult living.

YOUNG, KIMBALL. *Social Psychology.* New York: Appleton-Century-Crofts, Inc., 1956, Chaps. 3, 4 and 5.

Part IV

ORGANIZATION AND ADMINISTRATION OF PLAY AND RECREATION

14

Promotion of Play and Recreation

In the light of the universality of play, the basic need for it, and the value placed upon it, one is not surprised to find many varying types of agencies organized to promote and administer it. Moreover, these agencies provide many varied types of recreational opportunities. Recreation is the sole function of many of these agencies, while to others, it is an incidental interest only. Some serve the entire community while others limit their facilities to their own membership. Some are organized to promote a single type of play while others give as wide a variety as possible. Some operate as a business, with profit as the objective, and others exist for service. The purpose of this chapter is to analyze this rather complex development of play, indicating under broad headings present-day play and recreation activities as they are now engaged in and promoted in various settings in our society.

DEVELOPMENT OF RECREATION SERVICES

Recreation programs and services in the United States developed along with public schools, libraries, and similar institutions. During the early part of the play movement, the recreation function was carried on mainly by philanthropic individuals and groups. Social welfare agencies operated community centers, playgrounds, camps, and similar programs as part of their overall approach to meet the needs of both children and adults caught in a rapidly changing world impelled by mass immigration and by deplorable economic and social conditions prevalent in heavily populated, industrial cities.

The need for recreation services grew so rapidly that by 1910 it had become a major problem. Philanthropic agencies alone were no longer able, because of expanding financial demands, to meet these needs. The public schools at that time failed to accept the responsibility of extending their services to offer adequate year-round recreation programs. Public park and recreation services grew in a rather haphazard manner, primarily on a local basis. Consequently, the major responsibility was left to no one particular existing private or governmental agency.

It is to be expected, then, that the present-day promotion of recreation programs and services throughout this country presents a rather complex pattern. It is not uncommon to find little or no public recreation services in one community; in another there may be a number of overlapping public, voluntary, and private recreation and leisure-time service agencies; and in still another, private and voluntary services might be well-coordinated along with a public recreation system involving the city, the park board, and the school board, all legally separate bodies, which may be engaged in the promotion of different phases of the various community recreation services.

For the purpose of this analysis, the various community recreation services are classified according to the setting in which they occur. Community recreation in this context means all recreation services and activities provided by public, private, and commercial agencies for persons who have in common a geographical or institutional bond and a community of interest. This classification, in some instances, also reflects the source of funds supporting the particular service involved. Definitions of the various types of play promotion are included in order to differentiate as clearly as possible one type of promotion from another. The following is an organizational pattern of nine classifications used, to some degree, in recreation survey studies and in a wide variety of research which reflects directly the changing trends in the field of recreation promotion: (1) informal and home play, (2) public recreation, (3) voluntary or private agency, (4) institutional recreation, (5) industrial recreation, (6) recreation in rural areas, (7) informal and organized camping, (8) private programs, and (9) commercial recreation.

INFORMAL AND HOME PLAY

The type of promotion referred to here is that of self-promotion. Its scope includes all the forms of play that are planned by single individuals or small groups without a definite organization. This type of play is the essence of free self-expression—it is self-impelled action on the part of the individual to engage in wholesome, healthful recreation during leisure time. There are always enthusiasts, singly or collectively, for such outdoor recreations as hiking, fishing, hunting, swimming, canoeing, skating, touring, camping, picnics, and informal "scrub" games; and similarly, for such indoor play as reading, cards, checkers, chess, and music. In addition, there are the congenial groups which will come together of their own accord for dances, card parties, informal conversation sessions, and similar social occasions. Since these groups are local and informal, it is difficult to measure their growth but their popularity and influence in everyday life is unmistakable.

Even more personal than the informal play group is the home and the family group. Family recreation may be defined as play and recreation activities performed by the family within the framework of the home or outside the home in conjunction with other families. In the complexity of modern industrial life, the home and the family group still remain as man's first playground, school, and workshop. Family experiences formulate deep influences on the individual's sense of values, condition his emotional stability, and have lifelong effects on the development of one's personality. It is in the family environment that the individual tests his abilities, first discovers the effects of his actions, secures satisfactions of basic affectional response needs, and develops his personality to the point of being able to adjust himself satisfactorily in society.

It would be unwise, however, to ignore the drastic changes in the structure of family life during the past thirty years. The function of the family as consumer has increased while its function as producer has virtually disappeared. Parents today are not independent of devastating unemployment fluctuations. Limited space in the home, the increase in the number of working mothers, and a trend toward indifference to family responsibilities is the cause of deterioration of many neighborhoods. Tensions in industrial life often are transferred to the home, and individuals often wish to escape the home to find solace in unrelated jobs, amusements, and separate interests of their own.

Despite these influences, great progress has been made in developing sound play and recreation patterns in the American home and family group. J. A. Wylie, in a survey of family recreation, found that 60 per cent of the 504 families studied were positive that they had achieved stronger family units as a result of cooperative participation in family recreation programs. In similar studies, recreation in the family has been found to rank third in importance behind money and housing as a major factor in family happiness and unity.

Planning and carrying out play activities in the home is taking advantage of a situation which is already organized and has a great potential for development. Despite outside activities, more leisure-time hours are spent in the home than elsewhere. The backyard is still the child's best playground. Present-day architects and builders are including in apartments and residences play space known as playrooms, rumpus rooms, and rathskellers; particular attention is given to the design of outdoor areas and facilities including ample turf area for swings, slides, sandpiles, and home-play apparatus, as well as out-of-door meals.

Within the possibilities of home play are toys, card games, table games such as checkers and dominoes, ping

pong, billards, and table golf; there is also reading, storytelling, handcrafts, music, radio, dancing, gardening,
motoring, picnics, family excursions, and trips. Finally,
the home recreation pattern has been changed by television. This medium has made the movie available in the
home. The possibilities of education for leisure through
television have great potential for developing more recreation centered around the family or informal groups in the
home.

Although recreation has great potential for improving
family life and the quality of living, desirable recreation
patterns do not develop in the family without integrated
planning for recreation throughout the entire community.
Life in the family group is conditioned, to a great extent,
by the individual's experiences and opportunities outside
the home.

PUBLIC RECREATION PROMOTION

Public recreation involves the provision of recreation opportunities and services, available to all the people, by governmental units at various levels. These units are financed
primarily by taxation and include establishment, operation,
conduct, control and maintenance of programs, services,
areas, and facilities. This is the type of play promotion
which gives greatest promise of meeting the needs of all
stratifications of society. Through such support as the
community gives, a broad field of play activities is furnished without direct charge to the players. Although
minor charges to cover maintenance may be made for
some types of public recreation such as the use of golf
courses, swimming pools, and the like, for the most part
the facilities are free.

CONTRIBUTIONS OF GOVERNMENT. All branches of government from federal to municipal are concerned in varying degrees with providing recreation facilities. Perhaps
the more conspicuous of federal contributions are the parks
of the National Park Service, the forests of the U. S. Forest

Service, and in the conservation of wild life and the restora-
tion of natural conditions by the Bureau of Biological Survey. The U. S. Office of Education makes available helpful
recreation literature and through multiple techniques encourages schools to place a greater emphasis on a wide
variety of activities having play value. The Children's
Bureau also carries on research and makes available valuable literature. Through its Extension Service the Department of Agriculture contributes outstanding service in conducting leadership-training institutes and operating clubs
and camps for rural residents. These are but a few of the
federal agencies concerned with phases of recreation.

The contributions of the state governments are similar
to those of the federal—providing basic services through
public parks and areas, publishing literature, and training
leadership. The county, although previously confined to
administering large metropolitan recreation systems, is
gradually accepting major responsibilities for administering
broader recreation programs in many areas of California,
Wisconsin, Kentucky, and several other states.

It is the municipal government that is closest to the
people and able to carry facilities into the neighborhoods
where the people live. The municipal program is financed
for the most part by property taxes but may have help from
other sources. Many playgrounds bear the names of local
benefactors who have donated expensive grounds. Recreation funds are frequently swelled by contributions from
organizations such as Parent-Teacher Associations, luncheon clubs, foundations, churches, and others similarly interested in civil improvement. Industrial concerns, too,
may throw open their privately supported play spaces to
the general community use.

PARKS. Parks range all the way from the great national
areas of famed natural beauty to the little neighborhood
plot of grass, flowers, and trees amid the city's concrete
piles. Whatever their size, and wherever found, their recreational importance is not to be underestimated.

Federal Lands. One of America's greatest assets recreationally is its national parks, administered by the National Park Service, including as they do those areas of most spectacular scenic value, and those of greatest historic and scientific interest. In other words, these are the areas of greatest natural recreational interest. The property of the government, they are preserved for all time against the woodsman's ax and the encroachment of profit-minded private interests.

Remote to most people as they are, they serve their greatest function during vacation periods. With the urge for auto travel what it is, the parks become the vacation goal of hundreds of thousands annually. So that the parks may be enjoyed to the fullest and with the least discomfort, modern highways lead through them and well-kept trails accommodate the thousands of individuals who wish to explore the parks on foot; hotels and low-cost camping areas supply accommodations; and naturalists and guides offer their services. The areas and facilities of the National Park Service include about 175 separate national parks, monuments, and sites of historical interest. The attendance at all National Park locations has increased from thirty-two million in 1949 to over fifty million in 1956, and this growth has been continuing to increase at from 10 to 15 per cent per year.

Typical of the coordination in federal and local park operation is the National Park Service program of recreation demonstration areas. These are wildwood areas of submarginal lands proximate to large centers of population on which organized camp facilities and overnight cabins are provided. Most of these areas have now been turned over to the states for permanent administration as units of their state park systems and their facilities are available to local agencies through regular channels.

An important recent development of National Park Services is "Mission 66." This is the result of a thorough research study of the physical and financial condition of the national parks and monuments, an evaluation of the objectives to be sought, and an estimate of the demands and requirements to be expected in 1966, the fiftieth anniversary of the service. It has been estimated that visitors at the National Parks by that time will reach eighty million persons annually.

In the same category as the national parks are the national forests administered by the U. S. Forest Service. Recreation is one of the most important uses of many of the forests. Although most of the areas remain more or less primitive and become a paradise for the more rugged types of campers who seek untouched wilderness, many of the forests provide easily accessible facilities for camping, hiking, fishing, hunting, riding, swimming, picnicking, and winter sports.

State Parks. State parks are established primarily for recreation. They vary greatly in size and attractiveness, from the magnificent 2,204,756 acre Adirondack Park in New York state down to the small roadside parks for overnight tourists and picnickers. State parks are increasing their acreage and types of services. From 1949 to 1954, the capacity for overnight accommodations was increased by 32 per cent, showing the trend toward camp and trailer vacation travel as well as toward expending facilities for overnight tourists. Although total attendance at these parks is difficult to determine, it is certainly well over two hundred million per year. The need for expanded state park services continues to increase.

County and City Parks. To the extent that city and county parks deal with organized play they are treated in a later chapter as an integral part of an adequate community-wide park and recreation system. City or special district local parks serve a variety of functions beyond playgrounds and organized game and court areas. Their inviting surroundings of trees and greens give opportunity to stroll, rest, and relax; to many they offer the only possible contact with the green earth. The park bench has long been linked with courtship. The natural surroundings are often improved by winding canals for quiet canoeing, and picturesque lagoons where swans, ducks, and fishes may be fed. Often a zoo or an aquarium adds interest. A trend in city and county park policy is the purchasing of larger areas of woodlands beyond the city limits where picnic tables and cooking grills are plentiful, nature trails abound, and where children's groups may pitch their tents overnight.

LOCAL RECREATION PROMOTION. Play as a public function requires an extensive range of general facilities in administering its program: playgrounds, playfields, field houses, social centers, parks, and camps. It is through these facilities that the public organization carries on and extends the varied activities which are included in the broad interpretation of play. The importance of adequate public play facilities, including specific standards for adequate community-wide services, is so great that Chapter 16, "Recreation Areas and Facilities," is devoted to this subject. The comments in this chapter are directed toward describing the overall effect of the public promotion of play, showing how recreation facilities and services are provided in a variety of settings. A more detailed discussion of the administration and operation of park and recreation systems by federal and state governments and by the various local subdivisions of government, including public school systems, is given special consideration in another separate chapter (15), "Responsibility for Public Recreation," found on page 345.

SPECIAL PROMOTION FOR ACTIVITIES. In addition to the extensive general facilities referred to in the previous discussion, there are a number of recreation interests that are served through special facilities and services for activities such as swimming, boating, and golf, as well as for cultural activities including reading, art, music, dramatics, and visits to museums, zoos, and botanical gardens.

Swimming. One of the most popular and widely participated in of all activities, and one of the most desirable physically and socially, swimming has become a major interest to recreation workers, and the operation of facilities for it a major aspect of public recreation.

Outdoor bathing facilities are of two types, the natural waterfront developed for the purpose, and the artificial swimming pool. Beaches that are considered ideal provide areas of varying water depth for the various gradations of swimming ability, each marked off from the others by buoylines or, if safety demands, with fences. Sand beaches contribute much to enjoyment and should not be sacrificed in the construction of other developments. Diving floats or platforms are desirable, located in not less than ten feet of water, and safety towers for lifeguards are essential. A bathhouse is necessary; it may range from a simple shed-like affair to a house with showers and lockers. Facilities for informal play, such as horseshoes, shuffleboard, volleyball, and picnic facilities are often added. Lighting facilities to permit night use add greatly to the beaches' usefulness.

Swimming pools and wading pools may be placed on a playground, playfield, or park, and operated as part of its program, or a separate swimming center may be developed. Pools vary from small rectangular tanks of the standard type to large developments accommodating hundreds of swimmers, often arranged in connecting units for varying ages and swimming abilities. The planning of pools is a technical matter involving complicated questions of engineering, safety, sanitation, and recreation, and should not be undertaken without competent advice in all of these fields.

Swimming facilities require specially qualified supervision, a director or manager of unquestioned authority, and trained lifeguards in numbers depending on the number of swimmers, the element of hazard the area offers, and the length of time open each day.

The waterfront program consists of informal swimming, competitive events, pageants and carnivals, and instruction in swimming. It must be remembered that most people seek the swimming beach just to swim, lie in the sun, enjoy platform or skin diving, and just relax. Too much effort at an organized program is therefore defeating to the beaches' primary recreational function, especially if the organized program utilizes the entire area. Aquatic meets with teams from various playgrounds and organizations add interest on occasion. Pageants, water carnivals, aquatic circuses, and comedy and novelty meets are highlights. Swimming instruction, important both from the standpoint of safety and increased joy to be found in the water, should be a part of every program, but should take place at specified times and in restricted, private areas. Achievement tests and the Red Cross lifesaving tests are often used.

Boating and Sailing. For the most part the use of boating by public recreation systems is limited to those cities which have natural facilities in lakes, rivers, or seashore, although some cities have developed small artificial ponds on playfields and in parks which bring canoeing joy to a public that otherwise might never experience it at all. Usually boating is limited to rowboats and canoes but some fortunately located cities provide motorboats, sailboats, passenger launches, and crew boats. Landing docks, mooring places, and boathouses for storage are necessary adjuncts, whatever the type of craft, and many public recreation agencies are providing these facilities as part of their overall community services. Recent statistics show that the total annual expenditures for boating in this country has reached nearly a billion dollars, thus pointing out clearly that boating is approaching the nationwide popularity of hunting and fishing as a general recreation activity.

Golf. One of the most conspicuous achievements of the last quarter century in public recreation has been the growth in golf facilities to accommodate to the ever increasing demand.

Golf requires large acreage (50 acres for 9 holes, 100 acres for 18 holes), and a particular type of terrain—rolling and partially wooded. Outlying areas therefore are used, made feasible by the fact that golfers will travel far for golf. Technical problems are involved in development, requiring the services of experts. Elaborate staffs are required, including a manager, a professional, greenskeepers, rangers, starter, caddie master, and, in addition, staff for the clubhouse.

The electric cart, a modern addition to golf course equipment, is making it possible for older persons and physically handicapped persons to continue their participation in the game. The small par three course is another useful innovation. It appeals to beginners as well as to older persons. It saves time, distance to be covered, and number of clubs carried; also, it appeals to players who wish to perfect their iron play.

Most public courses reduce their charge to as minimum a fee necessary to cover operating expenses only and thus encourage participation.

Public Libraries. Public libraries to which everyone has access are now to be found even in most of the very small villages. They are an integral part of the play movement and constitute a recreation-education institution of first magnitude in American life. Reading not only brings pleasure during the reading, but in the case of young children fires their imagination to the point where they live the story in imaginative play. Storytelling hours with gifted specialists in charge are operated by many libraries, and play rooms for children are sometimes found. Guidance service is provided in the selection of suitable reading material. Exhibits of books on timely subjects are displayed. In addition to the main library, centrally located, branch libraries are often established, thus bringing reading privileges into the neighborhoods. In rural districts, county bookmobiles and libraries-on-wheels cover outlying areas at regular intervals.

Recent years have witnessed the publication and eager reception of a great number of non-fiction books popularizing science, philosophy, and travel; and books on all forms of hobbies, sports, and leisure-time activities are now plentiful. The fact still remains, however, that most of the reading of America is fiction and is pursued for escape and the vicarious experience of the thrilling life which is impossible in the day by day routine of life.

A recent expansion of the service of many larger institutions is the record library with a broad selection of music, and often voice, dramatic and language records. Records may be taken out in the same way books are withdrawn or may be enjoyed in the library through earphones or in rooms for that purpose.

Public libraries are usually operated by a special board and are not part of the direct responsibility of the recreation commission, although many community centers under this commission have small libraries.

Museums. Museums such as those operated by state or large city governments are significant recreational and educational institutions, permitting visitors to picture more accurately the historic events of the country, the life of primitives, and the marvels of nature from far-flung areas of the world. Although visited by all ages, their sponsored activities are primarily for children, and include after-school and Saturday picture-talks and exhibit-talks, nature lore and nature-craft sessions, movies, and guided tours through the museum. The municipal museums operate under separate management, but the recreation commissions and park boards often have small nature museums of their own and sometimes provide separate buildings for them, with activity rooms for meetings and crafts.

Zoological and botanical gardens are of the same type as museums and serve a similar function. The zoos of many large cities are recreation centers of importance, setting forth their exhibits in delightful park-like surroundings, with picnic facilities so that groups and families can spend the day there with pleasure and profit.

Art. The art museum as well as gallery display masterpieces and noteworthy works of art ranging from the ancient to contemporary. The museum is a center of art activity, with lectures and concerts by outstanding artists, informative talks on all phases of art, travel, and science, classes in sketching, painting, sculpturing, crafts, nature lore, gardening, photography, and the like. Its function is both educational and recreational, and it performs the latter outstandingly well for many people with cultural inclinations.

Music. Although most of the promotion of music in American communities is sponsored by special clubs and associations headed by interested and public spirited boards, the recreation departments are placing an increasing emphasis on this type of promotion. Such promotion consists of participatory activities such as mass singing, glee clubs, bands, orchestras, harmonica bands, contests, and so forth, as well as concerts and entertainments in which the public listens rather than participates. Many of the larger systems carry music specialists on the staff. The activities are carried on for the most part through the regular facilities of the recreation departments, in connection with playgrounds, field houses, community centers, and parks.

Drama. Increasing emphasis has been placed on drama as a phase of recreation. The participatory activities range from the spontaneous make-believe of young children to the full-dress stage production or pageant. Large systems employ specialists to provide coaching for interested groups. In addition to playground and center dramas, play tournaments for adults, in which groups compete in one-act plays, are used in some cities and play festivals without competition are preferred in others. Little Theatre groups receive promotion, encouragement, and coaching. Puppets are widely employed and enjoyed.

Outdoor facilities range from a secluded corner of the playground to the large outdoor amphitheatre. Some cities use a stage built on a truck which is moved from playground to playground. A few cities have municipally owned theatres.

Other Public Recreation Services. In addition to the provision of facilities and leaders for play in definite play centers, the public recreation departments furnish guidance of far-reaching significance in the promotion of play in other institutions and agencies throughout the community. They conduct leadership-training courses for leaders from all recreation, group-work, and religious agencies who care to come; they cooperate with churches and neighborhood groups in program planning for recreational ends; they provide picnic and outing service to all who ask, by both supplying equipment and suggesting programs.

In general, the public recreation department is an influential factor in the promotion of community-wide play activities. This help is evidenced in granting the use of public facilities to organized groups; for example, permitting industrial and other teams to use the athletic fields in the playgrounds and parks. Consent is frequently given to groups to use gymnasiums for dances and games and to use available rooms for meetings. Often the play staff volunteers to furnish officials, to give advice, and to aid in organization.

VOLUNTARY OR PRIVATE AGENCY PROMOTION

These agencies and organized groups are mostly nonprofit or eleemosynary corporations, essentially private yet primarily supported by funds raised through general charities such as the Community Chest or through their own appeals to the public. In this position they retain a relatively private status, yet they are really semi-public in that they have an obligation to provide specific services on a community-wide basis. There is a wide variety of these agencies; the following is a representative list:

American Red Cross	Young Men's Christian Association
Boy Scouts of America	
Boys' Clubs of America	Young Women's Christian Association
Catholic Youth Organization	
Camp Fire Girls	Young Men's Hebrew Association
Girl Scouts of the United States	
Settlement Houses	

Since these agencies and organized groups have served and continue to serve such an important role in the promotion of leisure-time activities, their classification, objectives, organization, and programs are covered in a later chapter (17), "Private or Voluntary Agencies."

INSTITUTIONAL RECREATION PROMOTION

Of the various settings in which play activities are promoted, that of institutions, including hospitals, is most recent and perhaps most unique. Individuals are confined in institutions because they are socially, physically, or emotionally maladjusted. The recreation program in an institution is designed to meet many of the recreation needs and interests of its patients whether they be delinquents, defectives, or dependents. Furthermore, the purpose of recreation in this setting is to provide one element of the several types of treatment and services required to rehabilitate patients and return them to society useful and well-adjusted citizens as soon as possible.

Recreation therapy has developed very rapidly during and since World War II. Through a very active program of the American Red Cross and the Veterans Administration, important advances have been made in service and in Veterans Administration hospitals. Enlightened programs of rehabilitation, including recreation activities, have also been inaugurated in special schools as well as in prisons and similar institutions. Private efforts also, such as the work done by Dr. William C. Menninger at the Menninger Foundation, have done much to develop the field of recreation therapy. Vastly improved methods of professional preparation of recreation therapists have helped immeasurably to demonstrate the value of this work.

The scope of recreation work in institutions is broad. For example, the following is a partial list of the many settings in which these programs are being promoted with excellent results:

Prisons
Juvenile detention institutions
Institutions for the blind, deaf,
    and mentally deficient
Institutions for the handicapped

Institutions for the aged
Institutions for the mentally ill
General hospitals
Camps for the handicapped

Recreation activities in these institutions are patterned to meet the needs of the individual patient. Sustenance programs, involving general recreation activity for large numbers of patients at one time, as well as specific play activities prescribed for the individual patient are carried out under the careful supervision of trained recreation workers. These programs are carefully planned in joint staff meetings and carried out in conjunction with the over-all medical or psychiatric treatment program. Patients are encouraged to engage in recreation activities as normally as possible; of course, whenever necessary, adaptations are made to meet the special needs of the patient.

Special physical facilities of all types for institutional recreation programs are designed to meet the needs of the specific situation. For example, special play facilities are provided at juvenile detention homes, prisons, and other penal institutions. The various types of hospitals operated by the Veterans Administration have special recreation facilities for both patients and operating personnel. Such a station may have a swimming pool, gymnasium, ward playrooms, day rooms, physical therapy rooms, and areas specially equipped for music and drama. Special facilities such as auditoriums, theatres, and similar facilities are available. Outdoor facilities often include a golf course, games courts and athletic fields, and nature and outdoor recreation areas as needed. Special play equipment is found in institutions for the deaf, blind, physically handicapped, and emotionally upset individuals to enable them to engage in activities much the same as normal individuals do in everyday life.

The field of recreation therapy is a new, rapidly expanding, and fascinating profession. Workers in this field must have not only special skills and knowledge to work with the handicapped, but also the art of reaching those who temporarily are unable to help themselves. The field is a noble one, and many people have dedicated their lives to this essential. Play as therapy is destined to make a significant contribution to the happiness and adjustment of many individuals in our society.

INDUSTRIAL RECREATION PROMOTION

Industrial plants in recent years have regarded the provision of recreational facilities and leadership as essential to the health, welfare, and happiness of their workers and their families. They have accomplished this either by providing and administering the facilities themselves, or by supplying facilities to, or lending financial support to, the existing public recreation organization.

Large plants often provide on-the-grounds facilities for the use of employees during the working day, such as outdoor play space, gymnasiums, rest rooms, and lounging rooms with radio, piano, magazines, and clubroom games, which find use during the noon hour and after work. Athletic leagues are organized with teams representing the different units of the factory in such games as baseball, softball, basketball, volleyball, and bowling. Tournaments are conducted in such sports as tennis, horseshoes, and golf. Recreation specialists are employed to promote and administer this work.

Many large plants extend their service to the entire community, and in small centers dominated by a single large industry, elaborate facilities are often provided. Playgrounds and playfields, tennis courts, golf courses, and swimming facilities are developed and staffed by industrial plants in many cities. Community houses are occasionally included, and auditoriums made available. Garden associations are sponsored, orchestras, bands, and glee clubs organized, and amateur dramatics promoted. Outings and picnics are scheduled and, in some places, camps are operated.

In addition to the intramural plant athletic teams, selected teams representing the plant are sometimes sponsored. The play is usually confined to city-wide industrial leagues but occasionally includes competition with other cities. Care is taken, however, that the ideal of plant-wide participation is not lost.

The growing trend today is for industries not only to supply noon hour and clubroom opportunities, but to encourage workers to utilize the community facilities for their after-work and leisure-hour activities. The labor unions favor this trend and lend support to it since it removes influences of paternalism on the part of management. As a consequence, municipal recreation organizations are developing special programs for industrial workers, and most of the large cities have established industrial departments with special supervisors in charge.

RECREATION IN RURAL AREAS

With the rapid changes in rural society brought about by the automobile, improved highways, and mechanized farming, a new rural social interaction has developed. The rural society of present-day America has also been greatly influenced by increased educational facilities and rural social services rendered by the state and federal governments and influenced markedly by the personal contacts of rural people with the economy, social life, and standards of living enjoyed by people living in urban areas. There has been, however, no recognizable organized approach in rural areas to solve rural recreation problems which are comparable to the programs initiated to meet the play needs of people in urban areas. This has evidently been due to the following factors: (1) the relative isolation of farm residences, (2) lack of group contacts for rural children and young people, (3) the crowded work hours of many rural people, (4) lack of rural recreation facilities, and (5) the competition of local and regional commercial amusements.

In the process of the development of certain customs,

mores, and folkways, rural people have, from early colonial times, exhibited very definite characteristics in their adjustment to their physical and social environment. The county fair, the circus, farm festivals, the sleighing party, the Grange, husking bees, country folk dancing, and similar activities have been legendary activities with rural residents. In spite of many of the changes that have come to rural life, the rural area program in recreation is carried on principally by various social groups found within each area. In the interest of brevity, only the principal groups will be discussed here.

HOME RECREATION. Recreation in the home should be the greatest stronghold in rural recreation, since rural people are still, in some cases, isolated and must play among themselves. At the present time more rural parents are becoming aware of the play needs of children and youth, and they are conscious of the need to provide more facilities in the farm home for recreation. Television is also having its effect in the farm home, both from the standpoint of extending the type of amusement available and of expanding the horizons of rural people in leisure-time activities. Also, the automobile gives the farm family increased mobility to take part as a family group in all kinds of activities in nearby areas.

CHURCH ACTIVITIES. One of the most powerful socializing influences of the rural community is the church. In recent years, the church has set aside traditional objections to wholesome recreation. Ministers are training leaders in the conduct of recreational activities, and the church has actually embarked on providing extensive facilities and programs in this field. The rural church is limited, however, in financial means and in leadership personnel to conduct recreation. Furthermore, rural religious groups are often not able to cooperate adequately and should not be expected to become a major force in the establishment of a well-rounded recreation program without help from other community groups.

SCHOOL RECREATION. The organization possessing the greatest potentialities for the development of rural recrea-

tion is the school. The consolidation of many rural school
districts has answered the problems that exist in many rural
areas. However, in a majority of rural areas, the schools do
not have adequate facilities and equipment to conduct
recreation activities. Many school districts have been unable to secure adequate funds; rural teachers have not been
trained in recreation, and too often they have too little time
to devote to it; finally, many consolidated schools overem-
phasize athletics and do little in training the mass of pupils
in leisure-time pursuits. Nevertheless, even though the rural
schools of the nation are, in many states, in bad condition,
they represent the most promising area for the coordinated
development of local public recreation.

CLUB GROUPS. Club groups in rural areas have been taking a tremendous amount of the responsibility of providing
recreation. The activities carried on through rural extension work are very popular and educational. The Grange
is one of the most important socializing agencies for adults
in rural districts. Among other adult groups are the
Farmers' Club, the Farm Womens' Club, and the Parent-
Teachers organizations. Of the farm youth organizations,
the 4-H Club, sponsored by the Extension Service, is probably the most popular and the most effective. The National
4-H Recreation and Rural Arts program is now functioning
in every state. Workshops, special training, and award programs attract the participation of thousands of young
people. Besides these activities, 4-H camping has grown to
be a major recreation program for rural area girls and boys.
The Future Farmers of America, the YMCA, Camp Fire
Girls, and other similar groups are also important in play
promotion in town and country areas.

COUNTY PROGRAMS. Since World War II, several states
have initiated public recreation programs for rural areas administered through the county government. This has resulted in the employment of trained leaders as well as
securing facilities located within close proximity to rural
residents. The operation of these programs is discussed in

more detail in the next chapter, "Responsibility for Public Recreation."

INFORMAL AND ORGANIZED CAMPING

The camping movement in its rapid growth has become part of the programs of practically all agencies. As noted already in this chapter, camping is involved in the nine-fold classification that has been followed—it is promoted under the various types of informal, public, service, institutional, industrial, rural, private, and commercial auspices. Because, however, camping facilities and programs are of such a nature and importance detailed treatment is required. Chapter 18, "Camping in Education and Recreation," covers this area.

PRIVATE PROGRAM PROMOTION

This type of promotion includes a wide variety of informal education and recreation programs essentially private in nature. Although supported by gifts, donations, assessments, fees and charges, and the like, these programs differ widely in scope. They vary from nonprofit organizations such as the church to the strictly pay-as-you-go private commercial operation. Since each of these types of promotion involve different settings, their role and unique character in American society will be discussed separately.

CHURCH-SPONSORED ACTIVITIES. The church is viewed here as an integral part of the total community where (1) people gather for spiritual expression, community service, and fellowship meetings, and (2) as an agency to support special types of youth and adult (partly recreational) leisure-time activities, which have become national in character. The church provides facilities and leadership for many types of recreation activities—during informal fellowship sessions at regular church meetings, Boy Scout meetings, youth club gatherings, couples' club gatherings, and so forth. Furthermore, several national voluntary agencies have grown from church sponsorship. Although directly sponsored or closely related to the church, these voluntary leisure-time agencies promote a wide variety of recreation activities which are not engaged in on church property. Significant in these developments has been the growth of the Catholic Youth Organization (CYO), directly under church administration. It is a national organization which carries on an aggressive program of athletic and social recreation and moral guidance for boys and girls. Similarly, the Young Men's Hebrew Association and the Young Women's Hebrew Association conduct work featuring general programs of recreation for members of their faith. The Jewish Welfare Board, organized in 1917, has sponsored hundreds of community centers throughout the country.

The new socialized movement of the church gives to that institution something of the character of a social center. It is not uncommon for a church to possess a separate building that is used for the showing of movies, for dancing, basketball games and gymnasium work, social parties, lectures, dramatics, etc., or to have gymnasiums and play facilities in the church building itself. Many larger city churches have organized small missions in the thickly populated districts which combine religious, educational, social, and recreational features. Many churches also own and operate resident and day camping facilities and programs.

The function of the church as a community center is largely one of supplementing other agencies in the community: if adequate facilities are provided in the neighborhood, the church is relieved to a certain degree of the necessity of providing recreational activities. The church follows two methods in providing recreational facilities: (1) to provide the actual place and the leadership for an adequate program for the neighborhood; (2) to use its vast influence in educating and moulding public opinion so that other agencies will be established to care for these needs.

Religion is distinctly related to recreation and has been throughout all of history from earliest savage times to the present. Worship itself has a distinct recreational value in that, through it, people become relaxed and refreshed and find escape from the pressures of life. Sociable expression has always surrounded gatherings for religious purposes. To many people, church work is the major means of sociable and recreational activity. The church has an advantage as a recreational center in that it has a closer touch and more common aim among its members than the public play center; the feeling of sociability is already present and does not have to be stimulated.

CULTURAL ACTIVITY CLUBS. Thousands of private clubs devoted to the fine and applied arts are found throughout the country in communities of all sizes. This is true of music, art, and again of crafts clubs. Literary clubs, book review clubs, reading circles, and other culturally oriented organizations exist in every city. Dramatic clubs and Little Theatre groups have their following. Garden clubs, nature clubs, and similar groups prosper. All of these groups are held together by a mutuality of interest and are seeking a common goal. Some of them meet in churches, schools, public meeting places, or in private homes. Others construct and operate elaborate physical facilities and have special programs of community-wide interest to both participants and spectators. These groups select their own members but are usually open to all, and are supported by donations, dues and fees, and charges.

ATHLETIC CLUBS AND ORGANIZATIONS. Local athletic clubs began to appear during the middle of the last century and, during the first quarter of the present century, prospered tremendously. They were for the most part composed of young men interested in athletic sports, and their programs featured a wide range of physical activity. The Amateur Athletic Union (AAU), is a national federation of such clubs and other interested groups. It requires a fee for membership, also an amateur standing; and it rigidly controls the participation of its members in competitive sports. Its program features track and swimming competition in sectional meets as well as national ones.

The Amateur Athletic Union is tending increasingly to look to playgrounds and schools for future participants in its activities. Certainly the general athletic club, featuring a wide range of athletic activity, is giving way to specialized clubs made up of individuals interested in some specific sport. The local clubs of this type have affiliated into organizations of national scope, with rules and regulations for the activity they sponsor and a machinery for its promotion. As examples of these organizations with national or at least widespread jurisdiction, the following might be mentioned: Amateur Fencers League of America, National Association of Angling and Casting Clubs, National Archery Association, American Bowling Congress, American Canoe Association, United States Figure Skating Association, United States Golf Association, United States Field Hockey Association, American Amateur Hockey League, National Horseshoe Pitchers Association, United States Intercollegiate Lacrosse Association, American Lawn Bowling Association, American Roque League, National Ski Association, United States Lawn Tennis Association, National Association of Amateur Oarsmen, Amateur Trapshooting Association, American Snowshoe Union, National Cycling Association, and United States Football (Soccer) Association.

Some of these organizations may be regarded as exclusive, but for the most part their membership fees are not prohibitive to the average citizen and they are open to all who have an interest in the activity they sponsor.

EXCLUSIVE PLAY GROUPS. The membership of the organizations referred to as exclusive is limited to a considerable degree, eligibility being determined by such factors as wealth, social influence, and sanction of the active members. This group at large includes (1) fraternal orders for men and women, such as the Freemasonry, Order of the Eastern Star, Benevolent and Protective Order of the Elks, Knights of Pythias of the World, Independent Order of Odd Fellows, and the college fraternities and sororities; (2) the noonday luncheon clubs, such as Rotary Club, Kiwanis Club, and Exchange Club; (3) nationalistic organizations; (4) fellowship clubs; (5) private schools which limit their enrollment; and (6) the many exclusive city and country clubs.

Fraternal Orders. Fraternal orders and secret societies were largely a contribution of the past century, practically all important and well-known orders having their origin before 1900. They have enjoyed widespread popularity and growth, but reliable evidence seems to indicate that the peak has very nearly been reached. Masonic orders have in recent years shown membership gains which barely offset their losses, and other fraternal lodges taken as a whole have shown a marked decline in the last quarter century. In so far as the members are concerned, fraternal organizations maintain first of all the social club idea. In addition, celebrations, picnics, bazaars, athletic occasions, and dances are held. To a smaller extent, some of the fraternal orders have also given support to the public play movement.

Luncheon Clubs. Conspicuous among the recently developed leisure associations are the luncheon clubs, which have prospered to such a degree as to demand particular attention. The first Rotary Club was organized in Chicago in 1905 and by 1910 there were sixteen of these clubs which were affiliated into the Rotary International. The Exchange Club came into being in 1911. The Optimists Club first appeared in 1911 and was formulated into Optimists International in 1919. The first Kiwanis Club was started in Detroit in 1915 and the Kiwanis International organized the year following. The Lions International appeared in 1917. Zonta, a luncheon club for women, was organized in 1918. From these few there are now many different national organizations of luncheon clubs. In addition to sociability and fellowship for their members, the luncheon clubs are of particular interest to the recreation field because of the generous and aggressive support they give to public recreation. These clubs are also the key organizations in money-raising campaigns for the group-work organizations for youth.

Nationalistic Organizations. Immigrants and descendants from European countries in this country frequently affiliate into clubs for social activity along the lines characteristic of their own culture. These groups have rich contributions in the way of music, dancing, and festivals, and often gymnastics and games. The Turnverein as representative of the German nationality and the Sokols of Czechoslovakia illustrate this class.

COMMERCIAL RECREATION PROMOTION

By commercial recreation is meant the type that is provided by private concerns in order to make money from the patronage. This would include not only toys and games purchased and taken home for children and adults, but more especially the amusements for which one pays admission. In this class are the baseball parks, bowling lanes, pool rooms, carnivals, circuses, dance halls, excursion boats, fairs, gambling resorts, horse races, motion picture shows, roof gardens, skating rinks, music halls, theatres, and so forth. The sums spent for these amusements by people in our cities are enormous, and far exceed all that is spent for schools, playgrounds, streets, and municipal improvements met by public taxation.

Total expenditures for commercial recreation are difficult to determine. Statistics that are available regarding expenditures during leisure time show the economic importance of leisure as a commodity in our daily living.

In spite of the development of the public play movement, the commercial field continues to increase and is more profitable than ever. The demand for recreation has become so great that all of the development of the play movement reviewed here fails to meet the needs, and the commercial enterprises have been quick to expand their facilities and reap increased profit. This being true, considerable attention must be given to the nature of commercial recreation and its effect on conduct.

PROFESSIONAL SPORTS. The popularity of certain sports has led to their increasing professionalization. Baseball has long been commercialized to the point where it is a big business. More recently professional football has gained an immense following. Boxing, with a long background of commercialization, still makes enormous profits, and wrestling, basketball, tennis, ice hockey, bowling, and golf are being used as a source of profit for players. Another aspect of the commercialization of sport is found in the opportunities for noted college athletes to capitalize on their fame by entering the motion picture and television field.

Horse racing still continues to increase in popularity, judging from the annual increase in purses and stakes. Dog racing and jai alai are also gaining in favor.

POOL, BILLIARDS, AND BOWLING. Pool and billiard rooms were many in number and decidedly popular up to 1921 but in that year a decline set in, and in the five years following, the taxes paid by them decreased over 50 per cent. The number of bowling alleys, however, more than doubled during the same period. Bowling is today the fastest growing sport in America in the number of participants. The small, ill-kept, poorly ventilated pool room and bowling alley has given way to large, centrally located, well-equipped halls, many of them no longer under commercial auspices. The invention of the automatic pin-setter has been the key in bowling's phenomenal growth, since it makes the lanes available at all times. The new enthusiasm of women and children has also made bowling a family sport. Open bowling now has its place along with the organized league phase of participation.

THEATRES AND MOTION PICTURES. The legitimate drama, musical, vaudeville, burlesque, dime museum, and Chautauqua were all forced far into the background of commercial recreation operations by the motion picture. From 1921 to 1950, vaudeville faded and live entertainment in general was replaced by the films made in Hollywood. The motion picture had, and still has to a degree, a tremendous influence on conduct. Probably no means of suggestion or imitative pattern, aside from actual interaction, has had greater potentialities for influencing conduct. And the recreational value of the motion picture needs no description; it has brought the theatre to the masses as the legitimate stage never did and could not for obvious financial reasons. Available to all in their own neighborhoods and at prices all can afford, the movies have brought recreational benefits to the people; their influence, for good or bad, has been felt by a considerable percentage of the public.

Much as the movie has generally replaced live entertainment, television has begun to reduce the importance of the neighborhood movie theatre. Although there has been some reduction in attendance at local theatres, drive-in theatres have replaced much of this loss.

The objections to the motion picture that have been raised by thoughtful people revolve in no small part around the fact that most pictures are produced for adults, yet a great part of the audience is youth. Considerable pressure has been exerted to induce the production of more pictures suitable for children. While many outstanding fine movies for children are being produced, the public has difficulty in evaluating their suitability in advance of attendance. Assistance is furnished by magazines interested in parents' problems, and by organizations with such interests, in making available lists of recommended pictures for various age levels.

TELEVISION. With the perfection of television to the point that a child can operate the controls, the vast theatre of the air, with its remarkable facilities for entertainment, has been brought to the homes of a great number of people. In 1950, only 12 per cent of all households in the United States had television sets; in 1959, 86 per cent of all households had one or more sets. Through the advertising on the part of industries, programs of outstanding entertainment formerly seen in movies or live coverage from the scene of an event are available without cost beyond the purchase of the television set. There has been a strong movement to control television and provide a pay-as-you-view plan. This controversy between pay and free television continues unabated. Meanwhile, the permanent effects of this new media on social behavior and leisure-time play habits of children and adults are still relatively undetermined.

TRAVEL. Since 1948 the desire for travel has grown remarkably. One cannot ignore the fact that over fifteen billion dollars each year is spent by Americans for travel and vacations both here and abroad. With increased facilities for travel in the jet age, this type of commercial amusement will undoubtedly become even more widespread in the future. Convenient services are offered by travel bureaus for attractive, relatively inexpensive tours. The automobile, of course, has been a big factor in family travel.

OTHER COMMERCIAL DEVELOPMENTS. The commercially operated amusement park has long been popular in the United States and still is well patronized in larger cities during the summer months. In smaller cities, however, a large number of them have been abandoned.

Pavilions, cabarets, night clubs, and road houses are examples of provision for social recreation under commercial auspices. Dining and dancing are always popular, and are normal, satisfying, and relaxing types of recreation. Adequate facilities under wholesome conditions will always be needed. Public recreation departments occasionally operate dance halls with admission charged, but they are immediately confronted with the same problems of control as the commercial hall. Regulations are needed for the commercial hall regarding closing hours, admission of minors, and lighting of the hall and surroundings.

One of the outstanding commercial developments of the last quarter century has been the roller skating rink or rollerdrome. These large arenas with their perfectly kept floors, their orchestras or recorded music, and their careful supervision as to speed of skating, provide recreation of increasing popularity. In the large rinks instruction is offered in roller dancing and many people find this a favorite hobby. In northern communities the ice rink is also an attraction for people of all ages, with interest in skating fostered by the ice carnivals held locally and by "professional" exhibitions of skilled talent.

STANDARDS FOR COMMERCIAL PROMOTION. Commercialized forms of play are both good and bad; and, moreover, many of them that may have had evil influences can be converted into useful and artistic forms of play. There is no question but that the theatre, music halls, and the movies can all be molded from the standpoints of art, education, and recreation; and, many amusements like pool and billiards, often frowned upon, can be made very desirable simply by improving their environment. Commercial recreation cannot be expected to supply the variety of recreation interest that is needed or the opportunity for participation in all such activities. Stuart Chase's statement, made early in the development of commercial recreation in this country, emphasizes a basic philosophy regarding participation that is more true today than ever before:

The most rewarding forms of play, furthermore, are those in which the player participates directly with his own muscles, his own voice, his own rhythm. To exercise the faculty vicariously through the play of others, while frequently amusing enough, is far less helpful biologically. . . . If this distinction is a valid one, it follows that the value of play in a given culture may be roughly appraised by the volume of its participating as against its non-participating forms.

In general, commercial recreation needs to be controlled and elevated to more acceptable levels, and the road to reform is education, not censorship.

SUMMARY

The quest for challenging activities during leisure time by freedom-loving Americans has led to the growth of play in a variety of settings. The vast natural resources and high standard of living allows the individual citizen a wide range of choice in informal recreation activities. This is evident by the increased participation in hobbies, do-it-yourself types of activities, home play, and a wide variety of indoor and outdoor activities characteristic of the American way of life.

In the structure of a free society, public park and recreation systems have grown with the development of the play movement until today these agencies provide the foundation of recreation facilities and services. Although services affecting national and regional needs are provided at the federal and state levels, local citizens have created county, town, and city systems of parks and recreation to meet community and neighborhood needs. As in the provision of public education, local departments of the federal government provide a system of public recreation that best meets the needs of the particular situation.

Voluntary or private agency promotion is also a distinct contribution to the nation's need for leisure-time programs and services. In one way, through the close personal touch of their smaller groups which organized around special interests and needs, these agencies can accomplish many things better than public organizations can. The voluntary agencies have provided not only wholesome activities for youth but have provided purposeful activities for many adults who find expression through volunteering their services in these programs.

Play activities have also been promoted in such special settings as industries, institutions, and hospitals. These developments are a part of our changing social system and indicate clearly how recreation is meeting the new needs of our society.

The private groups also have their value in the community. Those interested in civic affairs should be kept informed as to the play needs of the entire community and their valuable support secured; fraternal orders, interest clubs, country clubs, athletic clubs, and similar groups play an important role in providing wholesome family and adult recreation opportunities. Even the exclusive clubs of privilege, in spite of the gulf between their programs and the public ones, do give needed recreation to many business and professional men.

And finally, commercial recreation offers much that is needed and desirable through the elevating of public taste and the building of an enlightened public opinion; those forms which are good can be encouraged and those which are bad can be suppressed.

This discussion makes it evident that community recreation includes all recreation opportunities existing in the community of a private, voluntary, commercial, and public nature. All of these programs are interrelated. Also, all of these programs are needed. The solution to the provision of more effective play and recreation services, as in other elements of our democratic system, lies in the cooperation achieved between the various agencies and groups concerned. This joint effort must be achieved through democratic processes. It must be guided by the effectiveness of each of the various agencies in supplying services to meet a given need. And finally, the publicly controlled play program, even though it can never function so as to take the place of all these various agencies that have been mentioned, must still accept the role of leader. It can provide the leadership needed for the future expansion of play and recreation so that maximum benefit may be forthcoming.

SELECTED REFERENCES

BUTLER, GEORGE D. *Introduction to Community Recreation.* New York: McGraw-Hill Book Co., Inc., 1959. Chapter 3, "Agencies Providing Recreation," and other parts of this book provide an excellent source of information on the conduct of recreation by various groups and agencies.

MEYER, HAROLD D., and BRIGHTBILL, CHARLES K. *Community Recreation: A Guide to Its Organization.* Englewood Cliffs, N.J.: Prentice-Hall, Inc., 1956. This is a comprehensive introductory text which outlines basic principles of recreation and includes a very thorough discussion of recreation as it exists in various settings, including the home, school, church, industry, institutions, and the voluntary and public agencies. Excellent questions and references are suggested by the authors for further study.

ANDERSON, JACKSON M. *Industrial Recreation.* New York: McGraw-Hill Book Co., Inc., 1955.

Athletic Institute. *Recreation for Community Living.* Chicago: Athletic Institute, 1952.

CHAPMAN, FREDERICK M. *Recreation Activities for the Handicapped.* New York: The Ronald Press Co., 1960.

CLAWSON, MARION. *Statistics on Outdoor Education.* Washington, D.C.: Resources for the Future, Inc., 1958.

CLEMENS, FRANCES, TULLY, ROBERT, and CRILL, EDWARD. *Recreation in the Local Church.* Elgin, Ill.: Brethren Publishing Co., 1956.

DEWHURST, J. FREDERICK, et al. *America's Needs and Resources: A New Survey.* New York: Twentieth Century Fund, Inc., 1955, Chap. 11.

EISENBERG, HELEN, and EISENBERG, LARRY. *The Family Fun Book.* New York: Association Press, 1953.

National Recreation Association. *Recreation: A Guide to Books on Recreation.* New York: National Recreation Association, 1959. Published annually.

————. *Recreation and Park Year Book. Ibid.,* 1956.

SESSOMS, H. D. *A Glossary of Public Recreation Terms.* Raleigh, N.C.: North Carolina Recreation Commission, 1956. Includes definitions of various recreation terms.

Social Work Year Book, 1957. New York: National Association of Social Workers, 1957. Selected readings in this publication provide information regarding recreation in its various aspects.

WYLIE, J. A. "A Survey of 504 Families to Determine Relationships Between Certain Factors and the Nature of the Family Recreation Program," *The Research Quarterly,* XXIV (May, 1953), 242.

Magazines containing further information on recreation include *Recreation, Sports Illustrated,* the *American Recreation Society Annual,* and the *American Recreation Journal.* See *Funspot: Amusement-Recreation Management,* for commercial recreation.

15

Responsibility for Public Recreation

Public recreation is the provision by government of recreation opportunities and services available to all people. These services are financed primarily by taxation and include the building or establishment, operation, conduct, control, and maintenance of program, services, areas, and facilities. Since recreation is so closely related to health, public morale, and general welfare, most states have considered it a government function. Thus it is conducted by various government units, most of which enjoy the operational privileges incident to the sovereignty vested in public agencies responsible for crime prevention, public health, prevention of fires, care of the poor, public education, and the like. Public recreation is regarded primarily as a function of local units of government such as the county, township, corporate municipality, or district. However, the administration of recreation through the federal government and the various state government agencies is also considered in this chapter.

RESPONSIBILITY FOR FEDERAL RECREATION SERVICES

The federal government has manifested an increasing interest in promoting recreation, a trend observable during the rapid growth of these services during the 1930's. This growth continued its great momentum after World War II. For example, attendance at U. S. Forest Service locations increased over 125 per cent from 1946 to 1956. Reference has also been made in earlier chapters to recent developments in the National Park Service, the Children's Bureau, and the Department of Agriculture regarding recreation services.

Following World War II, federal authorities became even more recreation conscious. In 1946, under the sponsorship of the Secretary of the Interior, the Federal Inter-Agency Committee on Recreation was organized. Essentially, the purpose of the committee was to serve as a clearing house for information and to develop basic principles and policies regarding the responsibilities and services of the federal government in the field of recreation; to discover and to fill, in so far as possible, existing gaps in federal recreation programs and services; and to coordinate the services of the federal government with state and local governments and other local groups offering recreation services. The member agencies of the Committee follow:

Agency	(Department)
Corps of Engineers	Army
National Park Service	Interior
Fish and Wildlife Service	Interior
Bureau of Reclamation	Interior
Bureau of Land Management	Interior
Federal Extension Service	Agriculture
Forest Service	Agriculture
Office of Education	Health, Education, and Welfare
Public Health Service	Health, Education, and Welfare

Today, eighteen major federal services in several departments and bureaus have important, far-reaching functions in recreation. These services, along with the lesser services of approximately an equal number offered by units in other federal government agencies, are described in detail in a special publication of the Federal Inter-Agency Committee on Recreation.

Although the Inter-Agency Committee on Recreation has done much to coordinate federal recreation services, there is, as yet, much more to be desired in this direction. True, the many federal agencies are continuing to develop and expand their services to meet increasing public demands; but there is an obvious need for coordinating federal, state, and local government efforts in recreation through national planning equivalent to that offered by the federal government in health, education, and welfare. At present the great needs are for: advisory and consultant services available to the states and communities, research in recreation problems, planning at the national level for immediate and long-range needs, coordination of existing and proposed developments affecting leisure-time activities, and a broad program of public information and education aimed at acquainting people with the importance and the implications of recreation as a fundamental public service.

LEGISLATION FOR STATE RECREATION SERVICES

Recreation legislation varies widely throughout the country. Each state has its own laws governing the conduct of public park and recreation programs and services operated at either the state or local level. Obviously this legislation has been enacted in the various states to meet specific local interests and needs. The result has been a variety of statutes that range from broad permissive laws to specific legislative provisions for various units of government on the local level to carry on these functions. It is difficult to evaluate the adequacy of these provisions because there are no norms by which to judge the adequacy of legislation in a given state: what is adequate depends entirely upon the local situation.

State legislation for public park and recreation operations may be classified into four major categories: permissive, regulatory, service, and special laws.

Permissive laws are state laws allowing the various agencies of local types of government to operate public park and recreation systems. They give broad powers to counties, townships, cities, and special districts to provide public park and recreation programs and services. Most of these laws prescribe the type of managing authority, broad administrative patterns for operation, and the general financial limitations regarding special taxes and bonded indebtedness. Such legislation is permissive in that local units of government may operate recreation services if the people approve such a system by local referendum vote or if the services are initiated by action of a local governmental body so empowered.

Regulatory laws are aimed at controlling both public and private operations of various leisure-time programs and services. The principal object of these laws is to protect the public and to regulate participation where the good of society is involved. Typical examples of such laws are state hunting, fishing, and boating regulations, censorship of movies, laws prescribing limits of participation on the Sabbath, the control of race tracks, and a wide variety of commercial amusements affecting the lives of millions of people.

Service laws allow the state as an agency to administer and operate many types of recreation services either directly or indirectly. Examples follow:

1. State park services are broad in nature. They involve a range of operation from roadside parks to large public properties with overnight accommodations and major recreation services.

2. Recreation programs are carried on in state institutions, including prisons, correctional institutions, hospitals, and the like.

3. State recreation commissions or similar state services to local municipalities have recently been created. In 1959, such commissions or state boards of recreation were operating in California, North Carolina, and Vermont. Michigan, Missouri, and several other states have similar types of services vested in a state inter-agency committee coordinating the recreation services of all state agencies.

4. Various departments of the state governments indirectly provide recreation services. These include such functions normally carried out by the Fish and Game Commission, Department of Conservation, Tourist Councils, Department of Agriculture, Youth Commission, and similar state agencies as provided in the various states.

Special laws allow local groups upon request special permission to build and operate local recreation and leisure-time facilities. These operations are not covered by existing legislation and meet only the particular needs of one locality. Legislation of special laws is often necessary in large metropolitan areas or to regulate special situations such as the proper construction of swimming pools, stadiums, community center buildings, and the subsequent operation of these facilities.

The trend in state legislation is toward expanding the power of the state to perform service functions. Several states have legislation pending for the creation of a state recreation commission or similar agency. The purpose of these agencies is to coordinate recreation planning and services at the state level and to render consultant services to local communities and groups seeking to initiate or to improve local services which are approved by permissive legislation.

It is apparent that people are becoming more conscious of the need for state as well as national planning for recreation. Many state permissive laws for recreation are complex and inadequate. In many instances, state legislation is being reviewed, laws are being codified, and new laws are being passed to authorize managing authorities to act jointly in coordinating state and local efforts to meet the increasing needs in recreation.

COUNTY, TOWNSHIP, AND DISTRICT UNITS

Counties are still a universal type of governmental unit in the United States. Likewise, although not as widespread, the township still occupies an important position in local government. Recent reforms in both county and township government have brought with them a new consciousness in local administration. The result has been expanded services on the part of these older local units in the form of agricultural extension work, public education, library services, park and recreation programs, and a variety of social welfare services.

In many rural areas the population is scattered and funds

for recreation are limited. Therefore, the most economical way that a small city, village, or isolated neighborhood can obtain adequate public recreation facilities and services is through county, township, or area-wide special district units of administration. Similarly, urban centers are in need of large open spaces nearby for recreation facilities which cannot be economically constructed within land-poor city areas. Consequently, along with rapid, efficient transportation and other changes, the administration of public park and recreation programs and services has also begun to develop in the following three ways:

1. County park or recreation departments operate directly under the county board of supervisors or a special lay board elected or appointed to operate these services. Many times this type of organization initiates and coordinates necessary provisions for physical facilities and supervisory services for a large metropolitan area, a densely populated suburban area or a limited rural population. Such systems are found in Cook County in Illinois, Los Angeles County in California, Milwaukee in Wisconsin, and in other locations. Some county systems, however, center more around services mainly for rural residents such as that operated so effectively in Jefferson County, Kentucky. Similar rural area services in recreation are developing in Florida and Wisconsin, as well as in several county administrative units now operating in California.

2. Township park and recreation departments are found in many states. They are usually organized to meet demands for large physical facilities to service regional areas. Such facilities often include race tracks, stadiums, regional park areas, and the like. Control is usually vested in a special board or exercised directly by one or more township supervisors.

3. Special park or recreation districts are special subdivisions of local government which usually include one or more urban areas and the surrounding rural or unincorporated areas. Special park districts of this type are found in Illinois, and, in many instances, the park maintenance and the program leadership are administered jointly by these districts. California recently provided legislation for the creation of special recreation districts which may include several corporate cities, unincorporated suburban areas, and rural areas. All of these special districts are separate corporate bodies, with their own taxing power and legal authority. They are usually operated by an elected lay board with the help of a trained park and recreation executive. Recreation planners and administrators in many parts of the country have expressed approval of the special district type of administration.

They contend that it provides a solution to many fringe area problems, to securing adequate assessed valuation for financing, and to providing a method of obtaining much needed, rural-urban cooperation in the administration of adequate public park and recreation services.

ADMINISTRATION OF MUNICIPAL RECREATION

The question of proper administration of public recreation in the city has been a perplexing one ever since the playground movement was inaugurated. In the early days, many cities maintained playgrounds through support from donations by popular subscription, and, in this case, the people primarily responsible and interested, continued in control in the form of a board of directors usually called a Playground and Recreation Association. The great majority of playgrounds, however, have been supported by public taxes, and, in this case, there has been no settled policy as to which municipal department should be in control. As a result, several different management plans have been followed. Often the authority has been vested in the school board, or the park board has been given this responsibility. Still another plan that has been followed is to divide the authority by allowing the schools to operate their own playgrounds, and the park boards to control the play in the public parks; however, the idea of a separate Recreation Commission has been growing in favor. The extreme of the divided type of management has come when in the same city there are found schools, parks, and private agencies conducting playgrounds independently of each other.

Each of the above plans has its special adherents, but in general it may be said that no one of them can be fully effective without a considerable amount of cooperation between the different parties whose properties are being used. The question of which department should control the play activities can only be settled by a careful survey of local conditions. There are certain advantages and drawbacks in each plan, as the following analysis will show.

SCHOOL BOARD PLAN. The modern type of school has facilities for both playgrounds and social centers and already conducts a play program of its own during the school day. Consequently, many feel that the school board is the logical branch of government to assume the responsibility for all of the community's play. The advocates of the school board plan advance the following defense of their position:

1. The school is usually convenient from the standpoint of location—it is already in the neighborhood, and there is no other agency that can compare with it in being in close touch with the children and neighborhood conditions.

2. Play is being increasingly looked upon as an activity of educational importance, and as such it would seem that the proper agency for its administration would be the board responsible for education in general.

3. The buildings and grounds possessed by the school board are needed in any city's recreation program. With the changing nature in school architecture and landscaping, these facilities are becoming increasingly valuable from the recreation standpoint.

4. The school is already administering a physical education program for children, which has been shown to be increasingly a play-motivated program.

5. The curriculum of the school also contains facilities and leadership for music, art, dramatics, and handcraft—activities which are a vital part of community recreational programs.

6. The teaching staff under the school board possesses a high degree of specialized skill in the wide variety of the activities which constitute a recreation program as well as a knowledge of teaching processes and experience in handling children.

7. In the interests of economy in smaller cities, the schools can administer recreation by employing part-time help to fill in the out-of-school hours and the summer months. There is then no duplication or separate overhead expense of administration.

Many feel, however, that the school board is not the proper agency in the community for the administration of recreation and offer the following objections:

1. A community recreation program must meet the needs of all age stratifications in the community and not be limited to school children only. The average school board has, in the past, been accustomed to think largely in the terms of children and their needs, and has given little attention to the problems of the pre-school and the post-school elements of the population. Even with the growing emphasis upon adult education as a function of the school, the scope of adult recreation is much broader than the interpretation school authorities are apt to put upon it.

2. The average school board has confined its efforts to activities which take place during school hours and has not been inclined to assume the responsibility for the out-of-school periods, such as late afternoon and evening, weekends, and summer vacations.

3. The average school board, thinking that its responsibility is for administration of education in the traditional sense, is inclined to include recreation in the budget as an extra item of less importance and, when the budget is reduced for any reason, the appropriation for recreation is apt to be the first to be eliminated.

4. An adequate recreation program must utilize all of the recreation facilities in the community—parks, waterfronts, churches, lodges, and various other institutions. School facilities represent only a small part of the needs. It is questionable whether the school board is the best agency to secure the cooperation of these other agencies.

5. Although adult recreation may be educational, it is not regarded as necessarily so to the same extent as that of children. School teachers, because of pedagogical backgrounds and experience in the school room, frequently do not make the best leaders for adult recreation. The tendency of teachers to carry over into the play program the classroom attitude with its formal approach and its disciplinary measures

often militates against the play spirit. While some teachers are successful play leaders, success as a teacher does not necessarily qualify a person for recreational leadership.

6. When schools administer recreation it is usually placed under the physical education department. While the training for such leadership may qualify it outstandingly for sports and games, it often lacks an appreciation of, or an inclination to employ, the many other areas of activities that must be included in the scope of an adequate recreation program.

7. School personnel, from boards and superintendents on down to janitors, often take a proprietary attitude toward the school building which makes its use for community functions difficult.

8. The use of school funds (and facilities) for recreation purposes is often affected by state laws, some states not permitting such use.

PARK BOARD MANAGEMENT. The responsibility for the administration of recreation in many cities rests with the park board. In the early days of the playground movement the park boards were a great help in sponsoring the movement. They already possessed grounds that could be converted to recreational uses, and so it was only natural that municipalities should turn to them for the help that was needed. There are still those who feel, and not without good argument, that the park board is the proper agency for the administration of recreation. In a sense, the park board is in the business of recreation to begin with, for recreation is one of its chief functions. Further, it controls many of the publicly owned properties best suited for recreation, such as playfields, golf courses, picnic grounds, camping and hiking areas, bathing beaches, and swimming pools; no municipal program can operate outside the park board. The development and maintenance of such facilities is a specialty of the park workers, and the park board already possesses a staff of engineering and landscape specialists of long experience. Moreover, the park board has a generous budget in most cities, which funds can be used for providing the needed facilities.

There is, on the other hand, considerable opposition among some authorities to placing recreation responsibility in the hands of the park board. This opposition is based on a number of reasons.

First, so much of the energy of the park board is consumed by the provision and upkeep of landscaping, road and bridge construction, tree surgery, and the like, and of botanical gardens, zoos, and similar facilities, that minor attention only is apt to be given to the development of a program and the provision and training of leadership. Recreation, after all, is primarily a question of activities and leadership. Park people are inclined to think more in terms of landscape development than of human service. Again, in case of budgetary cuts, program and leadership services would suffer first. In the selection of an executive, it is only natural that park boards would seek a man experienced in the major areas of park specialization, namely, engineering, landscape, and outdoor architecture, with the result that recreation programming and leadership would likely be relegated to the background.

Another objection to the use of park boards is that they, like school boards, think in terms of their own properties and are unaccustomed to the promotion of a broad program serving the needs of the entire community. Furthermore, park boards as a rule do not have adequate indoor facilities and, as a result, either no indoor program is carried on, or field houses are constructed which schools may already provide—a costly duplication of buildings. In very few cities have school buildings been turned over to park boards in which to conduct a recreational program. The experience all over the United States has indicated that school boards are less likely to turn their facilities over to a park board than to an independent recreation commission upon which they are represented.

RECREATION COMMISSION PLAN. There is a distinct tendency in America today, especially in large cities, toward the use of a separate recreation board plan—the creation of a board composed of individuals having an interest in, and an appreciation of, both school and park objectives, which will have administrative authority over all recreation activities. Owing to the wide range of activities which it is necessary for an administrative body to carry on and the many agencies which must be coordinated in an adequate community recreation project, it is held by many that a separate recreation board or commission can hope to achieve better results than either park or school boards. Such a board uses facilities provided by the park, the school, the street, the waterfront, and any other municipal board or department having equipment it needs, as well as special facilities secured for its own use or loaned to it by private groups. Members of the board may be elected but are much more frequently appointed by the mayor or city commission. They have the same relation toward the director of recreation as does the school board toward the superintendent of schools. Some states require representation from the board of education on the recreation commission.

Local conditions indicate that the tendency to establish recreation under a separate authority is most effective because recreation is important enough to require the extensive planning and administration which a separate authority can give it. This is being done in various communities with the realization of the importance of school and park facilities as such, and of the need for coordinating the use of physical facilities, leadership, and other resources in the community.

PRIVATE ASSOCIATION PLAN. The private playground and recreation associations were a great asset in the early history of the playground movement, when awareness had to be created in the different cities by people who were interested in social welfare work. In contrast to other plans, these associations were supported by private funds rather than public. Nearly always these bodies drop out of existence whenever the city takes over adequately the recreation needs.

The playground associations are organized the same as other organizations having a board of directors. The directors represent other important organizations of the city. Such a board is efficient if the members are really interested in the work; they are not paid and hold this position as an honor rather than because of any special ability in recreation work. Because of the standing and influence of these members in the community, the playground association is in a good position to influence public opinion, secure appropriations, and enlarge the scope of the work. The members are often found acting as volunteer leaders and serving in advisory capacities.

COORDINATED OR COMBINED PLAN. Many cities throughout the United States are using a coordinated plan of operating public park and recreation services. This is devised in several ways.

In one plan there is a close coordination between public school and public recreation boards so that, through their legally constituted authorities, contractual arrangements are made for the interchange of staff and the dual use of facilities. This is accomplished without either legal body losing its identity or its jurisdictions.

In a second type, there is a close coordination between park and school operations often referred to as the park-school plan. In such an arrangement, park and school officials arrange for joint ownership of land, interchange of leadership and maintenance personnel, and closely coordinated operations to obtain the maximum use of facilities and services for the funds expended. This plan has been adopted in a number of communities and has the approval of many city planners, designers, and park administrators.

A close cooperation between public recreation boards and city park boards or special park districts is also quite common. This is, of course, very natural and logical since these two services are most often directly responsible for the provision of public, leisure-time services in the community.

Close coordination of three separate agencies—the park departments, the public school, and the recreation commission—is found in many communities. In this plan, the corporate bodies involved agree to perform specific functions and operational procedures, and a close cooperation is the result. In many instances, however, coordination between the three groups is hampered by local laws and differences in the geographical boundaries of each of the agencies.

Finally, the combination of parks and recreation services into one department is increasing throughout the country, particularly since 1955. Under this type of system, public park and recreation services are operated under one legal board and administered as one function. Similarly, the recreation function has been, in some cities, combined with public school operations. Most notable of these has been the school-centered public recreation program in Milwaukee (Wis.), the Recreation Division of the Chicago Public Schools, and similar combined systems in smaller communities, particularly in New York, Wisconsin, and California.

FORMULATING A LOCAL RECREATION PLAN

EXPERIENCE IN LOCAL PLANNING. The plan of administration of recreation in any city must depend upon local conditions in that city. It is possible to point out cities where park boards are administering recreation with outstanding success. On the other hand, there are cities where the park board's efforts in this direction have been distinct failures. It is likewise possible to point out examples where the school board has administered recreation with conspicuous merit, and, on the other hand, there are, again, failures.

In studying the problems of a given city, it may be found that the park board is steeped in politics or whose leadership has no enthusiasm whatever for recreation. On the other hand, the school board may be extremely conservative in its attitude and very reluctant to give leadership to the newer recreation movement; or it may be overburdened with formal educational responsibility or not possessed of enough funds to administer adequately the school curriculum, let alone to take on the added burden of public recreation.

Any plan of recreation which does not make the fullest possible use of its school and park facilities for recreation will fail to meet the problem with fullest effectiveness. Then, too, the churches possess many facilities and resources that the community needs for recreation. Many industries supply recreational facilities which can be and often are made available to the community at large. A cooperative plan is needed, bringing into play and coordinating all of the resources in the community, seeking the enthusiastic contribution of every likely institution. With this in mind, some cities have found it more effective to use the separate commission plan in which all of the resources of the community are represented. Such a commission can best work out a comprehensive plan showing how to advance and organize public recreation.

No uniform plan can be advocated for every city in America. Instead of trying to make one plan uniform throughout the length and breadth of the land, the National Recreation Association advocates using all the existing facilities in a city for recreation, recommending that each community has at least one well-trained, experienced recreation executive, that there is an adequate plan of cooperation between all the different groups that are conducting play, and that all available recreation resources, whether in schools, churches, industries or parks, or elsewhere, are utilized.

PRINCIPLES IN LOCAL PLANNING. Regardless of local conditions which will influence the selection and operation of the public recreation plan, there are several essential principles which must be observed.

A board, commission, or other definite organized group should be placed in control of the community's recreation with the responsibility and power to give continuous and undivided attention to the study of the leisure-time problems of all elements of the city and to work out the most effective means of solving them. This board should contain representatives of the school board and the park commission, inasmuch as both school and park property are essential to an adequate and comprehensive program. In the pursuit of continuity in planning, it is recommended that the terms of office of the members overlap so that not more than one or two expire each year.

A full-time executive, with a broad social education, thoroughly trained in the administration of recreation, and familiar with the workings of municipal government, should be employed to direct the program. This task will require all of the time and energies of such an executive and, in an organization of any size, a number of assistants and specialists will be required.

A definite budget, set aside for recreational purposes only, is most desirable. Adequate recreation planning must take a long look into the future and, with this in mind, many cities have voted a mill tax for recreational purposes, thus assuring the board of a relatively definite amount of money upon which they can rely each year. Unless the director knows what he may expect from year to year, he cannot plan with any degree of security or thoroughness. Without a definite budget available for recreation only, the funds are apt to be diverted into other channels in times of financial emergency. In some cities, a percentage of the park or school budget is definitely set aside for recreation.

A comprehensive recreation plan is an integral part of the total community master plan. A cooperative planning process will result in the most effective functional use of school district, park, city, and other properties for community recreation purposes day by day.

The primary consideration in planning should be a vital, compelling, challenging program of recreation activities, suitable to meet the needs of all elements and age stratifications in the city. Such a program will include music, arts, crafts, drama, nature, camping, and social activities, as well as physical activities. Facilities are essential, and administrative machinery is necessary, but it is through the program that the objectives of recreation are accomplished. Behind the program is leadership.

SUMMARY

A variety of methods are followed in administering public recreation. Since no one agency or government unit has assumed total responsibility for these public services, they have developed rather haphazardly at all levels. Presently, it is obvious that the federal government has broad responsibilities in the park and recreation field; yet no agency comparable to the Department of Health, Education and Welfare has been established to plan and direct these vast services. A few states have developed effective plans to coordinate the many facets of the recreation movement, but as yet not many. Permissive legislation in most states is inadequate to meet the changing needs for recreation programs and services in the enormous expansion following World War II. Locally, the administration of public recreation is becoming more effective under heavy pressure to provide more inclusive services. The separate public recreation commission still is the predominant method of administering year-round public recreation programs and services. On the other hand, many park departments and recreation systems have recently combined their operations. Schools operate relatively few full-time, year-round recreation systems but are playing an increasingly important part in the development of coordinated recreation services in the community. Some recreation systems still are administered under various other local governmental units, but such administrative procedures are gradually being replaced by departments of recreation operating under the authority of the park department, or the school district, or as a separate recreation board.

Finally, local conditions and factors determine how a recreation system is administered. Advantages and disadvantages may be stated for any one system in a given locality. Where recreation is recognized as having a separate identity on a plane with education, health, welfare, and other public services, a sound administrative system is likely to develop. The essence of good administration in recreation is coordination among all jurisdictions and agencies to best utilize the total recreation resources in the community. With improved public relations and the development of qualified recreation administrators, there will evolve improved methods of administration to meet the complex, changing needs of the fast-growing recreation field in its various settings.

SELECTED REFERENCES

The following three texts are the most comprehensive and thorough references for the study of the administration of public recreation:

BUTLER, GEORGE D. *Introduction to Community Recreation.* New York: McGraw-Hill Book Co., Inc., 1959.

————. *Playgrounds: Their Administration and Operation,* 3d ed. New York: The Ronald Press Co., 1960.

MEYER, HAROLD D., and BRIGHTBILL, CHARLES K. *Recreation Administration: A Guide to Its Practices.* Englewood Cliffs, N.J.: Prentice-Hall, Inc., 1956.

The Institute for Training in Municipal Administration. *Municipal Recreation Administration.* Chicago: International City Managers' Association, 1960.

ARNOLD, SERENA E. *Desirable Practices for the Administration of Consolidated Municipal Park and Recreation Departments.* Aurora, Ill.: American Institute of Park Executives, 1955.

BRIGHTBILL, CHARLES K., and MEYER, HAROLD D. *Recreation: Texts and Readings.* Englewood Cliffs, N.J.: Prentice-Hall, Inc., 1953.

California Recreation Commission. *Public Recreation and Parks in California: Principles and Current Practices.* Sacramento, Cal.: State Printing Office, 1957.

The Role of the Federal Government in the Field of Public Recreation. Washington, D.C.: Federal Inter-Agency Committee on Recreation, 1956.

VAN DER SMISSEN, BETTY. *State Laws for Parks and Recreation.* Wheeling, W. Va.: American Institute of Park Executives, 1956.

FILM.

Town and Country. (20 min.). 16 mm. Sound. Color. Athletic Institute, Merchandise Mart, Room 805, Chicago, Ill.

16

Recreation Areas
and Facilities

In every community there is some degree of organization for community living. Whether this organization develops a pattern which allows for a wholesome and productive life for each citizen, through work as well as through play, depends entirely upon the efforts and desires of the people at large. Most often the organization for economic development receives both direction and the undivided personal attention of practically every adult. Also, the planning of necessary elements of the physical pattern of the community usually receives similar attention because it is closely related to the function of earning a living and to the provision of the minimum requirements for personal comfort and safety enjoyed by each individual in the community. But social planning in most rural areas, cities, and metropolitan areas in the United States has not kept pace with industrial growth and the consequent ecological conditions which have significantly changed the lives of people in our society.

GROWTH OF PLANNING

The public services and facilities that do exist today to improve general living conditions and to allow for the development of broad social communication between individuals and groups are the result of planning, or the lack of it, since the Civil War. The reservation of open places for parks and recreation gained national recognition in 1853 when New York City created its now famous Central Park in Manhattan. This was followed by large park developments in Chicago, Boston, Los Angeles, and many smaller cities and towns throughout the country. The work of Jacob Riis, Robert A. Woods, Jane Addams, and many others brought out clearly the folly of poor planning in urban areas. Joseph Lee, Luther Gulick, Clark Hetherington, and others demonstrated the need for play space for the typical American games and the need for special indoor as well as outdoor play spaces in the growing program of education for leisure.

Since World War II, the space requirements for play, as well as for industry, transportation arterials, commercial activities, and residential living have become increasingly acute. The automobile, along with other factors, has revolutionized the space needs of all cities as well as many rural areas. The supermarket, the drive-in theatre, the large shopping center, and new or expanding industry all require considerably more space. Added to this basic need for space is the complexity of modern living and the unusually rapid population growth that has taken place since 1947. Local as well as regional plans, developed by professional city planners working with citizens and legally responsible governmental officials, are an absolute necessity for the orderly development of our economy and adequate living conditions.

At the present time, cities and villages and vast outdoor spaces exhibit poor as well as excellent planning. During the developments from 1900 to 1930, many schools were built without adequate play space, many cities and other local corporate municipalities neglected to plan adequately for park and recreation space, and aesthetic beauty was obviously ignored by lack of urban planning. The trend, since the 1930's when considerable public works construction was accomplished and since World War II, has been toward the development of a specific master plan for each city, metropolitan area, or region.

The master plan for public park and recreation areas and facilities in this country is unique in its component elements.

Never before has there been such distinct planning for living, nor on a national scale—space devoted to broad leisure-time activities as well as to specialized urban facilities for sports and cultural programs. During the early play movement, Joseph Lee and others experimented extensively to develop what is now known as the neighborhood playground, a distinct American institution. As a result of experience, recreation and park practitioners discovered the needs of people and presented these facts to the professional planners, who have, in turn, created new architectural and landscaping designs. Thus specialized designs for golf courses, swimming pools, gymnasiums, community centers, playgrounds, camps, and the wide variety of physical facilities we have for recreation gradually evolved.

STANDARDS FOR RECREATION UNITS

Although standards for recreation and park areas and facilities adopted by various cities and groups differ, a basic similarity in the standards has become increasingly evident. The National Recreation Association standards have long been used as a guide to planners and recreation executives. Further, various standards to fit local needs have also been devised and adopted by Chicago, Kansas City, Cleveland, and other cities. The American Public Health Association has also drawn up standards for public recreation and park areas and facilities. While national-type standards are fundamentally applicable, they are not absolute and must be adapted to local needs and resources. In California, for example, standards have been developed so that space standards are given for the "Six Californias." This implies that there are many areas within the state, not contiguous, which all are recognized as having social, cultural, economic, climatic, and other conditions requiring special consideration in recreation planning.

Recreation *standards* serve as measures of quality or adequacy of particular recreation areas. They are concerned with definite details—specific size, facilities to be included, service radius, age groups to be serviced, and similar details. They cannot be applied without recognizing that certain principles must be followed whether planning is specifically for a small village or a large metropolitan area. *Principles* express broad concepts which, along with standards, form the basic tools required for planning a superior public recreation system.

Fundamental variables such as density of population, economic or educational level, social need, and similar factors may alter the emphasis in a particular part of the community to a limited extent, but the standards for public recreation have been devised to insure recreation opportunities for all individuals in all parts of the community in the same way that public education and other community services are provided.

ORGANIZATION ACCORDING TO AREA PLAN. The provision of recreation facilities and areas beyond the home are often developed on the principle of the neighborhood concept. This concept recognizes that in urban areas specific neighborhoods are planned providing immediate needs and services within one-quarter to one-half mile radius of each residence within the neighborhood. Services and facilities such as adequate residential traffic patterns, schools, shopping areas, and recreation areas are necessary because of the economic, social, cultural, ethnic, and physical factors which, in themselves, actually determine the neighborhood. Each neighborhood is, in turn, a part of a larger pattern, the community, composed of four or five neighborhoods.

Services in the community usually involve a secondary school, a large business and shopping area, large area parks, and recreation facilities and other services within approximately one mile of the center of the community. Finally, several communities make up an entire city or metropolitan area, and special recreation facilities are included which service all people in the various communities and the surrounding region.

Recreation areas, facilities, and services thus are provided according to the basic neighborhood, community, and regional plans in a given area. Generally, urban areas and facilities are organized on the following basis:

1. A total of approximately one acre of public park and recreation area per 100 persons or a gross acreage of 10 per cent of the total land space of the area should be allotted for recreation purposes. This includes public school property and similar publicly owned land.

2. The total or gross acreage for public recreation purposes should be allocated accordingly to meet the specific needs and interests of people.

   a) Twenty-five per cent of this space should be allocated to provide totlots, playgrounds, neighborhood park playgrounds, playfields, activity buildings with meeting rooms, auditoriums, game rooms, craft shops, and the like. These facilities are for activities, which, by their nature, involve organization and require special supervision and specific types of areas, facilities, and equipment.

   b) The remainder or 75 per cent of the space should be set aside for activities generally without special organization or leadership (except permit or custodial and similar limited supervision) in areas such as large park areas, camps, beaches, picnic areas, zoos, museums, and cultural centers. These types of space allow people to participate in a variety of recreation activities of their own choosing in an interesting, inexpensive, and safe environment.

3. There should be, besides the public facilities, voluntary agency and informal education facilities. These should be built and maintained by community funds donated to agencies and organizations to provide services to meet the special interests and needs of groups and individuals. Facilities such as those of the YMCA, YWCA, Jewish Community Center, Catholic Youth Organization, and Community Chest-supported centers provide areas and facilities for small group participation, special interest groups, and persons wishing to take part in activities centered on a religious, fraternal, or similar basis.

4. There should be ample private and commercial recreation facilities in the community to provide wholesome recre-

ation services of a private nature. Public and voluntary agencies cannot provide all community recreation facilities. Commercial enterprise should be encouraged to provide well-regulated, safe, and economically priced services of all types to the general public. Private clubs, fraternal groups, and similar private organizations should provide special facilities for their members to develop educationally sound and interesting programs for children, adults, and family groups.

DESCRIPTION OF MAJOR RECREATION UNITS. In describing public recreation facilities, it is necessary to clarify terminology. In the growth of the play movement and particularly during the rapid development of planning since World War II, various names have been used by planners and local park and recreation executives to describe specific units of park and recreation areas and facilities. The following is a general description of public recreation facilities, indicating that certain terms have gained definite recognition as the most commonly accepted names of units that are considered necessary to the operation of an adequate public recreation system.

The playlot or totlot is an area designed especially for children of pre-school age. Playlots are located in the interior of a city block in a high-density population area, in a court within an apartment building, or on the grounds of a neighborhood recreation center or elementary school. Such lots are often supervised by parents or other volunteers.

The playground is a sub-neighborhood play area of limited size, designed to supplement the more extensive park playground. The playground is usually found in neighborhoods where physical features, population density, or similar factors necessitate a sub-neighborhood service unit.

The neighborhood park playground is the major neighborhood recreation unit, either a park, school, or a park-school combination providing general neighborhood indoor as well as outdoor play space and facilities. Other terms such as neighborhood recreation center, neighborhood playground, or park-school playground have sometimes been used to describe this type of area.

The playfield or community park is a unit usually serving four to five neighborhoods. This unit is also called a community recreation park or a community recreation center. It involves a major sports and recreation center, with facilities for both children and adults, and may involve a large park with a large indoor center, a park adjacent to a secondary school, or perhaps only a secondary school site especially designed for both formal school purposes and community recreation.

The city-wide park serves an entire city or a considerable portion of a large urban area. Because of its location, size (usually over one hundred acres), and inclusive features, this unit is often called a district park.

The reservation is sometimes referred to as a regional park. It involves a large tract of land operated by local township or by county authorities. Reservations usually serve more than one city or metropolitan area and provide a variety of outdoor, but somewhat limited indoor, recreation facilities.

Other units provide space especially designed for one type of activity or for mass use by large numbers of persons. Stadiums, golf courses, diversified aquatic facilities, zoos, band shells, skating rinks, and camping areas are among these units. Mention should also be made of games, sports, and recreation facilities such as baseball and softball diamonds, horseshoe pits, spray or wading pools, and tennis courts, that are specifically designed for certain activities and are a part of a well-designed neighborhood or community recreation area.

The standards for the above seven major recreation units vary throughout the country. The following charts incorporate to some degree the standards of the National Recreation Association, the California Committee on Planning for Recreation, Park Areas and Facilities, the Chicago Recreation Commission, and several other agencies of local planners and of recreation officials.[1]

PLAYLOT OR TOTLOT

LOCATION	Specially designed and fenced-in area located at neighborhood playground or recreation center; also located in land adjacent to large housing projects, apartment buildings, or in other areas of high-density population.
AGE GROUP SERVED	Pre-school children, 6 years and under.
SERVICE RADIUS	¼ mile maximum to minimum of one block, depending on density of population.
POPULATION SERVED	100 children, or 40 children per 100 families at one time; serves neighborhood families.
ACREAGE RANGE	1,500 square feet to 8,000 square feet; 75 square feet per child.
FACILITIES	Open shelter or shade from sun; swings, slide, sandbox, climber, wheel toy freeway, playhouse, special play equipment, benches for parents, shrubs, trees for shade, and fencing.
OPERATION	Provision by public as part of larger play areas; development by private agencies, housing authorities or neighborhood groups when not located on larger public grounds.
LEADERSHIP	Special paid leadership, with voluntary help, when operated on public grounds; paid, volunteer, or informal leadership as desired when operated privately.

PLAYGROUND

LOCATION	In center of sub-neighborhood or in section of neighborhood not accessible to, or influenced by, larger neighborhood recreation center.
AGE GROUPS SERVED	15 years old and younger.

[1] Standards have also been published by recreation departments in Washington, D.C., Kansas City, Missouri, Cincinnati, Cleveland, St. Louis, and by the American Public Health Association.

SERVICE RADIUS	Generally, ¼ mile.
POPULATION SERVED	Up to 4,000 persons or 1,000 children.
ACREAGE RANGE	2 to 4 acres.
FACILITIES	Indoor—shelter house with game room, meeting room, office, toilets, and storage space; elementary school used if located on school grounds. Outdoor—play apparatus for pre-school and school-age children; multiple-use, paved court areas, small quiet area, turf area for softball and informal games.
OPERATION	Generally like that of a neighborhood park playground or neighborhood recreation center, as described on the following chart.
LEADERSHIP	Qualified full-time paid leadership, supplemented by qualified volunteer leadership.

NEIGHBORHOOD PARK PLAYGROUND

LOCATION	Center of neighborhood, preferably adjacent to, or in conjunction with, school grounds providing indoor facilities.
AGE GROUPS SERVED	All ages, with emphasis on school-age children 5 to 16 years of age.
SERVICE RADIUS	¼ to ⅜ mile, with ½ mile radius in low density areas; within walking distance of homes in the neighborhood.
POPULATION SERVED	4,000 to 10,000 persons.
ACREAGE RANGE	7 to 16 acres; approximately 1.5 acres per 1,000 persons.
FACILITIES	Indoor—community center building or elementary school with gymnasium, assembly hall, club and meeting rooms, game room, arts and crafts room, office, shower rooms, toilets, and service space. Outdoor—playlot, apparatus area, sports field, multiple-use paved area, family and group picnic area, quiet area, area for older people, hobby area, off-street parking space, and night lighting.

OPERATION   Year-round, with seasonal emphasis on indoor or outdoor program, coordinated with school, voluntary, and private agency operations.

LEADERSHIP   Qualified full-time leadership, supplemented with qualified volunteer leadership.

PLAYFIELD OR COMMUNITY PARK

LOCATION   Center of four to five neighborhoods, preferably adjoining high school property, field house, or large community center building providing extensive indoor facilities.

AGE GROUPS SERVED All ages.

SERVICE RADIUS   1 to 1½ miles in low density areas.

POPULATION SERVED 20,000 to 50,000 persons.

ACREAGE RANGE   20 to 40 acres.

FACILITIES   Indoor—Community center; junior high or senior high school building including gymnasiums, auditorium, multipurpose rooms, arts and crafts room, kitchen, lounge, offices, shower and locker rooms, and service space. Swimming pool should be included when location is at school site.
Outdoor—playground area (school and preschool ages), fields for athletics (baseball, football, soccer, etc.), multiple-use paved area, paved court games area, picnic and day camp area, concrete slab for skating and dancing, free play area, nature area, and area for older people. Outdoor pool should be included; off-street parking and night lighting should be provided.

OPERATION   Operation year-round, closely coordinated with schools, voluntary, and private agency needs and operations.

LEADERSHIP   Qualified full-time leadership, supplemented by qualified volunteer leadership.

SPACE ALLOTMENTS FOR VARIOUS USES. Play areas vary considerably in design and equipment. The ideal situation is found where the space is designed specifically to meet local needs. When complete indoor facilities are not provided, as on a sub-neighborhood playground, shelters are provided for necessary space to carry on an adequate program. In general, the following types of areas are designed, equipped, and located to meet best the play needs of various age groups. Designers have combined these areas and in some cases omitted them when neighborhood needs so indicate.

Area for Pre-School Children. An area is needed for little children where they can play safely and without interference. It should be isolated if possible, fenced in, easily accessible, and close to the shelter house. Furniture and apparatus should be cut down to size, and such appropriate items as spray pools and sandboxes featured.

Apparatus Area. It is considered good practice to allocate all the apparatus for older children in one area, easily accessible and close to the shelter house. If close to other playing areas, it should be fenced in. The present practice is to have both boys and girls use the same apparatus.

Spray Pool or Wading Pool. Spray pools are preferred by most recreation personnel. Wading pools, when used, should be carefully designed to meet sanitary standards. Location should be near shelter and apparatus areas where all the younger children can make use of the facility.

Area for Free Play. An area for free play and for games of low organization is desirable. Since its greatest use will be by pre-adolescents it should be strategically placed in respect to the apparatus and other activities this age prefers so much.

Multiple-Use Area. This is usually a paved area marked out for court games and used also for roller skating and dancing. It finds many other uses after rains when other areas are wet. Sometimes two such areas are provided, one for younger, and one for older children.

Field Game Area. This is a large area with facilities for such sports as softball, baseball, soccer, and touch football;

around its edges are often found box-hockey, goal-hi, tether-ball, quoits, badminton, deck tennis, and other lawn games. It is customary now to use the same facilities for girls and boys, setting separate times for use by each, if necessary.

Craft and Quiet Area. This area has benches and tables, and other facilities for arts and crafts, nature, music, story-telling, dramatics, and dancing. There also are the facilities for quiet play such as checkers, bean bags, darts, ring-toss, marbles, hopscotch, and croquet.

Area for Older People. While children may predominate, adults, including those over 60, are using playgrounds in increasing numbers. An area set aside and equipped to meet their needs is most desirable. It features benches and shade, and less strenuous games such as giant checkers, shuffleboard, and horseshoes.

Shelter House. The shelter house provides rain protection, toilet facilities, storage and equipment rooms, and sometimes an indoor playroom.

Family Picnic Area. A fireplace area with tables for picnic and day camping programs.

Landscaping. Shade trees, shrubs, grassy areas, and plantings should be a part of the total design of the area, both for aesthetic beauty and for practical recreation program operations.

Off-Street Parking. There should be some off-street parking to take care of immediate area needs. Design of the parking area will determine the number of automobiles accommodated, approximately 50, if possible.

The California Committee on Planning for Recreation, Park Areas, and Facilities offers specific information on space required for a school or a park area (see Selected References). Although these space allotments are based on needs in California, they furnish much basic information for planning of areas in other parts of the country, including types of space, ratio of space, and related factors.

EVALUATION OF PHYSICAL FACILITIES. The adequacy of local recreation areas and facilities can be determined by accurate appraisal of existing facilities and resources. Appraisal and survey studies of local park and recreation systems have accurately shown the status of, and the deficiencies in, physical facilities. From these analyses, the need for immediate and long range planning is revealed and priorities for developing specific areas and facilities have been indicated. The development of public physical facilities for leisure activities can no longer be left to chance. This function is an integral part of the total community master plan and an important factor in the creative design for living that will emerge to meet the needs of life in American communities in the present age.

EQUIPMENT FOR PLAY AREAS

The fully-equipped neighborhood play area must provide space and apparatus for play, and play materials of all sorts. There must be adequate provisions for the comfort and welfare of the children and parents. The accessories necessary for the general maintenance of everything pertaining to the playground must be on hand. The size of the ground, money available, ages of children, and the special neighborhood interests are all factors that enter in when playground equipment is being planned.

In respect to playground play, the equipment may be classified under four types: ground facilities, play apparatus, play supplies, and miscellaneous supplies. The following shows the areas, equipment, and materials for playgrounds and playfields:

Ground facilities		*Play apparatus*
Field house	Courts for games	Swings
Shelter house	Tennis	Sandbox
Toilets	Volleyball	Giant-stride
Drinking fountains	Handball	Horizontal bar
Water faucets	Basketball	Horizontal ladder
Flagpole	Croquet	Seesaws
Swimming pool	Tetherball	Slides
Wading pool	Quoits or horseshoes	Teeter ladders

Ground facilities

Track and field athletics
Running track
  Jumping pits
  Shot pits
Fields for games
  Baseball
  Softball
  Soccer or football
  Field hockey

Paddle tennis
Badminton
Hopscotch
Marbles
Box hockey
Giant checkers
Deck tennis
Goal-hi
Shuffleboard
Table tennis

Play apparatus

Parallel bars
Traveling rings
Swinging rings
Merry-go-round
Balancing board
Sliding pole
Vaulting horses
Jungle gym
Balance beam

Play Supplies

Ball for games
  Softball
  Basketball
  Volleyball
  Baseball
  Football
  Tennis
  Handball
  Field hockey
  Water polo
  Tetherball
  Table tennis
Vaulting standards
Measuring tape
Quoits
Horseshoes
Croquet sets
Deck tennis rings

Bean bags
Ring-toss
Target board
Medicine ball
Handcraft materials
Bows
Arrows
Archery target
Darts
Dart targets
Golf cage and net
Shots
Badminton rackets
Shuffleboard equip-
  ment
Giant checkers
Field hockey sticks

Miscellaneous supplies

First-aid kit
Repair kit
Benches
Tools for mainte-
  nance
Roller
Marker
Equipment chest
Awnings
Attendance blanks
Prizes
Cards for tests
Inflators
Lacing needles
Lime
Megaphones
Whistles
Starting guns
Blank cartridges
Stop watches

The experience of the years has standardized the equipment for many of the above facilities and has indicated the best types of development for all of them. The results of this experience have been accumulated in the literature of the National Recreation Association and should be consulted.

PREPARATION OF THE PLAY FACILITY

Special considerations in play areas should be given to shade, fencing, grading, surfacing, lighting, and winter usage.

SHADING. To the city child, especially, an aesthetic value arises in having shade trees, hedges, vines, plants, flowers, and grassy plots, but they should not be allowed to interfere with the play. There is the chance to place these things at the entrance to the grounds, on the borders, along walks, and close to buildings. Vines help beautify the appearance of a fence. When trees follow along the walks, it takes but little more space to have a double row (one on each side of the walk) instead of one alone, and this is what most cities do in this respect.

In all playgrounds, trees are needed for their shade, especially in the sections where the little children play, such as about the sandbox, swings, and other apparatus, and about the spray or wading pool. They are also needed to shelter the benches where parents sit and watch their children. During the hottest periods of the day, the shaded portions of the playgrounds are the only ones that are kept busy.

The hedge can also serve a practical purpose. Many cities use it as a fence, especially where it is desired to bound spaces within the playground.

FENCING. The general opinion favors fencing. The reasons given are several in number. The children are safe from the street traffic; otherwise they are apt to run into the street after a ball or to escape being tagged, and in the excitement of the game, forget the danger. Fencing will make the problem of supervision much easier, because it sets the playground apart from the outer world.

It is more essential that the small playground be fenced than the large one. In a sense the large park playground is fenced off by the park areas that usually surround it. In such a situation, any fence, unless a hedge, tends to detract from the appearance of the park as a whole.

Fences should be high enough to keep the balls inside;

and so constructed as to deter people from trying to climb over them, and to be strong enough to stand up under the strain they are subjected to when children run into them or use them to lean upon. There are many types of fences which are satisfactory. Woven wire fences are most commonly used, the meshes of which should be fine enough to keep in the balls that are being used in the games. A low hedge of evergreen is also accepted by some authorities, and is a type of fence that is especially well adapted to park uses.

Fences near sections where ball games are played should be at least ten feet high. In some places where they are needed as a backstop for the particular game, a height of twelve feet is required. Tennis and baseball backstops of adequate height are not only necessary for the convenience of the players but for the protection of neighboring property.

GRADING. The playground surface must be level, therefore the grading problem must be given consideration. If the playground is on a low level, it may be advantageous to have the grounds slope gradually to the center; then the drainage can be handled by having small catch basins leading to a larger catch basin at the center of the depression. This type of field can be easily flooded in the winter time for skating. Another type of playground is the one that has the high point in the middle so that the water will run off toward the sides. Still another type, and one that needs considerable grading, is the playground that is located along the side of the hill. Quite often some excavation is necessary before the playing space can be made level. This requires special attention, such as heavy sodding and arrangement of shrubbery on the terraces. The drainage in this case will be in one direction—in the general slope of the hill. Following heavy rains, however, the water will wash out the ground and leave gullies.

The problem of grading is a technical one requiring a lengthy discussion to handle it adequately. Those who are confronted with play areas needing much grading should seek expert assistance.

SURFACING. The surfacing problems differ according to the locality and nature of the grounds, and according to the games that are to be played. No one type of surface can meet all needs. A surface to meet all the demands made upon it should be smooth and level, and firm and springy under the feet; should resist wear, not be dusty, and absorb water readily.

For surfaces under apparatus, sand is serviceable and most economical; mixtures of tanbark, sand, and loam have also proved excellent, although more expensive. For general all-round use there is probably no better surface than grass turf, yet this is impossible to maintain where the grounds are being used intensively. Spaces that are being used all day long, like the ordinary school ground or the concentrated areas where popular competitive games like volleyball, tennis, and softball are played, require a much more durable surface.

The simplest type of surface and one that proves fairly satisfactory is sandy loam, or, better yet, the loam mixed with clay. The loam alone is not firm enough; and the clay alone stays muddy after a rain, and during a dry spell bakes too hard and cracks. This mixture is very dusty in dry weather and must be sprinkled frequently, or treated with calcium chloride. Another surface that is recommended is a mixture of clay, loam, and fine cinders, placed over a subsoil of coarse cinders, crushed brick, or gravel for drainage. Experiments for top surface drainage are being made with cork asphalt and other types of resilient material.

Surfaces of gravel, cinders, or concrete, such as are sometimes found, are very objectionable. The loose gravel makes an unsure footing, and children are tempted to throw the stones. Cinders lead to injuries when players fall. The concrete is not only too hot in the summer but the jar from playing on it is tiring. Yet concrete or asphalt are preferred for small-area games such as tennis, outdoor handball, and shuffleboard.

Special surfaces are needed for certain parts of the more

elaborate playgrounds. The cinder track and tennis courts are examples. Many cinder tracks are made simply by using cinders with loam (approximately three to one). This is placed over a porous surface such as crushed brick, stone, and so forth, and then watered and tamped.

Tennis courts need very careful construction. Asphalt or cement are the most practical types of tennis court surfaces for public outdoor play areas. A clay surface is excellent but limitation of play during wet weather and cost of continuous maintenance prohibits widespread use of this surface for public courts. On neighborhood play areas, tennis court areas should be so constructed that they can, where weather permits, be flooded for ice skating during the winter season.

Various mixtures of asphalt, depending on weather and soil factors, are adequate to provide playing surfaces for basketball, volleyball, handball, paddle tennis, and similar court games. The whole question of surfacing is a very technical one and requires the attention of experts.

LIGHTING. Playgrounds that are large enough to serve the older boys and girls and adults of the neighborhood should be kept open at night, and results show that this period is probably the busiest one of the whole day. There are many older people who will stay for volleyball, softball, horseshoe pitching, folk dancing, and other suitable activities if the playground is well lighted.

Also, modern lighting is a very necessary part of playfield or community-wide recreation facilities. Night lighting for softball, baseball, tennis, and other sports, as well as for special facilities such as bandshells, swimming pools, and ice rinks, should be included in plans for these areas. Lighted facilities increase the length of the day so that people of all age groups can take advantage of the wholesome activities offered at public play centers during hours when most of the population has leisure time to participate.

WINTER FACILITIES. Playgrounds and playfields located in cold climates can be adapted for flooding to develop natural ice during winter months. Areas for pleasure skating, speed skating, and ice hockey are thus provided. Outdoor public, artificial ice rinks have been installed in many cities and have proven to be very practical and popular. Special facilities to provide opportunities for coasting, tobogganing, and skiing should be provided at playfield, community center, or large park locations. For the development of facilities for winter use, technical references should be consulted.

FACILITIES FOR INDOOR RECREATION

In addition to neighborhood and community-wide outdoor facilities, there must be adequate public indoor facilities of various types to meet the needs and interests of people in the community. As previously indicated, the complete neighborhood play area and the playfield or community-wide facility now both include special types of indoor play space. During the early years of the play movement, public outdoor play areas often had only temporary or limited indoor facilities. But as the movement grew, it became evident that it was necessary to plan joint indoor-outdoor facilities to provide total public community recreation programs and services. In some instances special shelters, field houses, and community center buildings were erected. In other cases, public school buildings were utilized for public recreation. More recently, school buildings have been designed to be used for both formal school and public recreation programs. It has also proven advantageous to combine the school and park.

In order to meet new needs, facilities must be planned on a community-wide basis for multiple use. This is particularly true of indoor facilities, and without the application of sound planning principles the proper perspective in regard to total needs in the community cannot be maintained.

SCHOOL-COMMUNITY FACILITY. The use of play in the regular program of the school differs from its use on the playground in several respects: first, play is only a part of a wide curriculum; second, play attendance is often compulsory; third, the play is regulated on a time basis, each group receiving an allotted share; fourth, the required play lessons are definitely arranged in progression, and the physical fitness of each child is much more carefully looked after; and fifth, the individual may receive school credit for engaging in play.

The activities of the school program are somewhat modified from the ones that have been mentioned for outdoor use. Only games suited for small spaces can be used. When the program omits plays and games entirely, it is then called formalized. Much true play is inevitable, however: all the activities of the kindergarten, for instance, and the recess games of the grade pupils, the plays and games that are found in the physical education lessons, the athletic practice that takes place in the gymnasium after school, and the recreation activities that the older people indulge in when they come to the school in the evening are all of play nature.

Certain facilities are needed to conduct play in the school building. Of course the kindergarten room is a playroom. Then, too, the classrooms and the corridors are often used for active games; and when there is a community project, the auditorium and library may also be classed as play centers. But in the strict sense, the gymnasium and the swimming pool are the centers of the play activities.

In addition to the physical types of play, the school also has facilities and leadership for other rich play activities, such as music, dramatics, storytelling, arts and crafts, and nature lore. The classroom work in these activities, if they are handled in a modern and progressive way educationally, will take on the aspects of play. Aside from their use in the regular curriculum, these activities constitute no small part of the extracurricular program and are the source of countless hobby groups. Handled in this way, these activities carry over into the home and furnish material for home and club play activity.

PUBLIC INDOOR RECREATION CENTER. The neighborhood is an area served by a neighborhood recreation center, which is a combination indoor-outdoor space located at an elementary school or separate park area. When the park-school plan is followed, facilities for neighborhood programs, primarily for young people five to fourteen years of age but also for young people and adults, are provided jointly by these agencies. The building on a park-school location should be designed so that the gymnasium, auditorium, and other facilities may be used for public programs without opening the entire school. The park department is usually responsible for providing outdoor facilities and the school provides for all indoor needs. In other locations, the indoor building space is located away from the school and a recreation-type building is usually provided. The ideal plan, however, is to locate the neighborhood center at the elementary school location since it is provided by tax funds and has costly facilities that should not be duplicated, except under special conditions. Whether located separately or at a school site, the neighborhood indoor center should include the following facilities; gymnasium and assembly hall with stage, shower rooms, toilets, arts and crafts room, multipurpose game or club rooms, lounge, kitchen, and office and storage space. Hallways and large assembly-classrooms in schools may sometimes be used for recreation programs. The size and utilization of these facilities depends upon local neighborhood conditions. Like the elementary school, the neighborhood indoor facility should service people within walking distance of the building.

The community-wide indoor center involves a larger and more complex facility than that required in each neighborhood. Servicing a radius of approximately one mile, the community center is often located at a junior or senior high school site. When located separately, the center should involve adequate recreation facilities but should not duplicate unnecessarily those already in existence. In many instances it is very logical that a community center building be located away from the school. This gives children as well as adults opportunities to use the center at all hours of the day and to get completely away from the school atmosphere. Size and design of the community indoor center varies with local population and needs.

According to National Recreation Association standards, the community-type center, besides the outdoor facilities already mentioned, should have the following indoor facilities:

Gymnasium with all service facilities for use by men and women, seating capacity for special events, and designed for various types of games and sports. There should be a gymnasium for each 10,000 or less of the population.

Assembly hall or auditorium, with stage, designed especially to be used for a wide variety of social, dramatic, and similar community events. There should be an auditorium for each 20,000 or less of the population.

Game room for each 10,000 or less.

Social room or play room for each 10,000 or less.

Club or multiple-use room, one for each 4,000 or less.

Informal reading room and quiet game room, one for each 10,000 or less.

Indoor swimming pool, one for each 50,000 or less.

Kitchen, storage space and essential service rooms.

SUMMARY

Adequate recreation areas and facilities cannot be provided without careful planning. The need for such planning is evident in the older sections of cities as well as in the many new subdivisions that have developed along with the rapid growth of cities since 1950. Many neighborhoods lack recreation centers and facilities for music, dramatics, art, and similar activities; and in many parts of the country sufficient space for outdoor areas and facilities such as playgrounds, parks, swimming pools, public beaches and lakes, marinas, golf courses, camps and the like is not being reserved for the use of present and future generations.

At the same time, however, the road ahead is clear.

Standards have been established describing types and amounts of recreation facilities required to provide adequate services. These standards are guides to help local communities as well as the entire nation to provide for the present as well as the future recreation needs at all levels. Research is needed to provide more serviceable, more adaptable materials for facilities at lower cost, to discover ways of utilizing materials and space more efficiently, and to provide new and challenging areas and facilities to broaden the opportunities for people to participate in recreation activities of their own choice.

Perhaps most important of all is the growing realization of the need for coordinated planning. While public agencies assume the responsibility of providing the basic needs for recreation areas and facilities for public use, they are obligated to plan these facilities cooperatively. This enables cities, school districts, park districts, and other departments of government to achieve functional groupings of properties and facilities to give maximum services to the public. Such functional planning may be achieved through a comprehensive master plan to provide for the needs of each local community or regional area; comprehensive planning at the state and national level is also needed to meet the recreation needs of the entire nation, which varies considerably from extremely low- to extremely high-density areas.

SELECTED REFERENCES

Excellent detailed material is available in the following publications regarding indoor, as well as outdoor school, park, and general areas; equipment, and facilities for recreation:

Athletic Institute. *Planning Facilities for Health, Physical Education, and Recreation.* Chicago: Athletic Institute, 1956.

BUTLER, GEORGE D. *Recreation Areas: Their Design and Equipment.* 2d ed. New York: The Ronald Press Co., 1958.

CARTER, JOEL. *How To Make Athletic Equipment.* New York: The Ronald Press Co., 1960. A manual for constructing the equipment and supplies most commonly used in athletics and in physical education and recreation programs. This book gives step-by-step instructions for improvising and constructing more than 350 items of equipment.

GABRIELSON, M. ALEXANDER, and MILES, COSWELL M. *Sports and Recreation Facilities.* Englewood Cliffs, N.J.: Prentice-Hall, Inc., 1958.

References on Facilities and Equipment For Health, Physical Education, and Recreation. (Fitness Series No. 2.) Washington, D.C.: American Association For Health, Physical Education, and Recreation, 1958.

California Committee on Planning for Recreation, Park Areas and Facilities. *Guide for Planning Recreation Parks in California.* Sacramento, Cal.: Documents Section, Printing Division, 1956. See especially pp. 25–32; for space allotments, see p. 50.

COLBORN, FERN M. *Buildings of Tomorrow, Guide for Planning Settlements and Community Buildings.* New York: Whiteside, Inc., and William Morrow Co., 1955.

CONOVER, H. S. *Grounds Maintenance Handbook.* New York: F. W. Dodge Corp., 1958.

Institute for Training in Municipal Administration. *Local Planning Administration.* Chicago: International City Managers' Association, 1959, Chap. 9.

LEDERMANN, ALFRED, and TRACHSEL, ALFRED. *Creative Playgrounds and Recreation Centers.* New York: Frederick A. Praeger, Inc., 1959.

OSTROW, ALBERT A. *Planning Your Home for Play.* Atlanta, Ga.: Tupper and Love, Inc., 1954.

SAPORA, ALLEN V. *A Recreation Survey of the Rockford Park District.* Rockford, Ill.: Community Welfare Council of Winnebago County, 1955, Chap. 5.

SCHNEIDER, RAYMOND C., BOYCE, R. DUDLEY, and PATERSON, TED T. *Creative Planning of Parks and Play Areas for Learning, Living, and Leisure.* Stanford, Cal.: Stanford University, The School Planning Laboratory, 1957.

Schools for the New Needs: Educational, Social, Economic. New York: F. W. Dodge Corp., 1956.

SCHULTZ, ARTHUR L., and others. *Principles for Chicago's Comprehensive Recreation Plan.* Chicago: Chicago Recreation Commission, 1952, pp. 23–28.

17

Private or
Voluntary Agencies

Private or voluntary agencies have played a large part in the development of the leisure-time life of people in the United States. During the initial stages of the play movement and even until after World War II, these agencies in many cities assumed the major responsibility for providing a wide variety of leisure-time, recreation activities in many different settings. Essentially these agencies began providing recreation programs along with the broad social welfare services provided by groups and agencies supported mainly by philanthropic and other charity funds.

Many of the voluntary agencies began their operations in the latter half of the nineteenth century. The Young Men's Christian Association was started in Boston in 1851, the Boy's Club of Hartford, Connecticut, in 1860, and the Young Women's Christian Association in Boston in 1866. The first American Social Settlement, which became so prominent as a neighborhood social service unit, was opened in 1886. Not until much later, however, did any of these organizations set forth a program of recreation and of leisure-time education. Notable of these developments was the pioneer playground work conducted by Jane Addams at Hull House beginning in 1889. Between 1900 and 1920, programs offering specific services for youth first appeared with Ernest Thompson Seton's Woodcraft Indians. The Boy Scouts, started in England in 1908, were organized in the United States in 1910; the Camp Fire Girls also began in 1910, and the Girl Scouts of the United States of America in 1912.

The private or voluntary agencies are not generally considered to be recreation agencies and do not exist primarily to promote and operate recreation services. They are essentially nonprofit or eleemosynary corporations providing a wide variety of public services depending upon the objectives, functions, sponsorship, and constituency of the agency involved.

Furthermore, these agencies have been and still are referred to under various names; no set terminology has been evolved in reference to them. That different names and designations are given to them by practitioners as well as by writers in social work literature is evident from the following:

> Youth-serving organizations are numerous and well known. Some are governmental in auspice and operation and are financed through taxes. They generally are referred to as public agencies; examples are municipal departments of parks and recreation, and public schools. Other youth-serving organizations are voluntary in auspice and operation. Under citizen boards of directors who finance them through contributions solicited directly or through community chest or united fund campaigns, they usually are called private agencies. Examples of them are Boys' Clubs, Boy Scouts, Camp Fire Girls, Girl Scouts, Catholic Youth Organization, Jewish Community Centers, Salvation Army, settlement houses and neighborhood centers, the YMCA, YWCA, and YM-YWHA.
>
> These public and private organizations tend to be loosely classed together as "recreation-education," "group work," or "character-building" agencies. This stems largely from their using many identical program activities. Both types of organizations offer such things as athletics, group games, parties, dramatics, arts and crafts, singing, camping, teen canteens, and lounges.[1]

Although often referred to as youth-serving agencies, many of them have, throughout the years, expanded their programs to include adults as well. Although they are not private in the sense of the private country club, private social club, or commercial enterprise, they are considered private in the sense that they are not tax supported nor operated by some department of government but rather are chartered by the various states as private corporations. The

[1] Russell H. Kurtz (ed.), *Social Work Year Book* (New York: National Association of Social Workers, Inc., 1957), p. 598.

term private or voluntary agencies is thus used here to designate the multitude of nonprofit agencies and groups that offer leisure-time, informal education and recreation programs and services.

STRUCTURE OF PRIVATE OR VOLUNTARY AGENCIES

Private or voluntary organizations today are many in number and include a wide variety of services. The *Social Work Year Book 1960* lists 328 different national voluntary agencies. Many of these groups, such as the American Bar Association, the American Cancer Society, the National Committee on Alcoholism, and similar groups do not provide leisure-time services, and so are not included in the discussions that follow.

IDENTIFICATION OF SOCIAL GROUP WORK. Social work is a phase of human service. It originated when it became apparent that economic, social, intellectual, recreational, health, and other needs were no longer being met through personal services by people within society itself. Social work grew as a profession rapidly as the changing industrial and social conditions from 1880 to 1910 brought on acute social maladjustment. It became obvious, too, that after 1900 social workers began not only to work more and more with the individual in case work but with groups of individuals as well. At first, these group workers were identified by the agency with which they were associated; they were called, for example, settlement workers, "Y" secretaries, scout executives, playground directors, recreation workers. As soon as the school of social work at Western Reserve University in 1928 offered a training course for those who worked with groups, a classification in terms of method was set up to include persons in any agency who followed this group method. Shortly thereafter the term "social group work" became commonplace, and workers were called social group workers.

Social group work, then, is one of the important phases of the profession of social work; the other two major phases of this profession are social case work and community organization. Furthermore, social group work is a process—a method of working with people which may be applied in many settings. It is aimed at helping people to establish better social relations with each other, beginning with a better knowledge of their own situation and how they may solve their own problems.

OBJECTIVES OF SOCIAL GROUP WORK. Although social group work may be applied in many situations such as hospitals, guidance centers, schools, institutions, and similar settings, the method was developed in the voluntary agencies and finds its widest application there. The objective of these agencies, since their earliest work, has been to help people through broad services rendered to groups, yet not to lose sight of the importance of the individual in the group. In group work, the important thing is what happens to the outlook of these individuals as a result of their group experiences.

It is true that for some groups the service rendered for the common interest is regarded as of more importance than any service it might render the individual members. For example, in a men's service club the help given to the physically handicapped may very well be of more importance than any personal contribution the club might make to the men themselves. However, in that form of social work called group work the point of view is quite the reverse. The individuals are more important than the common interest which holds them together. The activities growing out of the common interest provide a congenial environment for the guidance of individuals by the group leader.

Frequently club leaders, in their enthusiasm for the club, lose sight of the individual as the paramount objective. They come to think of the club as such and to gauge success by how well the club functions as a club. If morale is strong, esprit de corps high, group consciousness evident, participation in activities enthusiastic, the club is regarded as outstandingly successful. The experienced worker does not permit this more glamorous group aspect to divert attention from the less spectacular but more fundamental matter of the growth of the individuals.

Again, activity-minded leaders frequently become engrossed in the teaching of skills to the point where guidance in other areas is lost from sight. The importance of a varied and compelling activities program cannot be minimized, and neither can the importance of developing skills in the activities; clubs devoted to developing athletic and swimming ability, for example, cannot and should not neglect the teaching of those skills. The very effort at teaching skills creates an unexcelled opportunity for general guidance, in that there are attendant and concomitant as well as direct learnings resulting from all such activity situations. (See Chapter 13.)

CLASSIFICATION OF AGENCIES. The voluntary agencies today have grown to occupy a much different position from that when they were originally founded. They still operate through settlement houses, neighborhood community centers, youth service groups, club organizations, schools, and churches. But in recent years these agencies are being classified, according to the following fundamental factors: (1) their general operational procedures, (2) the physical facilities they use, control, or own, and (3) their radius of service to people. The private or voluntary agencies are, accordingly, classified as indicated below:

Mobile or Non-Building-Centered Agencies. These organizations or groups usually operate on a club or neighborhood basis, with volunteer leadership. Most of them are under the direction of lay boards who hire professional field workers to supervise on a national or area-wide basis large numbers of volunteer workers. They are able to begin operations in any neighborhood as long as leaders and a meeting place can be obtained. Thus these agencies do not own their own local meeting places, but operate from schools, churches, community centers, and similar physical facilities. They usually have some special facilities like a central office, a resident or day camp, or similar properties. Typical examples of this type of organization are the Boy Scouts of

America, Girl Scouts of the United States of America, Camp Fire Girls, and many private and informal incorporated nonprofit interest groups of a regional or local nature.

Neighborhood Building-Centered Agencies. These agencies usually operate from a building-centered facility owned or controlled by the agency. The building or facility is often relatively limited in that it is large enough to serve only the neighborhood area in which it is located. Thus it most often provides services to people living within a radius of from three-eighths to one-half mile from the building. Most often operated independently by a local board, these agencies make up the bulk of the local neighborhod agencies that have been so prominent throughout the United States; some of these agencies are, however, linked with a national organization. Examples of this type of voluntary agency include neighborhood community centers supported by charitable funds, neighborhood settlement houses, housing development centers, youth centers, missions, and different types of social and service centers.

City-Wide, Building-Centered Agencies. Operating from a central building having extensive facilities to carry on a wide variety of leisure-time and recreation activities, these agencies service an entire city or a smaller metropolitan area; in very large cities they service a section of the city commensurate with the density of the section's population. Typical examples of the city-wide, building-centered agency are the YMCA, YWCA, Jewish Community Centers, Boys' Clubs of America, agencies serving racial or interracial groups, and local music or theatre groups.

ADMINISTRATION OF AGENCIES. Legally, as previously mentioned, a private or voluntary agency is usually a nonprofit corporation. Such a corporation must be registered and function under the general laws of the state in which it is operating. Most states have special legislation covering such corporations which usually (1) defines the minimum organizational structure of this type of corporation, (2) defines the limits of its operations, and (3) establishes its legal liability as either a government or proprietary function. A corporation is thus formed by each local board to conform with both the area-wide or national structure of the agency, as the case might be, as well as with the state regulations governing eleemosynary or charitable corporations.

A local lay board of directors or governing body represents both the community at large and the specific membership of the voluntary agency corporation. This is usually true since most of these agencies are Community Chest or United Fund agencies and receive funds collected from the community at large. The board usually includes individuals with diverse backgrounds and experiences representing people from all walks of life. Usually the board elects its own members, paying particular attention to selecting individuals who contribute funds as well as key leadership services to the agency. The primary purpose of the board is to establish objectives for the organization and to see that funds and professional as well as volunteer leaders are available to carry out these objectives. It must develop policies to guide the organization and procedures to evaluate its efforts periodically. Finally, boards of voluntary agencies should, through delegation to their professional staff, insure the organization of detailed operational procedures through the extensive use of well-oriented volunteer leaders.

The private or voluntary agencies depend upon the following three major sources of income to cover operating costs: (1) payments for service, including fees, charges, and dues, which most often provide a major source of income, (2) Community Chest or United Fund Campaign contributions, which also bear a considerable portion of these expenses and are widely used throughout the country, and (3) miscellaneous income such as special funds, endowments, gifts, and other income-producing operations such as dormitories, restaurants, and similar special services.

ROLE OF THE PRIVATE OR VOLUNTARY AGENCIES

Agencies and groups with different approaches to meeting the leisure-time needs and interests of people are essen-

tial in any community. Some needs are best met through
the case work approach; other needs are most appropriately
met through the mass approach in public recreation. And
some needs can be met most effectively through a group
work approach. Consequently, both voluntary and tax-supported, leisure-time services are necessary in the community.
This principle is based upon the fact that recreation is an
integral part of individual and group expression, and it follows that in a democratic society recreation activities will be
carried on in many different settings, supported by funds
from various sources, and conducted according to the needs
and the cultural patterns of the individuals and groups involved.

PLANNING. There must be a close coordination of programs and services offered by public and the private or
voluntary agencies. In too many instances poor planning
results in overlapping and duplication of efforts in certain
programs and serious gaps in other community leisure-time
services. The coordination of public and voluntary agencies
must stem from definition, understanding, and acceptance of
function based on the purpose and scope of each public or
private agency. These relationships must be constantly
studied and worked out through a local coordinating committee in many communities. Such leadership and planning
may emerge from a Council of Social Agencies, a Community Welfare Council, or similar group. The success of
joint planning rests upon the realization by the agencies that
in this capacity they constitute a council or coordinating
group, and that they must accept the general responsibilities of this body. Agencies cannot be forced to cooperate;
logical persuasion and facts should prevail to induce the
various local agencies to act cooperatively. Significant
progress in coordinating the planning and promotion of
leisure-time and recreation programs at the local as well as
the national level is now being made through the work of
the Education-Recreation Conference, a division of the National Welfare Assembly. Since its formation in 1945, the
National Welfare Assembly gradually has become recog-

nized as the national planning body for social welfare in the United States.

METHOD OF APPROACH. Since the private and voluntary agencies offer a wide variety of services of a recreational and informal educational nature, they use different approaches in dealing with the needs of their constituents. Participants may include what may be termed normal individuals of all age groups. They may also include groups with a large percentage of persons who need individualized attention and referral for more specialized treatment, or include persons in children's homes, institutions for the aged, reformatories, and special treatment groups where the programs are rehabilitative as well as educational or recreational. Thus it is especially important that the social group work method is particularly applicable in the private or voluntary agency setting. Whether the agency serves youth through the Scout movement, the aged in a special interest club, families in a neighborhood center or settlement house, or any of the myriad of other services these agencies offer, the principles of the methodology remain the same. These principles involve the refinement of the quality of the group experience to meet the needs of the entire group and at the same time provide the interaction processes between the individuals of the group so that each member will become an integral part of the group and receive maximum individual expression and satisfaction from the group participation.

PROGRAM PATTERN OF OPERATION. The private or voluntary agency program is characterized by a limitation of group size, a procedure which enables the leader to more easily accomplish his objectives. Indigenous group leadership is used and developed among participants who remain in the program over a long period of time. The size, membership, and continuity of the group permit the individual to develop a high degree of identification with the group and its overall objectives. The leader, then, using basic leadership methods, many of which are fundamental in the social group work process, carries out the program to meet the group and individual needs within the setting of the agency.

As the private or voluntary agencies grew in size throughout the years, their programs were tested, revised, and finally crystallized around certain age groups, religious doctrines, interest groups, or similar categories.

The growing emphasis on group work early in the twentieth century led to the formation of national organizations which provided program patterns for their local groups to follow. The program scheme is usually drawn up by a national headquarters and set forth in a manual or handbook which is placed in the hands of the members. In this way, a definite program guide is formulated and made readily available—one that can be utilized without exceedingly long preparation and effort. The program outline is particularly useful to volunteer leaders, unskilled and inexperienced in group work, who work under the supervision of trained professional leaders. Programs of national organizations are thus prearranged to a certain extent, since national leaders must, of necessity, formulate basic standards and an overall program by establishing definite goals for participants and a framework of valuable program resource material and workable activities suggestions for leaders.

It should also be noted, however, that some agencies have, even from their earliest activities, built their programs more exclusively around the interests of the local group. Through the years, there have been two approaches to this method of program operation. In the first type of interest approach the leader and the group, working together, plan their work. The leader prefers a definite systematic program, carefully planned in advance, but does not wish to superimpose his own choice of activities upon the members. He wants the group to have its full share in the planning. Consequently, he suggests as many types of activities as possible out of his experience, seeks to determine the reaction of the members to the suggestions, discovers by one means or another their own desires and interests, and together with them evolves a program for the month ahead and for the season.

The second type of interest approach begins with the situation the club is in at the moment, with the interests it now has, and then seeks to enlarge these interests and lead on to an ever-widening field of activities. This point of view is based on that principle of education which says that a gripping, compelling interest is essential to the learning process. The leader constantly looks for related interests or possible outgrowths of present interests, which will lead to a changing, growing program.

Since 1946 the pattern of operation by private and voluntary agencies, like other programs, has changed. There has been an increasing amount of competition from commercial recreation which draws people out of the neighborhood or local setting. The glorification of competitive sports in many quarters, the commercialization of sports for younger children, television, automobile, and other factors have dazzled and, at times, admittedly confused both children and adults. Certainly the leisure-time habits and activities of people have changed with the tempo of the times. As a result, the private and voluntary agencies have modified their approaches to meet the new needs.

Today, an adequate program presents an endless chain of fascinating and compelling activities, which are not only interesting in the execution but challenging to the imagination, and which are varied enough to satisfy every individual in the group, whatever his likes and interests may be. The adequate program must be of such a nature as to fulfill the laws of the learning process. Modern club work is thought of as a recreational-educational institution; it aims beyond mere entertainment and recreation and seeks growth and education for its members.

The following sections of this chapter are directed toward a more specific analysis of programs carried on by the three major types of agencies: neighborhood non-building-centered, neighborhood building-centered, and city-wide, building-centered organizations. Since space prevents a discussion of all these agencies or even a representative number of them, a few have been selected arbitrarily to illustrate the general program framework followed in many of them.

PROGRAMS OF NON-BUILDING-CENTERED AGENCIES

The programs of non-building-centered agencies are, in most cases, sponsored by national groups. They are conducted in facilities such as schools, churches, properties of civic groups, and sometimes in homes. Generally these programs focus attention upon the interests and needs of the immediate neighborhood through the methods and procedures followed by the particular agency. In this section, the programs of the Boy Scouts of America, the Girl Scouts of the United States of America, and the Camp Fire Girls are described, as representative of programs offered by non-building-centered agencies.

BOY SCOUTS OF AMERICA. Lord Robert Baden-Powell, an English general and hero of the Boer War, was the founder of the Boy Scout movement. As early as 1893, Baden-Powell had experimented with scouting and camping as a means of training soldiers. During the war he was impressed with the lack of camping and woodcraft knowledge on the part of English soldiers as compared with South Africans. His book, *Aids to Scouting*, prepared for soldiers, became immediately popular among the boys of England and opened to him the vision for a scouting and camping organization for boys of the pre-soldier age. He set about preparing a new book, *Scouting for Boys* (published in 1908), receiving inspiration and suggestions from Ernest Thompson Seton, artist, lecturer, and author of *The Birch Bark Roll of Woodcraft*. Seton had, in 1902, founded the Woodcraft Indians, the first organization in the United States emphasizing outdoor, camping, and handcraft activities with a program designed to be both recreational and educational.

In shaping the character of the boys' organization, Baden-Powell was influenced by his close personal knowledge of boys and by his notion of what was lacking in the training of the average school boy. He knew that boys in their teens were adventuresome and held as their heroes the knights, pioneers, Indians, and explorers. Hence, the term "scouts" seemed the best to convey the nature of the scheme. Character training, practical intelligence, manual skill, physical development, health habits, and a spirit of service for others and for the state were the things he thought necessary to incorporate into the scout training.

An American, William D. Boyce, traveling in England in 1909, was impressed with the nature of the English Boy Scouts, and later secured the cooperation of a number of American businessmen and leaders of youth to found the Boy Scouts of America, incorporated on February 8, 1910. In 1916, it was granted a federal charter by the United States Congress. In 1960, there were almost two million Cub Scouts, over 1.6 million Boy Scouts, approximately three hundred thousand Explorers, and over a million volunteer leaders, making a total membership in Boy Scouts of America of over five million persons.

The primary purpose of the Boy Scouts of America is to promote the ability of boys to do things for themselves and others, to train them in Scoutcraft, to teach them patriotism, courage, self-reliance, and kindred virtues. These traits are to be developed through a variety of activities, both recreational and educational, conducted by volunteer leaders under the guidance of trained professional leaders. The Boy Scout movement sets forth a series of virtues or character traits in its Scout Law which constitute the moral code governing the conduct of its members.

A Scout is:

trustworthy	courteous	thrifty
loyal	kind	brave
helpful	obedient	clean
friendly	cheerful	reverent

Members dedicate themselves to the Scout Oath which is given on page 400.

On my honor I will do my best
To do my duty to God and my country and to obey the
    Scout Law;
To help other people at all times;
To keep myself physically strong, mentally awake, and
    morally straight.

Organization. The Boy Scout movement is nonsectarian,
being open to those of all religions and denominations. It
is democratic in the sense that all races, classes, and stratifications of society are found in its membership. It holds
itself to be nonmilitary, although obviously distinctly nationalistic in tone and affiliations. Boys must be at least
eleven years of age to be in the Boy Scouts proper, whereas
the age groups in the movement range from eight to eighteen years of age and older. The needs of different age
groups are cared for by special phases of the organization
as follows:

Cub Scouts	8 through 10 years of age
Boy Scouts	11 through 17 years of age
Explorers	14 years of age and in the ninth grade; or 15 years or older in any grade, with privilege continued as long as a full-time high school student.
Volunteer Leaders	adult leaders

    A patrol consists of approximately eight boys. Two boys
out of each patrol act in the capacity of patrol leader and
assistant patrol leader, respectively.

    A troop is made up of patrols, totaling not more than 32
boys nor less than five boys, according to the groups of close
friends naturally existing among the boys. Troops must be
chartered by the National Council for a year at a time. It
is important to note again that Scouting is not an independent organization but is rather a movement with a program conducted through already existing neighborhood institutions, such as churches, schools, clubs, Parent-Teacher
Associations, and social centers. The parent institution

sponsoring the troop provides leadership and a place for meeting and appoints the necessary troop committee. The Scoutmaster must be at least 21 years of age and a citizen of the United States. It is all the better if he knows outdoor life. He is often assisted by men and older boys (18 years of age or over), who act as Assistant Scoutmasters.

The local troop is administered by a troop committee of the parent institution which sponsors the troop. The city or county or larger local area of scouting is administered by a local council with a professional Scout Executive and assistants. The nation is divided into twelve regions with regional Scout Executives in charge who are employed by the National Council, a body of over five thousand people made up of representatives of each local council. The National Council staff conducts many specialized departments and divisions. Financial support for the movement is secured through registration fees, funds from local Community Chests, United Funds, or similar agencies, and from gifts, donations and endowments from individuals and groups.

Method of Teaching. The method of teaching upon which the Boy Scout movement relies is summed up in the phrase, "learning by doing." Rather than instructing by the traditional methods of lecturing and textbook assignments, the Scouting program utilizes first, demonstration, observation, and experimentation; and second, the informal or play way of competition and dramatization while carrying out the activities program. Leaders and Scouts have definite goals to work toward in the system of badges and awards; equipment and basic procedures in the program are generally standardized; and the method of teaching is directed toward the accomplishment of goals through a home-centered program as in Cub Scouting, and through close group relationships in Boy Scouting and in Exploring. Teamwork, Scoutcraft and Scout spirit are emphasized by leaders directing all activities.

Activities and Program. The activities in the program fall under the following general headings: animal husbandry, aquatics, arts, building, campcraft, citizenship, communication, conservation, crafts and collections, nature, outdoor sports, personal development, plant cultivation, public service, and transportation. The program consists of a series of tests or groups of tests, described in the *Boy Scout Handbook,* which boys must pass if they are to advance in the organization. The following of these to the letter is mandatory. The program is an adult-conceived one, based on the assumptions that the activities which boys must enter into to get on in the organization, such as knot tying, first aid, swimming, camping, and map-making, are in themselves valuable to successful living.

The Boy Scout program of activities is so wide and comprehensive in nature that every boy, regardless of his individual differences, may find something to interest him. The program is carried on at three levels: Cub Scouting, Boy Scouting, and Exploring. Briefly, the program at these levels is discussed below.

Cub Scouting is a more recent development of the Scouting movement. Built around home and family interests, Cubbing has grown since its inception in 1930 to a membership of well over one and one-half million boys, eight through ten years of age. Its genius lies in the fact that the Cub Scout is assisted in his achievements by his own dad and mother, thus helping to knit the family group more closely. His den and pack correspond to the Scout patrol and troop, with the exception that pack meetings consist of boys and parents of all the dens, and usually occur monthly to demonstrate what the Cub Scout has learned.

Boy Scouting involves three ranks to be achieved in order, Tenderfoot, Second Class, and First Class, each requiring a longer, more difficult set of tests than the preceding. Having earned five merit badges and demonstrated satisfactorily his service and leadership, the Scout becomes a Star Scout; 10 merit badges (including 5 specified ones) lead to Life Scout; 21 merit badges (including 12 specified ones) lead to Eagle Scout. Candidates for the advanced honors appear before an adult board called a board of review.

Exploring is a program for Scouts which recognizes the

fact that young men need to be challenged beyond the program of activities offered in Boy Scouting. It provides an organization for older boys to form friendship groups and engage in a program of training in social, vocational, outdoor, personal fitness, service, and citizenship areas. The program involves outdoor adventure, social companionship, vocational exploration, and practice in citizenship responsibility through participation in local, state, and national civic affairs.

Evaluation of the Program. The breadth and comprehensiveness of the program of suggested activities in the *Boy Scout Handbook* leaves little to be desired in the way of program materials. Its outdoor emphasis is excellent and all in the right direction. It is gripping and compelling to countless thousands of American youth and satisfies drives and urges that to many could not be satisfied adequately and wholesomely without some organization to show the way.

The Boy Scout method of education in skills is a doing rather than a listening process, which, of course, is educationally sound. Furthermore, it has developed a scheme of games to teach subject matter which is unique and which makes a distinct, significant contribution to educational methodology. (The Girl Scouts have likewise made distinct contributions in this direction.) Its teaching by the play-way, by dramatization, and by competition is excellent. Its conception of its program as activities which boys teach each other is sound. As a scheme of self-education with the meetings aimed to inspire and arouse interest, with the thought that the boy will learn the skills in his leisure time at home, it is encouraging rather than destructive of home activity.

The Scout patrol system organizes the gang into patrols, each with its own leadership constituting a self-governing unit. Within this unit much of the educational work is carried on. The patrol system permits boys to meet in their own neighborhoods, organizing in their own churches, schools, and play centers; this method is sociologically more

sound than convening at a centralized, unfamiliar, out-of-
the-neighborhood headquarters.

GIRL SCOUTS OF THE UNITED STATES OF AMERICA. The
Girl Scout movement was also the result of the early pioneer
work of Lord Robert Baden-Powell. In 1909 the Girl Guides
were formed in London under the leadership of his sister,
Agnes Baden-Powell, to meet an overwhelming interest
shown by girls in Scouting. The movement spread to other
countries from England; the name Girl Guides was retained
in some countries, while in other countries the name of Girl
Scouts was adopted. Juliette Gordon Low founded the Girl
Scouts in the United States in 1912. Her untiring individual
efforts were rewarded by a rapid growth of the movement.
Today, in the United States there are over two and one-half
million Girl Scouts, over three-quarters of a million adult
men and women volunteer workers, and over five million
persons in fifty countries are linked with the World Association of Girl Guides and Girl Scouts.

Girl Scouting is based upon an ethical code expressed in
the Promise and the Laws of Girl Scouting. The movement
is designed to give girls citizenship training through activities that broaden their interests and help them to develop
new skills, explore the out-of-doors, learn democratic attitudes and procedures, and practice living in accordance with
the principles of Girl Scouting. As a preparation for their
responsibilities in the home and for service in the community, Girl Scout activities are designed to promote the
qualities of truth, loyalty, helpfulness, friendliness, courtesy,
purity, kindness, obedience, cheerfulness, thriftiness and
kindred virtues.

Organization. The Girl Scouts of the United States of
America is a corporation chartered by Congress. The purpose of the corporation is to promote the Girl Scout movement in the United States of America, its territories and possessions, by directing and coordinating the movement and
by providing and administering the Girl Scout program in
accordance with the purposes set forth in its Congressional

Charter. Its purposes shall be nonsectarian, nonpolitical, and nonprofit.

Membership in the movement is open to all girls seven through seventeen years of age and to adults eighteen years of age and over.

The National Council is the membership body of the Girl Scout corporation which meets triennially. Its membership consists of delegates elected by local Girl Scout councils in proportion to the number of Girl Scouts under each council's jurisdiction, of the National Board of Directors, and of other persons who may be elected by the National Council itself. Its powers include amending the Constitution and By-laws, establishing requirements for credentials and certificates of membership, determining the general lines of policy of the Girl Scout movement and program, and electing officers, a Board of Directors, and the National Nominating Committee.

The Board of Directors manages the affairs of the Girl Scout corporation between meetings of the National Council. The National Organization consists of a national headquarters which operates on a functional basis with board committees and employed staff in each area and twelve regions each with a committee and staff. The purpose of the National Organization is to assist in the organization of councils and provide necessary services to councils. It is financed by membership dues of one dollar annually, gifts and bequests, and the sale of official uniforms and equipment.

Local councils are chartered by the National Board of Directors to establish local responsibility for the further development of the Girl Scout movement and program. The territory within which a council is authorized to operate may be a city, all or part of a county or a number of counties. The council has an obligation to make the Girl Scout program available to all girls within its jurisdiction who wish to belong and to maintain standards of the highest quality in the program offered. Council financial support is secured through local organized or independent giving, gifts, bequests or contributions of interested individuals and groups, and product sales.

Within the council, girls are organized into troops consisting of from eight to thirty-two members with adult leadership and often with a troop committee and a sponsoring group. The two forms of government used are the representative form and the direct form. The representative form is called the patrol system, in which the troop divides itself into small working groups, each having a patrol leader and an assistant patrol leader. The troop has a Court of Honor, or executive body, including the patrol leaders, troop treasurer, troop scribe and troop leader. The Court of Honor deals with matters that affect the whole troop. It discusses ideas from the patrols and leaders and works them into a program for the troop, which it submits to the patrols for approval. The patrol system is the recommended method of government. However, for Brownie troops or troops of older girls consisting of less than twelve members, the club or direct form of government is suggested. Under this form the entire troop elects a president, vice-president, secretary and treasurer. The whole troop meets together for business sessions and then the troop officers meet with the adult leaders to work out the details of planning. The troop appoints short-term working committees when needed.

Method of Teaching. The approach in teaching and guidance in Girl Scouting is based upon the troop, which includes small, democratic working groups in which girls elect their own officers, make their own plans, and accept responsibility for carrying out these plans. Trained volunteer troop leaders assume major responsibility for guiding and leading the girls. In Brownie Scouts, for example, the program is not home-centered, but group-centered in the troop, with help and support provided when necessary by parents and adult volunteers. Although a national program is outlined, it is considered more as a guide for leaders and girls to develop their own initiative to meet the local needs and interests in each troop, and to offer the girls opportunities for fun, friendship, service and daily practice in living the Girl Scout Promise and Laws.

Activities. Activities in the Girl Scout program are designed to provide fun and opportunities to learn and practice both new and old skills. The activity program is a tool used to achieve the purposes of Girl Scouting. Basic to all programs in the out-of-doors, the arts, the home, and so forth, are training in citizenship and developing international understanding and proper regard for health and safety. Democratic troop government and service projects help girls develop an awareness and acceptance of civic responsibility. Girls progress from Brownie Scouts into the Senior Girl Scout program broadening their interests and abilities through participation in activities suggested in the handbooks. Notable, too, is the program of both resident and day camping carried on by the Girl Scouts of the U. S. A.

Evaluation of the Program. Although Girl Scouting clearly belongs to the established program classification, tremendous strides have been made in recent years toward flexibility and toward shifting from a program-centered to a girl-centered approach. Through its development of the unit camping system, the Court of Honor in the troop, the emphasis upon trained volunteer leaders, and the broad range of program activities, opportunities are given for development of the interests and abilities of each Girl Scout within the framework of the principles and the National program of Girl Scouts of the United States of America. With so many sports and other activities available to boys, the constructive and challenging program of the Girl Scouts is much needed and helps provide informal education for young girls in the United States today.

CAMP FIRE GIRLS.* The organization of the Camp Fire Girls, first national nonsectarian organization for girls of all races, creeds and economic levels, was the result of the

* This information has been taken from two publications of Camp Fire Girls, Inc.: *Purpose and Program* and *There's A Part for You.*

thinking of a group of men and women prominent in education, the arts, and social engineering, associated with Luther Halsey Gulick, M.D. As director of physical training in the New York City schools, author of *The Philosophy of Play*, and first president of the Playground and Recreation Association (now The National Recreation Association), Gulick's belief in the possibilities of personality development through play and through group association was well known.

Much of the experimental work in developing the program took place at the private camp for girls organized by Gulick and his wife in 1908. The personal philosophies of Dr. and Mrs. Gulick and their ideas of education as carried out with their daughters in their own family strongly influenced the program. A deeply spiritual couple, they believed in setting goals of idealism, beauty, and social responsibility. They saw the value of creative activities, of doing things with one's hands, making one's own designs, creating one's own music and of executing everything with imagination and zest. The program developed skills in homemaking, handcrafts, outdoor living, health, Indian lore, education, and administration.

The first experimental Camp Fire groups were formed in 1910, and the organization was incorporated in 1912, with Gulick as the first president. In accordance with its Certificate of Incorporation, the National Council of Camp Fire Girls seeks to make available to all girls an educational-recreational program of girlhood experience which will develop the best potentialities of each one and encourage in her:

the application of her religious, spiritual, and ethical teachings to her daily living;

a love of home and family that grows as she grows;

pride in woman's traditional qualities—tenderness, affection, and skill in human relationships;

deep love of her country, the practice of democracy, readiness to serve;

the capacity for fun, friendship, and happy group relations;

the formation of healthful habits;

the ability to take care of herself, to do her work skillfully, and to take pleasure in it;

interests and hobbies she can enjoy with others and alone;

love of the out-of-doors and skill in outdoor living;

a happy heart that will help her find beauty, romance, and
adventure in the common things of daily life.

To this end, Camp Fire Girls offers a creative, flexible
program of enjoyable leisure-time activities to girls from
seven through high school age, without discrimination as to
race, religion, or economic background.

The Law of the Camp Fire Girls epitomizes the aims of
the program, reminding each girl to:

> Worship God
> Seek Beauty
> Give Service
> Pursue Knowledge
> Be Trustworthy
> Hold on to Health
> Glorify Work
> Be Happy

Organization. The unit of organization is the Camp Fire
group under the guidance of a volunteer woman leader. As
the number of groups increases, a local council is formed
which engages an executive director. All councils are represented on the National Council which elects the National
Board of Directors, the administrative unit for the Council.

Although the individual group, with its leaders and sponsors, is the focal point of the program, this key unit is
strengthened and the group program is more effective when
there is organized community backing and support. Men
and women interested in making the program available as an
educational and recreational opportunity for all girls in the
community may apply to the national organization for au-
thorization to organize, support, develop, and direct the
overall local program.

The particular form of organization desirable in a given area is determined primarily by the size of the community to be served. In a community of less than 5,000, as few as five men and women may apply for a charter as a Camp Fire Girls Association. This is the simplest form of administrative structure, with an executive committee responsible for new group organization, leadership training, providing camping opportunities, interpreting and publicizing activities, and financing the overall program.

Camp Fire Girls councils, the chartered administrative organization in territories of larger population, all vary in size and stage of development and in community characteristics. Therefore, no two councils arc organized in an identical way. There is, however, a general framework which serves as a guide, adapted as needed, but always to provide sound, democratic structure and methods of operation.

Even in communities of less than 10,000 population, this administrative group numbers at least ten members. Larger councils find they need more—as many as thirty serving on the board, with additional members working on the various committees. These members are not the leaders or group sponsors. Theirs is a different and very important responsibility: making the best possible program available to every girl in the community.

Camp Fire Girls began as a program for teen-age girls, but it has grown with the years to meet the needs of all girls seven to eighteen. Blue Birds are seven, eight, and nine years old; Camp Fire Girls from ten through eighth grade; Horizon Club girls from ninth grade through senior high school. Each group is a democracy in miniature, with girls planning their activities, assuming responsibility, and cooperating with others to make everyday living richer and happier. In order that each girl may have individual attention and be helped to realize her fullest potentialities, Blue Bird and Camp Fire groups are limited to twenty members. Horizon Clubs may have as many as thirty girls. They meet weekly in homes, schools, churches or synagogues, or in community houses. Since Camp Fire Girls' founding fifty years ago, millions of girls have been strengthened in their growth toward happy responsible womanhood by the organization's creative, flexible program.

Activities and Programs. The soundness of "learning by doing," the program's cornerstone since its inception, has been proved by its continuing effectiveness. In keeping with Dr. Gulick's belief that character is formed predominantly during leisure hours, Camp Fire Girls offers a wide range of activities that are fun and, at the same time, character-building.

The program for Blue Birds is based on creative play activities designed to acquaint little girls with the world around them and to develop their ability to get along in a group of girls their own age through a series of broadening experiences. The program for Camp Fire Girls is based on activities in the Seven Crafts: Home, Outdoors, Creative Arts, Frontiers of Science, Business, Sports and Games, and Citizenship. The program for Horizon Clubs recognizes the maturing interests in teen-age girls and features co-ed activities, personality development and social skills, career explorations, and personal community service.

Cultivating skills is important, but a primary objective of the program of all three age groups is the development of personality. Camp Fire provides every girl the opportunity needed to make new friends and to become both self-reliant and cooperative with a group her own age.

Camp Fire Girls presents a practical training in citizenship, a prerequisite in developing tomorrow's community leaders. Girls are encouraged to take an active interest in the affairs of their own community, to respect the rights of others, to obey the laws of the land, and to give friendly, cooperative, generous service to their community.

Local service activities include cooperation with organizations such as American Red Cross, Community Chest, United Fund, Needlework Guild, hospital and health associations and churches. Wherever help is needed, Camp

Fire Girls are on hand to do their part—adopting lonely "grandmothers," baby sitting while mothers vote, cleaning up vacant lots. A special Camp Fire undertaking since its beginning has been the conservation of natural resources of wild life and beautification of outdoor areas. Camp Fire Girls work closely with federal, state, and local officials in all these developments.

Just as Camp Fire Girls believes that citizenship entails community responsibilities as well as privileges at home, so too does it believe in broadening a girl's understanding of other communities throughout the world. Groups show their interest in neighbors around the globe by exchanging "pen friend" letters, assisting in drives conducted by international relief agencies, and learning about other lands in international projects such as the People-to-People program.

Camping, which has become a year-round activity, is a high point in the lives of Camp Fire members. Camp Fire's founders pioneered in girls' camping. Today almost all Camp Fire Girls councils throughout the country offer girls the unforgettable experience of living out-of-doors in resident or day camps. Along with swimming, dramatics, cookouts, handicrafts, and nature lore, a camper learns to take care of herself and to work for the good of the whole camp community. Camping is one important way that Camp Fire members live democracy.

Evaluation of the Program. Camp Fire Girls is essentially a small group program rather than a mass recreational program. Although a basic program is provided, it permits wide choice, encouraging creativity and imagination. Emphasis is placed on home and family life, the unique role of women, and on beauty and aesthetic values. While individual achievement is encouraged and girls are helped to develop their special interests, talents, and goals, they are taught group relationships and made conscious of their value.

Dedicated to spiritual ideals since its founding, the Camp Fire Girls program has the warm endorsement of religious leaders and educators.

PROGRAMS OF NEIGHBORHOOD, BUILDING-CENTERED AGENCIES

This group of agencies represents a diversity of local neighborhood organizations characteristic of American social life. The mass of these organizations, of which no actual count exists, includes the many local nonprofit corporations operating local community centers and similar building-centered activities which service a particular neighborhood. Included in this type of agency is the neighborhood settlement house; special centers for racial, cultural, or religious neighborhood groups; and special interest clubs, such as garden clubs, sports clubs, theatre groups, and the like. Usually they are supported by funds from the local Community Chest, by gifts and donations, and through fees and charges paid by participants. Generally the following objectives determine the program of activities in these neighborhood service units:

1. To provide constructive, wholesome leisure-time programs for all people in the neighborhood, including all ages, nationalities, races, and interest groups.
2. To provide interesting activities through the development of talents, skills, special events, athletics, clubs, informal classes, and the like.
3. To teach good sportsmanship and develop leadership and a sense of responsibility through the practice of democracy and good citizenship.

Rather than describing any particular one of these diverse local agencies, their general program and activities will be reviewed.

Controlled by local lay citizen boards, the programs of these agencies are definitely centered around local neighborhood interests. The service radius of the unit is usually one-half mile, or in some cases a maximum of a mile from the central building. In most situations the building includes a gymnasium, showers and locker rooms, reading room, nursery school, game room, craft shop, music room, library, or special facilities to meet local needs. The building facilities can usually accommodate approximately two hundred participants at any one time; many more persons are usually accommodated at a special event program. Generally such a building serves approximately six hundred to one thousand members of the organization in the neighborhood.

Neighborhood center programs include nursery schools, various Girl and Boy Scout programs, teen-age clubs, arts and craft groups, dancing classes, music groups, adult interest clubs, a complete athletic program, summer play programs, and a variety of special events. The special events are often the high points of these agency programs and include holiday celebrations of all types, mother-daughter banquets, family nights, dances, special music and dramatic programs, and community service programs including civil defense, first aid classes, and the like.

The neighborhood building-centered program represents one of the most fundamental and characteristic patterns of local self-motivated social program services. The buildings of these groups are landmarks of a neighborhood's social customs and mores. The programs operated in them depict the efforts of local people to meet their needs through their own efforts and represent the type of neighborhood action and concern that is one of the most basic elements of a successful democracy.

PROGRAMS OF CITY-WIDE
BUILDING-CENTERED AGENCIES

The programs of the Young Men's Christian Associations and the Boys' Clubs of America are representative of a type of city-wide, building-centered program. Like agencies utilizing specialized buildings, there has been a trend for these organizations to work in local neighborhoods in the community as well as in the central building. This has been very pronounced with the YMCA. Often, in large cities, there are a number of organizations of Boys' Clubs, each Club serving a particular neighborhood. The Club may be either a unit of the larger organization or a separate entity.

THE YOUNG MEN'S CHRISTIAN ASSOCIATIONS OF THE UNITED STATES OF AMERICA. The Young Men's Christian Association began in London in 1844, through the work of George Williams, a dry-goods clerk, as a group to improve the spiritual condition of young men in the factories of London. The association was popular and its fame spread. In 1851, the first association in the United States was organized in Boston. The early YMCA groups were very much concerned about "the young man away from home in the great city," and their original programs were almost totally religion-centered.

As early as 1860 associations in the United States began to add baths to their meeting places and by 1866 several local units had gymnasiums as part of their facilities. From this point on the YMCA grew as a program, changing with the needs and interests of its members, until it has reached the broad, inclusive program it now encompasses. It has over 1,823 local associations and nearly three and one-half million registered members in the United States.

The purpose of the YMCA is to help youth and adults to maintain physical fitness, to develop skills in personal relationships, and to develop qualities of leadership. It is an organization based upon Christian principles, relating to its participants the Christian heritage and the need for a religious faith. It works cooperatively with other agencies of the community to achieve aims that all character-building organizations have in common.

Organization. A membership organization, the YMCA is open to individuals as outlined in policies adopted by each of the local associations. Generally, services are provided for both youth and adults, with a major emphasis upon activities for young people. The local YMCA is governed by a local Board of Directors composed of interested lay citizens in the community. This Board, by meeting certain requirements, is a member of a State or Area Council which coordinates YMCA activities at the state or regional level; and through this regional organization it also may be a member of the National Council. Local associations elect members to the National Council according to the number of members in the association. The National Council, with its National Board, provides general leadership to the movement, renders services to the State or Area Councils and Boards, and to the local associations. A special committee of the National Board, appointed jointly with the Young Men's Christian Associations of Canada, is responsible for offering North American aid for developing YMCA activities in about thirty other countries.

In the cities, YMCA's operate from central comprehensive buildings and branch buildings adapted to neighborhoods. The central buildings are usually equipped with residence rooms, club rooms, game rooms, craft shops, gymnasiums, swimming pools, assembly halls, and similar facilities. Extension programs from both central and branch buildings, recently becoming more prevalent, involve use of school and other local facilities to provide additional services where needed in the community. The local Board of Directors is responsible for determining policies, giving personal leadership, securing funds, and employing qualified professional leaders to supervise the program. A specific local program is not prescribed by the national body, and local associations carry on programs of informal recreation and education to meet the interests and needs of the community the association serves. However, the triangle, symbolizing all-round development—spirit, mind, body—is symbolic of the ideas that guide all YMCA's.

Method of Teaching. Conducting activities that appeal to all age groups, the YMCA develops program situations in which individual needs for development are met and young people discover leisure-time activities that are challenging and useful. The informal educational approach is emphasized to help persons develop new skills and insights that help them to lead richer and more productive lives. Small club groups, interest and hobby groups, father-son programs, and similar approaches are used; these cultivate close-knit group relationships.

In youth work, as in other aspects of the YMCA program,

the interest approach has been used successfully. Leaders discover the interests and needs of groups, retain these natural aids to program promotion, and seek to guide and assist individuals to fulfill their needs. Leaders are thus not overly concerned with the particular activities the club uses as long as there is a compelling interest on the part of the boys which leads to joyous, enthusiastic, and significant activity, all in contact with stimulating, wholesome leaders.

Counseling of individuals is undertaken to deal effectively with the personal, vocational, and educational problems of members. Through its basic teaching methods, the YMCA provides opportunities for individuals to participate in activities and a program of personal leadership development according to principles basic to the Christian faith.

Activities and Program. The program of the YMCA is developed in accordance with youth and adult needs and interests. Basic activities followed include arts and crafts, dramatics, sports, dance, camping, social recreation, and other general recreation programs. Although no specific program pattern is prescribed by the National Board, program activities in many local associations are grouped around the following major interest areas.

More than ninety percent of the YMCA's club activities with youth is related to one of the following clubs, for which manual materials are supplied:

Youth Activities.
> Father and Son Y Indian Guides, a father and son program that gives fathers and sons a chance to get together twice a month in fellowship program.
> Gra-Y for boys, Tri-Gra-Y for girls, meaningful club programs for grade school boys and girls.
> Junior Hi-Y for boys, Tri-Hi-Y for girls, club programs for junior high school girls and boys.
> Hi-Y for boys, Tri-Hi-Y for girls, a popular fellowship and service club for high school boys and girls.

Educational Services.
> The YMCA operates twenty-three schools and colleges,

with approximately forty-eight thousand students; over four hundred YMCA's offer night schools; there is an attendance of over thirty-two million persons annually in YMCA adult education programs.

Health and Physical Education.

Programs of this division are held for all age groups and include swimming, calisthenics, and sports of various types.

Citizenship and Public Affairs.

Through club and informal meetings, including forums on international affairs, discussions on local civic problems, adult classes, men's clubs and similar activities, the "Y's" provide education and information regarding the major political and civic issues facing the nation.

Counseling and Individual Services.

The well-conducted YMCA's provide for individual conferences to allow young men to share their problems with experienced advisors regarding family and marriage, job opportunities, vocational guidance, and education and to help youth through counseling sessions to develop a personal philosophy in an atmosphere of Christian fellowship.

World Service.

The program in the World Service serves to confirm the YMCA's objectives of developing a world-wide fellowship. World Service committees in local associations promote activities to raise funds to help people in other nations, exemplifying the spirit of fellowship and the sharing of one another's burdens.

Evaluation of the Program. The YMCA represents the interest-centered approach to informal education and recreation. Its programs are varied and each association has the freedom to provide the types of activity that meet the interests and needs of the local community. The work of the YMCA in this country and throughout the world provides worthwhile, necessary informal recreation and education services typical of the democratic way of life.

BOYS' CLUBS OF AMERICA. The first Boys' Club started in Hartford, Connecticut in 1860. After the Civil War, the idea spread to other New England communities. In 1906, some fifty existing clubs joined to form a national organization, now known as Boys' Clubs of America. In 1942, there were only 209 clubs; by 1959, the number had increased to 550 clubs with a total membership of over five hundred thousand boys.

The Boys' Clubs of America is a guidance and character-building organization using group-work, health, recreational and informal educational activities. It is nonsectarian and no proof of good character or pledge is required. It is open to boys approximately eight to eighteen years of age regardless of nationality, religion, or political belief, and provides activities and guidance to meet the individual needs of each boy.

Organization. Each Boys' Club belonging to Boys' Clubs of America is an autonomous organization. It is managed by a board of public spirited citizens and supported by Community Chests or United Funds or by contributions made directly to the Boys' Club.

Boys' Clubs of America, composed of member Clubs banded together in a national organization, establishes standards and methods; develops programs and program material; plans buildings and equipment; recruits, trains and places Club workers; publishes periodicals, booklets and bulletins; carries on national interpretation and publicity, and furnishes guidance, plans, and materials for the use of the Boys' Clubs themselves and, in general, promotes the development of the whole movement throughout the country.

There are seven regional offices with field staffs who visit Boys' Clubs and communities to give guidance and assistance to the Clubs in their plans and problems, and to aid communities in the organization and establishment of additional Boys' Clubs.

Boys' Clubs have a voice in matters of national policy through the National Council which meets annually. Each member Boys' Club may elect two delegates to the National Council yearly. Each organization is entitled to one vote.

Organizations must meet certain minimum requirements for membership: each member Club pays to Boys' Clubs of America minimum annual dues of 1 per cent of its total operating budget, exclusive of the operation of camps and the direct cost of raising money. Each Club is required to submit an annual report of its organization, membership, activities, attendance, and finances to Boys' Clubs of America.

The only exceptions to the above are the Associate and Provisional Boys' Clubs which do not quite meet all of the membership requirements. Although they enjoy most of the privileges and obligations, they are not entitled to delegates to the National Council or to any votes in National Council meetings.

Through its national staff, the national organization serves its members in all phases of Boys' Club organization and operation. Each member Club is entitled to identify itself with the Boys' Clubs of America and may use the official Boys' Club insignia.

Local Clubs subscribe to the suggested standards and procedures in program and operation which are developed by the national headquarters. These can be changed and adapted to local needs in any way as long as minimum membership requirements are not violated. Boys' Clubs find guidance in programming and management in the *Manual of Boys' Club Operation* and from the publications prepared by headquarters.

Method of Teaching. The program of Boys' Clubs is primarily a guidance program directed toward building character and good citizenship. Its methods and procedures revolve around the discovery of the interests and needs of boys within the area serviced by the club and directing its efforts toward meeting these needs. The uniqueness of the program lies in the opportunity for staff contacts with boys in a wide variety of leisure-time and informal situations. In these everyday contacts, the trained personnel and volunteer workers give individual service and guidance to assist boys in making satisfactory adjustments to problems in life. The informal or interest approach, providing a freedom of choice and action within reasonable limits, is basic to the methods followed in Boys' Clubs. The sense of loyalty, honesty, and respect for others is cultivated by practice of these traits in everyday club activities. Special methods followed include creating traditions and habits, maintaining a neat, orderly, and friendly club atmosphere, using group influences, and dealing directly and individually with the needs of each boy through personal interviews and guidance.

Activities and Program. The programs of Boys' Clubs are intended to develop lasting skills, awaken enthusiasms, reveal talents, and stimulate desirable relationships with other boys and with adults. The emphasis is no longer, as it was nearly a century ago, simply taking boys off the streets and upon recreation. The programs of Boys' Clubs are planned to promote the health, social, education, vocation, and character development of boys—the purpose for which Boys' Clubs of America was organized.

The Boys' Club program includes a wide range of activities in physical training and athletics, arts and crafts, and groups of various kinds organized around the different interests and the already established friendships of the boys. A quiet place for reading and studying is usually provided. At the older age levels, activities for boys and girls are carried on. Many Boys' Clubs have day, overnight, and resident camping. An important part of the program is training in citizenship and community service. The extent and variety of programs depend upon facilities, staff, and the support given the Club by the community.

While the Boys' Club is not a religious organization in any sectarian sense, its teachings are rooted in religious principles. The greatest emphasis is on leadership and guidance. In the day-to-day association with boys both in group and informal contact, Boys' Clubs leaders have unparalleled opportunity for guidance of boys in behavior and attitude as well as in their general development.

The administration of Boys' Clubs and the guidance of

boys is a profession. Men who enter the field not only possess basic qualifications, but also are especially trained for the work. Instructors and leaders are selected for their ability to guide and influence boys, in addition to their teaching and organizing skills.

Evaluation of the Program. The Boys' Clubs movement has grown rapidly since 1950. Particularly notable in Boys' Clubs operation is the "open door" policy which welcomes all boys to its program, and its work with the "hard to reach" boys and youth groups in conflict. An interest-centered program, Boys' Clubs has undoubtedly helped to redirect the behavior of thousands of boys into desirable, purposeful channels; their contribution to reducing the severity and frequency of offenses such as gang fights and youth conflict has been significant. Boys' Clubs programs have expanded and changed in recent years to meet the special needs and interests of boys and youth in large urban centers as well as in suburban areas and small towns.

SUMMARY

Among the social agencies there are many which, although multiple in purposes, place great stress on recreation as one of their offerings. This is particularly true of those agencies which are concerned with the individual and not with a cause. In the former case the individual member's health, education, and social adjustment are considered paramount. Such a responsibility may extend to children or youth mainly, as with the Boy Scouts, Girl Scouts, or 4-H Club organization, or it may also extend to adults as with the YMCA organization.

Social work is really a product of the twentieth century, although its origins, which were found first in the mid-nineteenth century, mainly evolved during the last quarter of the last century. Socially-motivated and public-spirited citizens were the first to perceive the pressing conditions of maladjustment occurring as populations grew, as rural life changed to city life, and as industrialized labor became more and more specialized, unsettled, and insecure. The private agencies usually preceded public support; and thereafter they supplemented public agencies. In social work the group becomes the focus through which the individual's needs may be met.

Voluntary agencies in general are classified in three ways: the mobile or non-building-centered agencies—those that do not have a centralized meeting place but operate from schools, churches, or homes as the case may be; the neighborhood building-centered agencies—those that operate within a limited area of a city from a central location; and the city-wide, building-centered agencies—those that service an entire community and its environs from a central location.

The private or voluntary agencies are as a rule nonprofit organizations, incorporated under existing state regulations. The members of the Board of Directors are usually elected by the Board itself, and the Board thereby becomes perpetuating. The responsibilities include the appointment of members, the administration of the budget, the planning and operation of policies and program, and the promotional work with the public.

There is usually the problem of coordinating the work of various agencies so that their programs do not overlap. Nevertheless, a number of agencies is necessary to provide for varied services that are needed. The private agency has a special role in bringing needed services to special interest groups, of which there is a wide range, based on such differentiating factors as age, sex, race, nationality, or educational and recreational preferences. It is argued that the private agency, dependent upon volunteer service, being smaller than the public agency, and operating in smaller groups, can give more individual consultation and help to those who need it.

In the field of recreation, the private agencies are in a unique position to render help to those individuals who would be lost in the overcrowded public recreation program. Public recreation has to give first attention to mass needs with the result that the individual who does not seem to fit into the group, the individual who is left alone on the fringes of the activity that is going on, does not receive special attention. Here is where the smaller private agency, with its breakdown into smaller groups, can step in and render a paternalistic service, in a sense adopting the lonely individual, boy or girl, man or woman, who needs to develop some interests that will bridge the way to adjustment to the group.

The services provided by the private or voluntary agencies reflect their flexibility and response to the dynamic social scene in which social needs are constantly changing. Modifications and extensions of these agency programs are being made to meet new needs. Notable among the new approaches has been the extension of the services of building-centered agencies to branch neighborhood units of service, the establishment of neighborhood and suburban agency programs, the initiation of mobile units and detached workers to work directly with local groups and individuals, and similar approaches to meet special needs. Finally, the need for community planning for private or voluntary agency services has never been greater. Admittedly there is great need for these services, but with rising costs, and funds becoming increasingly more difficult to obtain through voluntary giving, there is a pressing need to develop workable plans for establishing priorities for agency services, plans which have not been, as yet, worked out and adopted on a broad scale by communities.

SELECTED REFERENCES

Social Work Year Book, 1960. A Description of Organized Activities in Social Work and in Related Fields. New York: National Association of Social Workers, 1960. This volume is a primary source book for the most complete summary of information regarding all phases in the field of social work. Specific historical and other information is given regarding the present status, objectives, program, membership, and other details of the major national voluntary agencies. See especially pp. 523–28, 607–17, 651–730.

Each private or voluntary agency has basic books and supplementary material on the many special phases of organization and program. It is suggested that the headquarters of the organizations be contacted for lists of their publications.

18

Camping in Education
and Recreation

The American tradition is an outdoor tradition. It goes back to a rugged pioneer background in which the explorer, the Indian, the frontiersman, the settler, the trapper, the covered-wagon family, the lumberjack, the ranger, the cowboy, the gold miner, the rancher, and the farmer played prominent, heroic roles. The exploits of these hardy, colorful individuals still stir the imagination and the glamour of their deeds fills our fiction and our motion pictures. Naturally, the hardship of their life is overlooked and only the picturesque and adventurous aspects remain.

For many years, however, with but a few exceptions, the average American has been far removed from the wide, open spaces. It was inevitable that the rugged pioneer life should be supplanted by a crowded urban existence; for, as industries grew, they acted as magnets to draw the population toward the city. This adjustment to cooped, city-dwelling existence brought in time the accompanying realization that the old life still claimed much of man's allegiance and that he always would have a craving for it.

It is not surprising, therefore, to find Americans once more turning toward nature—with enhanced appreciation of the great outdoors that is America's own. From the grind of the city with its rush and hurry, its heated days and breathless nights, its odors of motors and its nerve-racking noises, its pavements and barren concrete walls, its monotonous repetition of the same task, its endless parade of strangers, the individual looks to the open country for ideal relief and relaxation. There in the woods he finds escape in a life rich in simple and colorful things—green fields, rippling water, sunlight on stirring leaves, the mirror magic of lakes, the sighing of pine tops. The thick woods, the darkness, the queer noises stir the imagination of childhood days, and the wild free self is aroused again. He drinks in the wine of the sunset and is lulled to sleep by that sweetest symphony in all the world, the patter of rain drops on the tent roof. From the prose of the city and the village, men turn to the poetry of the wilds. Thanks to the automobile this wild-wood life can now be enjoyed without the annoying discomforts and hardships that were necessary accompaniments of the wilderness period. While the wheel may have developed cities and congregated people in metropolitan areas, it has also been the means of the rediscovery of American soil. In the old Greek myth of Antaeus, power came to him whenever his feet were pressed against the solid ground: there is more than myth in this classic tale.

Today, it is the usual thing, therefore, as one drives along the well-paved, modern highway, to see little tents along the road, the automobile, and perhaps a trailer parked behind, folding chairs and folding tables near by, and the typical American family gathered around; and to see rows of cabins or a motel furnishing reasonable, often delightful overnight accommodations to the growing army of auto campers. Municipalities have provided and advertise their tourist camps and their outlying picnic grounds equipped with cooking grills and many conveniences. States have established their reserves, trails, and have provided shelters and rangers to assist the tourists. The federal government has opened its natural forest reserves and parks.

In the youthful heart, the zest and appeal of camping is undying. Witness the perennial popularity with youth of the Western movie star as a symbol of the rugged, roving, fighting life of the plains; the hero worship of the American Indian among the youth of all countries in Western civilization. Youth has a peculiar susceptibility to suggestion concerning the life and ways of the wild and open country.

The business of recreation is to teach these skills and to supply the opportunity for the fulfillment of these dreams. Many organizations today are dedicated to this end.

Camping, in common with all social movements, has not been without its prophets. Ernest Thompson Seton through the romantic and colorful appeal of his writings and lectures has led folks to nature and woodcraft. Nessmuk, Horace Kephart, Dan Beard, and scores of others have made available to all who will read, the skills of the woodsman. Magazines, sensing the public pulse, have depicted in compelling style the appeal of the open country. Outdoor organizations have aggressively preached their gospel.

THE ORGANIZED CAMP

Whereas once children found camping only on a family vacation or, if particularly enterprising, in small groups on their own while parents stayed home and worried, today the organized camp brings safe, thrilling wildwood adventure to the youth of the land. The organized camp is an institution operating on a permanent site, with a responsible director and leadership staff, providing lodging, food, guidance, and supervised activities for purposes of recreation, education, and personality development to groups of people (usually children), who remain for given periods ranging from one week to two months or longer. There are two types of camps falling into the category of organized camps that are exceptions to the above definition. The day camp does not provide lodging, the campers being transported to the camp for the day only. The travel camp often does not have a permanent site but, using buses or other means of transportation as its headquarters, keeps on the move.

The word camp is variously used to imply all gradations of woodland residence. Camping may imply either on-your-own living in the out-of-doors when the campers must provide for their own needs, or living in an organized institution in which the management provides in part for the needs. Since this book treats organized efforts for recreation primarily, it is the organized camp that will receive the major emphasis here. Further, one of the goals of organized camping is to train people so that they will be equipped to enjoy on-your-own camping safely and beneficially.

The development of the organized camp idea follows closely that of the play movement in America and is unquestionably an important phase of it. Historically, it differs in its development strictly as an American institution, without European antecedents. Like the playground movement it had its spasmodic beginnings in the closing years of the nineteenth century, but is primarily a product of the twentieth century. The first recorded was in 1861 when Freebuck H. Gunn, headmaster of Gunnery School for Boys, took his school boys on a two-weeks' camping trip near New Haven, Connecticut, and later established Gunnery Camp on Lake Waramaug. In 1876 a physician named Joseph T. Rothrack established an all-summer camp for boys on Lake Ganago near Wilkes-Barre, Pennsylvania. In 1880 a clergyman established the first church camp on Gardner's Island in Rhode Island, and in the same year Ernest Balch established Camp Chocorua on Chocorua Island. Camp Dudley, New York State YMCA camp, was established on Lake Champlain in 1885 and is the oldest existing camp. Until 1900 the growth was slow, there being no more than twenty-five camps at the turn of the century. Since then the movement has prospered amazingly.

In the earliest days standards were set as an individual matter, each director arriving at the standards he himself considered essential. In these early years, the American Camping Association (then called the Camp Director's Association) made a start by setting a few minimum requirements that had to be met for membership. Later, various local regions containing a number of camps developed standards for the camps in their areas. It was not until recent years that standards began to formulate for the camping movement as a whole. Various national organizations sponsoring camping, such as the Boy Scouts, Girl Scouts, YMCA, have contributed by setting standards for their own organizations. The American Camping Association in 1940 attempted to synthesize the current standards and formulate the requirements that could be considered as marks of good camping for all types of organized camps. A revision of these standards was completed in 1953 (see Selected References). These efforts are indicative of the development of camping toward filling its role as an educational agency of significance. They are symptomatic, also, of the efforts toward elevating camp leadership to the level of a profession.

CAMPING OBJECTIVES

What is the essential nature of organized camping? First, it is living in the wilderness environment. It is living close to nature, experimenting with mist and rain, sand and clay, sun and wind, and all the solitude of the wide, open spaces. It is simple living—strong, virile, robust living in the realm of nature.

It is living in a community of people. It is face-to-face contact with the ebb and flow of human life—it is the civilizing, socializing, humanizing process of people working and playing and living together, closely, intimately. It is group living—active, robust living together in the realm of people.

One thing more: organized camping implies leadership. It implies guidance to help its adherents navigate the churning rivers of the wilderness, as well as guidance to help them paddle the whirling stream of life.

The unique role of camping is the training of people to live in the out-of-doors. In all of its other roles camping shares with other agencies. To teach people to camp is the unchallenged obligation. Other institutions may touch upon it but with them it is always incidental.

But camping's responsibility does not stop here. There are other roles that come to mind, and even though in these the responsibility may be shared with other agencies, they are central to camping.

Role of Joy. Camping looms to a towering height among the country's recreational institutions; it looms large in the minds of recreation-minded people everywhere—so large that the camp director is confronted with a major recreational responsibility. It is the function of camping to develop skills that will carry into the recreational life of adulthood, and it is also its function to provide joy here and now.

It is not so much the typical activities of organized camping that give it great recreational significance, for these can be found in many other institutions—it is the conditions under which these activities take place. It is first the eternal appeal of the out-of-doors. Second, it is the perennially refreshing joy of fellowship that comes from living closely and intimately with others and creating with them the joyous activities that are called the program. It is these two factors—the wild natural setting and the fellowship of people living together—that give eternal appeal to organized camping and great eminence to its recreational role.

Health Role. Every agency dealing constructively with children has a health obligation, more or less, depending upon its nature. The camp leader is confronted with the plain fact that life in camps does affect health, for good or for bad. The aim is to develop to the utmost that capacity for abounding, zestful living that is called health. With this aim camp administrators mislead themselves if they sit complacently by and rely on "the health-giving environment of the out-of-doors."

Health, whether personal or national, is the quality of abundant living—it must be created, and it must be constantly remade. Through the stimulus of its environment and of its program and through the guidance of its leadership, the business of camping is to develop abundant health in strong, hardened bodies and to implant in youthful minds the necessary facts for healthful living.

Social Role. So great is the capacity of camping to affect the lives of people that the scope of its social role becomes sobering indeed. The fact that camping claims the undivided attention of the camper day and night to an extent that neither home nor school nor church nor gang can; the fact that camping groups are of the primary type in which attitudes and sentiments are affected profoundly; the fact that counselor-child relationships are often more natural and frank than parent-child relationships; the fact that the living situation is wholly natural with none of the artificiality of the school—these factors combine to give great social potentiality to camping and eminence to its social role.

More is involved, however, than personal qualities of character and refinement, more than personal adjustment to social living. Today's world demands the developing of a sense of social responsibility, a sense of obligation to the group, whether it be camp, home, city, or state. Herein camping has an unexcelled capacity for fostering an attitude of social obligation.

EDUCATIONAL AND DEMOCRATIC ROLE. In camping is an unmatched educational capacity. The opportunity for personality guidance, for social adjustment, for cooperative living, for democratic experience, for meaningful work, for sharing responsibility, for knowledge of the natural world, for the learning of skills, for appreciation of finer things—all in a natural, life-like situation, under accepted adult guidance—presents an educational situation that stands unique in the educational field today. Fresh and young, unhampered by stagnating tradition, camping has explored where others have feared to tread. In its better levels it has demonstrated the workability of so-called progressive methods. It has created a type of experience of demonstrable educational merit as compared to traditional types of schooling.

Chiefly, there is but one role for children's camping in America—to prepare people to live acceptably, successfully, and joyfully in a democracy. Camping is an instrument of the society it serves. The camp, operating according to democratic principles, has a potentiality for training for democracy that cannot be matched by any other agency, for it gives the child the opportunity actually to live the democratic life day and night in a little democracy of which he is a vital part.

EVALUATION. It is possible to determine just what is being accomplished in the attainment of objectives in the course of the camp season. The health and strong physique objective is rather definitely measurable and the modern camp is careful to determine the progress each individual is making in this direction. Education in skills is also measurable, as it is comparatively easy to show that more skill or knowledge is possessed by an individual in a certain activity or subject at the end of the season than at the start.

In the field of social learning the question is considerably more confused, since measuring sticks cannot be readily applied to changes in attitude as to the more tangible changes mentioned above. There is a distinct trend in camping, however, to use all possible devices for determining growth and social adjustment. The devices are, for the most part, attitude measuring scales, the camper's own story, observation of behavior, and behavior frequency scales.

CAMPING AGENCIES

Camps are classified according to the types of agencies promoting them as follows: (1) private camps, (2) organizational, voluntary, or private agency camps, and (3) public camps. (The day camp, a more recent development, as well as the resident camp are promoted by all three of these agencies.)

PRIVATE CAMPS. Any survey of camping must give a conspicuous place to private camps operated by individuals or corporations at a fee covering expenses and usually making a profit. Such camps have become firmly established as an American institution; they are many in number and are well patronized by those who can afford their superior advantages.

As a rule, the private camps run for eight weeks, their campers remaining for the full season, thus giving them an opportunity to do careful, constructive work in pursuit of their objectives. These camps usually have sufficient funds to make possible a varied, complete, and comprehensive program of recreational, educational, and personality-moulding activities and guidance; they have a larger percentage of counselors per camper, obtaining, as a general rule, an adult leader for every four or less campers; and they usually have a larger percentage of mature counselors trained in leadership, expert in the skills which they teach, and versed in educational principles. Although operating for a profit, their directors nevertheless are usually motivated by a service ideal and hold conscientious objectives for the accomplishment of constructive ends for their campers. Not all private camps measure up to these standards, but as a rule these facts hold.

In addition to the conventional private resident camps which offer a broad general camping and other outdoor education programs, many specialized types of camps are now in operation. Included among these are the wilderness camp, music camp, foreign language camp, ranch or riding camp, dance camp, gymnastics camp, sailing camp, and others. Although offering a general program of activities, these camps feature one particular activity and usually have both excellent facilities and staff members of outstanding reputation to carry on the feature program of the camp.

Much of the pioneering in the field of camping has been done by the private camps. In the early days of the movement they were a potent force in establishing the program pattern, developing standards, and giving shape to the organized camp as a unique American institution.

ORGANIZATIONAL CAMPS. Among organizational camps are thousands of camps operated by the private and voluntary agencies, group work, and character-building agencies such as the Boy and Girl Scouts, YMCA and YWCA, Camp Fire Girls, 4-H Clubs, Pioneer Youth, and Boys' Clubs of America; and also the camps operated by the churches, settlements, and other social agencies, and by foundations sponsored by philanthropic sources. They are rendering an outstanding service by making camping available at very low cost—at a nominal fee barely sufficient to care for the routine operation of the camp. These camps are usually located within easy access of the cities which they serve, and the cost of traveling a distance to reach the camp is thus eliminated. Such camps ordinarily operate in sessions of one or two weeks, the campers as a rule staying for one session only, although some continue for two or three sessions or, occasionally, all summer.

The program of the organizational camps is usually a continuation of the year-round program of the organization and complements it, and is thus not regarded as an isolated effort. While these camps serve well the purpose of vacation and recreation, their educational accomplishments are limited by the length of the period the campers remain in camp, but when the camp experience becomes an integral part of the year-round educational and guidance effort, its significance is greatly increased.

The 4-H clubs render a service to farm youth in providing summer camps for them. The tendency is to select outstanding boys and girls with leadership capacity from rural neighborhoods and attempt to give them during a week or two of training in camp the inspiration and skills which will enable them to return home and enrich the recreational life of their associates in the year-round program.

Social settlements operate camps for the neighborhoods in which they work. Owing to the fact that those neighborhoods are usually underprivileged, these camps operate at a much lower fee and often are entirely charitable. The program is affected by the immediate needs of the campers, and, when malnutrition is a factor, the health-building phase may overshadow all others. Children of all ages and often mothers of infants are taken.

Specialized health camps caring for children with specific handicaps have been developed in some of the large cities. Thus there are camps, for example, for crippled children, for those with speech defects, for diabetic children, and for children with cardiac handicaps.

Aside from the organizations operating camps as part of a year-round program, other agencies with a philanthropic spirit sponsor camps. Among these are the luncheon clubs such as the Rotary and Kiwanis Clubs, which sometimes operate camps themselves but more frequently lend support to organizational camps by contributing facilities and by financing the way of campers who otherwise could not attend. In this category also are the university camps, caring for underprivileged boys and financed by donations from students and alumni.

Reference should also be made to the industrial camp. This type of camp is operated by an industry or large store to give its employees a vacation at a very reasonable cost. The development in this field has been meager and experimental and, for the most part, industrial camps consist of equipped campsites where weekends and vacations may be spent.

PUBLIC CAMPS. Municipal camps were slow in development because of the immediate need confronting city recreation departments for concentration upon the development of city playgrounds. In recent years, however, there has been a growing emphasis upon camping as an important function of the recreation commission, and many larger city departments present camping facilities of some sort.

Organized municipal camps are supervised in two ways: one type resembles the organizational camps described previously, with campers registered for one- or two-week periods at low cost; the other type provides permanent leadership at the camp and assigns to each playground days when the camp facilities are reserved for it. Parties from one playground, accompanied by playground leaders who cooperate with the permanent camp leaders, spend one or two days at the camp paying a low fee covering meals, then vacate in favor of a group from another playground. Of the latter type, the day camp is more typical than the residence camp, with parties spending the day only and returning home at night.

A new trend which holds great promise is the appearance

of the public school camp. It has long been advocated by
some educators that training for outdoor living is in the area
of the school's function. This first led to an outdoor emphasis in science classes, centered more around nature information than camping techniques. Recently some schools have
moved toward taking their pupils to the open country. In
some cases this involves nothing more than the use of a
school-owned cabin to which science classes are taken occasionally for an afternoon. Again it might involve the use of
an organized campsite to which various schools may send
children for a period of several days, under school leadership. School camping, with its emphasis on outdoor education, is developing rapidly in various parts of the country.
It has become well organized and its role in general education has been clearly demonstrated. There is great value
in learning subject matter in the natural setting and educators visualize a great expansion in this direction as part
of the curriculum of tomorrow. Probably the most outstanding of the public school camps are those which receive support from public-spirited institutions or individuals, such as
the Kellogg Foundation and Mott Foundation camps in
Michigan.

There has been little indication of a move toward state-
operated camps, although some states contribute to the
training of camp leaders through institutes and literature.
Perhaps the most significant trend in the state's relationship
to camping is the leadership being given by some state departments of public instruction to the cause of outdoor education in the schools.

Similarly, it is not the policy of the federal government
to operate camps itself, but its greatest contribution has been
in the area of campsite selection and development, in which
case the demonstration camps and literature of the National
Park Service have been of inestimable value. Its recreation
demonstration areas, built in marginal lands near large centers of population contain model camps available for rental
by local agencies. Many agencies of the federal government

have promoted better camping through literature in their respective fields.

DAY CAMPS. In day camping campers are transported in the morning to a campsite within a reasonable distance of their homes and returned home late in the afternoon. In this way, children enjoy the benefits of a camping program while retaining close association with the home. A day camp may involve an experience for a one-day period, daily periods for a week, or daily attendance for periods of from six to eight weeks.

The day camp is not limited to a special type of promotion, being conducted successfully by the various agencies that have just been discussed.

The day camp movement started during the 1930's but received its big emphasis when mothers worked in the 40's in industry to further the war effort and their children needed safe care. Then, its benefits recognized, the movement was expanded after World War II under the sponsorship of county and municipal park and recreation departments, as well as by churches, Girl Scouts, 4-H clubs, and similar groups. Several factors have been significant in the steady growth of day camping. The cost is within the financial means of many families. Parents will more readily send their children to a local day camp operation which is usually close to home. Also, children learn the fundamentals of camping through the organized play activities.

The purpose of day camping is to provide an opportunity for boys and girls between the ages of seven and fourteen years to participate in creative, outdoor group experiences in a democratic setting. The program is not just a repetition of experiences found on the school grounds or playground, but primarily an experience in outdoor activities. More specifically, it utilizes natural outdoor settings to provide fun and adventure, teach skills and appreciations, and to develop a life-long interest in the out-of-doors. As much as possible the atmosphere of the traditional summer camp is retained, with emphasis levelled downward to a generally younger age group. Treasure hunts, field trips, nature collections and museums, storytelling, dramatic skits, water fun, and games are geared to the neophyte's experience.

CAMPSITE DEVELOPMENT

This section discusses (1) the selection of a campsite, (2) plan of layout, and (3) development of the camp after the layout plan has been adopted.

SELECTION OF CAMPSITE. The choice of a campsite depends so largely upon local conditions that only a few general rules can be laid down, as follows:

1. The source of water supply should be carefully inspected and a sample analyzed for typhoid fever germs.
2. A safe body of water for swimming should be located within easy access of the camp.
3. The grounds should be high, well-drained, and cleared of heavy timber growth. The buildings and tents should be located so as to get plenty of direct sunlight.
4. The camp should be fairly well secluded in order to permit the campers a certain amount of privacy.
5. A large open field should be available for games and activities.
6. There should be easy access to a source of food supplies, especially of fresh vegetables, milk, and butter.
7. The camp should be located with regard to ease of access, by both automobile and train.
8. There should be a large woods nearby for nature lore, woodcraft, and hiking.
9. The campsite should be beautiful and inspiring.

CAMP LAYOUT. Three types of camp layouts are common. In the formal plan the sleeping tents or cabins are placed in rows forming streets or a hollow square, with the other buildings such as dining hall, recreation building, and hospital in formal relation to the sleeping quarters. A variation of this plan arranges the tents in a semicircle or circle. In the topographical plan the layout avoids any semblance of a formal arrangement but seeks to place the living quarters more or less at random where they fit in naturally and attractively to the topography of the campsite. The larger buildings are likewise placed with a view to the natural setting. With the unit plan, a further development of the topographical idea, the cabins or tents are arranged in groups or units, each unit some distance from the others, the units arranged in equal radius from the central buildings (dining hall, administrative headquarters, etc.) which serve all units.

Selection among these plans is largely a matter of personal choice, affected by the limitations of the campsite. However, the trend in camping has for some time been decidedly away from formalism. The older camp emphasized formality in the method of programming, camper-counselor relationships, and discipline. The modern camp director feels that better results are obtained by a more natural, congenial, and life-like approach. Hence the topographical and unit plans have become more popular.

The extreme of decentralization is found in the unit plan. Isolated somewhat from each other as they are, the units are able to live more or less independently, as sort of miniature camps in themselves. This leads to flexibility, informality, and offers greater opportunity for self-expression. Too much separation, however, destroys the feeling of oneness with the larger whole and jeopardizes morale and *esprit de corps*, which are priceless goods in camp. The trend is toward pulling the units closer together through assemblies, joint activities, and special events. The Girl Scouts early accepted the unit plan and have doubtless done more to develop and perfect it than any other agency.

STRUCTURAL DEVELOPMENTS. The layout and development of a campsite involves a multitude of technical problems in engineering, sanitation, recreation, education, and forestry. The solution to these problems requires expert advice in all these areas.

Sleeping quarters may be tents, tent-cottages, or dormitories. Dormitories hold little favor in organized camps for children. As for tents and cottages or cabins there are points in favor of each:

Advantages of tents:

1. They are in keeping with the simple outdoor life which should characterize camping.
2. There is a romance and picturesqueness about life in them which is particularly appealing to the imagination of boys and girls.
3. The openness and airiness of tents provide a more healthful arrangement for sleeping than cottages or cabins, in which the housing of six or eight people in one room is a questionable health practice.
4. The original cost is low.
5. They are particularly adapted to use on temporary campsites or where permanent buildings are impossible.

Advantages of cottages or cabins:

1. They are longer lived than tents and do not require the constant care and upkeep.
2. They are more easily prepared for occupancy at the beginning of camp and more easily closed.
3. They furnish better protection against the weather and insects.

If the campsite is infested with mosquitoes, the advantage of a carefully screened cabin or cottage is so great as to offset the appeal of the open tent; also, flies awaken campers with the coming of daylight and cause the loss of much sleep. All tents should be equipped with a floor raised six to eight inches off the ground.

The dining hall should be fitted into the topography in such a way that it blends with the natural scenery and presents if possible a beautiful view of a lake or landscape. Some camps use the dining hall for a recreation building by clearing the tables away, but this is undesirable, and if possible a separate recreation building should be provided. All buildings should be attractive and camplike, made to fit into the particular environment in which they are located. Camping is romance, beauty, and simplicity, and the buildings should reflect this spirit.

Special attention should be given to the sanitary location of toilets with respect to the tents and kitchen, of incinerators, washing facilities, stables, and drinking water. On all these matters of permanent equipment and layout, the standard books on camping should be consulted.

CAMP RESPONSIBILITIES AND LEADERSHIP

Camps are not entirely built around things; they are largely built around personalities. The thing that counts is leadership. One of the great tasks of the camp director is the selection and training of his leadership staff.

Most camps select counselors with a view to obtaining specialists in the various areas of the program. No matter how ideal an individual may be in character and personality, if he has no skill which he can contribute, it is difficult to consider him seriously. On the other hand, the most gifted teacher of a needed skill cannot be considered if his character falls short of the camp ideals.

In respect to age, the high level of skill and teaching ability usually requires mature leaders. The judgment of young counselors is often faulty, especially in emergencies. Too many middle-aged adults, however, often dampen the spirit of joy which must predominate in the camp. Youthful counselors as a rule carry with them a glamour that the more mature frequently do not have. The staff should be composed of both younger and older counselors—a preponderance of either would be unsatisfactory.

Regardless of age, camp leadership must have the spirit of youth—the spirit of joy. It must be friendly, approachable, sympathetic, and understanding. It must maintain respect and have the capacity to maintain order. It must be impartial and have no favorites.

Although all staff members have their special functions, they all share a general responsibility for the personal welfare and guidance of the campers. The area of social learnings, character growth, and personality development cannot be left to any one individual. It is a major function of the cabin counselor in respect to the campers in his cabin. It is also a function of the activity counselors, even though many of them in their enthusiasm for teaching the skills of their activity are inclined to overlook its importance. The concomitant learnings are as important as the direct learnings in these activities.

CAMP DIRECTOR. The Camp Director is the executive of the camp, possessing organizing ability and financial experience. He is responsible for the budgeting of the funds and the handling of all financial matters. In large camps he has a bookkeeper and office secretary. He is responsible for publicity, advertising, and the enrollment of campers. He advises with parents regarding their problems and complaints and is responsible to them for the accomplishment of objectives. Some directors prefer to direct the program personally, but a director as a rule employs a program director who works under him. He selects and employs counselors, although, if he is wise, he will confer with his program director regarding the acceptability of these counselors for they will have to handle activities in which the program director must work with them personally.

The director, for the best results, must be a well-socialized individual able to work harmoniously with others, especially with his staff. He must be a man of sympathy and tact in that he is arbiter in the disputes and conflicts of personalities which arise when people live together in the close relationship of camp. Although a good executive he must be more than a cold, analytical businessman, for he must symbolize all in the way of idealism, educational philosophy, and objectives that he hopes his camp will stand for.

PROGRAM DIRECTOR OR HEAD COUNSELOR. Next in authority under the director is the Program Director or Head Counselor, or, less frequently, Assistant Director. His duties are to formulate, set in operation, and direct in general the program and activities of the camp. He keeps up morale and is for the most part the moving force and inspiration behind the program. All activity leaders are responsible directly to him.

The program director should be well informed in modern educational principles and equipped to build a program on these principles. He trains and supervises the leadership staff and educates them in the philosophy and principles of education on which the camp operates. He must be equally well versed in recreational activities.

PERSONNEL DIRECTOR. Some large camps carry a personnel director whose task it is to give guidance to campers needing individual attention and to advise with counselors in the handling of the campers. He is the head of the guidance program. This program works along two lines: first, it seeks to guide the personality and physical development of campers, giving special individual guidance to those most in need of help; for this reason, some camps feel a man best qualified for this phase should have training in psychology and recreation therapy. Second, it seeks to guide campers in the skill-training phase of the program. Camps using a flexible, informal program based on interest and individual incentive have need for a person to observe and advise those campers who need direction given to their efforts. Both are phases of the personnel director's responsibilities and he often becomes the program director's first assistant.

SUPERVISOR OF ROUTINE OPERATIONS. Many matters of routine need constant supervision to keep the camp operating in orderly fashion. If the director is wise he will not burden himself with these routine details, and certainly such duties do not square with the areas to which the program director should address his energies.

Upon this staff man fall two main areas of duties. The first is keeping the living quarters and grounds in order, and the permanent equipment in repair and operating. This involves daily inspection of cabins and of the entire inhabited area of the campsite; also frequent inspection of permanent equipment, referring matters needing repair to the maintenance man. The second is keeping the daily life moving along on schedule. Many camps use an officer-of-the-day system to see that calls are sounded on schedule and campers assembled as need be. Such officers-of-the-day are responsible to the supervisor of routine operations.

SECTIONAL HEADS. In the decentralized or unit camp, each unit has a director who is responsible to the camp director. In centralized camps, the campers are usually divided into age groups such as midgets, juniors, intermediates, and seniors, and the campers in each section are housed in neighboring cabins. It is customary to provide a sectional head for each of these sections who has supervisory duties over the cabin counselors. He may be an older or more experienced counselor and may have charge of one of the cabins himself in addition to his supervisory duties.

DEPARTMENT HEADS. Under the program director are the heads of the various departments of the camp program. These directors of activities are usually specialists in their lines and responsible for their departments. Some camps object to a departmentalized program and to specialists, in the sense that they work exclusively with their specialty. The use of the term department does not necessarily mean a formalized, school-like program, nor does the specialist necessarily confine his activity exclusively to his specialty. In addition to their specialties, these counselors should have varied interests and should contribute to every activity within their capacities.

In larger, well-programmed camps, experienced staff men are sought to head such areas as the following:

Swimming	Campcraft and woodcraft
Canoeing	Woodsmanship
Sailing	Pioneering
Athletics	Indian lore and Indian dancing
Tennis (usually separate from athletics)	Arts and crafts
	Music
Horseback riding	Dramatics
Riflery	Dancing (including folk)
Archery	Trips
Nature lore	

The waterfront involves a large element of danger. One individual should be in absolute charge of all waterfront activities. Usually, this is the swimming director—a highly skilled, mature, and experienced individual. In small camps this counselor may handle swimming, canoeing, and sailing. But in a camp of any size, while he is responsible for all regulations and supervision of water activities, he confines his teaching to swimming, with other counselors handling canoeing and sailing under him.

In camps with a limited staff some of the departments may be combined. For instance, one individual may handle campcraft, pioneering, woodsmanship, and Indian lore. Music, dramatics, and dancing often fall under one head. Organizing off-campus trips and overnights are frequently handled by the canoeing or the campcraft counselor.

DIRECTOR OF EVENING ACTIVITIES. Some camps carry a counselor giving special attention to evening programs. These evening programs are of such importance, however, that often the program director desires to give them his personal attention. In some camps the dramatics counselor is assigned the duty of giving attention to the details of all evening programs, whether dramatic or not, and plans with the program director. The music counselor also plays a large part. The whole camp program, evenings and otherwise, must be integrated and all should be headed by one man, the program director.

OTHER STAFF MEMBERS. A dietitian plans menus, supervises the kitchen staff, and purchases, or is responsible for purchasing, food supplies. He is usually given a strict budget for the purchasing of supplies.

A doctor should be on the camp staff if at all possible. In case of serious illness, an outside doctor is usually called in to confirm the diagnosis of the camp doctor. In addition, camps often carry a trained nurse. Some eliminate the doctor and rely on a trained nurse with the help of doctors in nearby communities.

The camp store, open a few minutes each day and handling candy and routine necessities, is under the supervision of a counselor with capacities in this direction, often the bookkeeper or financial assistant to the camp director.

The mail is usually a minor assignment to some activity counselor. He, as postmaster, not only handles mail but is responsible for seeing that all campers write home frequently, for keeping a chart of letters written home by all campers and often for posting lists of suggested subjects for campers to write about.

While some mature staff personnel may not have cabin responsibility, most counselors have the dual responsibility of giving direction to a camp activity and supervising a cabin of campers. The cabin counselor is the head of the family group of the cabin, and the good performance of his duties is of paramount importance to the accomplishment of the camp's objectives. Much of the individual guidance work stems through the cabin counselor. Enthusiasm for his favorite activities should never lead to neglect of this counseling responsibility.

SCOPE AND SELECTION OF ACTIVITIES

In the light of the objectives of camping stated earlier, four considerations appear paramount in affecting the selection of activities for the program.

First, in view of the fact that the training of people to live in the out-of-doors is camping's unchallenged obligation, activities that serve this purpose should receive a major emphasis. In a considerable percentage of the camps the only exposure to the skills of on-your-own camping takes place on occasional trips off the campsite. The pendulum has swung back somewhat toward basic, on-your-own camping. For camping to fill its role of training for outdoor living, it is necessary that the pendulum swing much farther.

Second, in the light of camping's objective to bring joy to its campers, a varied program is indicated. The years have standardized the program and the tendency is to use the traditional activities only. There are many individuals in camp, all with different interests, and the activities must be broad enough in scope to satisfy all individual inclinations. Specialized camps giving the major emphasis to one type of activity are acceptable enough, provided their limitations are duly stated in the advertising so that those whose interests differ may go camping elsewhere. The program must be always changing and growing.

Third, the objective of educating in skills implies not only the learning of skills for the present but for the future years of adulthood. Education for leisure looms large in the camping scheme of things. One of the chief criteria applied to a camp activity is: will it carry on throughout the long years of tomorrow, leading to a larger and fuller recreational life in adulthood? If not, its value is limited.

Fourth, the objective of developing appreciation of finer things is indicative of the need of emphasis on broadly cultural areas rather than physical activities only. It would point to a search for beauty in dramatics, storytelling, dancing, nature, religion, and human personality.

Mention has already been made of the major activity departments of the camp: swimming, canoeing, sailing, athletics, tennis, campcraft and woodcraft, woodsmanship, pioneering, nature lore, Indian lore, riding, riflery, archery, dancing, arts and crafts, music, dramatics. These activities break up into many, many activities. The following list is merely suggestive.

Water actitivies:
  Swimming, lifesaving, diving
  Swimming meets, regular and
    novelty
  Canoeing, canoeing meets, tilting
  Stunt canoeing
  Portaging
  Sailing
  Motor boating
  Row boating
  Water polo
  Water cageball
  Water baseball
  Water pillow-fighting
  Log rolling
  Water skiing
  Skin diving

Athletic sports:
  Baseball
  Softball
  Volleyball
  Cageball
  Speedball
  Soccer
  Basketball
  Tennis
  Golf
  Boxing
  Wrestling
  Touch football
  Track and field events

Other sports or "fillers":
  Paddle tennis
  Deck tennis

Hand tennis
Tetherball
Badminton
Horseshoes
Darts
Blow guns
Table tennis

Horseback riding activities:
Riding shows
Riding and pack trips
Early morning and moonlight rides
Saddling races
Flag raids, etc.
Stunt riding

Shooting:
Rifle
Pistol
Trap
Skeet

Fishing:
Bait casting
Fly casting
Trolling

Archery:
Target shooting
Roving and field shooting
Dummy deer hunting
Making bows, arrows, targets

Campcraft and Woodcraft:
Fire building
Campfire cooking
Trail refrigeration
Trail shelters
Trail sanitation
Trail beds
Back-packing
Signals
Tracking
Weather signs

Woodsmanship:
Axemanship

Sawing
Tree felling
Bucking
Handling logs
Cording wood
Splitting
Brushing
Log cabin construction

Pioneering:
Shelter building
Bridges and towers
Rustic furniture
Whittling
Horn craft
Rawhide craft
Buckskin craft

Indian lore:
Indian dancing
Costume-making
Drum- and rattle-making
Pipe-making
Feather craft
Rawhide craft
Buckskin-making
Council fires
Pageants
Tomahawk throwing
Symbolism and art
Tepee- and wigwam-making
Sweat bath construction
Beading
Silver and shell beadwork

Nature lore:
Familiarity with nature objects (trees, birds, animals)
Nature trails
Spatter prints
Smoke prints
Ink prints
Leaf collections
Wood collections
Twig collections
Seed collections
Plaster casts

Recording animal tricks
Aquariums
Mounting insects
Star overnights

Music:
  Orchestra
  Group singing
  Solo work (on high level)
  Goodnight song
  Musical shows
  Operettas

Wild West activities:
  Lariat throwing
  Rope spinning
  Whip cracking
  Western riding
  Stunt riding
  Circus

Arts and crafts:
  Basketry
  Leather plaiting
  Leather tooling
  Jewelry making
  Brass, silver, copper, pewter,
    wrought iron activities
  Design
  Wood painting
  Canoe paddle painting

Pottery
Dyeing
Weaving

Dramatics and storytelling:
  Stunt nights
  Dramatic productions
  Musical shows
  Dramatic reading
  Pageants
  Circuses
  Concerts
  Storytelling
  Poetry
  Costume-making
  Make-up
  Scenery painting
  Stage lighting

Council fires:
  Grand council
  Little council

Dancing:
  Tap and clog
  Indian
  Folk
  Social
  Modern

Library

Camping provides for one's needs in the wilderness. On camping trips real experience is encountered. So that they are most meaningful and enjoyed to the fullest, it is important that they be geared to an in-camp instructional program in campcraft. It is the policy in most camps to provide opportunity for each camper to go on a trip once a week. Older campers are often provided trips of a week or longer in duration. Some camps in wilderness locations make long trips the main feature; the campers, after they return from one trip, remain on the main base camp only long enough to rest up and re-equip before starting on the next. Trips are taken by canoe, motorboat, horseback, pack-mule, truck, horse and wagon, and on foot.

Evenings are regarded by many camp authorities as perhaps the most important part of the whole day. It is in the after-dark activities that the camp spirit reaches its highest pitch. So important are evening activities that the time on which a camp operates may well be set so that there is a full hour of darkness before bedtime.

Evening activities are of four general types: (1) dramatics on the camp stage (these may be more or less impromptu such as dramatized stories and mock trials, or of the type of vaudeville and stunt nights in which each tent or cabin group presents an act, or they may be coached and rehearsed productions such as a play or operetta in which every effort is made to do a worthy piece of artistic work); (2) storytelling; (3) councils; and (4) tent or cabin campfires.

Storytelling nights have proved to be one of the most popular of camp events and a good storyteller is a most valuable asset. No one can fail completely as a storyteller if he is willing to make the necessary effort. There are several excellent treatises on the subject. Appreciation hours in which the reading of poetry predominates are common in some camps, particularly girls' camps.

The best single approach to evening work is the council fire held in the council ring which is copied after Indian council rings. Councils are of two types—grand and little. The grand council is an Indian ceremonial featuring Indian dancing and is colorful, ritualistic, and symbolic. Little council consists of challenges or dual contests with two competitors in the ring performing before the gallery in the stands. The winner is challenged until a champion is determined. This council fire technique transcends all other activities in glamour, but it takes dynamic leadership on the part of the counselor in charge.

Open or unprogrammed evenings should be the exception, not the rule. An occasional open evening is appreciated, however. Tent campfires, in which each tent is by itself around its little fire, also offer variety and enjoy distinct popularity in camps where they are practiced.

SCHEDULING ACTIVITIES

The following schedule, indicative of how the camp day goes, is kept flexible and changed as the day's activities may indicate:

7:00 *First call.*

7:10 *Everybody out.* Flag raising (the tendency is away from a reveille formation and formal colors).
Morning dip—optional.

7:30 *Breakfast.* Counselor serves food family style. Family training in table manners is emphasized and table slang is avoided as much as possible. Eating is slowed in order to avoid rush, noise, and confusion. If at all possible, dish washers are employed to free campers for more constructive work.

8:00 *Counselors' staff meeting.*
Campers clean up tents or cabins. Counselors join campers at close of meeting.

8:50 *Inspection of tents or cabins.* No grades or awards—emphasis on cleanliness for the sake of cleanliness.
Personal inspection of each camper by doctor or nurse for cleanliness, infection or illness.

9:15 *Interest groups, 1st period.*

10:15 *Interest groups, 2nd period.*

11:15 *General swim.* No instruction—that is given in interest groups. General swim is for the joy of the sport. No swimming except at scheduled hours and place. Signal to enter the water is not given by the swimming counselor until lifeguards are all in place.

12:05 *Dinner.* Announcements follow each meal. Singing takes place at the noon and evening meals, usually camp singing at noon and solo work at night. This slows up the meal and relieves the rush and nervous tension which accompanies it.

12:45 *Store open.*

1:15 *Rest hour,* carefully supervised and enforced, counselors with their tent or cabin group.

2:15 *Interest groups, 3rd period.*

3:15 *Interest groups, 4th period, or athletic leagues.*

4:15 *General swim.*

5:45 *Supper.*

6:45 *Unscheduled,* and open for informal games, tournaments, and so forth.

7:30 *Evening entertainment.*

8:45 *Call to quarters.*

9:00 *Taps.*

All campers should receive ten hours sleep. This is not sufficient for some age levels in a strenuous program of activies, but it is very difficult in camp to secure longer hours. The needed extra hour is obtained during the rest hour. This is not an hour of sleep as a rule, but it affords rest and thereby helps. Quiet must prevail during rest hour. An additional hour of sleep is obtained every few days when it may seem necessary, by going to bed early or getting up late. This procedure usually takes place on rainy nights when campers go to bed willingly, or on rainy mornings when nothing is gained by arising early. On Sunday, the camp gets up a half-hour or an hour later, and the morning features a church service. The afternoon is characterized by special activities giving relief from the routine of weekdays.

There have been two schools of thought with respect to scheduling a camper's time, the older point of view holding that the camper should be subjected to a fixed and compulsory schedule of activities, the newer contending that the camper should be relieved of all such compulsory schedules with respect to activities and should be entirely free to do as he pleases.

Some sort of compromise between the two points of view should be reached. Individual differences in likes and dislikes are conspicuous and should be recognized. The element of interest is of outstanding importance. Today the program is regulated from the view of the total living situation in the camp, rather than as a series of classes or activity periods. Campers are therefore given interest sheets containing the names of the major departments of the camp program as listed above and asked to check those in which they would prefer to participate. This system amounts to a series of interest groups chosen by the campers. After selections are made, a schedule of interest groups is made up for each camper, so that he can work them into his day without conflicts. For instance, one camper's schedule might read as follows:

Monday   9:15 Horseback riding
         10:15 Woodcraft
          2:15 Riflery
          3:15 Swimming
Tuesday   9:15 Nature lore
         10:15 Riflery
          2:15 Arts and crafts
          3:15 Reserved throughout the camp for
                 athletic league games or special
                 events.

Wednesday and Friday duplicate Monday; Thursday and Saturday duplicate Tuesday. An effort is made to keep these interest groups down to six campers to the counselor, twelve if there are two counselors in the department. Sometimes a schedule is worked out on the basis of a two-hour period instead of one hour.

This may appear to have all the earmarks of a rigid, school-like schedule, but compulsory attendance does not necessarily follow. If interest groups are worthy of the name, the campers will attend as a rule; if interest ceases, the camper's schedule should be changed. Special projects growing out of the life situation in the camp are constantly arising to take campers away from the stated schedule of activities, such as making scenery for a show, or building a totem pole for the council ring. While working on them, campers abandon their basic schedule briefly, then return to it when the special project is completed.

For purposes of programming and to insure fair competition in contests, campers should be grouped by age. Four groupings are customary: midgets, juniors, intermediates, and seniors, based on age, weight, and height, with the camper entering the classification into which two of his measurements place him. In large camps as many as six groupings are sometimes used.

CAMP SAFETY PRECAUTIONS

In spite of all precautions, strenuous physical activity is sure to result in occasional minor injuries. These are to be expected and anticipated. Most of the injuries which occur in the organized camps, however, are not the result of strenuous activity but of carelessness in the casual life about the campsite. Holes in floors and broken steps, roots on paths, protruding stones, and such result in many a bruised foot and broken arm. Careful precautions should be taken to clear up all main travel paths and areas, particularly those frequented at night.

Of course, a thoroughly adequate sanitary system must be installed, including latrine and garbage disposal facilities, and the director should seek expert advice on these matters. Drinking water should be analyzed by the state department of health.

Each camper first should be given a careful health examination by a licensed physician. Preferably this should be done by the family physician and details recorded on a health examination record form, e.g., that approved by the American Academy of Pediatrics. This should also include comments by the parents regarding the physical examination record. The examination should be completed early in order to allow time to correct any major remediable physical defects. Campers should be checked briefly by a physician within forty-eight hours prior to admission or checked upon arrival at camp for contagious diseases. The medical record of each child should be available, through the camp nurse or physician, to all camp personnel. Brief summaries of each camper's medical history should be given to the counselor involved; specific instructions should be given counselors regarding daily health inspection to maintain the health of campers during the entire camp period. It is necessary for the camp to have a full-time, resident registered nurse. A resident physician is highly desirable, but if this is not possible, a physician must be on call for duty at the camp. Also important is the maintenance of a well-equipped infirmary, including an isolation ward.

The waterfront must be in the hands of a thoroughly competent and trained specialist, and no camp can be excused for allowing campers to enter the water unless every possible precaution is taken for safety. Swimmers should be carefully classified at the beginning of camp into at least three classifications: non-swimmers, beginners, and swimmers. Until these classifications are worked out all campers should be regarded as non-swimmers and limited to the non-swimmers' area. The swimming area should be divided, depending on depth, into carefully marked-off sections for each class. Likewise, to protect swimmers and divers, there should be a safe diving area and a roped-off area for power boats, canoes, sailboats, and other craft.

A lookout tower for the head lifeguard should be erected upon a swim beach so that there are no obstructions to his view. One or more life boats, equipped with crews of two, should patrol the beach during swimming periods. Care should be taken to see that rowboats are never overloaded, and the use of canoes should be limited to first-class swimmers. The American National Red Cross in *Life Saving and Water Safety* outlines details and offers instructions on water safety.

SPECIAL CAMP POLICIES

Administrators of camps are confronted with a number of special problems which can be alleviated if carefully thought-out policies are prepared in advance. For purposes of illustration a few of the more common policies are briefly discussed.

HONORS AND AWARDS. Experience has shown that extrinsic incentives are not needed in camp. In an environment that offers so much in the way of interesting and compelling activity, the situation can be relied upon to provide its own incentives. Many camp directors feel that a program educationally sound will result without the use of award badges, pins, and buttons on the grounds that compulsion should come from the lure of the activity itself. Any honor should be a recognition of achievement rather than an incentive for the camper to participate.

DISCIPLINE. Camp counselors are much too prone to

penalize. The goal should be to restore the offender to a normal state of participation and conformity, and what the child needs is help—sympathetic help. A little friendly, intelligent cooperation on the part of the leader will eliminate much of the need for punishment. If extreme measures are unavoidable, which will be seldom indeed, the curtailment of privileges is the course to follow.

Even though work is one of the most prevalent punishments in camps, it is the most undesirable of all types. Work is rather to be regarded as an honor and a privilege, a thing to be glorified.

A scheme of self-government in camp can do much in caring for administrative problems and in planning programs, but when this machinery includes a court for the trial and punishment of offenders, the policy is exceedingly questionable.

When the camp program is fascinating and compelling and life in the camp society is satisfying and contributing to the individual camper's well-being, few regulations will be broken. Widespread disregard for traditions indicates something vitally wrong with the program, and measures should be taken to reform it.

VISITORS. The problem of visitors is an important one to camp directors. Parents and sightseers do much to distract the attention of campers from their work and make the accomplishment of objectives more difficult. They consume endless time on the part of director and counselors, who must greet them and show them about the campsite. They often seek permission to take campers away on leave to nearby resorts, a practice which usually is not desirable. On the other hand, most camp directors like to have parents and the interested public see the campsite and the program in action, feeling that this is the best method of education of adults concerning what the camp is accomplishing. Most parents have a sincere interest in their children's camp and have a right to know what is being done there.

In order to safeguard against undue disturbance and at the same time display the camp program in action to those who are interested, most camps have set visitors' days on which the gates are open; but at other times keep the camp-site closed to guests. Some camps follow the policy of opening the camp to parents during the camp fire period with the thought that they will not only enjoy the performance but their presence will swell the audience and add incentives to the performers.

YOUTH HOSTEL MOVEMENT

The Youth Hostel movement is unquestionably recognized as an important phase of the growing trend toward outdoor living in the United States. Copied after the European movement and introduced here in 1934, it fosters travel for those who like to move "under their own steam"—usually by foot or bicycle. A series of hostels or overnight residence places (often farm houses) are provided along established hostel trails, each under the supervision of "houseparents," usually the permanent dwellers of the house. The hostels are available very reasonably to members displaying the membership card. Not more than three consecutive nights can be spent at any one hostel. Blankets and cots are provided but the hosteler is required to carry his own sheet-sack for sanitary reasons. Cooking rooms are provided but eating utensils must be carried. Each hosteler has his hand-book-knapsack which contains maps and locations of hostels.

Membership in the American Youth Hostels, Inc., which numbers over thirteen thousand, is required for the use of facilities. Membership is open to anyone, the word "youth" referring to spirit rather than years. Memberships are classified according to age with the privilege of selecting individual or family passes. Membership passes also give certain privileges in the International Youth Hostel Federation, which include hostels operating in over thirty foreign countries including Australia, New Zealand, Egypt, India, Japan, and many European countries.

There are well over one hundred councils with local headquarters organized in the larger urban areas. These councils develop trails and facilities in their areas and arrange special trip routes including canoeing and horseback riding trips. Bulletins are published describing these trips and stating the estimated cost of each.

While hosteling in the early days was an individual matter, now groups are organized giving the movement a club or group-work aspect. The groups have leaders, and leadership-training courses are conducted by the local council. Moreover, the councils conduct supervised trips under special leaders during vacation periods, there being several from which to choose. While previously the emphasis was on long trips of the vacation nature, now one-day and weekend trips are also featured, thus bringing to the members a continuous year-round program of varying interest.

SUMMARY

The organized camp and the informal camping activities that are engaged in by so many people today have grown out of the desire to seek recreation and personal expression through activities in the out-of-doors. Since today's environment has become more mechanized and devoid of natural settings, people are finding the wonders of nature to be a restful and refreshing change. Camping has been a channel through which children as well as adults have been able to participate in outdoor activities in a safe, satisfying manner. It has not only provided a variety of opportunities to have fun, but it has filled an important role in helping to develop and maintain physical fitness, to develop desirable ways of social adjustment and expression, to release emotional tensions, and to practice democratic living in a meaningful way.

Early camps were limited in the scope of their services. Many of them were poorly equipped and difficult to reach. But with the improvement of camp facilities and services and the widespread use of the automobile and other rapid means of transportation, people have migrated to the outdoors. Since 1946, organized resident camping as well as informal private camping has flourished throughout the country. Many different types of camps to meet the needs of the handicapped or special interest groups have appeared. Significant, too, has been the growth of public and agency day camping and the fact that many schools have begun to organize and operate camping and outdoor education programs as a part of the regular school instructional program.

Today the modern camp is a well-designed, safe, and appealing recreation area including facilities for a wide variety of activities. Professionally trained camp personnel provide interesting and educational programs. Since 1935, under the guidance of the American Camping Association, the professional approach to camping has been increasingly evident. Definite standards have been established through the more than six thousand members of the Association. There has been particular emphasis on programs utilizing the natural environment in contrast to activities normally carried on in urban leisure-time programs. At the same time there has been a coordination of the uses of camp facilities in day and school camping which has allowed many more children to receive a satisfying introductory experience in camping.

With the revolutionary improvements in methods of transportation that are now so evident, the opportunities for camping and outdoor living will undoubtedly greatly multiply. People must be informed of these opportunities and properly educated regarding the importance of preserving our great natural areas for not only their own use but for the benefit and pleasure of future generations. The field of camping and outdoor education plays an increasingly important role in helping people to discover satisfying and desirable leisure-time activities.

SELECTED REFERENCES

DOTY, RICHARD S. *The Character Dimension of Camping.* New York: Association Press, 1960. This work gives a scientific approach to the measurement of character changes that occur as a result of camping experiences. Camp objectives are analyzed, and techniques of measurement and approaches to the evaluation of the total camping experience are explained.

MITCHELL, A. VIOLA, and CRAWFORD, IDA B. *Camp Counselling*. Philadelphia: W. B. Saunders Co., 1955. An illustrated book of know-how for the camp worker, this book contains excellent material regarding the position of camp counselor and the conduct of all phases of the camp activities program; particular emphasis is given to campcraft and woodcraft.

REIMANN, LEWIS C. *The Successful Camp*. Ann Arbor, Mich.: University of Michigan Press, 1958. The major aspects of professional leadership and administration in the organized camping field are discussed. The material presented is inclusive and useful for a study of, and practical application to, camp administration and operation.

SALOMON, JULIAN H. *Campsite Development*. New York: Girl Scouts of the U. S. A., 1960. Basic concepts of preliminary planning, site selection, building planning, and construction of major facilities and buildings of the modern camp are included. Diagrams, illustrations, and descriptions in this publication make it a useful reference for the camp planner, builder, and operator.

American Camping Association. *Standards*. Chicago: American Camping Association, 1953.

American National Red Cross. *Life Saving and Water Safety*. New York: Doubleday & Company, Inc., 1956.

American Youth Hostels. *Hosteling*. New York: American Youth Hostels, Inc., 1958.

BENSON, REUEL A., GOLDBERG, JACOB A., and OTHERS. *The Camp Counselor*. New York: McGraw-Hill Book Co., Inc., 1951.

BERG, BELLE R. *Psychology in Children's Camping; A Dynamic Approach*. New York: Vantage Press, 1958. See especially Chap. 3.

Boy Scouts of America. *Camp Sites and Facilities*. New York: Boy Scouts of America, Inc., 1950.

BURNS, GERALD P. (ed.). *Program of the Modern Camp*. Englewood Cliffs, N.J.: Prentice-Hall, Inc., 1954.

DIMOCK, HADLEY S. (ed.). *Administration of the Modern Camp*. New York: Association Press, 1948.

Girl Scouts of the U. S. A. *Established Camp Book*. New York: Girl Scouts of the U. S. A., 1946. Excellent information is also available in the following Girl Scout publications: *Day Camp Standards*, 1953; *Day Camp Book*, 1942.

MACMILLAN, DOROTHY LOU. *School Camping and Outdoor Education*. Dubuque, Iowa: William C. Brown Co., 1956.

Outdoor Education for American Youth. Bulletin of the National Association of Secondary-School Principals. XLI, 229 (May, 1957). Entire issue.

SMITH, JULIAN W., and others. *Outdoor Education for American Youth*. Washington, D.C.: American Association for Health, Physical Education, and Recreation, 1957.

THURSTON, LARUE A. *The Complete Book of Campfire Programs*. New York: Association Press, 1958.

19

School and Community Sports and Athletics

School and community sports and athletics constitute one of the major elements of the total community education, recreation, and leisure-time program. Until recently, however, athletics and many types of sports were limited to only a few carefully trained members of school varsity teams or private club teams, and to those individuals who could afford the costs of special instruction—and these people alone received the benefits of specialized types of instruction and the satisfaction of participation.

Interscholastic, intercollegiate, and highly specialized community athletics are still somewhat limited to the few who are favored with outstanding ability. However, athletic games and sports have found their way into the physical education periods of the schools, into intramural programs, into recreation department playground and adult programs, into industrial recreation programs, and into many activities sponsored by private and voluntary agencies.

From impromptu teams in the sandlot and from the students' pastime in the schools, sports and athletics have grown to be a source of interest to the student bodies of schools, to the entire community, to the entire state and nation.

Activities associated with sports and athletics are, then, widespread in the United States. A variety of these activities are practiced widely under two basic patterns of organization: (1) the public and private schools, at all levels through physical education, interscholastic, intramural, in-

tercollegiate, and informal sports and athletic programs; and
(2) community sports, including community groups organized particularly through public park and recreation departments, private and voluntary agencies, churches, industries,
private clubs and the like, and through many types of informal play at the home, neighborhood, and primary group
level in a wide variety of situations.

During this growth of more integrated education and
recreation programs, many terms relating to the field of
sports and athletics have evolved. Sometimes these terms
have different regional or local meanings which have, at
times, contributed to the confusion of the issues involved.
The following definitions and explanations are used in this
book to establish definite points of reference in the discussion of matters relating to school and community sports and
athletics. Their source is *School Athletics, Problems and
Policies,* a publication at the Education Policies Commission
(see Selected References).

Community Sports and Athletics are inclusive terms which, in their
broader meaning, include all sports and athletic activities in the community. More specifically, the combined term refers to sports and
athletics carried on outside the formal control exercised by schools in
physical education, intramural, or interschool athletics. Community
sports and athletics may thus be controlled by a municipal recreation
department, park department, school-community recreation department, voluntary agency, private agency, or similar group.

Sports are selected activities which usually require a great deal of
physical movement and the use of specific equipment and areas. Examples are golf, tennis, hunting, fishing, horse racing, skiing, mountain
climbing, and similar activities. Athletics and sports, though often
confused, are not synonymous; athletics is one aspect—the competitive
one—of the many kinds of sporting activities.

Athletics refers to competitive games involving physical activity, accepted rules of play, and a system of scoring for determining winners
from among two or more contesting individuals or teams.

School Athletics refers to all athletics in which students participate
under school auspices. School athletics are considered a part, and
only a part, of the physical education program of a school.

Interscholastic athletics refers to the systems of play involving competition among teams representing different schools. The *school team*
or varsity in any sport is usually composed of the most skilled players

of one sex among all students in a school. In interscholastic athletics it is characteristic that school teams play a series of games throughout a sports season to determine champions and that great emphasis be placed on practice sessions designed to develop maximum skill. Interscholastic games are usually played before spectators.

Varsity refers to the school team selected to compete in interschool athletics. Varsity is virtually synonymous with interscholastic as a term for designating the pattern of athletic organization and competition described above.

Physical Education refers to that part of the school program that provides guidance and instruction through physical activities designed to meet the needs of students in developing their physical efficiency and recreational skills. The *physical education program* is a school's inclusive plan and provision for instruction in physical education.

Intramural refers to athletic competition in which all participants are students in the same school.

Extramural refers to athletic competition (other than interscholastic) in which participants are students from two or more schools. Extramurals differ from interscholastics in that they seek to involve all students irrespective of skill; they usually take place only a day or two at the end of an intramural season; and they usually require few or no systematic practice sessions. Extramural competition commonly takes place in the form of play days or sports days, but it also includes occasional informal games between teams (not varsity) from neighboring schools. Extramural athletics do not involve leagues, championships, or season-long schedules.

A *play day* is an extramural athletic activity in which each participating team is assembled on an impromptu basis including players from all (two or more) schools taking part.

A *sports day* is an extramural athletic activity in which each participating team is composed of players from the same school.

STAGES AND OBJECTIVES IN SCHOOL ATHLETICS

Sports and athletics first developed in this country outside the schools. Between 1880 and 1900, sports and athletics were considered as pastimes and only systematic gymnastic exercises were considered to be of value in the school physical education program. While school physical educators were debating the value of the various systems of European gymnastics, a number of other activities, such as sandlot baseball, football, and the new game of basketball, were being developed in local clubs and on an independent

basis among school students. The Playground Association
of America, the YMCA, and similar agencies on both the
local and national level began promoting all these new sports
activities. Youth as well as adults quickly realized the vast
difference between the two programs and soon clamored to
have sports activities taught in the public schools. Following World War I, sports in the physical education program
and athletic competition between schools became widespread throughout the United States.

The present status of athletics is the result of a process of
evolution which falls into eight well-defined stages in which
different objectives appeared and grew in importance.
Since the growth of athletic competition outside the schools
closely paralleled that found in the schools, these objectives
will be discussed with particular emphasis upon the development of athletics in the school setting.

The educational aspects of athletics have varied greatly
from period to period. New objectives have gradually made
their appearance as new conditions have arisen in the economic and social structure of our national life. The effect
of these changes has been cumulative. In no case none of
the eight objectives, which will be traced through their evolution, have entirely disappeared. The emphasis on one
may have lessened, and the emphasis on another may have
strengthened, but the influence of all has remained to affect
the total result. Consequently, at the same time that school
authorities have been conscientiously striving to exercise
more effective control over this phase of the educational
curriculum, problems have continued to face them. The assumption of new objectives has accordingly meant added
responsibilities, which in many cases were school-wide and
community-wide in their ramifications.

SAFETY VALVE FUNCTION. The first objective of athletics
was called the "safety valve" function. When desultory
forms of athletic activity first appeared on the scene in the
1880's and 1890's, educators at first, with but little enthusiasm, saw in them a possible value in the utilizing or diverting, in a harmless way, the excess energies of students who

were possessed of more than an average amount of physical vitality and vigor. It seemed that this superfluity of animal spirits might well be expended in the rough and tumble of vigorous sports and thereby diverted from the more vicious occupations of hazing, drinking, gambling, class rushes, "town and gown" brawls, general harassment of teachers, and the like. School literature of this period is replete with incidents of this nature. The period 1900 to 1905 might well be called an age of pranks in education.

In considering this early objective it should be kept in mind that athletics were merely considered negatively as an avenue of using up energy in out-of-school time. The positive values in the way of affecting character, personality, and sociability were not yet perceived, or, if perceived, not yet stressed. There was a definite relationship between this emphasis and the campaign slogans of the newly organized playground movement in the large cities to the effect that organized play would reduce the growing amount of juvenile delinquency. The same idea has vogue today in the constructive programs for combating Halloween vandalism.

It was only natural that the great impetus for extracurricular forms of education in which athletic activities are so strongly represented, should follow directly upon this period of student pranks, hazing, and vandalism.

Educators sometimes fail to realize and appreciate this value of the extracurricular program simply because they have never experienced so many annoyances such as have been described. The fact that these things do not exist so commonly today is one that should be attributed largely to these new educational interests, so valuable because the students themselves share in them and largely organize them.

RUGGED MANHOOD. The second objective that was claimed for athletics became most stressed in the days of Theodore Roosevelt's pre-eminence. This was the health and character-training side of athletics which has become one of the most important educational objectives of the athletic program. Certain preliminary events had helped to stimulate a dominating interest in athletics beginning with the year 1900. In 1896, with the revival of the Olympic Games, interest in competitive sports was stimulated. The games of basketball and volleyball had just been invented and were gaining in popularity in gymnastic circles. The Spanish-American war, as is true of all war experiences, left a strong realization of the need for physical fitness and courage.

To these actual events, there was added academic challenge in the writings of Karl Groos and Herbert Spencer, who gave scientific evidence that competitive play belonged to the race through the process of natural selection and that it was a most necessary factor in the struggle for existence. In the United States William James was asserting that sports were "a moral equivalent for war"; that games of personal contact sublimated the pugnacious and aggressive tendencies and emotions of man into higher channels guiding them toward more idealistic ends.

All these tendencies to emphasize the vigorous and self-reliant values of athletics were thrown into the spotlight by Roosevelt's ardent espousal of them. Roosevelt, himself, was the best and most quoted example of the value of a regimen of sports and outdoor life. From a childhood of semi-invalidism, he had gained health and confident personality from roughing it with men on a ranch. It was only natural that he should be intensely interested in vigorous sports and outdoor life as a means of training aggressive and self-reliant leaders and should preach the virtues of an active, strenuous life. In short, his athletic philosophy stressed leading a rugged outdoor life, winning modestly, losing gracefully, and never showing weakness.

The effect of athletics and sports upon health and character has always been a debatable subject. The evidence, however, seems to be in favor of the opinion that, when properly conducted, they can make a definite contribution to health and character.

SCHOOL SPIRIT. The third function of athletics which appeared is that of school spirit. There is probably no unifying agent in school activities as powerful as athletics. This was caused at first by the need to raise money for equipment and other expenses of the teams. The first affairs that involved the entire school in this connection took the form of dramatic entertainments, socials, and penny bazaars.

The homecoming game must be considered as more than an affair involving two teams of players and their respective crowds of rooters. Prior to it, there is the mass meeting, an occasion giving the orchestra or band an appreciative audience. Banners and posters made by the art department are displayed in the school halls. The school paper prints feature stories of the games and contests. The school band plays an indispensable part in making the game a colorful spectacle and furnishes the opportunity for a friendly display of courtesies; it also leads in the singing of the school songs. The athletic banquets are made possible by the efforts of the domestic science department which supervises or furnishes food and service. Moreover, the general interest in athletics provides a lively topic for school debates.

All these relationships make athletics the hub for many school activities and functions. These organic relationships all contribute to the "we" feeling of students and supporters, to the sharing of common interests and loyalties.

Games give the school an identity that reaches out beyond its walls. The old grads cling to and treasure this spirit, which for them furnishes many occasions for reunions and homecomings.

COMMUNITY SPECTACLE. The next objective claimed for athletics was that they afforded a community spectacle. In other words, emphasis began to be placed upon the spectacle aspect of the game. The unifying bond that was first formed within the school by the interest in athletics soon spread to the communities at large.

The spectator interest in athletic sports is a natural one. All forms of sport and recreation furnish a subject of common interest. Schiller many years ago called play "an offset to specialization." The specialization of business and the professions isolates men into small groups according to mutual interests and friendships. But sport is common to all

and is therefore a great leveler and humanizer. No wonder
that, next to the weather, sport is the most common topic of
conversation.

Indirectly, the varsity games serve as examples of skill for
the onlooker to emulate, a feeling that is stirred in all spectators who are watching a performance of merit—ending
often in a desire to test out their own skill in a like manner.
These games show the highest degree of technique and
teamplay; the beginner will be attracted by some special
feat of skill, which he will keep in mind and practice to
master for his own accomplishment. In every line of endeavor, whether it be art, music, science, business, or athletics, the outstanding figures who have achieved high attainment serve as the inspiration for those who are starting
out on their own careers and seek examples to emulate.

The situation brought about by the new spectator interest
was both encouraging and discouraging. On the one hand,
the intensified interest by the alumni and citizens in the athletic teams of their schools brought about community awareness of their schools and increased support for all departments of them. On the other hand, the schools found that
this new interest was a mixed blessing. By inviting the
community to support their games they invited at the same
time insistence by the public upon having a voice in many
school affairs. Far-seeing school administrators, however,
have been able to minimize this interference and even to use
it to advantage, by encouraging such progressive leadership
as that of the parent-teacher groups and the civic clubs.

SPORTSMANSHIP. The next objective of athletics appeared
as a result of shortcomings in the older system. There arose
a conscious effort to improve the standards of sportsmanship.
Because of the frequent problems that were foisted upon
the educators by partisan followers as well as by the players,
it became apparent to all that better standards of sportsmanship were absolutely necessary.

Many measures to improve the existing situation were
taken by educational authorities. State authorities drew up
rules of conduct for players, coaches, spectators, and officials.

Moreover, a national movement, the Sportsmanship Brotherhood, was inaugurated in 1923 by a group of sporting enthusiasts, the purpose of which was to foster, by publicity and encouragement, the ideals of sportsmanship. It drew up a Sportsman's Code and promoted it through posters. This code became a familiar sight on the walls of schoolrooms and gymnasiums.

The Code of Honor of a Sportsman is that—
       He keep the rules,
       He keep faith with his comrade,
       He keep himself fit,
       He keep his temper,
       He keep his pride under in victory,
       He keep a stout heart in defeat,
       He keep a sound soul, and a clean mind and a healthy body.

These measures were supplemented by local, district, and state meetings to bring together officials and coaches on a common interpretation of rules and other procedures. This was an important measure in preventing misunderstandings and it resulted in a much higher grade of officiating. Again, as the spectators became more educated in the finer points of sport, there came a new appreciation of the technical features of the play, apart from the interest in merely winning or losing.

ATHLETICS FOR ALL. Mention has been made of the steadfast efforts of educators to improve the older system of athletics by removing the abuses which crept in and by emphasizing a positive campaign to create sportsmanship and good will. Another need, too, had been apparent for some time, and in its turn was vigorously championed and promoted—athletics for all. Assuming prominence at the end of the 1920's, this movement has grown with cumulative force as more and more athletic participants have been enlisted.

In attempting to broaden the older program of athletics, the intramural movement at first fell into a natural error. In its early beginnings, it accepted the varsity program of sports as an example to be followed, with the result that football, basketball, baseball, and track were the first intramural sports. It was soon found, however, that on the whole these sports demanded too much equipment, training, and endurance for promotion on such a widespread scale. The intramural leaders, therefore, began to experiment with many recreative sports that could be played more informally. Consequently, the curriculum of athletics and sports expanded to include swimming, tennis, golf, handball, archery, soccer, speedball, volleyball, softball, bowling, touch football, and many others.

In general the intramural program has developed three lines of procedure: that of featuring and popularizing many new sports; that of surrounding the more strenuous activities with training regulations and health safeguards; and that of offering skilled instruction to novices who would have been entirely neglected under the older system of athletic participation.

Once introduced and under way, the intramural movement has affected the entire athletic structure. By promoting a wide variety of sports, it greatly broadened not only its own program, but eventually the interscholastic program as well. It was only natural that in these newer sports a nucleus of skilled players should develop who would eventually demand the privilege of interschool competition.

Indirectly, the intramural movement also developed new interests which eventually led to experiments in a new type of interschool competition, such as the play days and sports days, in which many activities are featured and large numbers of players and teams are engaged. Probably the greatest educational contribution, however, was placing of value upon informal recreation as well as upon the organized athletic competition. By this emphasis the intramural movement directly anticipated the concept of education for leisure which eventually became a definite objective in itself.

FINANCIAL SUPPORT FOR STUDENT RECREATION. The objective of athletics which followed is really a concomitant need but at the same time is inseparably bound to recent athletic developments. It came as a result of the crowd-drawing power of athletic events. Athletics, particularly in the case of the larger colleges and the larger high schools, became a money-making institution. Fortunately, surplus funds began to be used for very worthy projects, such as, the providing of facilities and equipment for the rapidly growing movement of intramural athletics, the purchase of uniforms for the school band, providing gymnasium clothes for indigent students, and financing of institutes in health and physical education. In the colleges, many stadium drives were won on the argument that the profits would provide increased opportunities for wholesome recreation for the entire student body, both men and women.

There are many questions which could be raised on this commercial practice of utilizing gate receipts for financing recreation for all. The most obvious is whether the end justifies the means. However, the consensus is that it is entirely justifiable to assess gate receipts and direct them to worthy purposes and a promotion of recreation for all, if standards are rightly upheld.

EDUCATION FOR LEISURE. The eighth and most recent objective refers to education in sports for leisure, which has been a direct outgrowth of the more recent trends in the physical education and intramural programs. While originally the aim of the intramural department was to provide wholesome recreation for the immediate needs of the students, it gradually became apparent that many of the newer activities developed interests that carried over into the leisure hours of adult life. Since the increasing hours of leisure comprise a great social problem for the present generation, it is imperative that the schools anticipate this need.

In connection with this objective it is essential to bear in mind that exercise can easily be made a habit. The problem for education is simply to create the right habits and attitudes during the plastic years of youth. The play spirit is so strong that the boy or girl will undergo the practice necessary to acquire the skills for reasonable proficiency, and these skills, once acquired, give lasting enjoyment.

The rapid rise in popularity of the intramural movement

has had a decided effect upon the make-up of the required physical education program. An evidence of this influence is found in the newer methods of teaching athletic and sports skills. Exercises have been devised which teach swimming strokes, track techniques, basketball skills, golf form, and so forth, to large groups of students in class formation. Students apply themselves to such instruction with zest. Their imagination is captured, and the incentive to utilize the newly acquired techniques in the voluntary after-school intramural activities is added.

Another influence of intramurals is the policy of permitting students in physical education classes to elect the sports they prefer and to give credit for participating in them as satisfying part of the requirements of the course. This is in keeping with the modern educational philosophy of permitting considerable freedom of choice within the general requirements.

Finally, the knowledge of popular games brings other enjoyments besides active participation in them. Many curriculums of physical education now include material designed to give a better understanding of the place of sports in our social environment. Through the use of lectures, demonstrations, and visual aids, students are shown the positive values of reading of sporting events in their appropriate seasons, listening to sports commentators, and watching thrilling moments in sports on television. All of these learning activities are directed toward the individual's education for leisure and giving him opportunities to learn how to enjoy sports and athletics.

In the future, athletics will no doubt find new objectives, and no doubt changed social conditions will bring stronger emphasis to certain of these objectives and will weaken others. The trends in athletics largely adjust themselves. Where evils clearly exist, they should be opposed by education and restrictive legislation; but where opinion is divided on the merits of certain athletic trends, the rule of laissez faire may better apply. The process of social evolution will inevitably decide the matters in question.

PROGRESS IN STANDARDS AND PROGRAMMING

Athletics sprang up so rapidly as a student innovation that school authorities at first lacked the insight to grasp the educational advantages which they offered and for a long time gave but little supervision to them, with the result that many problems developed. Today such problems, although constantly tending to recur, are minimized where there is strict supervision of athletics in school circles. In the colleges, in particular, the problems of proselytizing, scholarships, and professionalism still persist to vex the conscientious administrator.

SECONDARY SCHOOL AND COLLEGE ATHLETICS. Today, trained leadership is present. Athletic coaching is a profession. Almost universally, the coach is a regular member of the teaching faculty; he has had teaching preparation and holds a teaching certificate. Consequently, under trained leadership, much more attention is being given constantly to safeguarding the players' welfare. While the element of danger is always inherent in vigorous athletic exercise, this has been minimized by: (1) careful supervision in the form of health examinations, (2) improved facilities and equipment, (3) application of the physiological principles of training, (4) equalized competition, (5) modification of rules, (6) limitations on length of season, (7) limitation on amount of participation by any one player, (8) improved coaching and officiating, and (9) accident-benefit plans.

At the same time that athletic practices were being improved, the standards of sportsmanship were being raised. Cases of unsporting conduct still occur in athletics; but it is significant that they are exceptions, whereas in earlier days they frequently occurred. Sportsmanship is the Golden Rule in action; it depends upon strong leadership in the school to set the example for the teams, spectators, and community to follow.

Organization in the form of state athletic associations has played a leading role in the developments that have been recounted. Included within their scope are the smaller state organizations, such as district associations, county associations, and city associations, which follow in general the state rules, useful for purposes of scheduling and so on. To state athletic associations goes credit for placing limitations on national meets and tournaments, requiring approval of invitational tournaments, adapting rules to the high school age level, abolishing spring football practice in secondary schools, developing uniform eligibility and contract forms, classifying schools, registering athletic officials, conducting rules clinics, acting in a judicial capacity for protests and interpretations, and, in general, insisting upon school control of interscholastic sports. The work of all the associations was further coordinated by the founding in 1920 of a national body, the National Federation of State High School Athletic Associations. It has served to develop uniform practices among states relative to their school athletic competition.

ATHLETICS FOR JUNIOR BOYS. While steady progress in the development of standards for secondary school and college athletics has been made through the years, another area of definite need for control has arisen through the rapid growth of competitive sports for boys under twelve years of age. Sports participation in this age group has been organized locally as well as nationally on a large scale, particularly since World War II. Most notable has been the organization of Little League Baseball, Inc., Biddy Basketball, Pee Wee Football, Inc., and similar nationally organized groups promoting sports for younger boys.

The question of desirable practices in regard to highly competitive or any type of competitive athletics for boys aged six to twelve has become one of important national concern. It is obvious that, in other than school or organized recreation departments, there are thousands of youngsters of this age throughout the country playing baseball and other sports. In 1946, the official Little League had only 48 teams in 12 leagues and was centered in Pennsylvania. Seven years later it had become a nation-wide movement with more than 250,000 boys playing official Little League baseball. This figure represents over 11,946 teams and 2,812 leagues in 46 states, and does not include the thousands of youngsters that are playing on "farm teams," nor the many umpires, committees, parents, and other adults involved. Along with this promotion, most often outside the schools and public recreation departments, has come the organization of district, state, and national tournaments, the construction of specialized sports facilities, night play, and many other promotional operations characteristic of adult competitive sports.

There is need for more direction regarding what is most beneficial for the growth and development of children this age—not only for boys but also for girls. The question is not the promotion of any one sport or activity, but what types of activities best motivate children and at the same time are most beneficial to their physical, psychological, and social development.

From 1950 to 1955, the question of highly competitive athletics for children under twelve years of age was discussed and argued by laymen and those considered authorities. A great deal of time and effort was expended in research and study of the problem. The Committee of the National Recreation Association in 1952 stated that:

Highly organized competitive athletics are any athletic activity which involves a considerable amount of the leisure time of the youngster in formalized practice, which encourages extensive attendance by adult spectators, which is limited to the outstanding players, and which involves the selection of winners on a state, regional, or national basis. It should be clear from this definition that intramural competition in football, basketball, baseball, tennis or any other sport would not be considered highly organized. Intra-city competition may or may not be highly organized; state, regional or national competition usually is.[1]

Despite these studies and the above definition, many persons feel that there is little or no harm in competitive athletics for this age group—even highly organized types of competitive athletics. Nationally, however, this is not en-

[1] National Recreation Association. "Are Highly Competitive Sports Desirable For Juniors?" *Recreation*, XLV (December, 1952), pp. 164-66.

tirely the opinion of school authorities and recreation groups.
So many joint authoritative reports and summaries of this
entire question exist that they cannot all be discussed here.
However, the major national reports are cited, and the study
of these will lead the reader to references summarizing the
many opinions of authoritative groups. The problem is so
controversial that it is important to become acquainted with
the arguments, pro and con, on the issues involved.

The following questions and answers dealing with the
issues and conclusions regarding competitive athletics for
junior aged boys state clearly the thoughts of many recreation leaders throughout the country:

1. Can a highly organized competitive athletic program
   satisfactorily meet the needs of all boys of this age?

   No community athletic program for boys under twelve
   is adequate unless it provides the opportunity for every
   boy to participate with other boys of comparable age and
   skill in a variety of sports within the neighborhood and
   community.

2. Can an intramural type competitive athletic program satisfactorily meet the needs of all boys of this age?

   A community-wide intramural type program is the basic
   means of providing satisfactory opportunity for all boys to
   participate in competitive athletics.

3. Can community enthusiasm and resources be mobilized
   for a local intramural type program?

   Although community enthusiasm and resources may not
   be as quickly mobilized for an intramural type program
   as for the more highly organized, there is the evidence
   from many years of experience to indicate that effective
   community support is forthcoming for this type program,
   when adequately interpreted to the public.

4. Is exclusive use of areas and facilities for competitive athletics for boys of this age desirable?

   A community should avoid establishing installations for
   the exclusive use of any one age or interest group. Adequate scheduling and supervision will provide the most
   equitable use of facilities and areas.

5. Are highly organized competitive athletics financially sound?

Until a community is providing the basic essentials of a genuinely well-balanced, total recreation program, it is financially unsound to spend large sums of money on a few participants.

6. Are highly organized competitive athletics harmful to the healthy physical development of boys this age?

The greater the percentage of boys twelve and under participating in a highly organized competitive program, the more likely is the possibility of physical injury to the less physically mature participants.

7. Are highly organized competitive athletics harmful to the healthy emotional development of boys of this age?

Competitive athletics hold greater danger of being harmful to the healthy emotional development of boys of this age when they are highly organized and imitate the tensions, excitement, and pressures of high school varsity, college, semi-professional and professional athletics.

8. Are state and national tournaments desirable objectives for boys this age?

From the point of view of growth and development of the child of this age there is little justification for state or national tournaments.[2]

The solution of the problems growing out of widespread competitive athletic activities for boys six to twelve years of age can be reached only through continued cooperation, study, and research. Harmful practices must be boldly pointed out and desirable practices encouraged. Most of all, the movement needs leadership and channels through which people may relate their opinions, experiences, and differences and then develop a sound plan which will result in what is best for child growth and development.

SPORTS AND ATHLETICS FOR GIRLS AND WOMEN. Sports and athletics for girls have become an accepted part of the general education program, but there is a wide difference in their policy administration from that used for boys. The

[2] *Ibid.*, p. 166.

principle that girls should participate is generally accepted today, but distinct problems of control and conduct are involved. Girls' athletics should be directed towards the goals of physical development, the enjoyment of action, the development of sportsmanlike attitudes, and the acquiring of skills in a wide variety of games and activities of the type which may carry over into later life.

It follows from the above that girls' and women's sports and athletic competition, aside from that which is carried on in connection with physical education, should be in the form of intramural sports, play days, and carefully controlled game activities. Methods of classifying the participants are discussed on page 514.

The objectives and standards for the conduct of sports and athletics for girls and women are stated in the platform adopted by the American Association for Health, Physical Education, and Recreation as follows:

1. The construction of the program of sports activities must be based upon a knowledge of the elements of individual differences, which are age, physique, interests, ability, experience, health, and stage of physiological, emotional, and social maturity.

2. Sports activities must be selected and classified on the basis of the best current research and in terms of the many interrelated factors entering into play.

3. The selection of sports activities must be based upon an awareness of three aspects; first, the analysis of activities from simple to complex; second, the classification of individuals in ability from novice to expert; and, third, the application to present and future use.

4. Each community must be studied to ascertain how to use, to improve, and to increase all available places for wholesome play.

5. Wise conduct of a sports program must make provision for every player to lead according to her merit and skill in leading, and to follow according to her willingness and ability to adapt herself to others and to a common end.

6. Wise conduct of the sports program must provide for continuous challenge to the ingenuity, organizing powers, and powers of appraisal of every player.

7. The acquisition of skill must be promoted by a wide variety of sound, effective methods aptly employed as progressive means to the desired ends.

8. Participation in sports must depend upon a comprehensive and reliable evaluation of the health status of the participant and upon a classification of fitness which takes into account the quality and extent of participation as well as the type of activity, together with individual differences as well as general organic normality.

9. Special restrictions upon participation, such as participation during the menstrual period, must be determined by reference to the findings on the individual's health inventory, with conservatism in the absence of final evidence.

10. The activities schedule should conform to an optimum plan of regular play periods of limited length at frequent intervals, held out-of-doors whenever possible, at times of day when vital energy is at a high level and when interference with a hygienic regimen is minimal.

11. The element of competition, present in all organized group play, must be made to function as a fundamental constructive factor in the sports program.

12. Provision must be made in equal terms for all players to participate and to compete in terms of actual ability and maximum expertness.

13. The method of organizing competition must be determined by the desirable possibilities it provides, not by the type into which it can be classified.

14. The official in a contest must measure up to all of the qualifications set for leadership; and exercise of her authority must be sound, consistent, and expert.

15. The official rules authorized by the Division of Girls and Women's Sports of the American Association for Health, Physical Education and Recreation must be used.

16. The sports program must progressively educate the participant to bona fide incentives rather than awards. When awards are used, they should be symbolic, inexpensive, and of secondary importance.

Suggested age groupings are as follows:

Pre-adolescent   10 to 12 years
Adolescent   early adolescent—13 to 15 years
                      late adolescent—15 to 18 years
Young adult   19 to 24 years
Mature adult   over 24 years.[3]

INTRAMURAL AND EXTRAMURAL ATHLETICS. Intramural refers to all athletics of a non-varsity nature. The scope of its work takes it everywhere within the high school or college, the goal in view being to reach every student who is interested in any form of sport. Aristotle said: "The principal aim of gymnastics is the education of all youth and not simply that minority of people highly favored by Nature," and again, "The measure which the state should adopt for public welfare should always aim at the grand mass of citizens; for only the education of all the citizens, with no exceptions, will give birth to collective virtue." The rapid growth of intramural activities has largely offset the "athletics by proxy" criticism that has identified itself with the varsity exhibitions.

Intramural athletics sprang into prominence in colleges in 1913 and rapidly became one of the traditions of student life. The success of the intramural idea in college circles led to its introduction into high schools about 1925, and there it gained momentum rapidly. Much of the present-day popularity of intramural athletics is due to the generous approval with which the general public and the school authorities view this phase of athletic sports.

In order to reach all the students, a great variety of activities must be offered. Individual differences are so great that if every individual is to be successfully drawn into activity a varied and challenging program is necessary. In instituting the program it is best to rely at first on the well-established, better-known sports, and then gradually increase the scope.

[3] American Association For Health, Physical Education and Recreation, *Standards in Sports for Girls and Women* (Washington, D.C.: National Education Association, 1958), pp. 5-6.

Extramural refers to that type of competition found in play days or sports days—occasions on which a large number of teams and players from one school compete against teams and players similarly representative of another school. This competition is not varsity because there is no emphasis on crowds or on the display of the highest skill attainable by careful coaching. Neither is it intramural, because it is outside the boundaries of one school, hence, extramural.

COMMUNITY SPORTS AND ATHLETICS

One of the most important elements of administration of community sports and athletics is to set the stage for sound operation of the program, which includes young children as well as adults, the handicapped as well as the physically able, and the star as well as the tyro athlete. The program must be allowed to develop freely and spontaneously, yet with control and direction where and when necessary by volunteers, professional educators, and recreation leaders. Standards must be developed with national and local agencies cooperating. Finally, there must be continual re-evaluation and long-range planning which reflect changing times and insure the community the best in organization, finance, leadership, and areas and facilities for sports and athletics.

NATIONAL AND STATE ORGANIZATION. As in the development of school sports programs, national organizations and groups have taken a direct part in organizing community sports and athletic activities outside the school. The National Amateur Athletic Union has established standards and has provided central organization for the vast interest in various kinds of amateur athletic competition in the United States; through its organization, American athletes compete in national and in world competitions. Also, organizations such as the National Recreation Association have been influential in directing the growth and development of community sports and athletics. The Association has published literature extensively indicating accepted practices in the field, maintains consultant services to help local groups to develop all types of sports and recreation programs, and co-operates with professional and lay groups to develop standards for sports and athletic play at all levels. Furthermore, the American Red Cross (with its aquatic standards program), the YMCA, the Boy's Clubs of America, the National Industrial Recreation Association, the National Public Parks and Playgrounds Tennis Association, and similar groups have developed special programs to motivate people of all ages to take part in wholesome sports, athletics, and physical play activities.

Regional and state organizations, paralleling state high school athletic associations and other school groups, have been formed to guide and to coordinate the efforts of recreation and civic leaders in conducting out-of-school sports and athletic programs. Regional groups such as the Southern California Municipal Athletic Federation have been formed to meet particular needs in one area; state recreation societies in Michigan, Wisconsin, and many other states have taken the leadership in developing competitive athletics at the state level with full consideration of all state problems involved.

LOCAL ORGANIZATION. As cities grew and space for both indoor and outdoor play became more scarce, sports and athletic activities gradually became more highly organized. Then, too, there was a national interest in sports, and participation in them was sought not only by groups especially organized to promote sports but by many other informal social agencies and groups that used them merely as one part of their total program. As a result, the local other-than-school sports organizations in this country now represent a diversified pattern. They are enthusiastically sponsored by public park and recreation agencies, the voluntary agencies, fraternal groups, churches, industries, private sports clubs, and similar organizations.

Although these organizations promote the development of local sports participation, the major direction of neighborhood and city-wide sports is carried out by specific organizations in the community. There is the problem of providing adequate facilities, giving instruction in sports and athletics, organizing competition, scheduling, and many other details which have to be carried out. These functions in local community sports are met by (1) public recreation agencies, (2) voluntary agencies, (3) private industry, and (4) private organizations.

Public Recreation Agencies. Whether the public recreation agency be a park department, city recreation department, or a public recreation service operated under a school system, their responsibilities are clear. It is their function to provide the foundation of sports programs for all groups, since the funds supporting public agencies are derived mainly from taxes. Thus, the public agency should best provide community sports facilities in accordance with national standards. Through this agency and in cooperation with the above-mentioned city-wide and area-wide sports groups, facilities are scheduled, areas supervised, leagues organized, and activities conducted on a city-wide basis. The public agency provides basic instruction in all sports; also, it provides equipment and leadership for all children's games and sports on playgrounds and in community centers. For adult leagues and sports participation, the public agency usually provides (1) supervisory personnel to help organize and administer the activities, (2) personnel to directly supervise play, and (3) areas and basic physical facilities needed for play. Adult groups usually provide, through special fees and the like, the funds necessary to insure adequate equipment and supplies such as bats and balls, and to pay officials and meet other expenses incurred by giving awards or providing other special services desired in the conduct of their competitions.

Besides conducting organized sports and athletic activities in the community, the public recreation agency provides facilities and supervision for many types of informal sports participation. The recreation department encourages and educates the community to participate in sports in and around the home and provides areas and facilities for informal play such as ice skating, softball, golf, swimming, tennis, and many other sports and games. Through this informal type of play, people are encouraged to engage in sports activities in the family group or with friends and to participate in sports for fun and relaxation. More specific information on the content of the community sports program is given in the following chapter.

Voluntary Agencies. Voluntary agencies, such as the YMCA, Boy's Clubs of America, Girl Scouts of the U.S.A., church groups, and the like, conduct gymnastic activities, sports, and athletics on a wide scale. Usually they provide special periods of instruction in sports and games for the different age groups. Also, utilizing their own as well as public facilities in the community, they conduct sports and athletic competitions and informal participation for their members. These activities include leagues, play days, and participation at all levels and for different age groups. In communities where public sports services do not exist, the voluntary agencies, through funds from the Community Chest or other sources, coordinate the community sports program. Through the years, these agencies have given valuable service to communities in maintaining public interest in physical fitness and sports participation; also the standards they have created, such as those in aquatics by the American Red Cross, have been important contributions to the growth and development of community sports and athletics throughout the nation.

Private Industry. Special consideration must be given to organized as well as informal programs conducted under the auspices of private industry. The trend is to coordinate these programs very closely with community programs, and in many instances industrial groups contribute funds for the support and use of community facilities with the municipal sports director fully in charge of the use of facilities as well as of the scheduling of events. On the other hand, many industrial groups have their own organization, use mostly their own facilities, conduct instructional programs, and carry on an extensive program of competitive athletics. It is not uncommon for industries to own and operate gymnasiums for informal play and physical fitness activities, golf courses, resident camps, winter sports centers, swimming pools, and other special sports facilities.

Private Organizations. The conduct of sports and athletics by private clubs and groups is both diverse and extensive. Most closely associated with community sports is the recent growth of private, unincorporated sports organizations conducting programs such as Little League Baseball and similar athletic competitions for younger children. Along with these are organizations such as United Commercial Travelers, the long-established Police Athletic League, the fraternal organization sponsorship by groups such as the American Legion, the service clubs, and many other such community groups too numerous to mention. In addition, many private clubs sponsor their own activities in sports such as archery, bocce, curling, hunting, fishing, boating, coasting, gliding, soccer, and practically every kind of sport. Finally, there are the commercial sports services offered through bowling alleys, roller skating rinks, and many other facilities which promote participation and conduct sports contests either on a semi-professional or professional basis.

SUMMARY

Sports and athletics are an integral part of American life. With the passing of the frontier, people in the United States have transferred to sports and athletics much of the love of adventure, the love of competition, and the challenge they experienced in building America. First developing outside the schools, sports of the Old World were played for a short time. In the frontier environment they were soon revamped to meet local needs and interests. Where needs were not met, new sports such as basketball were invented and have become established as national pastimes.

In tracing the evolution of sports and athletics, it should be pointed out that the original interest in them was centered in local neighborhood or private community clubs that conducted competitions on a rather informal basis. As interest in participation grew, the skill level of the players improved; with the tremendous desire of Americans to excel performances in competitive sports improved rapidly, and sports contests began to attract many spectators.

Colleges, then secondary schools, accepted varsity competition as a part of the total education program of the school. It became common by the 1920's for thousands of persons to pay admission to see athletic contests between school or other amateur sports teams or individuals. Spectator interest in sports gradually grew to be dependent upon (1) the expertness of the players, (2) the ability of the competitors to play a colorful style of game, and (3) the ability of an individual performer or a team to win.

The attention given to the high quality of competition and the importance of winning has tended to develop overemphasis in athletics both at the college and the secondary school level. For the most part, however, control of sports and athletics by school and community authorities has led to the development of national as well as local standards for these programs. The National Intercollegiate Athletic Association governs college sports; state athletic associations direct the sports activities of secondary schools; and national standards have been evolved to develop physical education programs and to regulate the sports and physical activities conducted in the junior high school and the elementary school. Very important, too, is the fact that sports have become more and more the basic material of the school physical education program. The result has been sports for all— a closer coordination of physical education, intramural sports, and varsity sports competition.

Closer coordination has also been gradually developing between the total program of sports education in the schools and the community sports and athletics program. The ultimate objective of the school sports program is (1) to insure participation by all during the formative years, and (2) to instill in young people the desire for life-long participation in a variety of sports activities for fitness and wholesome recreation. Public park and recreation agencies, schools, voluntary agencies, and other groups all have a tremendous responsibility in providing facilities and leadership to perpetuate and cultivate the sports interests of individuals in the home, in local interest groups, and in organized community-wide sports activities of all types. It is only through their combined promotional efforts that sports participation, a necessary and dynamic part of American life, can continue to increase and make its maximum contribution to a changing American society.

SELECTED REFERENCES

Cozens, Frederick W., and Stumpf, Florence S. *Sports in American Life.* Chicago: University of Chicago Press, 1953. This work provides an analysis and the social significance of the large place sport fills in the public consciousness throughout all classes of society. Sport, in all its phases, is discussed, with particular emphasis upon its form, as well as upon its social and cultural implications in promoting desirable human relationships and reducing prejudice and intolerance in our democratic way of life.

Education Policies Commission. *School Athletics, Problems and Policies.* Washington, D.C.: National Education Association, 1954. An excellent summary of basic policies and desirable practices in school athletics is given. It includes definitions of terms used in sports and athletics on pages 3, 6, 8, 23, and 301.

Mueller, Pat, and Mitchell, Elmer D. *Intramural Sports.* 3d ed. New York: The Ronald Press Co., 1960. A well-illustrated text which covers the entire intramural sports program for schools, colleges, clubs, and organizations. This work includes definite suggestions on how to adapt adult-directed intramural sports to military, industrial, and community sports and to recreation programs.

National Recreation Association. *Community Sports and Athletics.* New York: The Ronald Press Co., 1949. This text represents the most complete coverage of the administration, organization, and operation of community sports programs other than those operated as part of the school educational program.

These two reports are major studies and summaries of authoritative groups regarding highly organized competitive athletics for children under twelve:

North Carolina Recreation Commission. *Competitive Athletics for Children.* Raleigh, N. C.: Recreation Commission, 1952.

Report of the Joint Committee on Elementary Competition for Children of Elementary and Junior High School. *Desirable Athletic Competition for Children.* Washington, D.C.: American Association for Health, Physical Education, and Recreation, 1952.

Ainsworth, Dorothy S. (ed.). *Individual Sports for Women.* Philadelphia: W. B. Saunders Co., 1955.

American Association for Health, Physical Education, and Recreation. *Standards in Sports for Girls and Women.* Washington, D.C.: National Education Association, 1958.

American Recreation Society. *Sports for Girls and Women.* Chicago: Athletic Institute, 1958.

FORSYTHE, CHARLES E. *The Administration of High School Athletics.* New York: Prentice-Hall, Inc., 1954.

LEAVITT, NORMA M., and PRICE, HARTLEY D. *Intramural and Recreational Sports for High School and College.* 2d ed. New York: The Ronald Press Co., 1958.

MENKE, FRANK G. *The Encyclopedia of Sports.* 2d rev. ed. New York: A. S. Barnes & Co., Inc., 1960.

MEYER, MARGARET H., and SCHWARZ, MARGUERITE M. *Team Sports for Women and Girls.* Philadelphia: W. B. Saunders and Co., 1957.

SCOTT, HARRY A. *Competitive Sports in School and Colleges.* New York: Harper & Bros., 1951.

WILLIAMS, JESSE F. *The Principles of Physical Education.* 7th ed. Philadelphia: W. B. Saunders Co., 1959.

20

Organization and Content
of Recreation Programs

The administration of play programs where large numbers of people are involved calls for a definite scheme of organization. The first step in such an organization is to decide upon what types of activities are to be pursued. It is wise to make available the widest possible variety of activities in order that the participants will have the opportunity to make selections that will be both beneficial and interesting to them. Definite consideration must be given to time schedules so that all activities are included and the available leadership and facilities are utilized most efficiently. Special methods of organizing the various types of play programs in different settings must be devised, taking into consideration the age and sex of the participants, the activities to be engaged in, and the numbers involved.

SCOPE OF PLAY AND RECREATION ACTIVITIES

The classification of fundamental play forms, play movements, and play interests, and the influence of age and sex upon play have been discussed in previous chapters. It is essential, however, that some general classification be made describing the broad program of organized play and recreation activities usually conducted by schools, recreation departments, voluntary agencies, and other organizations. It is difficult and really unnecessary to make a rigid classification of these activities, yet their scope should be generally defined.

Whether these play programs represent instruction in play activities in the schools or informal free play on playgrounds or other settings, it is important that the interrelationship between them be clearly recognized. For example, the sports program involves dramatics, since many sports contests include aspects which are essentially dramatic in nature; the arts and crafts program becomes functional when puppets are made for the dramatization of a story; and the music program is closely related to performance in the dance. Social recreation involves skills and attitudes that are learned in several different activities in a total community play and recreation program.

Classifications of the scope of community play and recreation activities were made in 1954 at the Second National Workshop on Recreation, where approximately eighty school and recreation program specialists worked together to classify recreation program activities and to indicate the scope and interrelationship between the eleven major classifications they had selected. These eleven major program areas are presented here.[1] How they are incorporated into the general community school and recreation program is described later in this chapter.

Arts and Crafts.

Elementary

Paper bag crafts	Drawing, crayon work	Finger weaving
Puppets	Stenciling (one color)	Hooking
Plaster casting, carving	Vegetable printing	Spatter painting
Finger painting	Basketry	Papier mâché
Clay modeling	Gimp craft	Whittling
Copper foil	Candlemaking	Tie dyeing
Soap carving	Shell craft	

Intermediate

Games such as:	Simple metal jewelry	Painting and sketching
Checkers	Tin can craft	Block printing
Puzzles	Plastics	Hand and simple loom work
Bean bag	Wood carving	Art metal craft
	Basic ceramics	Leather
		Leather modeling
		Leather tooling

[1] The Second National Workshop and Recreation, *The Recreation Program* (Chicago: Athletic Institute, 1954).

Advanced

Specialized work in leather, plastics, wood, jewelry enameling, painting, and sketching and similar types of arts and crafts.

Dance.

Folk dance
  Square dance
  Round dance
  Circle dance
Social dance
Ballet

Dance mixers
Modern dance
Creative rhythms for children
  Free rhythms
  Identification rhythms
  Rhythm games
Tap, clog, character dance

Drama.

Blackouts
Ceremonials
Charades
Children's theatre
Choral speech
Community theatre
Creative drama
Demonstrations
Dramatic games
Dramatizations
Festivals
Formal drama

Grand opera
Imaginative play
Impersonations
Light opera
Marionettes
Monodrama
Monologue
Musical comedy
Observances
Operetta
Pageants
Pantomime

Peep-box
Plays
Puppetry
Script-in-hand
Shadow plays
Shows
Skits
Story-reading
Storytelling
Stunts
Symphonic drama
Tableaus
Theatre-in-the-round

Sports, Games and Athletics.

Informal games and activities
Individual and dual sports
Team sports

Combative sports
Women's and girls' sports
Co-recreation sports activities

Hobbies.

Collecting:
  Stamps
  Phonograph records
  Guns
  Antiques, and
  Others

Creative:
  Writing
  Painting
  Home mechanics
  Photography
  Cooking
  Gardening, and
  Others

Educational:
  Reading
  Languages
  Religion
  Sciences
  Arts, and
  Others

Performing activities based on
body skills:
  Hunting
  Fishing
  Dancing
  Boating
  Magic, and
  Others

Music.

Singing:
  Community sings
  Choruses
  Quartets
  Ensembles
  Glee clubs
  Madrigal groups
  Solos

Playing:
  Rhythm instruments
  Simple melody instruments
  Fretted instruments (guitar,
    etc.)
  Bands
  Orchestras

Listening:
  Home music
  Records
  Radio
  Television
  Live concerts

Rhythmic Movement:
  Purely rhythmic
  Singing games
  Play party games

Creative:
  Songmaking
  Other musicmaking

Outdoor Recreation.

Nature Activities:
  Collecting
  Care of living things
  Nature trails, exhibits
  Nature talks and demonstra-
    tions
  Nature games
  Study of natural sciences

Outdoor Living:
  Picnics and informal outdoor
    fun
  Camping—
    Day camping
    Resident camping
    Family camping

Trips, Outings and Travel

Miscellaneous Activities:
  Museums and Zoos
  Arboretums and the like

Outdoor Arts and Crafts:
  Projects using bark, fibre, seeds,
    nuts, etc.
  Weaving
  Wood carving
  Clay projects
  Shells, horns, fungi, and
  Others

Outdoor Sports:
  Orienteering
  Hiking
  Fishing—
    bait and fly casting
  Riflery, and others

Plant Culture and Husbandry:
  Forestry
  Gardening
  Landscaping
  Flower shows
  Animal care, pet training

Reading, Writing, and Speaking.

Reading:
  Book review clubs
  Expressive reading
  Reading for others
  The Great Books Program
  Reading the classics

Writing:
  Business and social letter writing
  Creative writing for stage, radio, magazines
  Poetry
  Technical writing
  Book writing

Speaking:
  Debates
  Voice and diction clubs
  Public speaking
  Forums
  Storytelling
  Toastmasters clubs
  Foreign language clubs

Social Recreation.

Games
Informal drama—
  skits and stunts
Dance
Family recreation

Co-recreation sports
Parties
Banquets
Outings
Teas and coffee hours

Special Events.

These activities involve a departure from the normal type of operation and require special planning and assistance. Special events are community-wide activities; special activities involve only local or neighborhood groups. Some of these events include:

Play Day
Circus
Talent Show
Arts and Crafts Exhibit
Music Festival
Winter Carnival
Halloween Celebration

Championship Athletic Contest
Doll Show
Fishing Derby
Holiday Parade
Science Fair
Hobby Show

Volunteer Service.

A volunteer is a person who performs necessary services without remuneration. The services may be of a professional quality or of an unskilled nature. Many persons derive a great deal of self-expression

and recreation from helping others through volunteer service. These
may be:

Administrative:
  Board members
  Committee workers
  Planning with professional staff
  Public relations
  Adult council

Program:
  Assistant leader in sports,
    drama and the like
  Camp counselors
  Chaperons, and the like

SCHOOL PLAY ACTIVITIES

Since 1918, probably the most widely accepted summary
of the aims or values of education has been the following
Seven Cardinal Principles of Education: (1) Health, (2)
Command of Fundamental Processes, (3) Worthy Home
Membership, (4) Vocation, (5) Civic Education, (6)
Worthy Use of Leisure Time, and (7) Ethical Character.
One of the major functions of the school, then, is to assist
parents and other individuals and groups in the community
to give each individual ample opportunity to develop interests that will lead to good health and the wholesome use
of leisure time. Actually all subjects in the school curriculum—art, drama, music, biology, history, and so on—help
the student gain broad experiences for living.

The school has, through the total education program, the
responsibility to teach a variety of games, sports, and physical activities in the elementary and secondary schools.

PLAY DAYS AND SPORTS DAYS. The school play program
should feature occasional special events, demonstrations,
play days, sports days, festivals, and the like. Play days
bring together groups from two or more schools to play together informally in a variety of games and contests, including sports. Care must be taken to choose the activities carefully, not to overcrowd the program, and to plan for proper
safety and, if necessary, for transportation to and from the
location. A loud speaker is essential, leaders should be
carefully briefed, and the activities carried off according to
schedule.

Sports days are, for the most part, held for the older age

groups. Usually during play days, color teams are improvised with team members selected at random, including everyone who wishes to participate. On the other hand, for the sports day, teams have been previously made up of players best qualified to represent their group. In order to bring larger numbers into action, representative teams in several sports play at the same time throughout the day, and no player is permitted to take part in more than one game in the same sport, although he may compete in more than one sport. Most often, there are few spectators. At the end of the program an informal fellowship program usually is scheduled where players can talk over their experiences and become better acquainted.

EXTRACURRICULAR ACTIVITIES. In addition to play days, sports days, and intramural and interscholastic sports, most junior and senior high schools provide opportunities for students to engage in a wide variety of school-sponsored extracurricular activities. These are usually organized on a club basis, supervised by school staff members who are specialists in the interest area concerned. Some of these programs include, among the more popular, photography club, foreign language club, science club, dance club, debating society, glee club, safety club, band, orchestra, and other pursuits that may lead to the development of lifelong leisure-time interests. The effectiveness and extent of these programs depends upon local resources present in different sections of the country and upon the philosophy of the community and the policies followed in administering the school system.

COMMUNITY RECREATION PROGRAMS

As previously stated, community recreation generally refers to all recreation opportunities existing in the community of a private, voluntary, commercial, and public character. It is important to consider this concept when planning the total community recreation program. Reference has been made in Chapters 14, 15, and 17 to the different roles of the various agencies and groups in the conduct of the community recreation program. Although reference in this chapter is made mainly to public recreation operations, the suggested activities and the principles and methods of conducting them may well be applied in other agencies in the community.

Several factors must be considered in planning and conducting community recreation activities. The fact that children, in most cases, are not required to attend school from June to September puts greater responsibilities upon the community to provide leisure-time programs for school-aged children during these months. Also, seasonal changes dictate a great increase in program operation during the summer months in areas having a winter climate; changes in weather often are reflected in the program in southern parts of the country. Some other major factors include differences in topography, population density, educational level, natural and economic resources available, and general philosophy, customs, and cultural background of the people.

The general recreation program will be discussed in regard to (1) summer program, (2) fall and spring programs, (3) winter program, and (4) special programs, including activities for the family, the aged, the handicapped, and other programs warranting special mention.

SUMMER PLAYGROUND PROGRAM. The problem of program planning and operation involves consideration of various local conditions that affect the total program plan. The hours at which people are able to participate, their interests and needs, and the availability of staff and facilities to meet peak-load needs are important in selecting and scheduling activities. Definite schedules must be made for each season and for the entire year, also made far enough in advance and include sufficient detail so that the program can be carried out efficiently. On the other hand, a reasonable flexibility must be maintained in seasonal schedules to meet specific local interests and needs and to take advantage of situations which encourage participant planning and spontaneous program development.

The summer playground operation is the major play program in the community during these months. There is, however, need to coordinate the playground program with day camp operations; with aquatic events (such as learn-to-swim campaigns, water pageants, and lifesaving courses); with a variety of special events; with special offerings in sports, music and dramatics; and also with family recreation programs, special interest groups, and services to help groups and individuals to carry on their own informal recreation.

In planning the season's playground program, care should be taken not to attempt to introduce all the activities at once but to build the program up gradually and progressively throughout the summer. The first few weeks should be spent in organizing teams and in building up attendance. A good idea is to run off some of the individualistic tournaments of minor importance first on the home playgrounds, the winners competing later for the all-city championship. Suitable events for this purpose are horseshoe pitching, croquet, clock golf, shuffleboard, table tennis, hand tennis, handball, first trial for achievement tests, and so forth. As soon as the teams are organized, the director should start the interplayground schedules, playing on a league basis, or, where the number of playgrounds is too large, on the combined league and elimination plan. He should carry the leagues in the popular team sports, such as baseball and volleyball, along until the end of the season, providing a home-and-home series between the teams that are matched against each other.

The season's program should be built up progressively throughout the summer, inserting new activities constantly. For example, tournaments start one week, the finals carry over into the next week, and at the same time new tournaments start which extend into the week following. In this way something new is provided all the time to challenge the interest of children and keep them in regular attendance. The schedules should all be finished in time so that the last week of the season may be devoted to arranging for a final festival day to close the activities.

There are different ways of approaching the problem of planning the summer playground schedule. Many program planners feel there should be a major theme which links many of the program elements into an all-inclusive special event at the end of the summer season; others feel a general theme is unnecessary and provide several minor themes which lead to a series of special events during the entire playground season. Usually the playground program is from eight to ten weeks in duration, depending on the local situation. A basic weekly program is made up in the pre-season schedule so that supervisors and playground directors have a definite overall program from which to make more specific plans for each neighborhood playground. In this way an overall progression is insured, yet there is flexibility to meet unusual situations.

Master Pre-Season Schedule. A master pre-season schedule can be outlined in several different ways. One way is to make a general one-page master scheme for all playgrounds, supplementing it with a limited number of special events including movies, adult night programs, and similar attractions. This type of schedule shows the progression of activities, the dates of all special events, and the key activities in arts and crafts, dramatics, music, nature lore, and so forth. The following summer playground master schedule illustrates this type of planning.[2]

Weekly Seasonal Schedule. Another effective method of outlining the seasonal schedule is to be somewhat more specific about various events, indicating for each week the details of the program. Such a program outline is shown on pages 500–502 outlining an eight-week schedule indicating the activities planned, the preparation for coming events, and the progression of activities throughout the summer playground program.

Weekly Forecast. The summer weekly master schedule is easily utilized by the playground director to develop the daily program for each neighborhood playground. The

[2] *Summer Program Outline*, Moline, Ill.: Department of Parks and Recreation, 1959.

SUMMER PLAYGROUND PROGRAM
MASTER PRE-SEASON SCHEDULE

I. *Operational Dates*
June 19 to August 9
(Playgrounds will be open from 9:00 A.M.–12:00 and 1:00 P.M.–4:30 P.M., Monday through Friday)

II. *Age Groups*
6–8: Midgets
9–12: Juniors
13–15: Seniors

III. *Dancing (City Wide)*
Social Dance:
Junior Teens (13–15)
Wed.-Fri, 7:00 P.M. to 9:30 P.M.
Senior Teens (16–18)
Mon.-Wed.-Fri., 7:30 to 10:00 P.M.
Square and Folk Dance:
Tue. & Thu., 7:30 P.M. to 10:00 P.M.

IV. *Family Nights and Movies*
Playgrounds should plan a family night activity at least twice monthly. Various playgrounds will have movies every other week.

V. *Special Instructional Activities*
(1) Golf
(2) Archery
(3) Tennis
(4) Swimming
(5) Fly casting
(6) Tumbling
(7) Dance
(8) Baton Twirling
(9) Drama–Music
(10) Crafts
(11) Sports (including softball)
(12) Hobbies and clubs

VI. *Weekly Athletic Tournaments*
(1) Clock Golf
(2) Table Tennis
(3) Volleyball
(4) Newcomb
(5) Paddle Tennis
(6) Checkers
(7) Small Fry Athletic Tournament
(8) Horseshoes, Ring Toss

VII. *Softball League*
Midgets–Tue., 1:30 P.M.
Juniors–Wed., 1:30 P.M.
Seniors–Thu., 1:30 P.M.
Girls' League–Wed., 1:30 P.M.

VIII. *City-Wide Special Events*
(1) Pet & Costume Parade
June 26, 6:00 P.M.
(2) Play Day
July 10, 9:00 A.M.–3:00 P.M.
(3) Fishing Rodeo
July 17, 9:00 A.M.
(4) All-Sports Day
Aug. 1, 9:00 A.M.–12:00 noon

IX. *Suggested Special Playground Activities*
(1) Pet Parade
(2) Doll Show
(3) Wheel Day
(4) Tumbling Show
(5) Marble Tournament
(6) Kite Tournament
(7) Hobby Show
(8) Trips and Tours
(9) Carnival Week
(Aug. 5–9)

WEEKLY SEASONAL SCHEDULE

Week	Designation	Playground Duties	Activities for Emphasis	Special Events

First	Organization Week	Register Participants
		Get acquainted with children
		Lay out activity courts
		Organize equipment
		Teach proper use of apparatus
		Classify players for competitive activities, especially softball, clock golf
		Organize groups for:
		  Leadership
		  Safety
		  Newspaper
		Post weekly schedule
		Display weekly crafts projects
		Keep attendance records
			Low-organization games
			Softball practice
			Clock golf
			Checkers
			Crafts—plan and make costumes for parade
			
			Work on family night program
			Prepare for costume parade
			Announce and arrange for hobby show
				Clock golf tournament
				Playground picnic
				Costume parade (city-wide)
				Teen-age record dance

Second	Hobby Week	Start softball league Hold playground checker tournament Prepare for city-wide Play Day Announce horseshoe contest Meet with club officers Start baton twirling classes	Low-organization games Horseshoes and ring toss Baton twirling Crafts & Dramatics (Skits & costumes for Play Day) Prepare playground newspaper	Checker tournament Hobby show Family night & movie Teen-age record dance

WEEKLY SEASONAL SCHEDULE (*Continued*)

Week	Designation	Playground Duties	Activities for Emphasis	Special Events
Third	All Play-Day Week	Hold playground horseshoe tournament Announce table tennis tourney Start tumbling Plan family night Announce playground picnic	Low-organization games Table tennis Dancing Prepare family night program (dramatic skits, crafts display, baton twirling & tumbling) Distribute playground newspaper	Horseshoe & ring toss tournament City-wide Play-Day Teen-age record dance
Fourth	On Wheels Week	Hold table tennis tournament Announce paddle tennis tournament Introduce golf Plan playground picnic Announce Doll show	Low-organization games Paddle tennis Crafts—start making doll houses & dresses Make final plans for dance & family night Golf; prepare playground newspaper	Table tennis tournament Family night Teen-age record dance On wheels parade
Fifth	Doll Week	Hold playground paddle tennis Announce Volleyball—Newcomb Announce family night Start nature collections Introduce Archery	Low-organization games Volleyball—Newcomb Crafts—start bird houses for show Stories on nature Final plans for doll show Distribute playground newspaper Archery—Begin plans for trip to the zoo	Paddle tennis tournament Teen-age record dance Doll show and parade

WEEKLY SEASONAL SCHEDULE (*Continued*)

Week	Designation	Playground Duties	Activities for Emphasis	Special Events
Sixth	Nature Week	Hold playground volleyball tournament Announce athletic contest Work on athletic skills tests Complete softball leagues Bring all attendance records to date Plan picnic of all club members	Low-organization games Athletic skills Neighborhood nature hike Final plans for trip to zoo, birdhouse show Plan for All-Sports Day	Volleyball–Newcomb tournament Teen-age record dance Trip to zoo Birdhouse show Family night
Seventh	Sports Week	Hold athletic skills contests Announce playground carnival Announce softball winners	Low-organization games Prepare for carnival Plan for final family night Prepare playground newspaper	All-Sport Day
Eighth	Carnival Week	Complete all playground records Check and return all playground supplies Write final playground evaluation Plan picnic for all club members	Final plans for carnival Complete crafts projects Distribute playground newspapers	Playground carnival Family night

daily program for the coming week is written out on Thursday or Friday by each playground director, assisted by the playground staff and presented to the playground supervisor in time for the supervisor and the program director to review the prepared schedule. These day-by-day weekly programs of each operating playground are discussed at the general weekly staff meeting, usually held Monday morning. At the staff meeting the basic activities for the coming week are reviewed, games and craft projects demonstrated, special events explained, operational problems discussed, and plans synthesized. A sample form of a playground director's weekly program forecast follows. It outlines both the entire weekly schedule and the schedule for each hour of the day for the entire week.

Daily Program. The scheduled program of daily activities is useful in letting the child who likes certain events know approximately at what time to come to participate in them; it places the various activities at the most convenient hours for the players; and it provides storytelling, arts and crafts, nature recreation, and other play that is not vigorous for the heated hours of the day. While holding to routine, however, the director must be careful not to rob play of its spontaneity.

The planning of the daily program should consider that the early part of the morning or afternoon, or likewise late, is a good time for individualistic play or scrub games, as the maximum attendance is not present. The team games should be put at the time when all the players are most apt to be present, usually the middle of the morning or afternoon. The quiet activities should come at the hot part of the day. In the morning many younger children will be present; the older boys and girls may be attending summer school or assisting about the home. In the afternoon the older children will predominate and the director should give them the most personal attention; likewise in the evening, he should remember that working boys and girls and adults should receive the first consideration.

WEEKLY FORECAST

At the _____ playground   For Week Beginning _____, 196__

Time	MONDAY	TUESDAY	WEDNESDAY	THURSDAY	FRIDAY	SATURDAY
8:30– 8:45	Distribute equipment—supplies—mark courts—inspect playground					
8:45– 9:00	Playground Staff Meeting	Low-Organization Games	Group and Singing Games	Low-Organization Games	Group and Singing Games	Low Organization Games and Free Play
9:00– 9:45		Playground Athletic Tournament	Softball Practice	City-Wide Athletic Tournament	Free Play	
9:45–11:00	Handcraft Daily					
11:00–11:45		Storytelling and Simple Dramatics	Music	Dance	Baton Twirling	
11:45–12:00	Call in all Playground Equipment					
12:00– 1:00	Lunch		Playground Picnic		Lunch	
1:00– 1:15	Distribute Playground Equipment and Supplies					
1:15– 1:30	Low organized games and free play					
1:30– 2:30	Handcraft	Dramatics	Storytelling	Clubs	Preparation for Special Event	
2:30– 4:00	Tumbling	Organized Softball League Play			Weekly Special Event Hobby Show	
4:00– 4:45	Intra-Playground Contests	Archery	Preparation for Family Night	Social and Square Dancing		
4:45– 5:00	Call in all Playground Equipment					
6:30– 8:00	League Games		Family Night (Every 2 weeks)		Informal Play	

Special Events and Activities. Special events are distinct and unusual, differing from the daily program features in scope and organization. They are carefully planned to develop city-wide interest, many times to be the culmination of a sequence of preliminary events. Every effort should be made to enlist the interest of parents. Activities in which adults may participate as well as observe, should be provided. These major events serve to punctuate the customary program and relieve the monotony of routine activities for the regular attendants of the playground. The cooperation of parents may be enlisted as entertainers, special officials, and leaders for the day.

In utilizing the talent in the neighborhood the play leader is able not only to present a much more attractive program but at the same time to interest influential citizens in the work and in public recreation in general. Historical pageants may be given that call for the participation of hundreds of people; and, if properly organized, such spectacles attract large crowds of interested spectators and promote civic spirit.

Events of this description must be made out well ahead of time and featured on the bulletin board and in the newspapers. This allows the director to plan with definiteness and also permits parents and children to look forward expectantly to a variety of interests. When the children know in advance about these occasions they are aroused to a climax of enthusiasm.

There are many types of special events, since many of them originate from local customs and interests. A representative list includes the following:

Amateur Night	Circus or Carnival	Football Field Day
Apparatus Contest	Coaster Derby	Garden Show
Arts and Crafts	Dart Throwing	Golf Putting
Exhibit	Deck Tennis	Halloween Parade
Band Concert	Demonstration Day	Harmonica Contest
Baseball Field Day	Doll Village	Hobby Show
Checker Tourna-	Easter Egg Hunt	Hopscotch
ments	Fishing Derby	Horseshoe Tourna-
Chess Tournament	Folk Dancing	ment

Ice Carnivals
Ice Skating
Jackstones
Kite Tournaments
Marble Tournament
Model Airplane
    Contest
Music Festival
O'Leary Tourna-
    ments

Outdoor Movies
Paddle Tennis
Pet Show
Play Day
Play or Pageant
Roller Skating
    Tournament
Rope Skipping
Rope Spinning
Shuffleboard

Sled Meets
Snow Modeling
Stilt Tournament
Table Tennis
Top Tournaments
Track and Field Meet
Ukulele Contest
Water Pageant
Whistling Contest
Winter Sports Festival

Special activities are those special types of programs that are also unusual and different from the daily program but are confined to neighborhood or local area promotion. These are specially designed to meet neighborhood needs; should they become city-wide, they would then be considered special events. Some of these local special activities include:

Athletic Carnival
Block Party
Campfire Program
Costume Parade
Doll Show

Family Night
Pet Show
Playground Dance
Puppet Show
Wheel Day

Suggestions follow for conducting a play day or special event where large numbers of participants and spectators will be present:

1. Put the slow events of individualistic nature first, while the crowd is assembling; display exhibits where crowd can see them.

2. Put exhibition games and drills on next and run off together at same time to give an idea of extent and scope of play activities. Have all ages represented.

3. Put races at time of afternoon when crowd is fully assembled. The spectators always like races, which are exciting and can be run off one after the other without delay.

4. Put the novelty events, which leave the crowd in good humor, at the end. These are not affected by the departure of a part of the crowd and contestants.

5. End up with award of prizes won during the season. Such a ceremony adds to the importance with which the prize is considered.

6. Advertise the occasion well. Use newspapers, bulletin boards, posters, and handbills, well in advance with sufficient repetition.

7. Let each playground be responsible for specific exhibitions.

8. Have the fields marked off and roped to keep the spectators at a proper distance. Have a monitor to watch each of these.

9. Have the distances for the races all marked out; one course can be used with the shorter distances indicated. Use the same starting line and vary the finishing points.

10. Portion off the administration of events. Have a capable person responsible for the running off of each event.

11. Divide the field into different assembly places, so each playground will have a common meeting place to receive directions.

12. Have two or more information bureaus.

13. Have competent officials; starters, judges, scorer, announcer, custodian of prizes, and sideline officials.

14. Have all the equipment in readiness; whistles, measuring tape, stop-watches, megaphone, basketballs, volleyballs, softballs and bats, yarn for finish line, etc.

15. Before starting an event, announce the one to follow. Repeat instructions in different directions.

16. Secure names of all winners in various events; keep an accurate record of events on sheets attached to clip boards.

17. Have a time schedule. Run each event off as scheduled.

18. Have policemen on hand to help with traffic control.

19. Have photographers and press representatives on hand, invited for the occasion.

20. Have some of the events flexible so that they can be omitted if scheduled events are behind time.

21. Do not have long waits or hesitations as a crowd loses interest quickly.

22. Have a physician on call; a first-aid outfit on hand.

23. Adapt the program to the occasion; if a holiday, introduce appropriate ceremonies; if a picnic, introduce many novelties; if for educational demonstration for parents, limit the novelty events and give a wide scope of games and folk plays.

24. If swimming pools are handy insert a few water events into the program.
25. Have a meeting place of all the directors and officials.
26. Rehearse each one's part in putting on the program.
27. Do not leave anything to chance.
28. Use neighborhood leaders and prominent persons in official capacities.

DAY CAMP PROGRAM. The day camp program should be carefully coordinated with the playground schedule. The general practice of determining the order of camp attendance is either to take each week children from a neighborhood playground for a one-week camp session or to take a limited number of children from each of several neighborhood playgrounds for each day or each week. The number of children attending day camp varies, but a camp with seventy to eighty children may be considered a unit of operation. In some programs, children register and go to day camp for several weeks or the entire summer period. The size of the community and other factors determine which practice will be followed.

Playground programs should include demonstrations of outdoor recreation activities and fundamental skills in camping. These activities are important for every child to learn; also, many children develop an interest in the day camp program through orientation programs held on local park and playground areas. Parents should be encouraged to attend campfire programs and similar demonstration activities at the day camp location.

ACTIVITIES FOR ADULTS. During the summer months many adults in the community may participate in a number of different activities in a well-conducted recreation program. The services of adults may be enlisted to volunteer assistance in a number of ways, among them, coaching sports teams, instructing in music or dramatics, and helping with hobby clubs. Many adults enjoy this experience and find self-expression in teaching their skills and knowledges to others.

Adults also take part in various program activities as participants. For example, they organize and manage many of their own softball leagues, depending upon the local recreation department to provide adequate physical facilities and areas as well as the necessary administrative supervision. Softball leagues often include senior or young men's leagues, open competition for men, leagues for men over forty years of age, church leagues, co-recreation leagues, fraternal organization leagues, and industrial leagues. Special instruction for men and women in tennis, golf, swimming, and other recreation sports should be culminated by summer competitions with contestants seeded according to ability. Music festivals, special bands, informal choral groups, special classes in arts and crafts, summer drama groups and hobby clubs hold interest for many adults. Square dancing in an outdoor setting often attracts older people, especially when combined with picnic or similar informal occasions. Then adults also may participate in holiday celebrations and informal club groups.

Perhaps more important than these community recreation activities for adults are two family types of programs that have an important impact on our society.

Recreation In and Around the Home. The community recreation program should provide special services through the schools, public recreation departments, voluntary agencies, and other groups to enable people to develop their own resources for wholesome family recreation. Typical of this kind of service is the promotion of backyard playground contests, where the public recreation agency provides advice and data for building home play areas and where recognition is given to family groups that develop the most effective plans. Special bulletins for holiday activities, consultant services, and other program aids for the home encourage parents to develop the home as the primary play area. The importance of family recreation was discussed in more detail in Chapter 14.

Evening Recreation. The development of night-lighted recreation areas and facilities has made it possible to conduct many activities that enhance the total program. The entire family may attend a night-lighted play area and engage in activities as a family group. Many recreation departments are using Joseph Lee's original slogan, "the family that plays together stays together." With improvements in effective ways of lighting play areas, evening recreation programs are becoming increasingly attractive and popular.

FALL AND SPRING RECREATION PROGRAMS. During the fall and spring seasons, particularly in northern climates, interest is high in vigorous games and a number of activities singularly associated with these times of the year. In the fall, favorable weather and the beauty of the changing foliage attract participants; in the spring, the spectacle of nature awakening from the winter—flowers, birds, and colorful shrubbery—and people wishing to get outdoors again are all natural bases for special program features. Some of these are as follows:

Fall	*Spring*
Camping	Easter Egg Hunt
Fishing	Fishing
Football (spectator)	Gardening
Halloween Celebration	Jackstones
Hiking	Kite Flying
Hunting	Marbles
Single Wall Handball	Picnics
Soccer	Rope Skipping
Touch Football	Sports Clinics
Trap and Skeet Shooting	Spring Softball
Turkey Shoot	Track Meets

WINTER SEASON PROGRAM. The winter program varies widely according to particular climatic and other factors. Many communities operate playgrounds year-round and combine community center activities with outdoor activities as well. Generally, however, in winter there is (1) an outdoor program, and (2) a community center program.

In southern parts of the country outdoor activity is accelerated during the winter months; schools conduct many of their physical education, intramural, and even competitive sports programs outdoors either during daylight hours or on lighted areas. In northern climates, activities are geared to climatic conditions.

Ice skating is promoted on both outdoor rinks with ice made by flooding areas such as tennis courts or multiple-use play areas, and on permanent or portable outdoor rinks. Recent technical improvements have made outdoor artificial rinks operable and economically within the reach of many communities. Many of these areas are made so that tennis courts have the necessary pipes under them to freeze ice, and the area is within reach of the pool bath house which is used as a warming shelter during the ice skating season. Special program features include figure skating, hockey, ice skating carnivals, and general skating instruction.

Skiing is carried on by many communities, especially where the topography is favorable. Where the terrain is flat, ski slides are often built for special skiing competitions. Many northern communities have extensive winter sports carnivals which include skiing as well as other winter sports.

Tobogganing has become a popular winter sports activity. Toboggan slides are constructed in many public and private play areas.

Coasting is still popular with children and youth. Special hilly areas, sometimes including city streets, are blocked off; the activities are supervised by play leaders and the best facilities are provided to insure safe areas for this popular pastime.

Additional outdoor activities include hiking, school or day camping, hunting, ice fishing, curling, learning how to use a compass, and many others.

COMMUNITY CENTER ACTIVITIES

As pointed out in Chapter 16, the community center facilities include mainly those of the public school system used on a coordinated basis with the public recreation department or other agencies and groups.

On the other hand, with the expansion of public recreation as the years have gone by, more and more buildings have appeared as part of the facilities of the public recreation agencies. Some of these are limited in their services, while others are all-inclusive, with gymnasiums, pools, auditoriums, social halls, club meeting rooms, quiet game rooms, library, craft shops, and cooking facilities. As contrasted to the school as a play center, they are administered exclusively for recreation and community-center use and thus are usually more readily and constantly available for all such uses, both day and night. Moreover, recreation is the main and usually the full-time task of the leadership staff and is not a side issue.

Many classifications have been made of the great round of activities which is conducted in the community center. For the general purposes there are four categories: (1) games and sports, (2) social activities, (3) cultural activities and (4) civic activities.

GAMES AND SPORTS. Games and sports consist of the active physical exercises and games that are played in the gymnasium, swimming, bowling, if lanes are available, games of skill like pool and billiards, and mental contest games like checkers and cards. A suggestive list of games and sports activities follows:

Basketball	Newcomb
Captain basketball	Hand tennis
Gymnastics	Paddleball
Calisthenics	Table tennis
Apparatus	Shuffleboard
Swimming	Deck tennis
Endball	Dart-throwing
Badminton	Bowling
Relay races	Golf-driving
Active group games	Roller skating
Centerball	Rope jumping
Squash	Folk dancing
Handball	Pool
Codeball	Billiards
Boxing	Checkers
Wrestling	Dominoes
Tennis (indoor)	Chess
Softball	Cards
Volleyball	

SOCIAL ACTIVITIES. Everything partaking of the nature of comradeship and hospitality is considered a social activity. Social activities overlap the other divisions because they may have value of recreational, educational, and civic nature as well as purely social. The following list gives an idea of the more popular social features:

Motion pictures
Social dancing
Social dramatic activities
Social games
Folk dancing
Social music activities
Community celebrations
Holiday and special play celebrations

Boys' and girls' clubs
Adult clubs
Parties
Fun nights
Banquets
Bridge and other card clubs
Community sings

CULTURAL ACTIVITIES. The educational group also overlaps in the sense that it is possible for its activities to be recreational and social at the same time.

The following list suggests the type of activities that relate to the cultural group:

Dramatic
  Elementary dramatic expression:
    Dramatic games
    Pantomimes—simple character impersonations
    Drama tournaments
    Charades
    Dramatic stunts
  Storytelling and story acting
Musical
  Community singing
  Community choruses
  Community concerts
  Glee clubs
  Orchestras and bands
  Musical competition—vocal and instrumental
  Music festivals
  Toy symphonies
  Ukulele playing
  Harmonica playing

Easter music
Christmas music
Community opera
Music memory contests
Music weeks
Oratorios
Community drama:
  One-act and full length plays
  Shows and skits
  Play making
  Pageantry
  Religious drama
  Educational plays:
    Safety—Health—Thrift
    Historical—Mythological
Creative and Constructive
  Sand box play
  Arts and crafts
  Paper work
  Sewing, knitting, etc.
  Cooking

Art	Linguistic
Community art exhibits	Reading
Painting	Debating
Sketching	Forums
Plastic art	Public speaking
Photography	Lectures

CIVIC ACTIVITIES. The civic group includes all activities of a civic, social, or patriotic nature. The following list suggests a few of the possibilities:

> Public forums
> Lectures on current topics
> Historical pageants
> Dramatic activities
> Holiday celebrations
> Language classes
> Industrial and civic inspection trips
> Civic improvement societies
> Service to community
> Welfare campaigns
> Parent-teacher associations.

When combined, the programs of the playground, athletic field, and community center building make an attractive offering.

SPECIAL OPERATIONAL PROCEDURES

Specific mention should also be made of two important operations fundamental to the conduct of the year-round play and recreation program. These procedures are (1) the classification of participants, and (2) honor point systems and awards.

CLASSIFICATION OF PARTICIPANTS. In order to divide boys and girls so that the competition is on a fair basis, also to give a chance for more participants to take part, some form of classification is necessary. Reference is made to the principles stated in Chapters 8 and 9 in which the forms of play, as well as the influence of age and sex upon play, are discussed in detail.

Although there are many systems of grouping participants, no uniform classification system prevails. Methods that may be chosen include (1) grade in school, (2) age, (3) sex, (4) height, (5) weight, (6) some combination of factors such as age and height, age and weight, weight and height, or age, weight and height, and (7) skill. The classification system best suited for a situation varies with the age and sex of the participants and with the type of activity involved.

In public schools, classification by sex and by grade level is by far the most common and the most practical. In public recreation programs and similar out-of-school operations, sex and age are the two most common factors used. Age is the most practical, since school age records are available. The age factor is also effective in equalizing competition despite individual differences. In some schools weight is used as a basic classification since it is rather easily administered; height alone is the least satisfactory of all methods used. Skill is an important factor, and the combination of age, sex, and skill, coupled with the sound judgment of qualified personnel to take care of the unusual situations, is a very satisfactory method of classification. Skill is undoubtedly the most effective way of classifying adults.

The age, height, and weight combination has been used effectively by some leaders for many years; but the fact that the participants must be checked periodically introduces time-consuming administrative detail and makes the method more difficult to use in practical operations. When groupings are made on the basis of the three measurements of age, weight, and height, the player is usually placed in the group into which two of his measurements place him.

Weight is very effectively used in classifying participants for combative sports such as touch football, wrestling, and boxing where weight is a major advantage to the participant. Also, further classification in weight categories might include a novice or inexperienced class, and an open class for experienced participants. Weight may also be used for the general classification of players in other types of games, sports, and recreation activities. A good weight classification follows. Some of the following divisions can be omitted in case the group is a small one; for instance, two groups,

Juniors and Seniors, could be used with the dividing point at 115 lbs.

Midgets	Under	80 lbs.
Juniors	"	95 "
Intermediates	"	115 "
Lightweight Seniors	"	135 "
Heavyweight Seniors	Unlimited	

The following two age classifications, with some slight variations, are used by many public recreation departments:

Boys or Girls		Boys or Girls	
Tot Lot	4– 7	Tot Lot	4– 6
Midgets	8–11	Midgets	7– 9
Juniors	12–14	Junior	10–12
Intermediate	15–17	Intermediate	13–15
Senior	18–21	Senior	16–18
Adult	over 21	Adult	over 18

Adult classifications, other than skill, are often employed to equalize competition in sports or to bring people of the same age group together. Often men have sports leagues called by such names as "Over Forty League," or "Old Timers." Suggested age classifications for adult groups may include the following:

18–21	Seniors (eligible for adult activities)
18–25	Young Adults (single)
18–35	Young Adults (married)
36–50	Young Middle-aged adults
51–65	Older Middle-aged adults
over 65	Oldsters: Senior Citizens; Golden Age Group

Regardless of the classification system used, the importance of inspired, trained leadership cannot be overemphasized. Through study and research in practical situations, classification for participation is being refined; it is being used more logically to insure safety and to develop and sustain interests in activities through best meeting the needs of participants in each particular instance.

POINT SYSTEMS AND AWARDS. The honor point system was introduced into a large number of playground and school systems several years ago, and various schemes have been devised for awarding points for participation and achievement in all types of activities on the playground, both physical and non-physical. Some of these systems are simple, being based on a few activities and a limited number of points, whereas others are elaborate, necessitating considerable record keeping. Some are restricted to the individual boy or girl, whereas others involve group participation or achievement.

There is not a complete agreement among recreational authorities as to the desirability of point systems. Those who favor such a system feel that its use is desirable for the following reasons:

1. It stimulates interest in new activities, introducing or exposing children to activities which they might not otherwise engage in and which may become a real and enduring interest in their lives. While they may engage in the activity at first merely for the award or recognition, their motive may shift to an interest in the activity itself.
2. It adds zest to old activities.
3. It encourages practice for proficiency in activities when children are away from the leaders.
4. It encourages greater participation and more regular attendance.
5. Leaders of average ability who must deal with large numbers can arouse interest and produce results more effectively with such a system than without.
6. It leads to a wider, more varied, and more careful thought-out program.
7. It sets standards for achievement and makes possible a measure of individual and group progress.
8. If properly worked out, it gives an opportunity to everyone, even the physically handicapped child, to excel and gain recognition and respect.
9. The desire for recognition is universal. All worthy effort should bring recognition to the participant.

The authorities opposed to the use of honor systems and awards advance the following arguments against them:

1. Play should be for play's sake; an activity should be carried on because of interest in it, because of the joy of participation.
2. Honors and awards set false goals and encourage children to be more interested in the award than the activity.
3. Honor systems are after all a form of compulsion. Programs should be built on interest, not force.
4. Children are forced into activities before they are ready for them. When they are ready, they can be relied upon to participate of their own free will.
5. There is no assurance that interest in the award will shift to interest in the activity. Awards may, and frequently do, develop a dislike on the part of the child for an activity into which he is forced before he is ready.
6. The system often places a premium upon native capacity and causes unhappiness among many who cannot achieve so readily.
7. Good leaders do not need to depend upon honors and awards—they can achieve full participation without them.
8. The system is expensive in time, effort, and money.

If honors are to be used, it is important that they be inexpensive. Ribbons of different colors for first, second, and third places, and celluloid lapel buttons containing a picture of the activity, are among the types sometimes used on playgrounds. Pennants and cups are traditional types of trophies for teams.

There are no uniform honor point systems in use in the playground and school systems of the country today. Various systems have been worked out by different recreation organizations and physical education departments. Some of these offer points for participation only; some for both participation and achievement; some include additional points for sportsmanship; and others, used particularly by schools, emphasize in addition health, leadership, and scholarship. In addition to the individual point systems many organizations use group point systems.

A plan which ties up an individual point system with a group point system is shown in the following table. In the team games, each member of the team is awarded the same number of points that the team is given. The points are awarded as follows: A member of the championship baseball team gets 10 points; second team, 6 points; third team, 4 points; and thereafter 2 points for participation. In the case of interplayground meets like swimming or track, a boy winning a first place would be awarded 10 points; and similarly on down to the 2 points given for participation. The inclusion of points for attendance and sportsmanship is optional with the individual director.

BOYS		GIRLS	
Sports	*Points*	*Sports*	*Points*
	1–2–3–P*		1–2–3–P*
Baseball	10–6–4–2	Swimming	10–6–4–2
Volleyball	10 "	Achievement Test ..	10 "
Swimming	10 "	Tennis	10 "
Achievement Test ..	10 "	Track	10 "
Tennis	10 "	Baseball	10 "
Track	10 "	Basketball or Group	
Basketball	10 "	Game	10 "
Badminton	5–3–2–1	Newcomb	10 "
Quoits	5 "	Novelty Relay	10 "
Target Throw	5 "	Badminton	5–3–2–1
Novelty Events	5 "	Target Throw	5–3–2–1
Attendance and		Attendance and	
Sportsmanship ...	10–6–4–2	Sportsmanship ...	10–6–4–2
Possible Total	100 points	Possible Total	100 points

* 1—1st place; 2—2nd place; 3—3rd place; P—participation.

The above scoring plan is based on athletic achievement, but the idea can be carried over to include other forms of play participation. Numerous suggestions for such inclusion are found in the list of special events given earlier in this chapter.

SPECIAL RECREATION PROGRAMS

In recent years, several special situations have developed as a direct result of changes in today's way of living. Some of the needs of individuals and groups affected by these conditions have been met by conducting recreation programs

specifically designed for the people involved. Mention is
made here of only a few of these special program operations.

RECREATION FOR OLDER ADULTS.   In 1940, there were only
nine million people in this country over sixty-five years of
age; in 1954 this number had grown to thirteen million, and
now it is estimated that there are more than fifteen million
aged persons in the United States.   These people are mostly
retired and with Social Security and pensions meeting their
major economic needs have a great deal of leisure time.   Yet
many of these adults are left without relatives or friends,
live alone, know very few people, and have little of the incentive to live previously supplied by work and family responsibilities.

Recreation programs can be of great help to older adults.
Thereby they can become a part of a group and find normal
companionship with persons of their own age.   Older adults
can find methods of self-expression through selected recreation activities and gain additional satisfaction by rendering
valuable services to the community.

Many communities of the nation have developed
municipal recreation programs for older adults.   Following
the research information on the subject provided by such
pioneer groups as the University of Michigan Division of
Gerontology, the North Carolina Recreation Commission,
and the California Recreation Commission, recreation programs for the aged have been well developed in Chicago,
Milwaukee, Dallas, San Francisco and many other communities, large and small, throughout the United States.   These
programs have been organized by the municipal recreation
departments with facilities and specially qualified leadership.   In some communities where the public agency has
not existed, voluntary agencies or private groups have taken
the leadership in promoting programs for older adults.

The recreation program for older adults centers mainly
around club organization.   These clubs have taken various
names such as The Golden Age Club, Senior Citizens, and
Golden Circle.   Typical activities of these clubs include
drop-in-hour, arts and crafts, coffee hour, cards and table

games, television hour, birthday parties, cooking demonstrations, personal counseling, and square dances.

Finally, it is important that the entire community realize its responsibility in developing a program for older adults. Through the local Council of Social Agencies or other coordinating agencies, not only the needs of the healthy aged person should be met but also those of the home-bound and shut-in as well.

RECREATION IN HOUSING DEVELOPMENTS. Since 1946, many large private as well as federal housing developments have been built throughout the country. These special housing areas have a high density of population without the crowded conditions of the tenement areas and have people with different social, cultural, and racial backgrounds who do not know each other. Special programs and conveniently located facilities are needed in these housing areas. The programs should be planned to meet peak-load needs at times when most people have their leisure time. This means special scheduling and providing a diversified educational program to interest the people in getting better acquainted and eventually organizing their own informal recreation activities.

RECREATION IN THE ARMED FORCES. Previous to 1942, recreation services for members of the Armed Forces were supplied through informal activities at military installations and by civic organizations such as the United Service Organizations. Control of recreation services was decentralized and relatively unorganized, professional leadership was limited, and physical facilities for recreation at military installations were inadequate. After the outbreak of World War II, the need for recreation services on a more organized basis became immediately evident; it was obvious that the provision of such services would require a large number of trained leaders in this country and throughout the world.

By 1943, the recreation program had become a functional responsibility of the components of the Armed Forces, Army, Navy, Marines, and later the Air Force, and each of these groups developed a definite recreation program to meet the needs of the military personnel under its command.

The Special Services branch was designated to carry out the recreation program in all components except the Navy, which has organized this service under Welfare and Recreation. Army Special Services is responsible for planning and conducting the recreation program and related activities, including library services, wherever Army personnel is stationed. The recreation program is planned and carried out by officers and men specially trained in recreation, assisted by highly trained civilian recreation specialists wherever necessary. This same general plan is followed in all Armed Forces units, each plan differing within the various components as organizational and specific needs differ. Many Armed Forces installations in this country and overseas have adequate recreation facilities including Service Clubs (social center clubs), movie theatres, arts and crafts shops, music rooms, libraries, gymnasiums, outdoor sports fields, golf courses, swimming pools, and other types of recreation facilities usually found in a community.

The recreation program in the Armed Forces varies with the needs of the personnel. The program has special features such as social recreation in the Service Clubs, tours and trips, professional entertainment, and activities arranged to meet specific needs of units stationed in unusual places. Otherwise, there is a complete program of sports and athletics, arts and crafts, dramatics, music, social recreation, and other activities organized around the military work-day and the resources within the camp and the surrounding community.

Similar to the recreation services of the community, the Armed Forces recreation program has required special direction and is effectively serving millions of America's Service personnel throughout the world.

RECREATION FOR THE HANDICAPPED. The rapid development of recreation therapy in hospitals and other institutions was discussed in Chapter 14. Reference here is made specifically to community recreation services to individuals who are not institutionalized. These people include older adults who are bedridden or unable to move about easily; persons who are temporarily incapacitated by the many automobile, industrial, and other accidents; and many children who are physically or otherwise handicapped and unable to participate in the general recreation activities of neighborhood play groups.

Many schools have instituted programs of exercise therapy or corrective exercises in physical education. Also, there is a trend toward public recreation departments providing special services for the handicapped. These include playground programs with selected equipment and specially trained leaders, programs for the orthopedically handicapped, day camp programs for handicapped children, programs for handicapped adults, and parties and entertainment programs for shut-ins.

In many cases the schools and public recreation agencies are taking the lead in organizing these activities, and various community organizations such as the service clubs, fraternal organizations, and other groups provide funds and personnel to carry out the program. The need for this type of recreation therapy program is growing.

SUMMARY

In this chapter the technical aspects of organizing play and recreation are outlined. This coverage includes a brief description of the general principles of programming. Samples of year-round, seasonal, weekly, and daily schedules are included, along with practical ideas for carrying them out successfully. Special events also are an important part of the play administrator's responsibility; so, too, are especially adapted programs for adult groups, handicapped individuals, and the military services.

One important aspect of organizing procedures is the classification of play and recreation activities. This occurs prior to the actual work of scheduling. During the conduct of recreation programs another type of classification is

needed, that of classifying participants so as to equalize
their chances for successful performance. Following the
conclusion of play programs there is the necessity for adopting policies on honors and awards. These matters, prior,
during, and following the conduct of play activities, are
essential to the successful organization of play and recreation
programs, whatever the nature of them may be and whatever the nature of the participating groups may be.

People in the United States are a mixture of individuals
from many national groups and different cultural backgrounds. This, coupled with the pioneer life of early
America and the freedom of the people to express themselves, has resulted in the development of many diverse
forms of play and recreation. Some of these activities are
a direct carry-over from other cultures; others are indigenous and reflect the changing social conditions which have
paralleled the economic and political development of the
United States.

The purpose of this chapter is to point out the many
different types of play and recreation activities and how
they are organized by groups and individuals within the
community. These activities are carried on in schools,
public recreation agencies, churches, and private or voluntary agencies, as well as in the home and other informal
settings in the community. Those who wish to study
further the nature of play forms and the total program of
activities should review the material already cited in
previous Chapters and also consult their Selected Reference
Lists.

The leisure-time activities referred to above are not
carried on without careful organization and supervision.
The objective is not to limit or restrict the individual's play
interests or habits but rather to allow him the widest possible choice and freedom in selecting wholesome leisure-
time activities. Consequently, the types of play programs
and their organization in the schools assure children a
broad orientation in play and sports in physical education
classes. Additional individual experiences are provided

in school intramural and interscholastic sports. Also, school subjects such as dramatics, art, and music, as well as the many extracurricular club and informal activities, help young people to develop wholesome life-long, leisure-time interests. The public recreation agencies in their capacity must develop programs to service the greatest number of persons and yet give reasonable attention to the desires of each individual. Furthermore, the conduct of play and recreation activities by all community groups should be coordinated to provide the most adequate total community recreation program.

It is very obvious that the summer community recreation program involves many people and a variety of activities. There is a sharp increase in play activities when schools close for the summer and children and youth have a considerable amount of leisure time. Many adults vacation from work during the summer, daylight saving time makes the day for play longer, and favorable weather usually results in a greatly accelerated recreation program. It must be pointed out that the summer play program is an intensified playground program; also that it is not exclusively for children of elementary school age. Furthermore, playground and community play programs should not consist only of sports and athletic activities but should include a broad, balanced program designed to best meet the needs and interests of individuals of all ages and both sexes. At the same time there should be provision for wholesome group and family activities that make the community a better place in which to live.

Finally, it should be pointed out that the organization of play and recreation involves more than the conduct of aimless activities to keep young people off the streets or to occupy somehow the leisure time of children and adults. Planned and carefully worked out schedules of activities are needed today to foster leisure-time education and the recreational life of the nation. They must be inspiring and meet the interests of people; if they do not, individuals possibly will turn to pastimes that are antisocial. Play and recreation activities should be organized to allow for equality of opportunity and to provide an environment which encourages the development of good health, leadership qualities, self-confidence, desirable competitive as well as cooperative experiences, self-expression, and actual practice of the principles of living in a democratic society. The orderly and effective conduct of play and recreation activities does not just happen; these activities are planned and directed by qualified personnel and, at the same time, they reflect the best in our culture and the wishes and desires of the people.

SELECTED REFERENCES

The following three publications include basic material for planning and operating recreation programs:

Athletic Institute. *The Recreation Program.* Chicago: Athletic Institute, 1954.

BUTLER, GEORGE D. *Introduction to Community Recreation.* New York: McGraw-Hill Book Co., Inc., 1959. Parts IV, V, & VI.

MEYER, HAROLD D., and BRIGHTBILL, CHARLES K. *Recreation Administration: A Guide to Its Practices.* Englewood Cliffs, N.J.: Prentice-Hall, Inc., 1956. Part V.

BORST, EVELYNE, and MITCHELL, ELMER D. *Social Games for Recreation.* 2d ed. New York: The Ronald Press Co., 1959.

BOYDEN, E. DOUGLAS, and BURTON, ROGER G. *Staging Successful Tournaments.* New York: Association Press, 1957.

BUTLER, GEORGE D. *Playgrounds: Their Administration and Operation.* 3d ed. New York: The Ronald Press Co., 1960.

Community Project for the Aged of the Welfare Council of Metropolitan Chicago. *Community Services For Older People.* Chicago: Wilcox and Follett Company, 1952.

COX, DORIS, and WARREN, BARBARA. *Creative Hands: An Introduction to Craft Techniques.* New York: John Wiley and Sons, Inc., 1951.

DONNELLY, RICHARD J., HELMS, WILLIAM G., and MITCHELL, ELMER D. *Active Games and Contests.* 2d ed. New York: The Ronald Press Co., 1958.

HINDMAN, DARWIN A. *Complete Book of Games and Stunts.* Englewood Cliffs, N.J.: Prentice-Hall, Inc., 1956.

KRAUS, RICHARD. *Play Activities for Boys and Girls, Six Through Twelve.* New York: McGraw-Hill Book Co., Inc., 1957.

————. *Square Dances of Today, How to Teach and Call Them.* New York: The Ronald Press Co., 1950.

LEONARD, CHARLES. *Recreation Through Music.* New York: The Ronald Press Co., 1952.

National Recreation Association. *The Playground Summer Notebook.* New York: National Recreation Association. Issued annually.

NEILSON, N. P., and VAN HAGAN, WINIFRED. *Physical Education for the Elementary Schools.* 2d ed. New York: The Ronald Press Co., 1956.

SIKS, GERALDINE B. *Creative Dramatics, An Art for Children.* New York: Harper and Bros., 1958.

Public Health Service, U. S. Department of Health, Education, and Welfare, *Looking Forward in Later Years.* Washington, D.C.: Superintendent of Documents, 1955.

VINAL, WILLIAM G. *Nature Recreation.* Boston: American Humane Education Association, 1954.

21

Leadership in Recreation

The recreation leader is a creature of the twentieth century. In the early years of the play movement it was considered quite absurd to engage a person solely for the purpose of directing play. It was enough to supply the space for play and a limited amount of apparatus and play materials—the children could then take care of themselves. Even the things in the way of equipment were considered more of a luxury than a necessity. But the playgrounds came, and the play leaders have followed.

At first many parents who were quite in sympathy with the idea of providing play spaces for the congested districts in the cities still maintained that "play cannot be taught." Having seen and experienced only the forms of play used by the isolated country child, they could comprehend no other kind that would be of value and they stood out for the old-fashioned free play. Their thought was that the children should play together of their own accord and that older people should not interfere with them. Quite naturally, then, many critics were disturbed at the mere thought of paying teachers to "play" with children.

This attitude toward play leadership has changed through the years; private and public groups have established organized programs employing trained leaders. This chapter deals with an analysis of early attitudes toward play leadership, the nature of play leadership, the role of the modern play leader, the qualifications for play leadership, and professional leadership education programs designed to prepare qualified play and recreation leaders.

NEED FOR PLAYGROUND SUPERVISION

Because of this general opinion that free, untaught play was desirable, many cities in their earlier experiences put all available funds into land and equipment and opened playgrounds without supervision. The seriousness of this mistake became immediately apparent and with such an impact as to threaten to defeat the purpose of the whole project.

Children will play, with or without guidance. It does not take the presence of a trained adult to engender the play spirit—it is there to begin with, and it will find expression regardless. The impulse is natural but, as the founders of the playground movement found, the forms of play are not natural—they must be learned. Play in itself is a natural drive but the forms are good or bad. The boys who throw stones at windows and street lights are following the same impulse as those who throw darts at a target or balls to a catcher. Just as much misdirected play can take place on a playground as in an alley; the mere shifting of the scene does not mean that all rowdyism and antisocial conduct will be left in the alley. Experience in the early playground days proved this point conclusively.

To assume that play will take place without leadership is to misunderstand both the nature of play and of people. Whenever a game starts, someone must assert leadership, and someone always does. This is to say that if there is no adult leader, a self-appointed leader will take over from among the more aggressive of the players. Unfortunately, an aggressive disposition is not always associated with good judgment and with social purpose.

All this is said by way of explanation of the results that followed the opening of playgrounds without supervision: (1) the equipment was destroyed or damaged through improper use, theft, and vandalism; (2) leadership of the bullying type often held sway, with the resultant lack of protection for the weaker and less aggressive; (3) and monopolization of the equipment and apparatus was exerted by the more assertive individuals.

Conditions such as have been describe became so extreme in the first decade of the century that the whole play movement was temporarily placed in disrepute, and property-holders objected strenuously to having playgrounds established in their neighborhoods. The Playground and Recreation Association of America (now called the National Recreation Association), recognizing the setback that was likely if things were allowed to continue, was obliged to issue through its field secretaries and institute workers the following warning: "Equip no more playgrounds until you have provided adequate supervision for all you now have."

Neither was the expedient, utilized by many municipalities, of hiring cheap help in the way of a caretaker or monitor, who was to watch the apparatus and keep order on the grounds, much more successful. The unruly element, finding their activities curbed and nothing else offered in place of them, went back to their old haunts in the streets and alleys. The playgrounds simply became vacant lots, holding little attraction and unpatronized except for the smaller children who came to use the swings and teeters, and for an occasional group of larger children who came to play a scrub game of ball.

Experience has shown conclusively that the effective operation of a modern public park and recreation system requires both adequate areas and facilities and dedicated, professionally trained and experienced leaders. The recreation plan is part of the city or regional master play. The careful selection and design of sites and the coordinated development of parks, schools, and other public recreation properties enhance property values and allow maximum use of the tax dollar spent for these purposes; furthermore, such a plan also makes provision for professional recreation personnel to insure proper maintenance and operation of facilities and employment of leadership personnel to carry on the activities and services provided through an adequate public recreation program. All this evidence has been pointed out by leaders in city planning, sociology, and other related disciplines. Also, this fact is portrayed vividly in the color and sound film "Playtown U.S.A.," and in the Athletic Institute's films depicting community recreation— "Leaders For Leisure" and "Town and Country."

NATURE OF LEADERSHIP

When one recognizes that an individual has unquestioned influence over large numbers of people, the thought comes to mind, "Why is this person a leader? Why do others accept him as a leader?" Essentially, two attributes belong to the nature of leadership.

The first attribute of leadership is a significant personality. This does not mean that to function as a leader a man must have a striking personal appearance, that he must be the type to walk into a crowded room and make everyone aware of his presence by sheer dominance of his personality. This quality may help and may make his task easier, but is by no means vital; many great leaders have not possessed it. What is meant by a significant personality is that the person represents something that people want. A person is regarded of value over others as he symbolizes what they want, and as he gives promise of realizing these wants for them.

The leader, then, is a symbol who represents in his life the hopes and aspirations, the needs of people. He is symbolic of the ideals of his followers, but he is in advance of them—he carries the torch—the light to help them see where their path directs. To the extent that he does this, he is effective as a leader, that is, is effective in controlling or affecting the lives of others; and as he ceases to be a symbol of what people want, his leadership diminishes. A boy with athletic ambitions sees in his coach a symbol of the life he hopes to achieve, of the kind of person he hopes to be, with the result that an ardent sympathy and adulation go out to the coach, and the boy's life is deeply affected by the kind of a model he is.

The second attribute of a leader is a sympathetic understanding of the people whom he is leading. The first attribute relates to his personal qualities which give him prestige in the minds of people, that cause people to move toward him; this second involves his understanding of the people which permits him to draw them to him. The people must come to feel that he is one of them and understands their hopes and aspirations, their frailties and inadequacies, and that he is in fullest sympathy with them and their lot. An example is well given in Abraham Lincoln. He seemed to understand his people so well that they in turn, feeling understood, possessed full confidence that he would not go contrary to their interests.

Translated into terms of play leadership, the leader in his personal equipment of training, information, and skills must represent something all his followers want—the athletes, the nature lovers, the craft enthusiasts, the music and dramatics devotees—for he will function as a leader to all these types only as he symbolizes their interests. He also must have a sympathetic understanding of all with whom he is expected to deal, regardless of age and type, and the people must come to sense this sympathy and this understanding of them.

Leadership is often imposed, coming to a person because of the kind of person he is, because, better than others in the group, he symbolizes their wants. At the other extreme, some people are very desirous of becoming leaders and try too overtly and directly to acquire and maintain such a position. The result of direct striving is that the person often condemns himself to second-rate leadership—because in his zeal to please, he hesitates to disturb any existing situation that is in need of change and that would bring him into disfavor with powerful interests.

Even though a leader is fully accepted as such and is ardently admired by his followers, he must not expect to be free from criticism by them, or even from open hostility, on occasion. The very fact of his position invites criticism.

Whenever he falls short of the ideal in which he is held, his followers are quick to subject him to criticism, quick to display antagonism toward him. This mixture of admiration and indorsement on the one hand and criticism and hostility on the other is the paradox of the leader's position. Failure to understand this hostility as a typical human reaction and to react properly to it has been the undoing of many an otherwise capable leader. For to meet hostility with hostility is to destroy one's leadership.

Conversely, to meet criticism gracefully is a basic essential of leadership. The wise leader thereby relieves his critics of their feelings of hostility and establishes a stronger tie than ever with them.

It becomes apparent from this discussion that the recreation leader not only needs to know the technical material of his chosen field but also must have an intimate understanding of human nature as well. Leadership is a job in human manipulation, and the more one knows of the workings of the human mind, the better equipped he is.

ROLE OF THE LEADER

That the success of a playground is dependent on the quality of its leadership has been proven conclusively by the attendance histories of playgrounds. The various areas wherein the play leader demonstrates the importance of his services fall under several headings.

CONTROL. The qualified recreation leader brings order out of chaos, not by force or suppression, not by rules, regulations, and penalties; he does it by getting people to move in the direction of their interests and by lending his services to the fullest satisfaction of these interests, by keeping people happily occupied in activities of their choice, and by developing an atmosphere of mutual confidence through constant cooperation in a joyous setting. People cooperate when they come to realize their own interests are best served by keeping their conduct in line with the leader's wishes.

ORGANIZATION. The qualified leader arranges the time and place for various kinds of play in a systematic way. This has several important advantages. In play, proper use is made of the apparatus; many more can play at the same time in a given space without interfering with each other, thereby making the best possible use of the space; and those seeking recreation can be sure of finding their favorite form of play going on at a regular hour. The systematic handling of equipment insures that it is in good order, ample in quantity, and at the proper place at the time it is needed.

The trained leader not only organizes his space to best advantage but classifies those desiring to play so that large numbers of teams can be organized instead of just one composed of the best performers; he also organizes them in such a way that many activities can operate at the same time. Moreover, he organizes more experienced or older players into leaders to assist him in supervision and officiating. He knows how to organize round-robin leagues and elimination tournaments.

PROGRAM. The qualified leader offers a basic program of such a wide variety of activities that no two days are exactly alike. He brings to the patrons of the playground a vastly wider variety of activities than they could ever know if left to themselves. Through change and variety he keeps his program fresh, challenging, and constantly growing. He does this not only in the area of games and contests, but also in the areas of dramatics, storytelling, music, crafts, and nature. In addition to this basic program, he brings in special and major events of interest to the whole neighborhood at frequent intervals.

The qualified leader realizes that the basic program he establishes, while designed to satisfy the largest number, will not meet the needs of all; he knows that individual differences are many in number and so diversified that no basic program could include them all. He seeks to locate the interests of those who do not participate, to preserve the initiative of those who have set purposes they are pursuing, and to give opportunity to those who seek to direct their own play. He senses the danger of oversupervision and domination. He realizes that his own program is an adult-conceived one which, although resulting from his training based on knowledge of, and long experience with, children's interests, may not fit all groups or individuals.

INSTRUCTION AND GUIDANCE. The qualified leader realizes that only with the acquisition of skill can a sport or activity be enjoyed fully. Skill is a prerequisite for a sport to function as play, for only then comes the sense of achievement and success which is an essential element of play. He regards the developing of skill (which is commonly called coaching) as a major phase of his job. He is cognizant of the need not only to develop skills in activities that will bring joy at the moment, but in activities which will carry on throughout the years of adulthood.

Although most recreation authorities hold that social learnings take a secondary place to the play leader's major task of providing as happy a childhood as possible through play, the qualified leader never forgets that play activity is a means to developing the man or woman and that all that occurs on the playground contributes to such learnings. In the teaching of skills and in leading play, he does not forget that concomitant social learnings, either good or bad, are actually being acquired; and he strives to see that they are good. He seizes the rare opportunity for guidance of individuals when the need is indicated.

SPIRIT OF PLAY. The qualified leader sees beyond the confines of his playground and regards the horizon of the neighborhood as the boundary line of his working ground. He lends his support to all worthy neighborhood projects, gives responsible leadership to all neighborhood projects that have recreation value, and seeks the support for his work of all agencies and individuals in the neighborhood.

The qualified leader realizes that much of his success in providing happiness through play will depend on his reflecting the spirit of play in his own personality. He realizes that as he goes, so goes his following. He knows that a buoyant spirit on his part engenders enthusiasm in others. He knows that if he reflects too much concern over the accomplishment of his serious adult objectives, his playground may become staid and adultlike. He reflects in his own mood whatever the spirit or mood or emotional tone of the activity he is conducting, with the full knowledge that others will join him in it. But above all he realizes he is selling the youthful spirit. Youthfulness in spirit does not depend on mere age alone—a person is young enough for play leadership just so long as he or she is dynamic and full of life, and radiates this same contagious spirit.

RECREATION POSITIONS AND QUALIFICATIONS

Technical knowledge of his field of specialization is expected of the play and recreation leader, but this is not enough to qualify him or to give promise of success. In few, if any other, fields of effort are personal qualifications more important. From the city executive down to the local play leader, the commodity with which the recreation worker deals is human relationships. This makes of it one of the most difficult fields in which to work; unless one is especially qualified for dealing in human relationships, one would do well to look to fields other than recreation leadership as a life-time profession.

As one moves from the community recreation executive on down through the supervisors to the local play leaders on the playgrounds, one finds the same breadth of outlook and the same capacity for human relationships needed in greater or lesser degree. In each case, mastery of technical material is assumed; what is more pertinent is how well can the play leader organize and how successfully can he lead people. Does the recreation leader have a desire to serve, can he lead democratically, is he friendly and sociable, does he possess a sense of humor, does he share an interest in the many-sided phases of the recreation program, does he radiate energy and enthusiasm, does he have organizing ability? If the aspiring leader's qualities be affirmative then the attributes of success are present.

Types of Leadership Positions.   As the scope of the play movement broadened, no uniform terminology developed concurrently to describe the various types of work done by professional recreation and park workers. At first the professional service was mainly that of front-line teaching and leadership work in conducting playground and community center activities. But as the movement grew, it was soon evident that there was need for personnel with special professional education to plan, administer, and conduct public recreation and park programs. In 1929, the National Recreation Association studied the problems of personnel standards for recreation workers; its first report in 1930, followed by subsequent reports in 1935, 1938, 1948, and, most recently, 1957, have been basic guides to the development of personnel standards for recreation workers throughout the nation.

Meanwhile, the California Committee on Recreation Personnel, through the State Recreation Commission, published a report in which fifty-seven different recreation position titles and job specifications were described. Recommendations were made relating to the employment of recreation personnel by public agencies, institutions and hospitals, industry, and commercial enterprises. In 1952 the National Advisory Committee on Recruitment, Training, and Placement of Recreation Personnel was created to advise and work with the National Recreation Association. In 1956 this committee undertook a special study of personnel standards and procedures; it profited from previous personnel studies by association groups, by state groups in California and elsewhere, and from field practices in other parts of the country.

Many changes have taken place in the terminologies used to describe recreation and park positions.[1]   Now, the term "Recreation Director" refers to the head of a municipal recreation department. The titles "Executive" or "Admin-

[1] National Advisory Committee on Recruitment, Training, and Placement of Recreation Personnel, *Personnel Standards in Community Recreation Leadership* (New York: National Recreation Association, 1957).

istrator" describe the professional leader who is head of a recreation or park department. The "General Manager" is frequently applied to the head of a park system or a combined park and recreation system, although "Superintendent" is more widely used. "Supervisor" indicates a worker who oversees and exercises more general guidance over a large part of a total municipal recreation system; "Director" denotes individuals who personally and immediately control and guide the conduct of activities by other workers. "Leader" is a generic term for all who practice the profession of recreation; at the same time, it specifically indicates the front-line worker who meets face-to-face with participants in the conduct of recreation activities. The terms "Recreationist" and "Recreator" are also generic terms, employed somewhat like educator is in the field education. The following are the major leadership positions as recommended by the National Advisory Committee:

I Executive
 1. Superintendent of Recreation
 2. Superintendent of Parks and Recreation
 3. Assistant Superintendent
II Supervisor
 1. Recreation Supervisor (General)
 2. Recreation Supervisor (Special Activity)
III Center Director
 1. Recreation Center Director
 2. Assistant Recreation Center Director
IV Leader
 1. Recreation Leader (General)
 2. Recreation Leader (Special Activity)
V Trainee
 1. Recreation Intern
 2. Student Recreation Leader
 3. Junior Recreation Assistant [2]

In smaller cities, some of these leadership positions may not be necessary. The superintendent of recreation administrating through a one-man department in a small community will have different duties from an executive with

[2] *Ibid.*

the same title who administers a program for a community of fifty thousand. In turn, the superintendent of recreation for a large metropolitan city of several million persons has still a different administrative operation, delegating many duties to the assisting staff members. One of the qualifications of all the major positions (except student recreation leader and junior recreation assistant who are trainees), is a college degree, if not in recreation then a related field with adequate recreation work experience.

JOB ANALYSES AND QUALIFICATIONS. The following is a brief summary of the job analyses and qualifications of the various positions in recreation.[3] Park administrators and park technical personnel are not considered in this discourse, except in the case of one, the Superintendent of Parks and Recreation.

Superintendent of Recreation. The superintendent of recreation is the general administrative head. His duties are analogous to the superintendent of schools. These duties include the planning for recreation facilities for the city, both immediate and long-range, the construction of facilities, the planning of the program, the choice of activities, the setting of standards, the selection of staff, and the training and supervision of all workers. The superintendent supervises the work of the recreation department in accordance with the general policies established by the recreation board or other local authority.

Minimum qualifications for this position include graduation from a college or university of recognized standing with a Bachelor's degree in recreation leadership, including supervised recreation field work. Further recommended qualifications include completion of the Master's degree in recreation or a closely related field such as public administration; graduate study should include courses in recreation administration, personnel management, city planning, research techniques, and the theory and philosophy of recreation. From two to five years of progressive, successful

[3] *Ibid.*

experience in a supervisory or executive position is recommended as prerequisite to assuming the responsibilities of a superintendency.

The Superintendent of Recreation must be a competent executive and a versatile individual with a broad social outlook, thoroughly familiar with the social needs of his community. He should be an aggressive and enthusiastic promoter of recreation, capable of stimulating the imagination of the community and arousing its enthusiasm for the advancement of his programs. He should be a good organizer and an aggressive publicist. As an administrator he should be familiar with business management and capable of efficiently handling budgets and finances, and should be able to supervise his staff of paid workers and volunteers. He should possess a technical knowledge of a wide range of recreation skills and be able to train his staff of workers, both paid and volunteer, a task which will call for a knowledge of the latest educational methods.

Superintendent of Recreation and Parks. The superintendent of recreation and parks is the chief executive officer in charge of a recreation and park department and its personnel. He is responsible for the administration of a comprehensive recreation program for the entire community and also for the administrative management of the public parks, playgrounds, and other recreation facilities. The superintendent serves as technical advisor and consultant to the recreation and park board or other authority responsible for community recreation and administers the policies laid down by that authority. The superintendent of recreation and parks has executive responsibility for both the recreation and the park functions and for the maintenance of a high level of recreation service through the efficient administration of both. This type of position is becoming more prevalent throughout the country.

Minimum qualifications for this combined position include graduation from a college or university with a Bachelor's degree based on recreation leadership or a Bachelor's degree in park administration or closely related field. Further qualifications are completion of a Master's degree in recreation, park administration, or a related field; and from two to five years of successful experience as assistant superintendent or supervisor of parks and recreation is recommended.

Assistant Superintendent of Recreation. The assistant superintendent of recreation is responsible for administrative planning, organization, and supervision of the recreation program as general assistant to the superintendent of recreation. He represents the superintendent at conferences and meetings and in other relationships as assigned by the superintendent and acts for the superintendent in his absence. The assistant superintendent exercises professional judgment with considerable latitude for independent action and initiative in the formulation, promotion, and guidance of a comprehensive recreation program. The assistant superintendent receives supervision from his superior through advisory conferences and review of the department's work. The qualifications of the assistant superintendent are similar to those of the superintendent.

General Recreation Supervisor. The general recreation supervisor is an administrative official having charge of the program for the entire city or a section of it, depending upon its size. As executive officer for the promotion of the program, the supervisor serves as a deputy to the superintendent of recreation and exercises responsible professional judgment in administration; as a rule, he plans new areas and trains and supervises play directors. The general supervisor receives broad policy and administrative guidance from the superintendent. His qualifications are similar to those of the assistant superintendent.

Special Activity Supervisor. Under the administrative supervision of the superintendent of recreation, the special activity supervisor is responsible for a specialized activity phase of the community-wide program of recreation. Special activities which may require such supervisors include: athletics, sports, and aquatics; drama, puppetry, and storytelling; arts and crafts; music; dance; older adult programs; and nature and camping.

The special activity supervisor exercises responsible professional judgment and technical skill in his specialty, reporting to and receiving guidance from the superintendent.

Recreation Center Director. The recreation center director is responsible for the direction of a comprehensive recreation program for a single recreation center which may include a recreation building or indoor center, playground, playfield, camp or day camp, or a combination of any of these. The recreation center director has full charge of the operation of program, staff, and facility, and receives general supervision through intermittent visitation and consultation by superiors. The director of a specific type of recreation center may be assigned a descriptive title, such as Playground Director or Community Center Director.

Assistant Recreation Center Director. Under the supervision of the recreation center director, the assistant recreation center director is responsible for personal direction of portions of the recreation program for a large recreation center assigned him. The assistant director aids in the administration of the center and supervises full-time recreation leaders and seasonal and part-time personnel. The assistant recreation center director acts for the recreation center director in his absence.

General Recreation Leader. Under close supervision the recreation leader is responsible for the promotion, organization, and personal leadership of a variety of recreation activities at an indoor or outdoor recreation center. The leader conducts activities with assigned groups, assists in the administration of recreation programs, and may supervise the work of non-professional personnel. The leader's work is subject to review and direction by the recreation center director.

Special Activity Recreation Leader. Under close administrative supervision, the special activity recreation leader is responsible for one or more closely related recreation activities. This leader is responsible to the recreation center director and serves as his staff consultant in his special activity. The special activity leader exercises professional judgment and responsibility in the conduct of appropriate recreation within a specialty area for all ages. He may oversee the work of non-professionals and may lead programs at more than one recreation center. Program activities requiring specialized leadership of this type include those activities handled by special activity supervisors.

Recreation Intern. Under supervision of appropriate staff members, the recreation intern is responsible for a variety of tasks in a rotated program involving work, directed reading, conferences, and examinations. This type of position is intended to serve as a postgraduate training program for selected students who have completed undergraduate education for recreation, at least, and are capable of carrying full professional responsibility; therefore, the position incorporates all important phases of administration and supervision, including projects during which the recreation intern works both with and without close supervision.

The recreation intern is administratively responsible to the superintendent of recreation but may be assigned temporarily to work with any staff member. The position requires a full-time staff experience for a period of approximately one year.

On successful completion of the internship program and a comprehensive final examination, the intern may either remain in a more permanent position, subject to departmental needs and requirements or may be placed in a supervisory or administrative position elsewhere. Successful completion of this internship would be credited as one year of qualifying experience for such positions as those of superintendent of recreation, assistant superintendent of recreation, and recreation supervisor.

Student Recreation Leader. Under close supervision, the student recreation leader is responsible for the promotion, organization, and personal leadership of a variety of recreation activities. The work of this position is designed to contribute both to the recreation service provided for the participants and to the professional development of the student leader who has completed at least two years of basic undergraduate preparation in recreation. Responsibility entrusted is gradually increased during the field experience period. Direct supervision is exercised by the recreation superintendent or an authorized supervisor from the leadership staff, in cooperation with a representative of a college or university recreation department. The student recreation leader's duties and responsibilities will vary according to the amount of professional training he has completed.

Junior Recreation Assistant. Under continuous supervision, the junior recreation assistant helps the recreation leaders conduct games, special events, and other recreation activities, and also oversees free play activities at areas such as the sandbox, apparatus, or wading pool. Routine tasks such as the maintenance and issuance of supplies and materials, the recording of attendance, the setting-up of equipment, and related work are characteristic of this position. The junior recreation assistant works at a sub-professional level, gaining practical experience while at the same time freeing leadership personnel from non-professional routine tasks. Ordinarily, the junior recreation assistant is employed on a seasonal or part-time basis for service at a single recreation center.

VOLUNTEER RECREATION LEADERSHIP. Volunteer leadership played a large part in the early development of the public recreation movement. As professional staffs have been employed, the number and importance of the volunteer workers have diminished, but the consensus among superintendents in the field is that the values to be gained from such leadership are conspicuous and that there will always be a need for the volunteer.

Motivated by nothing but his own desire to help, the volunteer brings an enthusiasm to the work that often diminishes in professional workers. By use of volunteer specialists, a much wider range of skills and often a higher level of specialized skill in certain activities can be supplied. This applies in particular to hobbies and specialized interests. In addition to actual assistance in leading activities, volunteer specialists can be of advisory help to paid workers. Volunteers on planning committees can render priceless service. They become supporters for public recreation and are ready enthusiastically to interpret it and promote it among the people of the neighborhood.

On the other hand, the volunteer presents certain problems: he cannot be regulated as to time and schedule as paid workers are; nor is there assurance that the volunteer's enthusiasm will hold out until the project is completed. Also, volunteers need training in policies and leadership methods.

When volunteers are used, particular care must be exercised in their selection. Their character and personal conduct must be acceptable, and they must be emotionally mature and stable. They must be dependable, businesslike, and conscientious in completing projects undertaken. They must be willing to accept fully the department's policies, methods, and standards.

PROFESSIONAL RECREATION EDUCATION

The demand for qualified recreation leadership has focused attention on specialized recreation education as a major need in furthering the growth of the recreation profession. An early attempt to provide professional recreation education at the university level was made at Harvard University in 1912, but a full course leading to a Bachelor's degree in recreation was not established at that time. In 1908 the *Normal Course in Play* was published by the Playground Association of America, and it served as a personnel guide for many years. From 1926 to 1935, the National Recreation Association conducted a nine-month, postgraduate course in recreation. No special college degree, however, was conferred upon the approximately three hundred persons who completed the course. These leaders include a considerable number of the experienced recreation administrators throughout the country today.

Recreation education was studied seriously at the first College Conference on Training Recreation Leaders held at the University of Minnesota in 1937. At that time about five institutions were offering what was interpreted as a major curriculum in recreation. Conferences on development of the college curriculum in recreation were later held at the University of North Carolina and New York University; and a National Conference on Undergraduate Professional Preparation in Physical Education, Health Education, and Recreation was held in 1948.

In 1949 there were 787 undergraduate students enrolled in professional recreation education programs; in 1955 it was estimated that there were over four thousand undergraduates majoring in recreation. In 1959 reliable research showed that there were 72 institutions of higher learning offering curriculums leadings to the Bachelor's Degree in recreation. Graduate work in professional recreation education developed rapidly following the 1950 National Conference on Graduate Study in Health, Physical Education, and Recreation.

The provision of trained personnel is perhaps the most serious problem of the fast-growing recreation profession. The present urgent need, as well as the future need for professional recreation workers, can be met only by a co-ordinated, intensive, nation-wide recruitment program involving institutions of higher learning, various recreation agencies, and the national and local recreation organizations, both professional and service, that might influence young men and women to enter the profession.

In 1956 the National Recreation Association initiated an effective personnel program similar to, but far more extensive than, the apprenticeship program which it established in 1937. Under the newly-established internship program, graduates of recreation curriculums are placed in recreation agencies by the Association in work-study programs for one year. During this time, the student works in an activities leadership capacity in recreation and also studies the total operation of the agency under its executive staff, whether it be a public park department, a city recreation system, a hospital, or other recreation setting.

Paralleling specialized education of recreation personnel has been the initiation of state plans for the registration or certification of recreation workers. Before 1950 state departments of education in Florida, Pennsylvania, Washington, Minnesota, and Indiana provided for certification of recreation personnel connected with school-centered recreation programs. It was not until after 1950, however, that state-wide registration plans for non-school recreation personnel were established in several states. In 1957, the Council for the Advancement of Hospital Recreation established a voluntary registration plan for hospital workers on three levels, namely, hospital recreation director, hospital recreation leader, and hospital recreation aide.

The present voluntary registration plans have already served to establish minimum standards for professional recreation employees, and they represent the first basic step toward eventual identification of recreation personnel through legal certification.

Finally, specialization is occurring in the professional recreation education programs that are preparing young men and women for the recreation profession. However important this specialized education may be, a broad educational background must be looked upon as the major prerequisite in recreation. The essential factor is that a general cultural background be secured and that it is not sacrificed for technical training.

Although a great variety of professional recreation education programs now exist in the colleges and universities offering major courses in recreation education, the programs have gradually become well defined. As a result of several conferences held by college recreation educators, the national conferences held on training of recreation leaders, and in more recent years the close cooperation of the recreation practitioners in the field, a core program has developed. A few schools have developed specialized programs for park management, hospital recreation, and industrial recreation; others usually offer a general recreation education program including a basic liberal arts background with a professional major in recreation and minors in hospital recreation, industrial recreation, park management, and special skill areas, such as arts and crafts, dramatics, music, camping and outdoor education, and the like. Further details regarding the status of professional recreation education may be found in the Selected References listed at the end of this chapter.

SUMMARY

The person who takes up recreational leadership as a life work has the satisfaction of knowing that he is making a distinct contribution to the happiness of mankind. He is not only providing opportunities for the immediate enjoyment of leisure to all children and adults but is equipping children for a richer and fuller life through the building of strong healthy bodies, desirable character, and a knowledge of many skills and techniques which they can use in the leisure which tomorrow will bring.

The profession is a new one; and, consequently, is not given full credit and recognition as yet. But this should not deter a potential recreation leader, for the leader who understands the nature of the objectives of recreation cannot fail to have unlimited confidence in the work he can accomplish. It is a profession that has excellent job opportunities and the great reward that comes from fulfillment of service. The recreation leader is a new kind of pioneer, and he must be animated by the spirit which makes all pioneers strong-hearted and venturesome, keen and alert to the challenges of his profession.

SELECTED REFERENCES

National Advisory Committee on Recruitment, Training, and Placement of Recreation Personnel. *Personnel Standards in Community Recreation Leadership*. New York: National Recreation Association, 1957. The most complete statement of standards for recreation personnel, including job titles, duties, and minimum education and experience requirements for recreation leadership positions, is given.

BALL, EDITH L. *Developing Volunteers for Service in Recreation Programs.* New York: National Recreation Association, 1958.

BLUMENTHAL, LOUIS B. *How to Work with Boards and Committees.* New York: Association Press, 1954.

DYER, DONALD B. *In-Service Education for Community Center Leadership.* New York: National Recreation Association, 1955.

The Education of Specialists in Hospital Recreation. Washington, D.C.: American Recreation Society.

FORSBERG, RAYMOND T. *Playground Leaders, Their Selection and Training.* New York: National Recreation Association, 1955.

The National Conference on Graduate Preparation in Physical Education, Health Education, and Recreation. *Graduate Study in Health, Physical Education, and Recreation.* Chicago: Athletic Institute, 1950.

The National Conference on Undergraduate Professional Preparation in Physical Education, Health Education, and Recreation. Published Report. Chicago: Athletic Institute, 1948.

National Recreation Association and The Southern Regional Education Board. *Recreation as a Profession in the Southern Region.* New York: National Recreation Association, 1955.

Personnel Practices Committee. *Personnel Practices for Recreation Departments and Agencies.* Washington, D.C.: American Recreation Society, 1959.

STONE, WALTER L., and STONE, CHARLES G. *Recreation Leadership.* New York: The William-Frederick Press, 1952.

VANNIER, MARYHELEN. *Methods and Materials in Recreation Leadership.* Philadelphia: W. B. Saunders Co., 1956.

FILMS

Careers in Recreation. (27 min.) 16 mm. Sound. Color. Rental $2.50.

Leaders for Leisure. (20 min.) 16 mm. Sound. Color. Both available from Athletic Institute, Merchandise Mart, Room 805, Chicago, Ill.

Index

abstract knowledge, 272–73
accommodation, 108
achievement tests, 164
acquisitiveness, 152
acquisitive play, 176
Addams, Jane, 60, 364, 387
adjustments, 270–71
adolescence, 188–91, 260, 284
adult play, 118, 119, 121
aesthetic play, 117
aesthetics, 145, 156
agencies
  for camps, 432–38
  public, 66–67
  voluntary, 67, 389 ff.
aggressiveness, 265
Aids to Scouting, 398
Alexander, Franz, 104–5
American Association for Health,
    Physical Education, and Rec-
    reation, 69–70
American Insitute of Park Execu-
    tives, 68–69
Americanization, 220–21
American Recreation Annual, 69
American Recreation Society, 69
Angell, James, 144
Aristotle, 18, 20, 88, 278
Armed Forces, 521–22
Arnold, Serena E., 37
Arnold, Thomas, 278
art, 16–19, 80, 98, 323–24
arts and crafts, 7, 490–91
Ascham, Roger, 20
assimilation, 108
association, 269–70
athletics
  for all, 469–70
  in community, 461–62, 481–85
  and community spectacle, 467–68
  financing of, 470–71

extramural, 463, 480
for girls and women, 477–80
intercollegiate, 461
interscholastic, 461, 462–63
intramural, 461, 463, 481
for junior boys, 474–77
and leisure, 471–72
objectives in, 463 ff.
programing of, 473–81
as safety valve, 464–65
in schools, 461–70, 473–81
and school spirit, 466–67
and sportsmanship, 468–69, 473
stages in, 463–64
standards in, 473–81
attitudes, 90, 21–23, 92–93, 279,
    304
Australia, 48–49, 54
automation, 25
awards, 455, 517

Back to Methuselah, 223
Baden-Powell, Agnes, 404
Baden-Powell, Robert, 398–99, 404
Balch, Ernest, 59, 428
baseball games, 169
Basedow, Johann, 34, 278
Bauer, W. W., 255
Beach, Frank A., 115
Beard, Dan, 427
billiards, 338
Binet, Alfred, 179
biosocial approaches to play, 109–10
Birch Bark Roll of Woodcraft, 398
boating, 321
Bode, B. H., 179
body control, 256–61
bowling, 338
Boyce, William D., 399
Boys' Clubs, 418–22
Boy Scouts of America, 398–404